IDEAS MATTER

Essays in Honour of Conor Cruise O'Brien

Edited by Richard English and Joseph Morrison Skelly

POOLBEG

Published 1998
by Poolbeg Press Ltd
123 Baldoyle Industrial Estate
Dublin 13, Ireland

A catalogue record for this book is available from the British Library.

ISBN 1 85371 882 3

Cover photography by Brigid Tiernan
Cover design by Artmark
Set by Poolbeg Group Services Ltd in AGarmond 10.5/13.5
Printed by The Guernsey Press Ltd,
Vale, Guernsey, Channel Islands.

Do Mháire Mhac an tSaoi

CONTENTS

NOTES ON CONTRIBUTORS

K Anthony Appiah is Professor of Afro-American Studies and Philosophy at Harvard University. He received his PhD in Philosophy from Cambridge University and has taught at Yale, Cornell and Duke. He is the co-author, with Amy Gutman, of *Color Consciousness: The Political Morality of Race*, which won the Ralphe J Bunche Award of the American Political Science Association. His other books include *In My Father's House: Africa in the Philosophy of Culture, Necessary Questions* and three novels. Professor Appiah is the co-editor, with Henry Louis Gates, Jr, of *the Dictionary of Global Culture* and he is the editor of the journal *Transition*.

Frank Callanan is a graduate of University College Dublin and of the College of Europe, Bruges. He is the author of *The Parnell Split* and *TM Healy*. He is a co-editor, with Edward Byrne, of *Parnell, A Memoir*. Currently, he is a barrister practising in Dublin.

John Patrick Diggins is Distinguished Professor of History at the City University of New York Graduate Centre. His many books include *Up From Communism, The Lost Soul of American Politics, The Rise and Fall of the American Left, The Promise of Pragmatism* and *The Liberal Persuasion: Arthur Schlesinger, Jr, and the Challenge of the American Past*. He has been nominated for a National Book Award and his forthcoming volume is entitled *The Cunning of American History*.

Susan Dunn teaches in the Department of Romance Languages at Williams College, Williamstown, Massachusetts. She is the author of *The Deaths of Louis the XVI: Regicide and the French Political Imagination*. Her forthcoming book, *Sister Revolutions: French Lightning, American Light*, will be published by Faber and Faber.

Owen Dudley Edwards lectures in the Department of History at the University of Edinburgh. His books include *1916: The Easter Rising, The Mind of an Activist: James Connolly, James Connolly: Selected Political Writings* and *Eamon de Valera*.

1

Ruth Dudley Edwards is a political commentator, historian and author. She was educated at University College Dublin and Cambridge University. She writes regularly for the *Sunday Independent* (Dublin) and contributes to numerous other newspapers and magazines in Ireland and Britain. Her many books include *Patrick Pearse: The Triumph of Failure*, *Victor Gollancz: A Biography*, *The Pursuit of Reason: The Economist, 1843-93*, *True Brits: Inside the Foreign Office* and several novels. Her forthcoming volumes are entitled *No Surrender: The Loyal Institutions* and *Cecil King: A Biography*.

Richard English is Reader in the School of Politics, Queen's University Belfast. His books include *Radicals and the Republic: Socialist Republicanism in the Irish Free State*, *Ernie O'Malley: IRA Intellectual* and *Unionism in Modern Ireland*.

Thomas Flanagan is the author of three novels based on Irish history: *The Year of the French*, *The Tenants of Time* and *The End of the Hunt*. He has written numerous books and articles on Irish literature and history and has served as Chair of the English Department at Berkeley and as Distinguished Professor at the State University of New York, Stony Brook. He holds honorary degrees from Amherst College, Iona College and the National University of Ireland.

Roy Foster is Carroll Professor of Irish History at Oxford University. He has written several highly-acclaimed books on Irish and British history, including *Charles Stewart Parnell: The Man and his Family*, *Lord Randolph Churchill: A Political Life*, *Modern Ireland, 1600-1972*, *The Oxford Illustrated History of Ireland* and *Paddy and Mr Punch*. The first volume of his biography, *WB Yeats: A Life*, was published by Oxford University Press in 1997, and he is now completing the second and final volume.

David Grene was born in Dublin and educated at Trinity College. After a period in Vienna and at Harvard University, he moved to the University of Chicago, where he has enjoyed a distinguished career teaching in Classics, the College and the Committee on Social Thought. His numerous publications include *Man in his Pride*, *Reality and the Heroic Pattern: The Last Plays of Ibsen, Shakespeare and Sophocles* and *The Actor in History: Studies in Shakespearean Stage Poetry*. He is best known as the editor and author, along with Richard Lattimore, of the University of Chicago series *The Complete Greek Tragedies*. Not only the excellence of Grene's own translations of Greek tragedy, of Herodotus and, most recently, of Hesiod's *Works and Plays* (published along with Stephanie Nelson's new book, *God and the Land*), but also the innovation of the Chicago series itself, has earned Grene the well-deserved reputation of making Greek classics accessible to a modern, general, educated public. He has received an honorary degree from Northwestern University and the Laing Prize from the University of Chicago Press.

Eoghan Harris is a screenwriter, playwright, political columnist and award-winning documentary film producer. His play *Souper Sullivan* was staged at the Abbey Theatre during the 1985 Dublin Theatre Festival. In 1990 he served as a political strategist on Mary Robinson's presidential campaign. His column regularly appears in *The Sunday Times* and he is currently working on a screenplay about Conor Cruise O'Brien's experiences in Katanga in 1961.

Seamus Heaney, winner of the 1995 Nobel Prize for Literature, received the 1997 Whitbread Book of the Year Award for his volume of poetry, *The Spirit Level*. He was Oxford Professor of Poetry from 1989-94 and is currently Ralph Waldo Emerson Poet in Residence at Harvard University. His recent publications include *The Redress of Poetry*, *Crediting Poetry* and *Opened Ground: Poems, 1966-1996*.

Dáire Keogh received a PhD in Modern Irish history from Trinity College Dublin and now lectures in the Department of History at Saint Patrick's College in Dublin. He is the author and co-editor of several books on late-eighteenth-century Irish history, including *The French Disease: The Catholic Church and Irish Radicalism, 1790-1800*, *The Mighty Wave: The 1798 Rebellion in Wexford*, *The Women of 1798* and *The United Irishmen: Republicanism, Radicalism and Rebellion*.

Enrique Krauze was born and educated in Mexico City, where he now lives. In 1982 he was named co-editor of the literary journal *Vuelta*. He has written numerous books, articles and essays on Mexican history, politics and culture. In the United States he has contributed to the *New York Times*, *Wall Street Journal*, *New Republic* and *Time*. His book *Siglo de Caudillo, 1810-1910* received the Premio Comillas, one of Spain's most prestigious literary awards. His most recent volume is *Mexico: Biography of Power*.

Alexander Kwapong was born in Ghana and currently resides in Accra. He holds a doctoral degree in Classsics from Cambridge University and has enjoyed a distinguished career at the University of Ghana, where he

3

was Professor of Classics, Dean of the Faculty of Arts and Vice-Chancellor from 1966 to 1975. He has been a visiting professor at Princeton University and the Lester Pearson Professor of Development Studies at Dalhousie University in Halifax. Professor Kwapong has published widely in the fields of Classics, educational theory and national development and is also the recipient of numerous awards, including honorary degrees from Princeton and the University of Warwick.

Deirdre Levinson was born and educated in Britain. From 1957 to 1962 she lived in South Africa, where she learnt her politics. Since 1965 she has lived in New York City. She has been an English teacher all her working life and has written two novels. *Five Years* (Deutsch, 1966) and *Modus Vivendi* (Viking, 1986).

Patrick Lynch is Emeritus Professor of Political Economy at University College Dublin. He has held numerous high-ranking positions in government and private industry, including terms as Personal Assistant to the Taoiseach (John A Costello), Chairman of Aer Lingus and Joint-Deputy Chairman of Allied Irish Bank. He has been an economic consultant to the OECD and is a former chairman of the Irish Anti-Apartheid Movement and the Institute of Public Administration. In 1973 he was named a member of the Club of Rome. His many publications include *Planning for Economic Development* and *Economic Development Planning* (with Basil Chubb). He has received numerous honorary degrees and is Fellow Commoner, Peterhouse College, Cambridge and Honorary Fellow, Trinity College Dublin. For over fifty years, through thick and thin, he has been a close friend of Conor Cruise O'Brien's.

John Lukacs is Emeritus Professor of History at Chestnut Hill College in Chestnut Hill, Pennsylvania. He has been a visiting professor at Columbia, Princeton, Johns Hopkins and the University of Pennsylvania. He is the author of nineteen books and the recipient of the 1991 Ingersoll Prize. His most recent publications include *The Hitler of History* (Alfred A Knopf) and *A Thread of Years* (Yale University Press).

Robert McCartney, MP, is the leader of the United Kingdom Unionist Party in Northern Ireland. In 1995 he was elected to represent the North Down constituency in the British Parliament. He is also a member of the Northern Ireland Assembly. Mr McCartney has written several pamphlets on political life in Northern Ireland, including *The McCartney Report on Consent.* He is a Queen's Counsel and lives in Belfast.

Kevin Myers is a journalist, political analyst, radio commentator and television presenter. He writes a regular column for the *Irish Times* and the *Sunday Telegraph*. He has also contributed articles and essays to numerous journals and magazines in Ireland, Britain and the United States.

John A Murphy is Emeritus Professor of Irish History at University College Cork, where he was Professor of Irish History from 1971 to 1990. He has been a visiting professor at Boston College, Loyola University in Chicago and James Madison University and has lectured extensively throughout Europe, North America and Australia. He is the author and editor of several books, including *Ireland in the Twentieth Century, The French are in the Bay* and *The College: A History of University College Cork*. He is a frequent contributor to scholarly journals and newspapers and often appears on Irish radio and television. He represented the National University of Ireland in Seanad Éireann and is currently a member of the NUI's Senate.

Darcy O'Brien authored eleven books, including *Power to Hurt*, which won the 1997 Edgar Allan Poe Award for nonfiction, and *A Way of Life, Like Any Other*, which was awarded the 1978 Ernest Hemingway Award for Best First Novel. He was a Fulbright Scholar at Cambridge University and the recipient of a Guggenheim Fellowship. From 1965-77 he was Professor of English at Pomona College and from 1978-95 Graduate Professor of English at the University of Tulsa. His last book, *The Hidden Pope*, a nonfiction account of changing relations between Catholicism and Judaism, was published in 1998.

Daniel Pipes is editor of the *Middle East Quarterly* and author of ten books, most recently *Conspiracy: How the Paranoid Style Flourishes, and Where it Comes From* (Free Press). He has taught at the University of Chicago, Harvard University and the United States Naval War College. He has served in the Departments of State and Defence and has helped three US presidential campaigns.

Gideon Rafael currently lives in Jerusalem. He was one of the founding members of the Foreign Ministry of Israel in 1948 and later its Director-General. He has served as Ambassador to the United Kingdom and Ireland; Ambassador to Belgium and the European Community; Permanent Representative to the United Nations; Ambassador-at-Large;

and Senior Adviser to several foreign ministers. He is the author of *Destination Peace: Three Decades of Israeli Foreign Policy* and a contributor to the volumes *The Impact of the Six-Day War* and *The Six-Day War: A Retrospective*. He has been a visiting professor at Princeton University and Hamilton College and presently lectures and writes on international affairs for the Israeli and foreign media.

Mary Robinson is the United Nations High Commissioner for Human Rights. From 1990 until 1997 she was President of Ireland. During her tenure as President, Ms Robinson served as Special Rapporteur to the Council of Europe's Interregional Meeting on Human Rights in 1993 and traveled extensively – most notably to Somalia and Rwanda – to promote humanitarian causes, human rights and the needs of developing countries. Ms Robinson was a member of Seanad Éireann from 1969 to 1989. She was Reid Professor of Constitutional and Criminal Law at Trinity College Dublin between 1969 and 1975 and established the Irish Centre for European Law in 1988. Ms Robinson holds degrees from Trinity College, Dublin, the Kings Inns, Dublin and Harvard University.

Joseph Morrison Skelly lectures in the Department of History and Political Science at Iona College in New Rochelle, New York. He received a PhD in Modern Irish history from University College Dublin and was a Rotary International Research Fellow at Queen's University Belfast. He is the author of *Irish Diplomacy at the United Nations, 1945-65: National Interests and the International Order* and co-editor of the forthcoming *Irish Foreign Policy, 1919-69: From Independence to Internationalism* (Four Courts Press, Dublin).

David Welsh is Emeritus Professor, University of Cape Town. He lectured at the University of Cape Town from 1963 to 1997, retiring as Professor of Southern African Studies in the Political Studies Department.

Xiao-huang Yin is an associate professor of Asian-American Studies at Occidental College in Los Angeles. He received a PhD in the History of American Civilization from Harvard University. His research interests centre on the Asian American experience, US-China relations and cross-cultural analyses. He is the author of *Gold Mountain Dreams: Sociohistorical Aspects of Chinese-American Literature*, a co-translator of *Secret Speeches of Chairman Mao* and a contributor to *Atlantic Monthly*, *The World Today* (London), *Il Mondo* (Italy), *Los Angeles Times*, *Boston Globe* and *Philadelphia Inquirer*.

I

INTRODUCTION

CHAPTER 1

IDEAS MATTER

RICHARD ENGLISH AND JOSEPH MORRISON SKELLY

ACCLAIMED ABROAD AS A SCHOLAR, DECRIED AT HOME AS A SOURCE OF endless discord, considered by some of his countrymen to be a national treasure, by others to be not truly "Irish" at all, admired for his courage, disdained for his forthrightness – Conor Cruise O'Brien, in short, is one of the most intriguing intellectuals of our time. Throughout his diplomatic, political and literary career his friends and foes alike have attached contradictory labels to him: he has been called both a liberal and a reactionary; a leftist and a neo-conservative; an anti-colonialist and counter-revolutionary; a Marxist and a Burkean; an Irish nationalist and a Protestant unionist. Conor thus seems difficult to pin down. He himself, in fact, resists being categorised or reduced to a simple formula. Such tension would paralyse lesser minds, but it inspires Conor. His complexity is a source of creativity, a key to understanding his rich output over the past several decades. Yet the exterior dissonance Conor is noted for by some is not the full story: even more important is his internal intellectual consistency, the sturdy philosophical foundation of democratic, constitutional values that underpins the corpus of his work. If his audience fails to grasp this intrinsic logic, and instead is frustrated by his alleged disparities or his latest disconcerting pronouncement, Conor Cruise O'Brien is not in the least dismayed. It is more imperative, he believes, to challenge the public's most comfortable assumptions rather than soothe its collective conscience. What's more, he has accomplished this task – internationally and in Ireland – and in the

9

process has secured a prominent place in the firmament of twentieth-century scholarship.

In this regard, it is apparent that Conor's intellectual powers reached their apotheosis in *The Great Melody*, his towering study of Edmund Burke, which was published in 1992. Completing this volume has, for Conor, liberated new creative energies, and he is now drawing on even deeper reservoirs of imaginative potential. The several books he has written since *The Great Melody* have reinforced his sterling literary reputation – and have stoked the coals of controversy always glowing in his vicinity. These works include his incisive critique of religion and nationalism in Ireland – *Ancestral Voices*; his insightful ruminations on the future of our Enlightenment heritage – *On the Eve of the Millennium*; his iconoclastic study of Thomas Jefferson's dubious infatuation with the French Revolution – *The Long Affair*; and his eagerly-awaited memoirs – *My Life and Themes*. But that's not all. Evincing his famous passion, as well as his penchant for provocation, Conor has immersed himself in the political process in Ireland throughout the 1990s with the same fury that has marked every stage of his career, refusing, as always, to yield the field of battle to his opponents or to forsake his principles.

It is altogether fitting, therefore, that Conor Cruise O'Brien's colleagues should now honour him with this *Festschrift*. Comprising splendid essays relevant to his many interests, this volume acknowledges Conor's indispensable contribution to public life and letters in Ireland and abroad. This collection also has another purpose, one which focuses on its readers: it is designed to guide them back to Conor's accomplishments, to his books and essays, so that people may discover them anew in all of their vitality, originality and urgency. Its aim is the same shared by university officials around the world. Recognising the brilliance inherent in his *oeuvre*, academies everywhere – Harvard, Dartmouth, Williams, Berkeley, Chicago, Cape Town, Toronto, Cambridge, Canterbury and more – have invited Conor to inspire, with his words and his wit, eager audiences of students and faculty. The writers in this volume desire the same: that its readers gain new insights into, and a deeper appreciation of, the wisdom of Conor Cruise O'Brien.

MAN OF IDEAS

Conor has enjoyed a remarkable professional life. After graduating from Trinity College he entered the Irish Department of Finance in 1941.

Three years later he transferred to the Department of External Affairs, where he hit his stride. In 1954 he was appointed Counsellor in the Irish Embassy in Paris and in 1956 he was recalled to Dublin to head the newly-formed International Organisations Section. In this capacity he served as an essential member of the Irish delegation to the United Nations until 1961, when the UN Secretary General, Dag Hammarskjöld, appointed him as his personal representative in Katanga. After leaving the Irish diplomatic service in that year, Conor returned to Africa in 1962 as vice-chancellor of the University of Ghana, where he remained until 1965, when he was named Albert Schweitzer Professor of the Humanities at New York University.

In 1969 Conor returned home to enter into politics as a member of the Labour Party, won election to the Dáil and represented his Dublin North-East constituency until 1977. From 1973 until 1977 he was Minister for Posts and Telegraphs in the Fine Gael-Labour coalition government. He then served one term in Seanad Éireann. In 1978 Conor was named editor-in-chief of the *Observer*. Since the early 1980s he has been a columnist for several Irish and British newspapers, including *The Times*, the *Irish Times* and the *Irish Independent*, as well as a visiting professor at universities around the world.[1] What's more, throughout these momentous decades he has written more than twenty books and plays and has produced a steady stream of priceless essays on literary criticism, politics, history and international affairs.[2]

An abiding leitmotif conjoins these fascinating strands of Conor's career, which Darcy O'Brien accurately identified in his poignant contribution to this volume: Conor is, first and foremost, "a man of ideas". He possesses the intuitive knowledge that *ideas matter*. He grasps their inherent capacity to inspire, to lead, to provoke, to vex, to reassure, to calm. He recognises that ideas, these seemingly evanescent entities, in effect live and breathe. Their habitats are not the sea, the forest or the desert, but culture, art, literature, politics, history and science. Evolving within these environments, they lead us, individually and collectively, to good or ill. Their power invokes both awe and profound foreboding. As Isaiah Berlin, the twentieth century's most elegant historian of ideas, reminds us, the great movements of our time – communism, fascism, extreme nationalism and the democratic responses to them – "began with ideas in people's heads: ideas about what relations between men have been, are, might be and should be . . . "[3]

When it comes to the expression of ideas, Conor is an artist. He works the same magic on an empty page that a gifted painter works on an empty canvas; he breathes fresh life into ideas, just as a sculptor breathes life into hardened marble or gives new form to a mound of clay. In his hands ideas sparkle, they leap off the page, they delight the senses. At other times, when exploring a serious topic – Irish politics, Jeffersonian republicanism, political terrorism – his ideas jar us, startle us, arouse us from of our complacency. For those who do not see eye-to-eye with him Conor's thoughts can be unnerving, frustrating, even infuriating. This is often the case because he is right; it is always so because one "of the greatest pains to human nature is the pain of a new idea".[4] In fact, a painful remedy that works, rather than an analgesic that dulls the senses, is Conor's favourite antidote for a social ill. Regardless of the prescription, his ideas are often provocative, endlessly intriguing, always potent. They linger in our minds, where they work their singular magic long after we have pored over one of his eloquent essays, finished his latest book or absorbed one of his arresting lectures. His ideas frequently have a transformative effect, like any work of art.

* * *

William Butler Yeats once exhorted his fellow writers to "Hammer your thoughts into unity".[5] Conor has done just that. But he has not had to rely on Yeats' blunt instrument to shape his beliefs, for they exhibit a natural integrity, they flow effortlessly from a wellspring of inner conviction. More specifically, Conor's ideas emanate from a central core of distinguished first principles: a life-long commitment to constitutional democracy; pluralism – in politics and in thought; the preservation of individual liberty; the defence of human rights; undiluted academic freedom; religious tolerance; an implacable opposition to racism, especially its most virulent strain in Europe, anti-semitism; resistance to imperialism in all of its forms; and the rejection of illegitimate political violence.

As such, Conor's core values arise directly out of the western tradition of democratic liberalism. He has spent his life navigating this great river of philosophical, political and moral thought. The tributaries feeding into this deep current flow from the minds of the world's most profound thinkers. These figures include John Locke and David Hume, the architects of the British Enlightenment, the fountainhead of classical liberalism; equable representatives of the French Enlightenment such as Montesquieu; Edmund Burke, who defended ordered freedom against the flood of French revolutionary terror (and whom Conor, in *The Great Melody*, has freed from the ahistorical, reactionary straitjacket previous writers have wrapped him in[6]); liberal-democrats in post-revolution Europe – Tocqueville, Guizot, Constant – who tried to reconcile the "modern and anti-modern political passions" set free by the tumult in France;[7] Hamilton, Madison and Jay, the authors of *The Federalist*; John Stuart Mill and William James in the nineteenth century; and Isaiah Berlin in the twentieth. Conor's principles reflect the priorities of these men. They are also deeply rooted in the most laudable features of the Judeo-Christian heritage, notwithstanding his own healthy scepticism of organised religion, an outlook shared by the *philosophes* themselves.

By its nature, democratic liberalism is inclusive of various interrelated strands of thought, so it is necessary to sketch the contours of Conor Cruise O'Brien's point of view. Like other genuine thinkers of liberal democratic disposition, Conor is committed to ideas, but hostile to constricting ideologies. While his intellectual scope is global – he is an acknowledged expert on the Middle East, Africa, Ireland, America, the United Nations – his conclusions are never universal. He identifies parallels across cultures, but he never loses sight of the particulars in each case. Many analysts would rather ignore inconvenient facts in favour of overriding theories. But not Conor: he pays the closest attention to local details. Edmund Burke called them "circumstances". Of them he said: "Circumstances (which with some gentlemen pass for nothing) give in reality to every political principle its distinguishing colour and discriminating effect. The circumstances are what render every civil and political scheme beneficial or noxious to mankind."[8]

In philosophical terms, Conor Cruise O'Brien eschews a monist interpretation of knowledge in favour of the pluralism of ideas. In this respect, one of his close intellectual kin is Sir Isaiah Berlin, whose own thinking illuminates Conor's. Berlin has written that the "enemy of pluralism is monism – the ancient belief that there is a single harmony of truths into which everything, if it is genuine, in the end must fit. The consequence of this belief . . . is that those who know should command those who do not".[9] Pluralism, on the other hand, affirms that a range of legitimate values exist "which men can and do seek, and that these values differ". They are not limitless, Berlin insists: "the number of human values, of values which I can pursue while maintaining my human semblance, my human character, is finite . . . " Yet "the difference this makes is that if a man pursues one of these values, I, who do not, am able to understand why

13

he pursues it or what it would be like, in his circumstances, for me to be induced to pursue it. Hence the possibility of human understanding".[10]

In his seminal essay on Leo Tolstoy, *The Hedgehog and the Fox*, Isaiah Berlin discerns the difference between the monist and the pluralist within the fields of nature. He does so by distilling the essence of the Greek poet Archilochus' aphorism: "The fox knows many things, but the hedgehog knows one big thing." Interpreted imaginatively, Berlin asserts, these words "can be made to yield a sense in which they mark one of the deepest differences which divide writers and thinkers, and, it may be, human beings in general".[11] On one side sit the hedgehogs, those "who relate everything to a single central vision, one system more or less coherent or articulate, in terms of which they understand, think and feel – a single universal, organising principle in terms of which alone all that they are and say has significance . . . " On the other side circle the foxes, whose thought moves on "many levels, seizing upon the essence of a vast variety of experiences and objects for what they are in themselves, without, consciously or unconsciously, seeking to fit them into, or exclude them from, any one unchanging, all embracing, sometimes self-contradictory and incomplete, at times fanatical, unitary inner vision". Throughout history, and "without insisting on a rigid classification", Plato, Pascal, Dostoevsky, Nietzsche and Proust are hedgehogs; Aristotle, Shakespeare, Montaigne, Erasmus, Molière, Goethe, Balzac and Joyce are foxes.

In Isaiah Berlin's taxonomy, Conor Cruise O'Brien too is a fox. But he is *not* a relativist. He realises that all ideas are *not* equal: dangerous ideas exist and have destructive consequences. They compete with more judicious ones for the allegiance of individual consciences and the welfare of society's soul. Indeed, if the "best ideas are common property",[12] the worst undermine the common good. Throughout the course of western civilisation injurious ideas have coalesced, with the encouragement of ardent alchemists, into casts of mind hostile to democratic pluralism. In the late eighteenth century, for example, the corrupt Jean-Jacques Rousseau fathered the cult of the General Will, an authoritarian mindset that evolved into its own twisted branch of the Enlightenment. The lineaments of this viewpoint can be traced back to Niccolò Machiavelli and ahead to Maximilien Robespierre and Louis Antoine de Saint-Just, the regents of the Reign of Terror. In the early nineteenth century Rousseau's thought mutated into the devious Romanticism of Percy Bysshe Shelley. In Germany it fused with the malevolent nationalism of Fichte, Nietzsche and Wagner and gave rise to Heidegger and Hitler in the twentieth century.[13] Meanwhile, the revolutionary intellectualism of Marx, Lenin, Stalin and Mao on the extreme left stalked political life in Russia and China. In Ireland the messianic republicanism of Patrick Pearse overwhelmed the adherents of democratic, constitutional nationalism for several years from 1916 onwards, went into remission after the Free State forces defeated the Irregulars in the Irish Civil War of 1922-23 and then recrudesced in the shape of the Provisional IRA in the early 1970s.

These lethal strains of thought have engendered various forms of what one lucid critic calls "the heartless tyranny of ideas", a confused philosophical outlook that places concepts ahead of people.[14] In the past, this *Weltanschauung* has often manifested itself as ideologically-inspired Utopian ventures in search of the perfect society, schemes designed, in theory, to usher in human bliss, that have, in practice, generated much human misery. History is littered with failed enterprises of this sort – revolutionary republicanism in France, national socialism in Germany, communism in the Soviet Union, the cultural revolution in China – and their emblematic institutions: the guillotine, the death camp, the gulag and the killing fields. Isaiah Berlin's verdict on the excesses justified in pursuit of the ideal state during the twentieth century is apt:

> all the brutalities, sacrifices, brainwashing, all those revolutions, everything that has made this century perhaps the most appalling of any since the days of old, at any rate in the West – all this is for nothing, for the perfect universe is not merely unattainable but inconceivable, and everything done to bring it about is founded on an enormous intellectual fallacy.[15]

In the light of such distortion in theory, and devastation in practice, Edmund Burke's description of Jean-Jacques Rousseau, the philosophical progenitor of twentieth-century totalitarianism, is especially appropriate. Burke, who encountered Rousseau in London in the late 1760s, wryly noted:

> We have had the great professor and founder of the philosophy of *vanity* in England. As I had good opportunities of knowing his proceedings almost from day to day, he left no doubt in my mind, that he entertained no principle either to influence his heart, or to guide his understanding, but *vanity*. With this vice he was possessed to a degree little short of madness.[16]

How different is Conor Cruise O'Brien, that rarest of intellectuals, a man of letters who puts people first. His work is a sustained critique of attempts by ideologies located at any point along the political spectrum to impose their cruel systems on societies unwilling to act as experimental laboratories. In a review of Isaiah Berlin's exquisite collection of essays, *The*

Crooked Timber of Humanity, he states: "I agree fully with Isaiah Berlin's anti-Utopian position: that is, with his contention that the belief that a Utopia can be constructed on earth, combined with the urge to bring about its construction, has resulted in practice in a colossal multiplication of human misery."[17] Conor discerns the origins of this modern impulse in the French Revolution, an epoch that bulks large in his historical imagination. This era of upheaval actually "deserves consideration as the first major realisation of a Utopian project: the construction of a perfect society, owing nothing to the past". The steady erosion of the twin pillars of the French past – Christianity and the monarchy of the *ancien régime* – had, by the eve of the Revolution, created a moral and political vacuum. Meanwhile, as Conor has pointed out, "Jean-Jacques Rousseau, enchanting almost all the French, was showing how the void could be filled. Human goodness – *la vertu* – took the place of the old God of the churches; the nation (the General Will) took the place of the king".[18] Rousseau had enchanted most of all Robespierre, who, in 1792, defined virtue as the love of the Good, the Country and of Liberty: *"l'amour du bien, de la patrie et de la liberté"*.[19] One year later, at the height of the Reign of Terror, Conor reminds us, the "virtuous Maximilien was seen as the heir and interpreter of the virtuous Jean-Jacques, guide and censor, worthy of trust and guarantor of the gains of the Revolution and the integrity of the nation".

The outcome of the Rousseauian dialectic, therefore, was the Terror. The emblematic act of the Revolution, though, was the assassination of Louis XVI. In her stunning book, *The Deaths of Louis XVI*, Susan Dunn explores the execution of this monarch within the French political imagination. Haunted by its implications, the writer Jean-François Lyotard called it "a crime", plain and simple.[20] Conor Cruise O'Brien would agree. He believes that the French have endured a kind of mental anguish as a result of it. In his Foreword to Professor Dunn's volume he notes of the regicide – and this is not simply a reactionary or royalist pronouncement, but a profound argument against summary political justice – that "the French are still remembering, even in the late twentieth century, and can still be tormented by that historical memory".[21] This is so because "in killing a king *because* he was a king, the French were repudiating the history of their country". Their lethal act, in other words, contrasts with the English, who beheaded Charles I nearly 150 years earlier not because he was the monarch, but because he was a "wicked" one. The upshot of all this for the French, Dr

O'Brien notes, is that they inflicted "a huge psychic injury on themselves". This is true. Conor's insight is also significant to our discussion: like the French Revolution, *all* Utopian projects have inflicted deep wounds on those societies they have sought to transform. The most cursory glance across the former Soviet Union, parts of Central Europe and Cambodia reveals the unimaginable social cost of such enthusiasms.

In sum, Conor Cruise O'Brien's principles are best elucidated by the fundamental differences between liberal democracy, on the one hand, and dictatorships of the extreme right and the radical left, on the other; by the contrary worldviews imagined by Locke and Rousseau, Burke and Robespierre; by the richness of the Enlightenment heritage versus the barrenness of authoritarianism; by the social benefits that flow from the freedom of individual conscience measured against the human costs incurred by the tyranny of ideas; by the distinctions, in short, between the fox and the hedgehog. When considered within the conceptual framework of democratic pluralism, the inherent logic of Conor's work emerges with forthright clarity. Indeed, this paradigm reveals the underlying coherence of his thinking from the 1940s until today. Wherever he has cast his critical gaze, Conor Cruise O'Brien has consistently applied the same principles. His field of vision now merits a closer look.

SACRAL NATIONALISM

One of Conor Cruise O'Brien's great intellectual achievements has been his illumination of the volatile intersection of religion and nationalism throughout history, including its harsh reemergence in recent years. He has aptly labelled this phenomenon "sacral nationalism". Owing to its regrettable sanguinary consequences, he has also designated this intersection "the bloody crossroads". Conor's insights in this regard are the by-product of personal experience – in Ireland and overseas – and years of rigorous intellectual analysis. As he once remarked: "All my life I have been both fascinated and puzzled by nationalism and religion; by the interaction of the two forces, sometimes in unison, sometimes antagonistic; and by the manifold ambiguities in all of this."[22]

What accounts for the power of sacral nationalism? People in every age, Conor has observed, "need to feel that what we believe about the universe, how we order our affairs in society, what we read and what we write, are not totally separate and closed spheres of thought, feeling and activity, but somehow belong in one moral and spiritual field of force" –

the need for "the sacred", in other words.[23] For centuries nationalism and religion have satisfied this yearning, especially when they have mutually reinforced one another. As Conor observed on another occasion, even though it is typically understood as a modern concept:

> As an emotional force, nationalism is very ancient. It is present at the roots of our civilisation, on both sides of the Judeo-Hellenic heritage. The Hebrew Bible abounds in fiercely nationalistic passages, along with some matter of a contrary tendency. On the classical side we have the official religious and national cult of those who fell for the polis or the patria.[24]

In his book, *God Land: Reflections on Religion and Nationalism*, Conor illuminates these early origins of sacral nationalism, traces its passage through the culture of medieval Europe, Enlightenment France and early America and, finally, delineates its persistence today in Russia, Africa, Central America and the United States. Sacral nationalism has been equally resilient in Ireland, a nation whose history over the last four centuries, Conor notes, "seems to show that, where a dispute about God's will is doubled with a dispute about man's power on earth over a particular piece of land, that dispute is likely to prove remarkably durable".[25] In *Ancestral Voices: Religion and Nationalism in Ireland*, Conor pursues this theme in greater detail, often through the prism of his own life, an approach that confirms his invaluable insights.

O'Brien's concept of sacral nationalism not only casts light on the past, it is an invaluable model for interpreting developments in the post-Cold War world, where reawakening ethno-religious forces threaten to overshadow the next century, just as communism and fascism endangered this one. One respected American commentator has even said that "the twenty-first century will be the most religious in 500 years".[26] He believes that this will be a positive development, which may well be the case, but Conor Cruise O'Brien's analysis is a sobering reminder of just how volatile the fusion of religious and nationalistic fervour can be. In Southeastern Europe, for instance, the Balkans region has once again lived out the meaning of its name. Serbian Orthodox Christians, Croatian Roman Catholics and Bosnian Muslims have transformed the former Yugoslavia into the killing fields of the 1990s. In Israel Jews and Palestinians relive their Biblical struggle, while elsewhere in the Middle East Islamic fundamentalism takes a heavy toll on non-believers. Across the former Soviet Union religious conflicts fester in Chechyna, Armenia and Azerbiajan. Most ominously, on the Indian subcontinent the government in New Delhi, led by the Hindu nationalist Bharatiya Janata Party, has recently detonated several nuclear warheads, and, not to be outdone, Pakistan has followed suit with its own "Islamic bomb". As this century draws to a close sacral nationalism has once again fulfilled the need for "the sacred", while assuming, for the first time, atomic proportions.

ANTI-EMPIRIALISM

Another one of Conor Cruise O'Brien's core principles is his relentless opposition to imperialism. On this issue he has legitimately claimed "an underlying consistency and continuity".[27] Interestingly, he has broadened the definition of imperialism beyond its traditional meaning of great power interference in the southern hemisphere to include attempts by outsiders to assert control over any region not their own – north or south, east or west – and the abuse of power at *any* level – even the personal. It is, in short, an illegitimate effort to dominate other states, societies or individuals, often backed by the explicit use of violence or by the implicit threat to resort to force. Conor, therefore, has detected imperialism at work not only in the more traditional locations in Africa and Asia, but in places and in relationships that the less observant eye would overlook.

While a member of Ireland's United Nations delegation in the late 1950s, Conor was an outspoken critic of European imperialism, especially French colonialism in Algeria.[28] As Dag Hammarskjöld's representative in Katanga in 1961 he opposed Belgium's and Great Britain's "imperialist enterprise" in the region: their covert support for the province's secession from the Congo. His outspoken criticism prompted Harold Macmillan, the British Prime Minister, to ask: "Who is Conor O'Brien?"[29] He soon found out, much to his chagrin, and our pleasure.

Throughout the 1960s Conor vigorously protested against the American war in Vietnam, which he interpreted not as an anti-communist crusade, but an imperialist project. On the same grounds, and in the same decade, he opposed the Nigerian Federation's war against Biafran autonomy. From the 1960s until the 1990s he ardently resisted apartheid in South Africa; in fact, in 1966 he was named chairman of the Irish Anti-Apartheid Movement.[30] By the 1980s, however, Conor detected that an authoritarian impulse had arisen among the anti-apartheid protestors themselves and so he courageously battled the academic boycott they had imposed against South Africa by embarking on a lecture tour there. He rightly discerned that the anti-imperialists had become imperialists and the main casualties were likely to be free speech and academic freedom –

19

requisite values in post-apartheid South Africa and, indeed, principles that Conor had defended in Africa twenty years earlier while vice-chancellor of the University of Ghana.[31]

By the same token, in the 1970s Conor, in a *tour de force* of intellectual integrity and political consistency, began applying the imperialist paradigm to a faith few had suspected of harbouring colonial tendencies: Irish Catholic nationalism. With striking originality, and devastating effect, he demonstrated that Irish irredentism, especially in its violent, republican incarnation, presented as great a threat to Ulster Protestants as French imperialism posed to native Algerians. This time, he asserted, "it was the IRA who were the imperialists, since they were trying to annex by force a territory a large majority of whose inhabitants were opposed to them . . . "[32] Conor's imperialist critique of Irish nationalism met with fierce resistance at home, especially – and this is ironic – from those most critical of western colonialism in Africa and Asia. His courageous stand, though, has altered the terms of the debate about Northern Ireland in his native land; exactly how will be discussed below.

Conor Cruise O'Brien has pinpointed colonial tendencies operating outside of the political realm. Given his life-long inquiry into sacral nationalism, he knows that organised religions can be just as imperialistic as governments, if not more subtle in their methods. He has called the Catholic Church to task for many shortcomings, most notably for its refusal to sanction the use of contraception, which would stem population growth, and thereby alleviate suffering, in the Third World. Pope John Paul II has come under close scrutiny for this policy. In the mid-1980s Conor registered his respect for this "man of profound convictions, and of high personal courage, proved in the frightful conditions of wartime Poland", but at the same time he decried the Pontiff's "great astuteness, even deviousness, in tactical matters", which conceal "the full depths of his traditional Tridentine Catholicity and of an authoritarianism gentle and unassuming in style, but implacable in substance".[33] Recently, the Vatican's uncompromising stand against contraception at the UN-sponsored Cairo Conference on Population and Development in 1994 has hardened Conor's attitude toward the Pontiff: "I frankly abhor Pope John Paul II," he remarked that same year (while still admitting "a meed of grudging admiration for the scope of his grand design, and the energy and tactical craftiness which he has devoted to its fulfilment".)[34]

Nonetheless – and this is crucial – Conor has never sought to reform religion out of existence, to cripple it or to abolish it altogether. Why?

Because he grasps that just as destructive as the one religious extreme – "God Land", that furious amalgam of religion and nationalism – is its irreligious antithesis: godlessness. What transpires in the moral vacuum of godlessness is inimical to civilisation. Barbarous regimes – revolutionary republicanism, national socialism, communism – deify the nation, the volk and the party instead of God. In this new, chilling order the state no longer answers to a higher authority, only to itself; it becomes, in short, the final arbiter of righteousness. History has revealed the baleful consequences of such moral reversals. Acutely aware of them, Conor has waged a battle against godlessness. He denounces Nietzsche, for example, because the accumulated effects of his writings led, in twentieth-century Europe, to "the reversal of the Christian ethic, based on compassion, which had survived the decline of revealed religion and animated the Enlightenment tradition",[35] a process he describes elsewhere as "the destruction of the traditional Judeo-Christian morality in its post-Enlightenment form".[36] It is imperative, Conor asserts, that we shield the post-Enlightenment Judeo-Christian ethic from its foes and, likewise, preserve the Enlightenment's intellectual legacy. Thus he has cautioned, on the eve of the millennium, that:

> The Enlightenment we need is one that is aware of the dark, especially the dark in ourselves. An Enlightenment that is on guard against hubris. An Enlightenment that is aware that there is far more evidence extant in favour of the Christian doctrine of Original Sin than of Rousseau's doctrine of Original Virtue. An Enlightenment that respects the religious imagination, but not the claim of some religions to know what God wants from us and to have the duty to enforce that knowledge.[37]

In brief, Conor rejects godless amorality; he respects organised religions; yet he repudiates the imperialistic tendencies inherent in them, seeing no contradiction in enjoining these repositories of "the sacred" to be more humane.

On a similar note, O'Brien knows that interpersonal interactions provide fertile ground for imperialistic seeds to take root. In his arresting study, *The Suspecting Glance*, he explores the quality of "suspicion" in the writing of Machiavelli, Burke, Nietzsche and Yeats. "All four are suspicious," Conor informs us, "in that they are profoundly aware of the resource and versatility of violence and deception in man, in society and in themselves."[38] While he was teaching at New York University in the 1960s, however, he was disconcerted by the lack of suspicion among his students. On the one hand, he tells us, they did suspect "the president of the United States, the board of General Motors, J Edgar Hoover and the trustees of the university".[39] They were also quick to protest against American intervention in Southeast Asia, sometimes intentionally courting a violent reaction in the process. On the other hand, Conor's students "did not suspect their own slogans or sages, they suspected one another too little, they suspected their own individual selves not at all". And that, according to Conor, "was the worst of it. They had not the slightest suspicion that, in their own way of speaking to policemen, there might lurk the germ of some future Vietnam or Czechoslovakia". Likewise, they assumed that a "world of which they had the ordering would automatically be a Utopia, ensured by the correctness of their slogans and the sincerity of their beliefs in them".

In the face of this blissful ignorance, Conor decided to disconcert his students in turn. He argued against the replacement of one form of imperialism with another, including personal tyrannies imposed in the name of progress. And, as he recalls, instead of "telling them about Marcuse or even Shelley, I went on endlessly telling them about Edmund Burke, a thinker to whom no spontaneous inclination of their own would ever have drawn them". Conor, in short, refused to reflexively sanction his students' conviction "that great literature should always in some way aid or validate the revolutionary process". Life and art, in his eyes, are not so easily reduced.

THE IMAGINATION AND POLITICS
The mention of Burke, Shelley, Marcuse and revolution all in the same breath raises another compelling motif of Conor's work: the interrelationship between the creative imagination and politics. "All my adult life," he once said, "I have been interested both in the world of the imagination and in the world of politics and in forms of interaction between these two worlds." More specifically, he is curious about how the "imagined order" affects the "political order", how the life of the mind translates into life on the street. While exploring this fascinating link, Conor has paid great heed to literature, one of the strongest artistic influences on our political consciousness. Exactly how literature – when filtered through the imagination – influences reality is endlessly intriguing to Conor, who has explored this process to great effect. His earliest essays, written under the pseudonym "Donat O'Donnell" for the *Bell, Hudson Review, Kenyon Review* and other journals, grapple with this theme. His first book, *Maria Cross*, published in 1952, illumines the imaginative

22

world of a series of Catholic writers, including François Mauriac, Graham Greene, Evelyn Waugh and Charles Péguy. One decade later he navigated the political undercurrents and eddies frothing just beneath the surface of WB Yeats' poetry and produced what is, perhaps, his most profound essay, "Passion and Cunning". Of his subject O'Brien concluded: "The political man had his cautious understanding with Fascism, the diplomatic relation to a great force; the poet conveyed the nature of the force, the dimension of the tragedy."[40] Conor has also published an elegant biography of Albert Camus, a writer compelled, owing to the circumstances of his own life, to explore not the intersection, but the collision, of the imagination and politics. Conor has reservations about Camus' ultimate judgement – in favour of his personal history, his family, France; les colons of Algeria rather than les colonisés – but he acknowledges the writer's honesty. In his novel, The Fall, and elsewhere, Camus "faced the implications of the choice he made . . . with unmatched imaginative integrity".[41] Camus may have "flinched", but artistically "he explored with increasing subtlety and honesty the nature and the consequences of his flinching".

Conor's exploration of the nexus between the imagination and politics has confirmed his judgement that the world of the intellect does affect life in the polis. The imagination, where ideas are tested against reality, is the staging ground for the political arena. When this experiment assumes literary form the author is responsible for the consequences, Conor asserts. Why? Because the writer "is not just a symptom or a clinical indicator. The imagined order which he creates legitimises in others some image of that order. To legitimise means to free something which would otherwise be at least partly suppressed".[42] Conor first said these words about Friedrich Nietzsche, whom he called "one of the great liberators" – of Hitler, for instance. His words of caution, though, equally apply to all artisans of the pen, for writing "is a form of social communication, a cryptic signalling going on in society and history".[43] A poem, in other words, can be like a lit match dropped in a parched forest, its impact a series of ever-widening concentric circles of flame that engulf culture, politics and society – and sometimes become an apocalypse.

Conor Cruise O'Brien's inquiry into the relationship between the literary imagination and politics casts light on one of his related pursuits: the unrelenting application of ideas to reality. Never content to restrict his principles to the printed page, he has consistently correlated them to the real world – as a statesman, university president, parliamentary representative and government minister. The American writer Shelby

Steele, who, like Conor, is acutely aware of the influence of the cognitive world on the physical universe, calls this a search for "the right *fit* of idea to reality".[44] Steele even posits that "reality must always have priority, accepting only those ideas that truly illuminate it".

Conor seeks that right fit. His readiness to wade into the rough and tumble of everyday existence has enabled him to discover it. This real-life experience also distinguishes him from many intellectuals. Indeed, it accounts for the arresting opening sentence in his essay exploring the "ferocious wisdom" of the Machiavellian ethic: "The blood shed is real blood."[45] Niccolò Machiavelli, O'Brien reminds us, witnessed Cesare Borgia murder several men (Vitellozzo, Oliverotto, Ramiro) in cold – *real* – blood: such ruthlessness so impressed the Florentine that he translated it into his famous princely code of behaviour. About this homicidal context Conor insists: "The reality of the bloodshed needs to be stressed, because more than four centuries have set up screens of history and commentary between us and Machiavelli."[46] Only someone seeking the right fit of ideas to reality would take pains to excavate the detritus of the past. Conor has completed this archaeological task; by doing so he has revealed the foundation of Machiavelli's mindset: his witness to, and revelry in, political murder. Conor, in sum, is interested in life as it *is*, not how he would like it to be, a bond with reality that accounts for his accomplishments in so many areas of intellectual endeavour.

LEARNING AND LETTERS

Owing to his dedication to the principle that ideas matter, to uncovering the link between the imagination and politics, to finding the right fit between ideas and reality, Conor Cruise O'Brien has enriched intellectual and moral life in Ireland and beyond. His contribution to learning and letters is immeasurable. In his essay in this volume, the distinguished historian John Lukacs accurately identifies an existential hunger at the core of humanity on the eve of the twenty-first century: we are, he says, "famishing for the truth". We hope, therefore, that scholars today are fired by "what had once impelled Thucydides to write his first history: the purpose of reducing untruth". Conor certainly is. By no means, however, does he claim a monopoly on *knowing* the truth, this most elusive of entities. Such knowledge, after all, is the self-proclaimed holy writ of ideologues, his philosophical antipodes. Yet he has shared with us, through open, candid, public debate, the results of his honest efforts to understand it, or at least to dilute "untruth".

24

The rich fruits of Conor's harvest are his books, plays, essays and articles. They are so delectable because he brings to them what the Italian thinker Giambattista Vico defined as *fantasia*, meaning imaginative insight, or the creative artistry of a novelist – a quality that Conor once ascribed to the accomplished historian Frank Callanan, a contributor to this volume.[47] Another of the ingredients that makes Conor's writing so successful, his intellectual message so vibrant, is his unrivalled prose style, a gift that distinguishes him, according to his biographer, as "the most important Irish non-fiction writer of the twentieth century".[48]

Conor's writing is often witty, irreverent and delightfully funny, but it can also be incisive, sardonic, unforgiving. These characteristics often appear side-by-side in the same piece. In an impious reflection on James Joyce's *A Portrait of the Artist as a Young Man*, for example, Conor declares, in response to Stephen Dedalus' predilection for navel-gazing: "But surely I can't be the only reader of *A Portrait* who gets put off by all this relentless rapture about self . . . "[49] He treasures, instead, "those rare moments when members of the 'shadowy cast behind the brilliantly lit central figure' are allowed their brief time out in the light" – such as the epic "Christmas row between Dante, Mr Casey and Mr Dedalus over Parnell and his priests" – and therefore wonders if anyone else can "read *A Portrait* without wanting to hear more about Stephen's father, and less about Mr Dedalus' pompous prig of a son?" After dispensing with this humorous touch, Conor shifts gears, ending his review with a devastating remark about both book and country: "*A Portrait* is, as they say, a chapter in our intellectual and moral history. Perhaps that's among the reasons why I can't like it. Our intellectual and moral history is a lacerating sort of affair." Conor is merciless elsewhere. In an article discussing the legacy of Yeats' turn-of-the-century play *Cathleen Ní Houlihan*, he calls the eponymous main character, whose deathly prophecy about the youth of Ireland – "They that have red cheeks will have pale cheeks for my sake" – was fulfilled in 1916, a "blood-thirsty Irish Valkryie".[50] Generating such indignation is the slow burn of Conor's restless intellect; a bed of smouldering embers, it often erupts into incandescent language to singe our sensibilities.

Employing such forthright prose, Conor has broken down intellectual barriers. He has forced us to reevaluate our received notions about political ideologies (sacral nationalism, revolutionary republicanism, communism, anti-communism), individuals (Rousseau, Burke, Yeats, Jefferson) and regions (the Middle East, South Africa, the British Isles, North and Central America). His original interpretations have often reshaped the parameters of intellectual discourse; his ideas have insinuated themselves into debates to such an extent that they now define them.[51] Thus it can truly be said of Conor's readers, admirers and, definitely, his antagonists that he has, to borrow Edmund Burke's phrase, "set them on thinking".[52] This effect is a testament to the power of his ideas. So is the fact that Conor's work does not go unnoticed by others. Academics have made a living countering his arguments. Journalists too have profited: one of Conor's recent newspaper articles evincing empathy with Ian Paisley's efforts to preserve the union of Northern Ireland and Great Britain, for example, set off a flurry of frantic replies in the Irish media.[53] Perusing the Sunday papers in Ireland would be an extremely mundane exercise without the lightning rod of Conor Cruise O'Brien to excite readers!

The intellectual debt is real, however. By toppling so many totems Conor has created new, safe spaces for social reflection. He and his likeminded colleagues in academia and journalism have made it possible for other writers to take risks, to reexamine the icons of European, Irish and American life. Indeed, an entire generation of scholars stands on his shoulders (many of whom honour him in this book) and they are now building on the foundation of his work. Consequently, exciting new perspectives on the Enlightenment, the early American republic, Thomas Jefferson, WB Yeats, Charles Stewart Parnell, Irish nationalism, Northern Ireland, South Africa, Israel, China, international affairs and literature are emerging from the new intellectual landscape shaped by Conor Cruise O'Brien.

RACISM AND POLITICAL VIOLENCE
There is another debt as well, of a moral nature. It arises out of a contribution as genuine as the scholarly one: Conor's lifelong campaigns against racism and political violence. His opposition to racial prejudice formed early. As a young student whose father had been an agnostic, attending a liberal, non-denominational school in a devoutly Catholic country, Conor developed, he has said, "a certain bond" for outsiders: in Ireland this meant Protestants and Jews. This empathy soon translated into an instinctual suspicion of racism, particularly anti-semitism. If, Conor recalls in his book, *The Siege: The Saga of Israel and Zionism*, he "heard a Catholic priest or layman referring to Jews in a hostile manner", it was unlikely that person would be a friend to either his family or to himself.[54] This sentiment grew stronger later in life, and throughout his work – in *The Suspecting Glance, God Land, The Siege*, his literary essays

and newspaper articles – Conor has systematically refuted anti-semitism in theory, history and in practice.

Nor does Conor tolerate any other expression of racism. While an undergraduate at Trinity College he joined with Professor RB McDowell and several other students to protest the Dublin University Boat Club's discrimination against a visiting African student, an act they labelled, in a letter to the college paper, an "amazing case of race prejudice and bad manners".[55] The same sensibilities elucidate his opposition to apartheid in South Africa. During a UN General Assembly debate on apartheid in 1957, he urged the delegates, since they all agreed "that racial discrimination is in itself fundamentally wrong and immoral", to impress upon the government of South Africa "that its policies are reprobated by the overwhelming majority of mankind, must therefore fail and ought therefore to be changed". Conor has continued his critique of racism in *The Long Affair*, his recent book about Thomas Jefferson. He rejects all of the *à la mode* rationalisations about Jefferson's ownership of slaves and concludes that "Jefferson's status as the oracle of Liberty, within the American civil religion . . . is becoming unsustainable in a post-racist America".[56] Elsewhere he calls the putative author of the Declaration of Independence "very cold and very false in everything he says about race".[57] What's more, he finds something "most repugnant in that part of Jefferson which touches on the suppressed black population of the period".

Like racism, violence is equally corrosive of civilised life. One of the great tests of any person living in a democracy, therefore, is his or her relationship to the illicit use of force. This is emphatically true of intellectuals, for they are, in essence, shapers of public opinion. Reflecting on this issue, Paul Johnson once remarked:

> Now, here we come to the great crux of the intellectual life: the attitude to violence. It is the fence at which most secular intellectuals, be they pacifist or not, stumble and fall into inconsistency – or, indeed, into sheer incoherence. They may renounce it in theory, as indeed in logic they must since it is the antithesis of rational methods of solving problems. But in practice they find themselves from time to time endorsing it – what might be called the Necessary Murder Syndrome – or approving its use by those with whom they sympathise. Other intellectuals, confronted with the fact of violence practised by those they wish to defend, simply transfer the moral responsibility, by ingenious argument, to others whom they wish to attack.[58]

In this century of upheaval many renowned Irish and international figures have failed this test. But not Conor Cruise O'Brien. He has

27

relentlessly opposed the illegitimate use of violence in principle and in practice. Commentary on this subject interweaves throughout the body of his writing – we have already discussed his interpretations of Machiavelli and the regicide of Louis XVI – and is concentrated in his striking book *Herod: Reflections on Political Violence*. This volume gathers together some of his most robust essays about terrorism and the resort to unlawful force. It also includes three original plays – *King Herod Explains, Salome and the Wild Man* and *King Herod Advises* – all of which explore the legitimation of violence, a theme addressed in Conor's earlier drama about events in the Congo, *Murderous Angels*.

With regard to illicit violence, Conor has been bravest at home, in Ireland, where he has condemned terrorists *of all hues*, the republican and loyalist ideologies that have sustained them and their apologists who, like Machiavelli, have been seduced by the "whiff", the glamour, of political murder. He joined this battle in the early 1970s when the Provisional IRA opened its offensive in Northern Ireland and he has waged it ever since as a political analyst, politician and author.[59] In so doing, he certainly has reflected the attitudes of the vast majority of Irish citizens – North and South – who, as a whole, abhor terrorism. And, without a doubt, other likeminded politicians, journalists and scholars soon joined him, brave-hearted souls such as John A Murphy, Ruth Dudley Edwards, Kevin Myers and Eoghan Harris. Together, these commentators have forced Irish nationalism to reexamine its sacred values and to accept the legitimacy of Protestant unionism.

Yet within the Catholic, nationalist tradition Conor was the first to raise his head above the parapet. He was the lonely sceptic, the dissident voice in Ireland who defied Provisional IRA violence and the republican tradition. This stand was remarkable not only for its immediate bravery, but also in the light of Conor's strong personal links with Irish nationalism. Several members of his family – his grandfather David Sheehy, his uncle Tom Kettle – campaigned for Irish Home Rule during the late nineteenth and early twentieth centuries as members of the Irish Parliamentary Party.[60] His great-uncle Father Eugene Sheey was the famous Land League Priest. His father, Francis Cruise O'Brien, wrote for several nationalist newspapers; his mother, Kathleen Sheehy, and her sister Hanna were the inspirations for the patriotic Miss Ivors in James Joyce's unforgettable story "The Dead". Conor himself is a noted student of Irish history and culture, a fluent Irish speaker and an expert on the Irish Literary Renaissance. What's more, during the late 1960s and 1970s he served as a Dáil deputy and government minister, a period during which he operated at the heart of the Irish nationalist establishment.

By opposing Irish republican violence in support of Irish nationalist aims Conor, in effect, called into question not only the founding principles of his society, but some of the themes of his own family history. Visualising such an intellectual quantum leap requires great imaginative integrity. Few people possess this quality; of those who do, even fewer are prepared to act on it. Conor Cruise O'Brien is one of them. During his long campaign against terrorism, Conor disputed the comfortable orthodoxies of Catholic Ireland. He reminded nationalists of unpleasant realities: their cost-free ambiguity *vis-à-vis* Northern Ireland; how the assertion of sovereignty in Articles two and three of the Irish Constitution destabilised political life in Ulster; how *revanchist* language legitimates violent acts. In sum, as Conor notes in *Herod*:

> Ireland's right to unity; the corresponding non-right of the Northern Ireland majority to have a state of their own; the deluded and ridiculous nature of that majority; the baseness of the British, the absurdity of their institutions and the brutality of their forces; the identification of Irish patriotism with anti-British feeling – these were the dominant assumptions of the [Irish] press and of the vein of tribal self-righteousness which it fed, and on which it fed. Reading this stuff anyone who had lived among other tribes for any length of time had to feel choked with the sense of *déjà vu* and *déjà entendu* and with the sheer implacable, impenetrable cosiness of it all.[61]

At the same time, one fact must be emphasised: throughout his struggle against the IRA, Conor has never opposed a united Ireland *in principle*. Many people overlook this point. They fail to see that what has always inspired Conor's analysis is his conviction that the rights of the Protestant people of Northern Ireland, and their desire to remain a part of the United Kingdom, are as sacrosanct as the rights and wishes of Irish Catholics – and, most important, the aspirations of both communities must always be expressed through the democratic process.

Still, by voicing his heretical opinions about Irish republican violence Conor collided with the prevailing wisdom of a large segment of the political elite, most of the trendy intelligentsia, their sympathisers in the press and a slice of the electorate in thrall to the ghosts of Irish martyrs. Unnerved by Conor's acute analysis, the media lashed out at him. In the late 1970s Conor elucidated the origins of their disproportionate response: people who, in principle, "dislike anything to do with violence do not like to be reminded that their own habitual assumptions may be feeding that violence".[62] By the same token, Irish Catholic nationalists expected censure from hostile quarters (the British media, Ulster unionists) and reconciled themselves to it by reference to its origins, but "sacrilegious" criticism proffered by someone from their own heritage – and a government minister, to boot – overwhelmed their imaginative capabilities. And for a hard core of nationalists Conor's greatest sin has been to humanise Protestants in Ulster – the ancient enemy – and they have never forgiven him for it.

Revisited today, the carping is demeaning of its begetters ("begrudgers" is the appropriate Irish phrase!). But in the face of it Conor exhibited great moral and physical courage. Considering the resolute public figures that the IRA and other republican terrorists murdered (Airey Neave, Christopher Ewart-Biggs, Ian Gow) and how the criticism levelled at Conor sanctioned, in a real sense, an assault on him, it is fair to conclude that his own life was danger. But Conor did not bend. In the end, though – and this underscores his mettle – he did loosen his ties with a significant part of Irish culture, which is always a difficult step for a public intellectual to take. As Conor himself has written in his book, *Power and Consciousness*, "for the intellectual to make a clean break with a society which on the whole has favoured him requires extraordinary conditions".[63] Examples include the society's adherence "to an ideology which he finds to be intellectually unsatisfactory and which, therefore, his own integrity requires him to fight" or "intellectually indefensible social anarchisms within the society" itself.

Conditions in Ireland in the 1970s were extraordinary: the Provisional IRA's campaign, and its loyalist paramilitary counterpart, were taking a heavy toll in Northern Ireland and in the Republic; government ministers were on trial for allegedly channelling money and weapons to the IRA; democratic life on the island was in peril. To counter this threat, Conor acted decisively. Since then he has followed his political principles to their logical conclusions. In the mid-1980s he opposed the Anglo-Irish Agreement, which granted Dublin a consultative role on matters relating to Catholics in Northern Ireland, on the grounds that it represented creeping Irish irredentism aimed at Ulster. In the early 1990s Conor announced that he had forsaken part of his nationalist heritage to become a unionist. In a 1992 address to the "Friends of the Union" he labelled this leap an "existential metamorphosis".[64] It was a requisite move, he explained, because in the face of nationalist rhetoric demanding a united

Ireland and republican terrorism reinforcing this demand (a "nice cop, tough cop routine") it was not enough simply to criticise nationalism: it became necessary "to defend publicly the Union that was being subjected to that perfidious and murderous combined attack" – what Conor would designate as imperialism, in other words, an Irish variant as pernicious as its historical and international analogues.

Adhering to this line of reasoning, Conor became a member of the UK/Unionist Party in 1996. Led by the intrepid Robert McCartney, this party not only courageously opposes loyalist and republican violence, but utterly rejects sectarianism in all of its guises. Conor joined the UK/Unionists to demonstrate in the most unequivocal manner possible his solidarity with those people combating IRA/Sinn Féin's terrorist enterprise: its systematic campaign of murdering Ulster Protestants and intimidating the surviving members of that besieged community into a united Ireland against their consent. By taking this step Conor has asserted the fundamental human right of the citizens of Ulster – unionist and nationalist alike – to construct constitutional arrangements of their own design through exclusively democratic means.[65]

In the same vein, throughout the 1990s Conor has stridently criticised the peace process in Northern Ireland and, more recently, the Belfast Agreement of April 1998 due to what he considers their common inherent danger, namely, the appeasement of terrorists. More specifically, he has condemned allowing the representatives of paramilitary organisations on either end of the political spectrum to enter into both the democratic process and the Northern Ireland executive established by the peace settlement *before* they have handed over their arsenals. He has correctly argued that their cease-fires are not permanent, but temporary, and are punctuated by periodic acts of violence deliberately intended to extract further concessions from the British and Irish governments. For this reason Conor has objected to the release of prisoners convicted of terrorist offences when they can so easily rejoin paramilitary structures that remain intact. Conor has also repeatedly warned against crippling the Royal Ulster Constabulary (RUC) by sanctioning over-zealous reforms favoured by IRA/Sinn Féin, such as dropping the word "Royal" from its name or introducing community policing. The latter proposal is particularly sinister. Both loyalist and republican paramilitary groups will hijack community policing bodies in order to tighten their already lethal strangleholds on traumatised neighbourhoods throughout Ulster, turning them once and for all into local criminal fiefdoms. The combined effect of these reforms, as Conor accurately sees it, will be the demoralisation of the RUC, an outcome that will then pave the way for the Provisional IRA to resume its campaign of violence with, chillingly, greater prospects for success.[66]

As a result of this highly controversial stance – he has actually been accused of opposing *peace* in Ulster, which is patently untrue – Conor has incurred the wrath of his long-time antagonists, as one would expect. But on several tactical issues he has also parted with his erstwhile allies, including, quite interestingly, several contributors to this volume. The redoubtable political commentator Eoghan Harris, for example, has lauded David Trimble, the leader of the Ulster Unionist Party, for his courageous effort to hold the middle ground and he believes that the peace settlement and the Northern Ireland Assembly deserve a fair chance. Kevin Myers, who discounted the likelihood of a political settlement ever being reached, would tend to agree. The same holds true for the renowned historian Ruth Dudley Edwards, who also, despite her deep empathy for Ulster Protestants, has noted in her contribution to this *Festshrift* that "I did not follow Conor into membership of a unionist party, nor will I: I am neither nationalist nor unionist, just a democrat". Thomas Flanagan has expressed similar reservations about Conor's recent political choices in his own gallant essay: "Many of his oldest friends cannot follow him along that path, and at the moment I myself am one of them." John A Murphy, whose integrity is unassailable, could not countenance those who opposed the Northern Ireland peace negotiations: he once asserted in his own erudite newspaper column that "They want the talks to fail if only because they have predicted so often that the talks *will* fail. This applies especially to . . . Conor Cruise O'Brien, the most eloquent of the prophets of doom". Conor, however, while maintaining the highest regard for his peers, has stood fast by his principles. As he recently said, in contrasting himself with other Irish politicians (and their sympathisers):

> I should be ashamed to be an ally of anyone who was allied with the political representatives of armed paramilitaries of any kind. I should be ashamed to be associated with the political representatives of the IRA, as our Taoiseach and other leading Irish politicians are. I should be ashamed to be associated with the political representatives of loyalist paramilitaries . . . [67]

* * *

For the past twenty-five years Conor has challenged his compatriots to meet the highest standards of public life. In the process he has refuted – to everyone's benefit – Alexis de Tocqueville's dictum that "No man can struggle with advantage against the spirit of his age and his country . . . " Conor and his sympathetic colleagues in the media, politics and academic life – despite their current tactical differences – have interrogated the "spirit" of their times, to advantageous effect. They have ushered in a serious revision of Irish historical interpretation. They have forced Irish nationalists to accept responsibility for their rhetoric. A quarter of a century after Conor began stressing the need for Protestant unionist "consent" to any constitutional arrangement in Ireland it has become one of the cardinal precepts of Irish political life. And in April 1998 the people of Ireland voted to amend Articles two and three of the Republic's constitution so that they no longer claim sovereignty over Northern Ireland.

Underscoring these accomplishments is Conor's extraordinary gift of political intuition. In this regard, he is the heir of Edmund Burke, Abraham Lincoln, Winston Churchill and Franklin Roosevelt, all of whom possessed extraordinary political judgement, which was the by-product of imaginative insight fired by a searing analysis of reality. These men were able to discern the proper policies for their times even while swirling maelstroms obscured their vision: Burke was the first to anticipate the radical, irreversible, bloody turn the French Revolution was about to take; Lincoln instinctively knew that the North must fight the Civil War to preserve the Union for posterity; during the 1930s, Churchill predicted the malevolent consequences of a Hitlerian order in Europe; and Roosevelt guided a reluctant, isolationist America into war against Nazi Germany and Imperialist Japan, realising that only victory could preserve liberty for future generations.

Conor Cruise O'Brien possesses this same intuition – imagination, if you will – in an Irish context. When the Provisional IRA launched its offensive in the early 1970s he accurately anticipated the dire long-term consequences. More recently, the IRA's resumption of terrorism at Canary Wharf in early 1996 has validated his analysis of IRA/Sinn Féin's peace process strategy: tactical cessations of violence followed by bombings designed to pry loose concessions from London and Dublin. Since then Conor has continued to warn against negotiating with the representatives of republican and loyalist paramilitary groups, believing that their return to violence, in the absence of the decommissioning of their weapons, is inevitable. Recent appalling, savage outrages throughout Northern Ireland – in Ballymoney, Banbridge, Omagh – constitute the most tragic evidence of his prescience. In the wake of the

Omagh atrocity Conor has called for the internment of the dissident republicans responsible for this vile act.[68] But such a serious security proposal is not new: he has consistently advocated that internment be carried out simultaneously against *both* sets of terrorists on *both* sides of the border. Now other analysts and politicians are considering this option, with the growing support of the public in the United Kingdom and Ireland. Looking ahead, Conor foresees an added benefit to internment: once it is operational, this security regime can be swiftly employed – with popular approval – to shut down the Provisional IRA or loyalist terrorists should they return to violence in the future, as is likely. Finally, in his memoirs, Conor reminds Ulster unionists – a beleaguered group for whom his sympathy runs deep – that they may wish to consider their own options if the British government continues to appease IRA/Sinn Féin and carries our demoralising reforms of the RUC. In short, on Ireland Conor has been ahead of most people in Ireland. His analysis has anticipated events, not because he possesses bald clairvoyant powers, but because he commands an imaginative field of vision, an intellectual panorama that is the product of boundless creativity, steely intelligence and an iron grip on reality.

The foregoing references to Burke and Lincoln call to mind other figures who illuminate Conor's principled career. Alexander Solzhenitsyn, for instance, is an intellectual of towering moral stature. Unlike the Russian, however, Conor has never deliberately donned a virtuous mantle; he has been content to let his writings and actions speak for themselves. Eastern European political dissidents during the Cold War era, such as Vaclav Havel, also come to mind. Conor has certainly exhibited the same intellectual courage as many of these writers, but it is necessary to draw a distinction: because he did not live in an authoritarian state, Conor's actions never invoked state measures. Many liken Conor to George Orwell, another prose stylist, political essayist and fierce intellect, and this comparison is valid in many respects.

There is, perhaps, an even better historical precedent, one located in *fin-de-siècle* France. As gathering clouds of anti-semitism darkened the horizon – a warning of storms to come two generations later – as a nation prepared to sacrifice one of its own, an army officer unjustly accused of crimes he did not commit, a lone voice rang out in his defence. *"J'Accuse!"* thundered Émile Zola. With this bold, public indictment he halted the scapegoating of Captain Alfred Dreyfus in its tracks. He shredded the tissue of lies and deceit that had enshrouded the forsaken Frenchman. Indignant, his countrymen forced Zola to flee to England. In time, however, his fearless stand redeemed the honour of Captain Dreyfus and, some would say, what dignity his nation still possessed. Consequently, Zola will be forever immortalised by Anatole France's declaration: "He was a moment of the human conscience."

This same description holds true for Conor Cruise O'Brien – in Ireland and abroad. He has earned our respect; accordingly, we honour his achievements. He is richly deserving of this tribute, for his life calls to mind John Milton's description of Socrates – another learned citizen dedicated to the well-being of the commonweal:

> Whom well inspir'd the oracle pronounc'd
> Wisest of men.

His Irish and international accomplishments testify to his wisdom. Indeed, Conor's gifts to learning, to letters and to democratic society distinguish him – as David Welsh, one of the contributors to this volume, rightly notes – as "one of the great minds of our time".

THE BOOK AND THE MAN

Appropriately for a man inspired by the power and potential of the written word, this collection comprises a series of eloquent essays – and an original poem – that reflect upon the many dimensions of Conor's brilliant career. The contributions explore a wide range of international issues about which Conor is an acknowledged expert; as such, they underscore the universal scope of his world-class intellect. At the same time, many focus on Ireland, Conor's native land, soil in which he is deeply rooted. The chapter immediately following this introduction, and its author, capture this tension between the magnetic pull of distant shores and the irresistible call of home that lies at the heart of so much of Conor's work: Mary Robinson, now the United Nations High Commissioner of Human Rights and formerly President of Ireland, maps out a strategy for anchoring human rights in international law and throughout the international community in her splendid essay, "Developing Human Rights, Together".

Part III, "Poetry and Memoirs", opens with "The Stick", an enchanting poem by the Nobel Laureate Seamus Heaney that describes an inspirational Irish heirloom he once received from Conor and has now passed on to another promising young writer. The next three chapters – by John A Murphy, Darcy O'Brien and Thomas Flanagan – warmly reflect on personal aspects of Conor's life. These essays are welcome indeed: most people, after all, are aware of Conor's public and political activities, but they have little knowledge of his abiding commitment to family and friends, his good company and his irrepressible sense of humour. This imbalance can now be redressed.

The following section (IV) concentrates on the literature, history and politics of Ireland. Roy Foster's exquisite exposition, "Yeats at Fifty", traces the life of an Irish icon, a figure whom has endlessly engaged the intellectual energies of Conor Cruise O'Brien. Next, Kevin Myers, demonstrating his unrelenting honesty, boldly exposes a black hole within Ireland's historical memory: the nation's participation in the Great War. Frank Callanan, in a *tour de force* of historical interpretation, scrutinises one of the forces that suppressed this memory, Pearsean republicanism, and its predecessor, Parnellite nationalism. Patrick Lynch's invaluable narration of his experiences as Assistant to the Taoiseach, John A Costello, sheds new light on many of the leading members of the first Inter-Party government (1948-51) and two controversial issues whose fallout still lingers in the political atmosphere: Costello's announcement of the repeal of the External Relations Act in 1948 and the Mother and Child controversy. In her poignant memoir, Ruth Dudley Edwards recalls the family members, friends and social dynamics that shaped her personal outlook and political principles. Robert McCartney closes this section by forthrightly delineating a central element of his party's economic policy: how and why Northern Ireland's future economic well-being lies firmly within the United Kingdom.

Opening Part V, David Grene reflects on the teachers, professors, intellectual issues and eternal texts – encountered in Dublin and America – that transformed him into one of the leading Classicists of our day. Deirdre Levinson's exhilarating treatment of Shakespeare, "Politics as Psychology as Politics: a Reading of *Macbeth*", addresses one of Conor's major preoccupations: the interrelationship of literature and politics. John Lukacs takes up this theme in his essay, "Polite Letters and Clio's Fashions", a pathbreaking philosophical disquisition that also entreats us to consider history not as "A Science", but as a form of thought.

Part VI links two of the most profound political thinkers of the late-eighteenth and early-nineteenth centuries: Edmund Burke and Alexis de Tocqueville. Dáire Keogh presents a finely annotated version of Burke's December 1796 letter to Reverend Thomas Hussey, the president of the Catholic seminary at Maynooth. Written during a time of great tumult – in the wake of the French Revolution and on the eve of the United Irishmen's Rebellion of 1798 – Conor Cruise O'Brien has called this missive Burke's "political testament on Ireland". John Patrick Diggins, the distinguished American intellectual historian, eruditely portrays Alexis de Tocqueville grappling with the decline of aristocracy in France and the rise of democracy in America; bridging the gulf between these "old" and "new" worlds required this renowned commentator on the early American republic to summon all of his imaginative powers.

The proceeding section (VII) recognises Conor's life-long association with African affairs. By intertwining his reflections on African art with his deep knowledge of broader philosophical and historical issues, K Anthony Appiah weaves new, creative perspectives on African culture and its relationship with western society. Alex Kwapong fondly recalls Conor Cruise O'Brien's tenure as vice-chancellor of the University of Ghana in the mid-1960s, a period during which he firmly established the foundations of an institution vital to this nation's future development. In Ghana Conor went to great lengths to protect academic freedom. He then reprised this virtuoso performance twenty years later by defying the academic boycott imposed against South Africa; in his significant addition to this volume, David Welsh, Conor's host at the University of Cape Town, vividly recounts this episode.

Conor spent a good deal of his Irish diplomatic career at the United Nations, where the Middle East was often discussed; since then he has written extensively on both topics, which are highlighted in Part VIII. Gideon Rafael, who first met Conor when he represented Israel at the UN in the late 1950s, discusses the diplomatic challenges the new state faced in New York; he also includes a fascinating series of vignettes on the Secretaries General he cooperated with to resolve endless international crises. Daniel Pipes, the eminent Middle Eastern expert and author, explores the relationship between non-western societies, western culture and modernisation. For example, the rejection of classical music by fundamentalist Islamic societies, which is emblematic of their disdain for western culture generally, parallels their difficulties with modernisation. Japan, on the other hand, which has embraced classical music as well as other aspects of western culture, has successfully modernised in the twentieth century.

The themes of Part IX – democracy, history and culture – are quite relevant to Conor's career. In an essay redolent of the drama and richness of his award-winning books, Enrique Krauze identifies the political, economic and social forces working for – and against – the consolidation of democracy in Mexico. Xiao-huang Yin pinpoints the particular challenges democracy faces in China; he also notes how Conor's

37

comprehension of the interaction of global and local dynamics has deepened his own understanding of China. Eoghan Harris too acknowledges Conor's influence and links it to the trenchant analysis of Irish and European politics found in his polemic, "The Necessity of Social Democracy".

The final part of this book (X) returns to one of Conor Cruise O'Brien's earliest intellectual interests: the European literary tradition. Susan Dunn explores how the theme of her book – the regicide of Louis XVI – percolates throughout the work of Albert Camus, especially as he grappled with France's post-war tribulations and its traumatic withdrawal from Algeria. And then, the *pièce de resistance*: in his delightfully-entitled essay, "Maria Cross Roads", Owen Dudley Edwards revisits Conor's earliest literary criticism published in the *Bell* and traces the origins of his enduring study of European Catholic writers, *Maria Cross*. This chapter is a striking work of creative insight. It is also a fitting conclusion to a book dedicated to Conor Cruise O'Brien, a volume imbued with the promise of the imagination to recreate everyday life to our advantage.

II

THE FUTURE OF
HUMAN RIGHTS

CHAPTER 2

DEVELOPING HUMAN RIGHTS, TOGETHER

MARY ROBINSON

On 15 May 1997 I delivered the following address upon receiving the North-South Prize in Lisbon, Portugal. I now dedicate it, with admiration, to Conor Cruise O'Brien.

* * *

I AM HONOURED TO ACCEPT THIS PRIZE, TOGETHER WITH THE FORMER President of Chile, Patricio Aylwin, from President Jorge Sampaio on behalf of the North-South Centre. This Centre stands for the promotion of global interdependence and solidarity. The values you represent and the methods you choose to advance them – through education and inclusive dialogue – inspire the theme on which I would like to address you this evening: "Developing Human Rights, Together".

I say "together" in the sense that we need to forge coalitions of concern on human rights issues;

"Together" in the sense that we require effective ways of simultaneously advancing the two fundamental, indivisible and interdependent sets of rights: civil and political rights; and economic, social and cultural rights;

"Together" in the sense that we require greater effort to ensure that our local, national, regional and multilateral approaches to human rights complement and reinforce each other.

These are issues which I have addressed in various ways on other occasions. Indeed, they permeated discussion at the Council of Europe Interregional meeting in Strasbourg (at which I was honoured to act as rapporteur) in the lead up to the World Conference on Human Rights in Vienna in 1993. The intervening four years have not blunted the urgency of the discussion.

And during these past few years I have learned to value, with humility, the leadership on human rights issues which I have witnessed in difficult contexts and at different levels. In March of this year, for example, I returned to Rwanda to take part in the Pan-African Conference on Peace, Gender and Development. I was deeply impressed by the eloquence, passion and commitment of the women leaders from the nineteen African countries represented, who wasted no time, took the Beijing Programme of Action as a benchmark, and were determined to devise practical measures to implement it on the ground. Between conference sessions I also had a meeting with about thirty representatives of a local women's network, Pro-Femmes.

Each of these women represented a small, underfunded group dealing with the victims of the genocidal killing: the widows, orphans, homeless, rape victims and other wounded and traumatised. As I sat and heard their stories, and admired their commitment to promoting reconciliation while they rebuilt their lives and their communities, I was conscious that although they lacked access to minimal material resources they had harnessed great energies and empowered themselves to cope with daunting problems.

Their insights have prompted me to look, in this North-South forum, at the issue of tensions – real or perceived – between the developed and the developing worlds on issues of human rights protection. The reality is, of course, more complex, more differentiated than the broad-brush picture often presented. But I believe there is a problem which we need constantly to recognise and jointly address.

We are told about the different agendas of the developing and developed worlds, the different groupings in which they frequently find themselves in bodies such as the UN Commission on Human Rights. Stepping back from the debates about tactics, procedures and mechanisms, we need to constantly remind ourselves of the objectives of international human rights action. Everything begins and ends with a determination to secure a life of dignity – a truly human quality of life – for all the people in whose names we act. That is the only true measure of the worth of what we are doing. Fundamental to these discussions is the basic question: how best can those being denied their human rights be supported or helped?

I suggest that if we keep reminding ourselves of this basic question it will help us to steer a path through the difficulties and complexities. Defining those "being denied their human rights" requires rigorous fact-finding, free from any political or cultural bias, using internationally accepted standards as a yardstick. Asking ourselves "how best to support" means taking account of the particularities of each situation, the practical possibilities for action and self help, and assessing the full range of instruments for human rights protection and promotion in order to identify which are most likely to help in each situation.

I believe we should try to move away from the vocabulary and attitudes which shape the stereotyping of developed and developing countries' approaches to human rights issues. We are collective custodians of universal human rights standards, and any sense that we fall into camps of "accuser" and "accused" is absolutely corrosive of our joint purpose. The reality is that no group of countries has any grounds for complacency about its own human rights performance and no group of countries does itself justice by automatically slipping into the "victim" mode. Moreover, I noted with interest that at the recent annual session of the Commission on Human Rights in Geneva there were several instances where developed and developing countries voted together on issues of contention. The tensions which undoubtedly exist in regard to approaches to human rights internationally cannot, automatically, be characterised as representing a North-South divide. At the same time, it is also clear from the recent session of the Commission that there is a danger of such a divide emerging on more and more issues.

The two words I would most wish to see characterise the debate are "respect" and "responsibility".

Respect requires a readiness to listen to each other and really hear what is being said; an effort to understand why situations are as they are; and a willingness to take advice on the scope for effective preventive or remedial action. It also means a recognition of the contribution that different cultures bring to our collective work. Four years ago, at the Council of Europe Interregional meeting in Strasbourg, I emphasised that:

> more thought and effort must be given to enriching the human rights discourse by explicit reference to non-western religious and cultural

traditions. By tracing the linkages between constitutional values, on the one hand, and the concepts, ideas and institutions which are central to Islam and the Hindu-Buddhist tradition, or other traditions, the base of support for fundamental rights can be expanded and the claim to universality vindicated.

That broadening and enriching of the discourse has yet to happen; a renewed effort is required of all of us to ensure that it does. Above all, respect calls on our notions of dignity and moral obligation.

"Responsibility" is equally important. North or South, we have to be prepared to recognise problems where they exist, including in our own countries and our own regions. The claims of human solidarity with victims must be weighed alongside the claims of political solidarity with governments. If we are reluctant to take on our own responsibilities in our own regions, we risk creating a vacuum in which those who are more distant from the problem come to feel that they carry the sole burden of analysis and prescription.

I would suggest that the time is ripe for the formation of new coalitions of concern on human rights issues. The Cold War – whose divisions were inevitably projected into international debate on human rights issues – is now some years behind us. We have yet to forge the integrated approaches in the human rights area that might have been expected to emerge in the post-Cold War period. New working methods – infused by a renewed dedication to our basic purposes, a strengthened sense of respect, as well as a strengthened sense of responsibility – are urgently called for. It goes without saying that non-governmental organisations will have an important role to play as partners in such coalitions of concern.

The second sense in which I invoke the word "together" signifies the need to achieve simultaneous and complementary progress in relation to the two sets of rights enshrined, respectively, in the International Covenant on Civil and Political Rights and the International Covenant on Economic, Social and Cultural Rights.

The source document for all subsequent work, the 1948 Universal Declaration on Human Rights, represents a very balanced treatment of these two sets of rights. In the intervening years that balance has not always been respected; indeed, various commentators have pointed to serious neglect in the development of the concept of economic and social rights.

It is imperative that we get that balance right. It is not enough that our statements should proclaim the interdependence and indivisibility of both sets of rights; we have to know and live and feel the truth of what we are proclaiming.

This year marks the 150th anniversary of Ireland's Great Famine, which decimated our population and scarred our country in so many ways. The anniversary has given Irish people world-wide cause to reflect again on that terrible national trauma and to have an empathy with those who wonder what the "classical" human rights can mean to people dying of hunger on a massive scale.

But experience has taught us that beyond grief and outrage, beyond emergency responses to emergency situations, the only long-term answer is to advance with the two sets of rights – political and economic – in equilibrium. The Secretary General of the United Nations, Mr Kofi Annan, put it in these terms when he addressed the Commission on Human Rights in Geneva in April 1997:

> Truly sustainable development is possible only when the political, economic and social rights of all the people are fully respected. They help to create the social equilibrium which is vital if a society is to evolve in peace. The right to development is the measure of the respect of all other human rights. That should be our aim: a situation in which all individuals are enabled to maximise their potential and to contribute to the evolution of society as a whole.

An acceptance of the complementary nature of the two sets of rights means looking at how resources are allocated in the international bodies dealing with human rights; how agendas are structured; how outcomes are measured. It means better dialogue – and by this I do not mean conditionality – between the human rights community and the development community. It means that in assessing the human rights situation in a particular country we use criteria that reflect the importance and the complementarity of both sets of rights.

The third sense in which I use the word "together" is the need for mutually reinforcing mechanisms for human rights protection and promotion at national, regional and international levels.

It is perhaps tempting for those who are active in the international arena to see international action as a first and best response to a problem. In the human rights area that would represent a serious misordering of priorities. My firm belief remains that human rights are best protected at home, subject to the system of outer-protection afforded by international bodies.

A firmly rooted and resilient domestic system of protection and promotion is the best safeguard against human rights abuse. The development of such a system does not happen overnight; it requires time, care and commitment. It requires a variety of actions and a variety of actors. The international community can sometimes make a very effective contribution through the provision of advisory services and technical cooperation programmes; it should stand ready to do so.

The various regional bodies – such as the Council of Europe, the OSCE, the OAU, the OAS – also have a critical role to play. They offer an important intermediate point between national and international approaches, combining the "insiders" approach that flows from the regional relationship with the "outsiders" perspective that establishes a context beyond the domestic one.

We must avoid any sense of exclusivity or competition in trying to identify the respective roles for regional and international bodies. In some circumstances it may be more effective to allow time for a regional approach to achieve results; in other circumstances a sensitive interaction between regional and international consideration is likely to achieve greater impact.

At the international level the United Nations has, of course, a unique role and responsibility in human rights promotion and protection. The Universal Declaration of Human Rights is a clarion call whose note rings as true today as fifty years ago. Its first three lines provide the rationale for all our actions: "recognition of the inherent dignity and of the equal and inalienable rights of all members of the human family is the foundation of freedom, justice and peace in the world".

How to project the global role and authority of the United Nations is an issue receiving intensive examination under the leadership of the Secretary General. In the human rights area there is much to be done. There are major policy challenges, such as how to integrate human rights considerations into the political, humanitarian and peacekeeping tasks of the United Nations. There are also administrative and organisational challenges: how to ensure adequacy of resources for human rights activities; how to match growing tasks to limited resources; how to ensure that the Centre for Human Rights operates to the highest standards of efficiency and transparency.

In short, we need to look constantly both to the condition of the mechanisms and the quality of their interaction. International systems of human rights protection will be an empty shell without effective national systems; in their turn, national systems need the norms and protections afforded by international action; and regional mechanisms have a vital role in helping to mesh and reinforce action at both levels.

North or South, we inhabit a common territory when we come together on these issues of universal importance. Perhaps, to borrow language from the Irish poet and Nobel Prize winner, Seamus Heaney, we might entitle that common territory the Republic of Conscience. It is, indeed, as he says, a frugal republic, without privilege for any citizen; its symbols are simple – the eye, the ear, the mouth, the pen. And with his principled eloquence, Seamus Heaney conjures up a visit to that land for us in his poem "From the Republic of Conscience":

> The old man rose and gazed into my face
> and said that was official recognition
> that I was now a dual citizen.
>
> He therefore desired me when I got home
> to consider myself a representative
> and to speak on their behalf in my own tongue.
>
> Their embassies, he said, were everywhere
> but operated independently
> and no ambassador would ever be relieved.

We are all dual citizens; and there are many ambassadors of the Republic of Conscience in this room tonight. I am greatly honoured to receive your award.

III

POETRY AND MEMOIRS

CHAPTER 3

"THE STICK"

SEAMUS HEANEY

*This poem was read at a gathering in Dublin on 18 August 1998,
where Conor Cruise O'Brien was guest of honour. The lines were
specially written for the occasion and celebrate the passing on to the
poet Nuala Ní Dhomhnaill of a walking stick that had once belonged
to Charles Stewart Parnell. The provenance of this stick is rehearsed in
the poem: Conor had received it in 1962 from the poet WR Rodgers,
with the proviso that he pass it on at an appropriate time to another
Irish writer younger than himself. This Conor did, more than 20 years
ago, honouring me mightily and, at the same time, putting me faoi
gheasa to hand it on in turn. Now it is Nuala Ní Dhomhnaill's, and
she too will eventually have to "see it released /Back into the thickets
/And thick of the language".*

Whitethorn, not blackthorn,
More a staff than a switch,
So not like the one

The District Inspector
Tucked under the arm
Of his dress uniform

When he fronted processions,
As black as his boot
And neater than ninepence.

Mine came from Conor –
Illustrissimus donor –
Conor Cruise O'Brien

To whom it had come
Honoris causa
From WR Rodgers

And Bertie had got it
From Brinsley Mac
Namara, who'd got it

From a man in Avoca,
One Victor Byrne,
Collector, pub owner

And friend of the blacksmith
Who'd shod it with iron,
A hoof-angled ferrule

Put on by instruction
Of the one who had cut it
In Avondale Woods

(Rhyme him with "carnal"
Yourself if you want to)
Charles Stewart Parnell.

I'm amazed Conor parted
With it at all:
It was intellectual

Property nearly,
His who had written
Parnell and his Party.

The head of it's like
The head of a snake
Being banished by Patrick,

But poised for its comeback,
Rising to strike
As the knot and the curl

And the shine of the grain
Come clean in your palm
Like a *non serviam*

Now it's mine to pass on
I don't want this baton
Getting into the hands

Of what Mandelstam called
"The symphonic police."
I'd prefer it to go

To some finder or keeper,
Some rapt son or daughter
Astray like Aeneas

Conducting himself
By the light of the leaves.
I'd see it released

Back into the thickets
And thick of the language,
Into that *selva*

Selvaggia e forte
We cull and come through
As poets, if we're lucky.

53

CHAPTER 4

MYSELF AND "THE CRUISER"

JOHN A MURPHY

IN THE AUTUMN OF 1961 THE ISSUES OF THE CONGO CRISIS AND THE United Nations' role were fiercely debated in University College Cork by staff and students alike. It was the first time, certainly since the Spanish Civil War, that Cork academic minds were exercised by Ireland's part in international affairs. The debate was a reflection of the way in which the nation at large, experiencing somewhat of a cultural renaissance, was turning its face away from insular and arid discourse and towards the global political stage. Pride in the Irish army's UN role, and emotion stirred by the Niemba ambush fatalities the year before, explained much of the new public interest, but there was more to it than our national involvement.

Two conflicting worldviews emerged in the UCC debate. The conservative Irish Catholic mindset regarded the UN with considerable suspicion, seeing it as a secularising institution (and one of its agencies, UNESCO, as a proselytising body) and muttering darkly about the coercion of "Catholic" Katanga. On the other side, there was much enthusiasm for the idea of an independent Irish foreign policy favouring neither Cold War side and making a small, but notable, contribution – in keeping with our best historical traditions – to the cause of international peace and understanding through our policies in the UN forum and our Army's peacekeeping activities in various trouble-spots. From this perspective, the Congo crisis was seen as a crucial testcase.

As a recently-appointed and untenured young college lecturer, I found myself at odds on the whole issue with the senior members of what was then a very small history department. I passionately argued the UN case at student societies and public meetings. Almost inevitably, our cause found a personal focus in Conor Cruise O'Brien, the Irish diplomat who seemed to epitomise our country's exciting new departure in foreign policy. We were not unduly concerned with the complexities of how the UN mandate was being implemented or the precise circumstances surrounding the Irishman's resignation as the UN chief representative in the Congo. But he was certainly *our* man during those exciting weeks in UCC in late 1961.

In due course, I devoured *To Katanga and Back*, which remains my favourite Conor Cruise O'Brien publication. It is a fascinating insight into the UN politics of the day and Conor's own role in the Congo crisis. It containes a valuable exposition of the genesis and attempted development of an independent Irish foreign policy in the late 1950s and early 1960s. Moreover, it evinces in generous measure the author's characteristic and perennial qualities of stylishness, lucidity, wit and irony, which have not diminished in the long intervening years.

At this point, I must reassure the reader who may feel that I have already degenerated into unadulterated eulogy and hero-worship. From the mid-1970s, when I first met Conor, down to the present I have differed with him in varying degrees on what is generally, but unsatisfactorily, termed "the national question". The formative influences of my childhood and upbringing were significantly different from Conor's background. Born nearly ten years later, I grew up in small-town Co Cork in a strongly nationalist house during the intensely nationalist decade of the 1930s. My parents had been Sinn Féiners and Gaelic Leaguers and became ardent supporters of Eamon de Valera and Fianna Fáil. My native town of Macroom still had a Gaeltacht hinterland, and the cultural ambience of my boyhood was strongly Hiberno-English, to say the least. Not surprisingly, therefore, my instinctive – almost hereditary – dispositions coloured my views for a long time, being only slowly modified by my study of history and other influences.

I looked askance, for instance, at Conor's proposal (when he was Minister responsible for broadcasting in the 1973-77 coalition government) that BBC1 should become our second television channel. I rather pompously accused him of wishing to alienate "a national resource to another state".[1] I participated in the public debate in the matter, upholding the banner of cultural protectionism which, in the global village of the 1990s and the nightly multi-channel choices of my sitting room, is now shown to be a quaint delusion. Conor was probably right on that one. I think he was also right about "Section 31" of the Broadcasting

Act, which banned Sinn Féin, and other organisations with terrorist links, from the national airwaves. On balance, I believed that Section 31 should have been lifted so that spokesmen for terrorism would be ruthlessly exposed by fearless and vigorous media interviewers. As we now know, and as Conor predicted, when the ban was eventually suspended the spokesmen quickly became masters of the media and were given an easy ride, generally speaking, by the interviewers.

In the 1970s, however, my main opposition was to the politically-inspired historical revisionism promoted by the 1973-77 coalition government, notably by Conor.[2] The gist of this revisionist case was that the Provisional IRA (for whose works and bombs I frequently expressed abhorrence at an early stage) derived apparent justification from the physical force cult in modern Irish history.

In this respect, the debate about 1916 was central. The fiftieth anniversary of the Easter Rising had been celebrated in the Republic in 1966 with great pomp and triumphalism, unaffected, for the most part, by any self-questioning about what was commonly accepted as the great sacral event in modern Irish history. A decade or so later the atmosphere was totally changed, and in the context of the upsurge of violent nationalism in Northern Ireland, revisionists were suggesting that public commemorations of events such as 1916 contributed to the cult of physical force and blood sacrifice and gave aid and comfort to the Provisional IRA.[3]

Were the Provisionals the real heirs of 1916, as they themselves claimed and as Conor, from his perspective, also seemed to maintain? If, the argument ran, you applauded the actions of a small, self-appointed group in 1916 arrogating to themselves the right to make war in the name of the Irish people, then you could not consistently condemn latter-day republicans for acting on the same assumptions as Patrick Pearse and his comrades.

I argued publicly against various aspects of Conor's case. I disputed his view that our history classrooms were turning out "little IRA men" and I maintained that the IRA mind was formed by other, extramural influences.[4] At the 1976 Merriman Summer School I publicly suggested to Conor that, with regard to 1916, it was, to say the least, an incongruous position for a Labour minister in an independent Irish state to find himself in, namely, disapproving of the state's commemorating the insurrection in which James Connolly, the Labour Party's founder, had sacrificed himself for the cause of an Irish republic.

In April 1977 Conor (still a cabinet minister at that stage) and myself debated the 1916 question on RTÉ television. It was very much a single combat and both of us took it very seriously indeed. Conor put the anti-1916 revisionist case, of which he was the most eloquent and courageous exponent, if not, indeed, the "onlie begetter". My contention was that the Easter Rising was the wellspring of the flow of events leading to the foundation of the state, which should not, therefore, relinquish custody of the 1916 dynamic and its ideals to the Provisionals. The debate (which, it seems fair to say, ended in a draw) aroused considerable interest and a condensed printed version appeared in a daily newspaper some days later. The encounter gave *me*, at any rate, a lasting taste for arguing with Conor.

Not surprisingly, then, it was as an anti-Conor nationalist that I was perceived by many voters when I stood as an independent candidate for Seanad Éireann in the National University of Ireland constituency in August 1977. I recall the late Tomás Ó Fiaich, then President of Maynooth College and afterwards Cardinal Primate, promising me his first preference vote with the phrase "well, now, any man who can put Conor in his box . . . " I like to think, however, that there were other reasons why I won handsomely. Conor was also elected to the Seanad by Trinity College graduates, having failed to make it back to Dáil Éireann. During the brief time he spent in the Upper House, he and I got along amicably as fellow university senators.

In 1977-78, in *The Crane Bag* journal,[6] our argument about 1916 widened to a general debate on the nature of Irish nationalism. I praised the way in which Conor had, in the early 1970s:

> with characteristic pungency and courage, masterfully exposed the woolliness of Southern attitudes towards Northern Ireland and in particular the ambivalence of Southern thinking – or, more accurately, feeling – about the Provisional IRA. Because he persistently compelled people to make uncomfortable reappraisals of emotions cosily and lazily cherished, he incurred considerable personal and political hostility. He performed, then, a very great public service which will one day be appreciated as such.[7]

Having handed him this fragrant bouquet, I then proceeded to hurl brickbats at him, some of which had rougher corners than I would now wish:

> Having compelled us to ask questions, he provided no real answers. His pronouncements became increasingly abrasive and intolerant: those who disagreed with him he tended to see as conniving at subversion. Moreover, his magisterial tone became pedantic and supercilious, and this considerably diminished the force of the message he wished to convey.[8]

I suggested, somewhat presciently, that in his 1978 Ewart-Biggs memorial lecture he was already articulating "something like a neo-Unionist position".[9] But the nub of my criticism was in this passage:

He concentrates his attack on the excesses of nationalism and the ambivalences indubitably inherent in Irish nationalist attitudes but in so doing he indicts the whole nationalist population and especially anyone who articulates a unity aspiration. His attack on nationalism is a stalking-horse for an assault on nationality itself. Dr O'Brien's personal background and many-faceted career have made him a cosmopolitan *par excellence*, a man of the world in the literal sense, and he seems unable to realise that a sense of nationality (*pietas* towards the past, commitment to the present, hope for the future) is an integral and essential part of the common Irishman whose lifestyle, unlike that of Dr O'Brien, is of necessity bounded by domestic horizons.[10]

I now realise that the forceful observations and the caustic tone (in the best Conor Cruise O'Brien tradition!) of my *Crane Bag* article twenty years ago expressed the sharpness of differences between us then and contributed to a continuing edge in our relationship which, notwithstanding our deepening friendship, has not quite disappeared today.

At the time of the Falklands/Malvinas War, I supported Mr Haughey's government's neutral attitude as a responsible exercise of Irish foreign policy. In a newspaper article on the subject, I expressed regret that "Dr Conor Cruise O'Brien, who contributed substantially to the evolution of our independent foreign policy twenty years ago, should see the Government's present stance as Brit-bashing".[11] Thereupon, Conor promptly wrote me an open letter in his weekly *Irish Times* column, "arguing the toss with you, in a friendly way".[12] I replied in kind, expressing my great regard and admiration for him and reminding him that "in private conversation as in public utterances" I had defended him "against the yahoos who still rant incoherently whenever your name is mentioned".[13] Having concluded my argument, I expressed the wish in a postscript that "you're one Cruiser they won't sink".[14] Conor was graciousness itself in a final comment, responding to my accusation of his being patronising with a handsome apology.[15]

He was equally gracious when he made an extended commentary[16] on an article I wrote[17] in 1984 on the continuing 1916 debate. He divined correctly that I was increasingly uneasy – moving towards his position, in fact! – with the problems again posed by the Easter Rising in the context of the Provisional IRA's claim to legitimacy for their campaign. Conor found himself "agreeing with much of what John had to say but dissenting profoundly from his conclusions", while commenting that I had wrestled with the difficulty "honourably and honestly". On another occasion, when I protested publicly at a GAA game in Cork in 1981 against a minute's silence for the Maze hunger-strikers, he paid tribute to what he was kind enough to regard as a courageous action on my part.

Meanwhile, Conor had some fun, if not quite at my expense, certainly in my direction. In the course of a profile of myself, a journalist had this to say:

> When Conor Cruise O'Brien analyses our ambivalence about the North or lacerates Irish politicians, those who disagree with him can dismiss his views as those of someone who is "not really Irish". When John A Murphy casts a beady eye on our beliefs and institutions, his views cannot be so glibly dismissed – they are those of a man proud of his national identity. He's a native of Macroom . . . he's a lover of the Irish language and . . . he's a man not averse to pub conversations.[18]

The aspersions on his Irishness obviously riled Conor (and this is interesting in itself), but he dealt with the matter in mocking, playful and characteristically mischievous fashion.[19] He had a field day, applying what he called the Murphy Tests of Irishry to himself and satisfying himself that he had passed handsomely! However, he had to plead guilty to being somewhat removed from "Macroom, the declared epicentre of contemporary Hibernocentrism". Ouch! I knew then how people felt when he described them as a "bog oak monolith" and "inscrutable Bandonians".

But in between the brilliant clowning there were serious points to be made. While asserting that family and national pride could be both ludicrous and dangerous, nevertheless:

> I am proud of being an O'Brien. I am proud also of my mother's family, the Sheehy family, and the part they played in Irish history . . . I am Irish. I achieved this condition by being born in Ireland of Irish parents, many of whose ancestors were in this land before the Gaels blew in, those *parvenus*, bringing with them their outlandish Celtic *patois* and their foreign games.
>
> I am as autochthonous as it is humanly possible to be. I am older than the rocks among which I sit. I am proud – quite irrationally proud – of being Irish, even to an extravagant degree . . .

* * *

Over the years, my views and those of Conor, while not quite converging, have become different rather than conflicting, as he himself has remarked. Nevertheless, in recent months,[20] we have disagreed sharply in our views on the peace talks in Northern Ireland. While accepting Conor's active membership of the UK/Unionist Party as his own business, I regard his attitude to the talks as regrettably negative and, I fear, characteristically pessimistic. I said as much in January 1998 when I referred to those outside the talks process: "They want the talks to fail if only because they have predicted so often that the talks *will* fail. This applies especially to . . . Conor Cruise O'Brien, the most eloquent of the prophets of doom."[21] Though Conor did not reject my tribute to his eloquence, he (erroneously) interpreted my remarks as meaning he would like to see large-scale violence resume, which would make him "a monster of cruel egoism".[22] He suggested we should debate the matter, which we duly did in a dialogue on radio.[23] The tone was moderate and civilised: after all, it was twenty years on from our first media encounter, and the blood no longer coursed as hotly. However, the argument about the UKUP's role continued at a Trinity College Historical Society inaugural,[24] where Conor (as President of the Society) was in the chair. The old spark ignited when Conor shouted "Shame" at a point I made. "Observe," I said to the audience, "the admirable impartiality of the chair." Both of us enjoyed the moment, I think.

* * *

All of this is not the full story. I am extremely interested in the popular perception of Conor in the contemporary folklore, perhaps a distinctively Irish phenomenon. He has not escaped unscathed in song and story, so to speak. In the mid-1970s, when shades of power and responsibility began to close around Conor as a government minister, and as an authoritarian ring began to be heard, I tried to express this in parody:

I'm Conor Cruise O'Brien, I rule P and T,[25]
And I keep the subversives away from TV,
I once was a liberal but now I'm so tame,
Since first I togged out in the Coalition game.

This was about the time he was incurring the wrath of such Gaelic intellectuals as the poet Seán Ó Ríordáin, for whom "Crús" epitomised the worst spirit of latter-day Anglicisation.[26] The grotesque caricature of Conor as the leading post-colonial lackey is coarsely drawn in a verse of a satirical song[27] popular in West Cork:

And then I was told of a war in the North
Invaded by an ancient oul Cruiser,
Bombarding all round him with blather and talk,
Never knowing he was born as a loser.
Although once a Gaeilgeoir, he had now changed his mind,
Preferring instead his new Queen's behind,
So now he is leading the bland and the blind
To the land of the Irish Dung Beetle.

60

The late Breandán Ó hEithir satirised revisionists in a mordant ballad called "The Gentle Black and Tan".[28] The last stanza goes as follows:

> So farewell you blinkered nationalists
> A warning take from me,
> If you want to seem progressive
> Then revise your history.
> And pay heed to our three heroes
> Murphy, Edwards and Your Man
> Who clear the name and sing the fame
> Of the gentle Black and Tan

Myself, Ruth Dudley Edwards and Conor are thus seen (in 1986) as the arch-revisionists. "Your man" is a long-established Irish colloquial usage where the person referred to obliquely is not named because everybody knows his identity; or the speaker and the company like the conspiratorial undertone; or it may be prudent to refer to him anonymously; or, in Conor's case, the phrase suggests a revisionism so extreme that it dare not speak its name! The more mundane explanation may be that "your man" conveniently rhymes with "Black and Tan".

There is no doubt that Conor provokes (indeed, he does little to avoid provoking) that rabid anti-intellectualism which lies beneath the surface of Irish politics and society. This was expressed, at an early stage, in a bilious jibe about him: "brilliant but useless, like a lighthouse on the Bog of Allen". And yet there is a grudging compliment here.

The nickname "the Cruiser" has persisted over the decades, and it calls for comment. It exemplifies a favourite Irish device to bring the remote, the Olympian, the difficult, the contrary, into the range of the familiar. As "the Cruiser", Conor becomes "one of us", "one of our own". It is a jesting image, and could occasionally be used with contempt and ill-will, but by and large it has tones of affection and sometimes even of pride. It recognises Ireland's foremost intellectual as a unique national asset.

* * *

I suppose I could be described as a semi-detached fan of Conor's.[29] Though I have never been in the legion of his rhapsodic admirers, by the same token, I was never to be numbered in the ranks of his hostile (and often ill-informed) critics. I once facetiously remarked that my support for his views swung between 69% and 83%.[30] It has since stabilised around the upper figure, despite my recent disagreement with his UK/Unionist Party stance.

We have broken bread and drunk wine together and enjoyed great company and sparkling conversation. I have vivid memories of his and Máire's hospitality when he was visiting scholar at Dartmouth, New Hampshire, in 1984, a year I spent in Boston College in a similar capacity. When he was researching his fine work on Edmund Burke, I was delighted to be able to put him in touch with people who were knowledgeable about Burke's native roots and the local tradition. It was also an honour for me to promote his name for the award of an Honorary DLitt of the National University of Ireland, which was conferred on him in 1993: at an earlier period, the NUI, with its Catholic and "national" ethos, might not have been so well disposed to honouring the personification of a very different ethos, secular and liberal.

I stand in awe of Conor's literary achievements and I was glad to have reviewed his books from time to time.[31] I admire his energetic application to work in his later years. I buy the *Irish Independent* every Saturday, since Conor is never less than immensely readable, even when – particularly when – his articles seem miraculously wrought *ex nihilo*. I identify with his sense of irreverent fun in life and literature (coexisting with a philosophical bleakness) and with his dismissal of sacred cows and political correctness, as when he exposed the pretentiousness of Yeats or refused to let the anti-apartheid movement be his conscience.

Nor was he impressed recently by the collective wisdom of the learned body, Aosdána, in refusing to condemn the writer Francis Stuart for his alleged sympathies with Nazism in the past. Conor's wife, Máire Mhac an tSaoi, was the sole exception to the consensus at the Aosdána meeting. Conor subsequently remarked: "I think of a consoling precedent from French history. When the French Assembly elected Napoleon emperor of the French there was just one vote against: that of Lazare Carnot. Napoleon made only one comment on the vote: 'The opposition,' he said, 'is distinguished.' '*L'opposition est de choix.*'"[32] Conor's comment exemplifies, *par excellence*, his wit, style and erudition, as well as his staunch loyalty to Máire.

Conor is, *inter alia*, the happy warrior, though we may not first think of him in that way. He has also stoically observed Horace's injunction: *aequam memento rebus in arduis/ servare mentem.* I am, indeed, glad to call him my friend.

Finally, he has been very good for Ireland. We can amend Goldsmith's lines (in *Retaliation*) on Edmund Burke and apply them in the best sense to Conor:

Born for the universe he focused his mind
And to country gave up what was meant for mankind.

He has done the nation, or the two nations, much service. And in time they will come to know it.

CHAPTER 5

CONOR CRUISE O'BRIEN AND *LA POLITESSE DE L'ESPRIT*

DARCY O'BRIEN

ALTHOUGH I HAVE HAD COUNTLESS POLITICAL CONVERSATIONS AND MUCH
such correspondence with Conor Cruise O'Brien since we first met thirty
years ago, it is as a friend that I have enjoyed him most and wish to write
of him here. I have no secrets to divulge, certainly none of a salacious kind,
which I offer at once as a disclaimer in this era when the President of the
United States reveals on television what sort of underwear he favours. I do
recall Conor's amusement – and that of his wife, Máire Mhac an tSaoi –
when his opponents charged that if he was elected to the Dáil there would
be a second wife under every bed in Ireland. (The effect on the electorate
of this calumny, one way or another, was never calculated; he did,
however, win a seat.) I can say that of Conor's many admirable personal
qualities, he is incapable of dullness.

Conor unfailingly makes of life's most banal circumstances something
more pleasurable than they are. When I think of him, it is this that comes
to mind rather than the risks he has taken, the threats defied, the lawsuits
fought or even the physical assaults he has endured. I did learn from him
that controversy is an essential ingredient of most writing worth reading;
that if you don't make a good number of people angry by what you write
you are almost certainly wasting your time – and theirs. But as a friend his
most prized quality to me, other than his kindness and generosity, has
been his knack of transforming the commonplace. Like the brush strokes
that animate a still life or the voice that rearranges nightfall or the sea, this
is an artist's gift that he has. As Patrick Kavanagh phrased it:

. . . nothing whatever is by love debarred,
The common and banal her heat can know.
The corridor led to a stairway and below
Was the inexhaustible adventure of a gravelled yard.

So Kavanagh wrote of a hospital; Conor does the same with anywhere.

He cannot resist doing it, any more than another artist could keep himself from transforming such unspeakably dull subjects as the gold standard, the farm lobby, the industrial – or rust – belt and political timidity into the Yellow Brick Road, the Scarecrow, the Tin Man and the Cowardly Lion. One evening during the winter of 1973-74 I was visiting the Cruise O'Briens at their cottage near Dunquin, at the tip of the Dingle peninsula, where, as Flann O'Brien wrote, "from the window on the left you could see the Great Blasket, bare and forbidding as a horrible otherworldly eel, lying languidly on the wave tops . . . " This is the cottage, made of wood, where Máire's uncle, the redoubtable romantic Monsignor Paddy Browne, translated Dante and Homer into Irish, asking local fishermen for help with similes, and edited the *Collected Works of Patrick Pearse*. This is where Máire spent the summers of her youth, learning Irish and stockpiling her word-hoard for future poems.

It was a cold day when I arrived there after the long drive from Dublin, with a strong wind off the Atlantic, Mount Brandon snow-covered to the northeast and the rich smell of smouldering turf escaping from every chimney. Although Conor at the time was Minister for Posts and Telegraphs, with authority over the national telephone system, the cottage had no phone; Conor, who was also the government's spokesman on Northern Ireland, could be reached, if necessary, through the gardaí or through Kruger's, the Dunquin pub, entities of equal reliability. The wind; the cold; the remoteness; the few other dwellings within sight; the angry Atlantic; the beauty of those stonewalled fields that crept up the hillsides; the sound of sheep and a donkey's bray on the wind – no other place in Europe could have seemed as remote from modern life, unless it was Albania. Inside the cottage it was warm, and one felt safe from contemporary anxieties, content with tea, bread, a bit of meat, plenty of potatoes and a measure of whiskey.

When the night had fully established itself, and outside there were more stars than one had ever remembered, Conor took up a book before the fire and began to read a bedtime story to the children, Patrick and Margaret, who were at his feet. In my experience most parents, including myself, read to children in their bedrooms, especially if there are guests; but such was not the custom in the cottage. I was glad of this, as it occurred to me that hearing Conor Cruise O'Brien read a bedtime story was probably something that even few heads of state had enjoyed. I doubted that a statesman of such world-historical importance as the late Secretary General of the United Nations, Dag Hammarskjöld, had ever been granted the privilege, though he might have benefited from it, especially on the eve of a certain airplane ride. The text Conor chose this evening was a chapter from L Frank Baum's *The Wonderful Wizard of Oz* (the original, 1900 version). "When last we saw them," Conor began, in the manner of the announcer on a children's radio serial from long ago, "Dorothy and her companions were approaching the gates of the Emerald City." The name of my favourite programme from childhood, *Let's Pretend*, floated into my mind; that was what we were all doing now, through the medium of Conor's voice, with its precise diction and that ironic slant, characteristic of his prose and irrepressible, even among schoolchildren.

That irony grew more pronounced and began to transform the familiar narrative into something altogether different from itself as the description of the Emerald City proceeded. Everything in and about that metropolis, you will recall, is monochromatic, that is to say, green. The city walls are green and all the buildings and the Wizard's palace, which I always envision as exactly like my childhood dentist's office building in Los Angeles, a graceful art-deco edifice faced with green tile that shines in the sun and once housed the old Wiltern movie palace, where I first saw Judy Garland sing "Over the Rainbow" to Bert Lahr and the others along the yellow brick road. Momentarily, I was back in the dentist's chair – happily, as he never caused me pain – until Conor, piling on one green image after another, could repress his sense of fun no longer and interrupted the story to ask his children: "What do you think this Emerald City must be? Where do you think it is? You, Darcy, what do you say?"

"I was thinking of my dentist," I said.

"Really? That is very peculiar. No, all green? It's Ireland, of course! Dorothy has ridden a tornado all the way to the Emerald Isle! The most beautiful place on earth!"

"It's the colour of American money," I said.

"Spoken like an American imperialist capitalist running dog. I'm ashamed of you. No, 'tis Ireland, the lamp of civilisation and the cradle of the faith and home of martyrs."

"Baum is a fine Irish name."

"O'Baum it was, before he changed it to protect himself from bigotry and murder. And O'Brien before that! We've added another O'Brien to the roll call of noble ghosts. And we have identified another classic in the canon of Irish literature, no denying it. Isn't that right, children?"

They seemed pleased to assent.

Later, before I made my way through that frozen night in Oz to my green hotel, Máire signed and presented me with a copy of her new book of poems, *Codladh an Ghaiscigh* (1973), that I have beside me as I write this. I could not read it, nor even the inscription; but on my voyage home to America, aboard the SS *Eurybates,* a tramp freighter that took twenty-six days to reach Bayonne, New Jersey, via Rotterdam, Antwerp and Sheerness on the Thames estuary, the radioman turned out to be an Irishman fluent in his ancestral tongue. One night somewhere near the Azores he entertained me and the other ten passengers by translating spontaneously from Máire's poems. In my mind I was back in the Right Reverend Monsignor Paddy Browne's cottage, by the fire, and may as well have been in Oz, for all I knew, listening to this green rhapsodist, who, I could see, was greatly moved by what he was reading, his voice cracking under pressure from the guttural muse.

Later, about fifteen days out, the radioman confided to me that the poems and speaking Irish again had filled him with a terrible homesickness. He had decided to jump ship in Bayonne.

"Off to see the Wizard?" I said. He looked at me as If I were daft, which I probably was by then, but I said that it was too complicated a matter to explain.

* * *

Some people, Texans for instance, can be far more appealing on their home grounds than elsewhere. A big fellow in boots and Stetson might charm everyone in the lobby of the Adolphus Hotel in Dallas; in Claridge's he becomes a loudmouth; at the Waldorf he should watch his step, as he might be mistaken for West Village chic. Not so, Conor. He takes his alchemical abilities with him. Wherever he is, be it Beverly Hills or Ballybunion – and I have been with him in both places – the locale becomes Oz. (I cannot speak of Elisabethville, but on the evidence of *To Katanga and Back* his effect there was the same; his political enemies in Ireland, of course, would place a different, less admiring value on this effect.)

About a dozen years ago, I think it was in 1985, his plane touched down one evening in Tulsa, Oklahoma, where I was living and he had come to deliver a lecture. I drove him straight from the airport to the Fifteenth Street Grill, about the closest thing to a Parisian bistro in a city better known for oil than gastronomy, a room done up pleasingly with bentwood chairs, Lautrec and Pernod posters and the like, a place that I knew would appeal to Conor's Francophilia. I ordered a bottle of red wine. Decades before it became popular in connection with the American health mania, or Ponce de León syndrome, Conor was devoted to vin rouge; the combination of this artery-cleansing drink and frequent, brisk walks of punishing duration explains his vigour in what for ordinary mortals is old age. That evening he was attired in what appeared to be a sort of après-ski outfit consisting of a hooded waterproof jacket, leggings and sturdy black shoes. It had been snowing in New Hampshire, from where he had travelled; no doubt he had walked through a blizzard to the airport.

I noted that as our waiter recited the night's specials Conor studied him with intensity. Obviously, the accent intrigued him. It was not the twang Conor probably had expected, but distinctly British upper-class, hardly what one would anticipate to issue in all its plummy hauteur from the lips of a waiter in Oklahoma or, for that matter, anywhere else.

"Confession time! Confession time, Darcy!" Conor confided, as soon as our waiter was out of earshot. The word makes me nervous. Was I to confess something or was he? A general confession, it seemed, was required. "Does it not please you, as I confess it does me immensely, to hear that man speak?"

"What do you mean?" I replied uneasily. Surely, I worried to myself, Conor was not revealing that he derived secret pleasure from the noises the British ruling class, or what is left of it, makes? Was it true after all, what his Irish enemies said of him, that he was a Brit at heart, or what in Joyce's day was called derisively a West Briton? But he explained, *au contraire*:

"My meaning is, does it not give you pleasure, of a certain malicious kind, to think that this man, very obviously a member of the British upper class, a direct descendant of the very people who persecuted our people and *held them in bondage* for seven hundred years, should be *serving us* tonight? What a delectable reversal of fortune! It does thrill you, doesn't it?"

"Not exactly," I admitted. I explained that the waiter in question, Gerard Campbell, was, indeed, British upper class and an Old Etonian to boot, although he had been expelled from that institution for general recalcitrance in his youth. His mother was a Gore; an uncle was David Ormsby-Gore, whom Conor would remember as the British Ambassador to the United States when John F Kennedy was President – just at the time when Conor was denouncing the British in the Congo. His father, Robin Campbell, had been chairman of the British Arts Council.

"I know him," Conor said. "How extraordinary."

I added that Gerard was, as he remains, a delightful person and a very good friend of mine. I had planned to introduce him formally when he brought the wine. I noted that Gerard had come to America as the chef for a rock star, whose career and entourage had since declined. As I did not have to explain to Conor, there were few professions appropriate to an upper-class gentleman who by birth was forbidden from showing any sign of ambition or venality. Cooking and waiting left him plenty of time for reading and playing golf and shooting holidays. Needless to say, money and property in the family had passed to another male line.

Others drifting away, Gerard sat down with us, and the evening turned into a geopolitical and literary excursion, covering life in various embassies as Gerard had experienced it, his father's friendship with Evelyn Waugh, the state of modern letters, and so on. I listened attentively to the harmonies and disharmonies of their accents, the one Etonian and the other Trinity College Dublin, more alike than not to the untrained ear, but as different as Harvard and Virginia in nuance and turn of phrase. Both sounds, like the profusion of historical and literary allusions carried in them, were anachronisms, vestigial as the old San Francisco-Irish accent my father had been among the last to voice. The conversation itself, energised less by class and ethnic differences than by shared knowledge of books, poems and the past, and by respect for all of these, was like the end of something. Soon there would be no one to remember this scintillating verbal world, unless some Plutarch came along to recover it.

Outside in the deserted streets of Tulsa I had to remind myself where we were. I recalled another evening, ten years before in Beverly Hills, when Conor had suggested that the ideal dinner companion, of anyone who had ever lived, would be Thucydides. By the time we departed that Californian bistro I believed that we had entered an *At Swim-Two-Birds* world and fully expected the author of *The Peloponnesian War* to emerge at any moment from the gents and join our table.

The next day at the University of Tulsa Conor delivered his lecture on religion and nationalism, part of what became *God Land*, to loud applause, although I sensed that some in the audience were made uneasy by his irreverence. He then, during a visit to the Gilcrease Museum, spent his entire honorarium (more than a thousand dollars) on a Navajo rug as a present for Máire. This romantic mood appears to have persisted, indirectly, when I introduced him to a certain woman of whom I had grown very fond and who entertained us at dinner that evening. I recall, I think it was during dessert, that he spontaneously began reciting Edmund Burke's description of the Queen of France. Conor's conversation, as you will have gathered, is usually pitched at an exalted level, rarely descending to the personal.

As I was driving him to his hotel, however – I distinctly remember being stopped in a left-turn lane – Conor said something that surprised me more than anything else he has ever said to me, because of its bluntly personal nature.

"I think you should marry Suzanne," he asserted, referring to our hostess. I had neither asked for his advice nor so much as solicited his opinion of her.

"I've been thinking of asking her," I admitted.

"Do not think too much about it. Act, my friend."

And so I did. We were married two years later. It was excellent advice. Perhaps, I often think, Conor is right about other matters too, political ones, for instance. Only history will tell.

* * *

"They order, said I, this matter better in France" – as Yorick complained to his gentleman, deciding then and there to set sail for Calais. Yorick was referring to a dish of fricasseed chicken, yet his words often enter my mind when I think about Conor and his place in the scheme of our world. Diplomat, literary critic, commander of troops, historian, professor, politician, memoirist, playwright, journalist, editor, columnist – what is he? What word or term best would describe him, to, say, a student who had not yet heard of him or read him? There is no word in English, or more precisely none within the context of Anglo-Saxon culture, that adequately encompasses all that he has been and what he continues to do. Yorick was correct. They do order this matter better in France.

Conor Cruise O'Brien is what the French call an intellectual – which in France is a perfectly plausible thing to be, indicative of a certain definable role in French society, as acceptable as being any other singular thing, a poet or a stockbroker or a pastry chef. He has sometimes been compared to André Malraux, as the *Atlantic Monthly* did on its cover for January 1994, which is a portrait of Conor that, although a good likeness, somewhat softens him around the edges. Fair enough, this Malraux analogy, if unfair to the sharpness of Conor's prose style, his abhorrence of persiflage and his preference for the concrete over the abstract. But any fuller comparison between the Frenchman and the Irishman shows how different was the place of the former in his society as compared to Conor's place, or the uncertainty of it, in his. Malraux, apart from his ending up as Minister for Culture under de Gaulle, attained, like Sartre on the far left and others at various points on the political spectrum, the status of intellectual, or man of ideas, which meant a definite function as a keeper of the flame of *la civilisation française*.

We, by which I mean British and Americans as well as Irish, do order things differently, or less well, or not at all for the intellectual, who, in truth, has no place among us, except perhaps as a professor, constrained within arbitrary academic disciplines. A man of ideas such as Conor – are there any others like him? – who may deal with one subject one minute, another the next, and in one literary form or another on impulse, must make up his role as he goes along if he is to remain true to his kaleidoscopic talents and not starve to death. For Conor this has meant a peripatetic life, hither and thither, which, fortunately, has suited his temperament. Had he stayed in one place, scribbling in Bewley's, say, like Sartre in the Deux Magots, he would long ago have disappeared from view or taken to wandering up and down Grafton Street like the pensioned-off former professor I remember there, who sang "Oh, What a Beautiful Morning" over and over at the top of his voice, all day long for a generation. Or like another I encountered in McDaid's (the Dublin intellectuals' and artists' pub of thirty years ago), a fellow wrapped in a cape and carrying a sketchbook filled with drawings of men huddled conspiratorially together in darkened rooms, who confided: "I have been educated to an effing standstill!" Nor could Conor ever have aspired to become the Irish Minister for Culture, for there was no such post until quite recently.

Like an actor in a repertory company, the intellectual not in France must learn many parts and have as his motto: "Have tux. Will travel." For his friends, Conor's various roles have been a blessing, as they have meant that one might encounter him almost anywhere. Late in the 1980s, I see from his inscription in a book of mine, I came upon him at a certain college in the East, where he was a visiting professor for the semester. I arrived to deliver a lecture on Seamus Heaney one afternoon, an exercise I found nerve-wracking with Conor's bright, unblinking eyes looking on. Afterwards, at a Chinese restaurant with other faculty, Conor appeared uncharacteristically forlorn and mumbled something to me about our lives as "mendicant scholars". I had the impression that this was a part he played less happily than others. He soon attempted to elevate the ambience, although he could do nothing about the chop suey or the absence of wine, by telling a professor who was sitting next to me that she looked like a Modigliani. He asked me to confirm the aptness of the comparison. I kept my mouth shut. He repeated the Modigliani analogy.

"A what?" she said.

"He said you look like a Modigliani," I offered helpfully. Her heavy-browed, orangey-complexioned face remained impassive. "The painter," I added. Still a blank.

"No," she said. "I'm in the English department. Semiotics."

"Actually I meant *zabaglione*," Conor replied. She expressed no mirth. Nothing.

"Your friend is sort of strange, isn't he," she whispered to me.

"Very," I said.

"Like he's speaking some other language."

"Exactly. He might as well be speaking French."

"Are you," she raised her voice to a normal level, "related to him? I mean with the same name and all."

"O'Briens are prolific breeders," I said. "My own grandmother, if you can believe it, had eight brothers. She played shortstop."

"All O'Briens," Conor said, "are descended from the admirable Brian Boru, who defeated the Vikings at the Battle of Clontarf. Certainly, Darcy and I are descended from the same tree, as it were, in the Dalcassian period. At that time our ancestors were traders. They exported dirt to the Egyptians, as a snakebite remedy."

"Are there written records of this?" asked the semioticist.

"Oh, no, alas!" Conor said. "The brutal conquerors of our people burned every scrap!"

* * *

What distinguishes Conor as an intellectual in the French sense is the delight he takes in exercising what they call *la politesse de l'esprit*, for which there is no adequate translation. "The good manners of the mind" is as close as I can come. He uses his mind gracefully and joyfully and daringly, as an acrobat uses his body, to the excitement, wonder and pleasure of his audience. As with any performance, the wrong crowd can make it fall flat. In that event the only remedy is to move on to the next arena.

It is pleasant to withdraw into the kingdom of my mind to recall these scenes that have punctuated the middle of my life, or maybe more than that, with delight. At home with Máire in their house on Howth summit, Conor is always in top form. Perhaps even the semioticist might appreciate how significant it is that they live on a hill, with a sweeping view from the sunporch of the swerve of Dublin Bay and the Hibernian metropolis. In the dining-room a portrait of Conor's father presides above a sideboard arrayed with squadrons of bottles of Burgundy and Bordeaux, breathing in welcome. Many are the times I have partaken there of Máire's salmon, that wisest of fishes, and often in the company of our mutual friend, the learned Thomas Flanagan, to enjoy hearing him engage Conor in arcane disputation concerning ancestral ghosts. To that table I brought my daughter, Molly, when she was fifteen, so she could be inspired by the heights some O'Briens can achieve in wit and hospitality. Máire pointed to a spot on the sunporch and welcomed Molly to curl up in her sleeping bag there any time she liked in the future; discreetly, Máire neglected to mention how often Molly's father had done that when it was too late to call a taxi.

But I have reason to know, fortunately, that one doesn't have to journey all the way to Howth and its courtesies, or even to depend on chance encounters beyond Ireland, to be invigorated by Conor's *politesse de l'esprit*. One of the requirements for canonisation is, or used to be before television gave the power to anyone, the capacity of bilocation, the ability to appear in two places at the same time. If Conor has no other saintly qualities, in print and in talk his word-play gives him that one. What's more, I have personally experienced apparitions of the man – and in the most unlikely places.

The Vatican, for instance. On 11 November 1996, at ten in the morning – these matters must be scrupulously documented – I visited the offices of Archbishop Jean-Louis Tauran, whose official title is *Segretario per i Rapporti con gli Stati*, or Secretary for Relations with the States or, succinctly, Foreign Minister. Archbishop Tauran, who was born in Bordeaux in 1943, presides over the Vatican's foreign policy and its diplomatic service, a position that has become more important than at any time in recent history with the accession of Pope John Paul II and that pontiff's vigorously activist role in the affairs of nations. I was on a mission of research in connection with my book *The Hidden Pope* (1998), which deals with the radically changed relationship between Catholics and Jews, as encouraged and promoted by Pope John Paul. In 1994 the Vatican at last reached agreement with the state of Israel for the exchange of ambassadors and formal diplomatic recognition between the political authorities of Judaism and Catholicism, an event of major historical and theological importance. The recognition had long been sought by Israel, but resisted by the Vatican. I wanted to ask His Excellency, Foreign Minister Tauran, why negotiations had taken so long. Were there theological as well as political barriers to recognition of Israel?

Perhaps Conor would, but I did not view a personal encounter with the Vatican Foreign Minister insouciantly. As I approached the archbishop's chambers down the cavernous, vaulted loggia, with its murals done by Raphael, awed by where I was and what lay before me, as I think even an infidel would be, I took heart from being fairly well prepared. I knew that my basic questions would derive from a meeting that took place in this very building in 1904 between Pope Pius X and the founder of political Zionism, Theodor Herzl. Herzl had come to the Vatican to ask for a papal endorsement, if not a blessing, of the idea of a homeland in Palestine for European Jews who wished to emigrate there. His Holiness had replied that as "the Jews have not recognised Our Lord, therefore we cannot recognise the Jewish people". Only on condition that the Jews convert to Christianity could the Holy Father support their return to the Holy Land. The source for this exchange is Herzl's diaries. As it happened, I had first read of the exchange in Conor Cruise O'Brien's *The Siege: The Saga of Israel and Zionism.* I had never discussed the matter with Conor, but had no doubt of his factual reliability as an historian. In that sense, I was taking Conor with me in to meet the archbishop, a circumstance that made me feel both less and more nervous.

A priest ushered me into a room perhaps thirty by twenty feet, with highly ornate furnishings showing the French influence on Italian design and therefore dating from no earlier than the eighteenth century. A tall window at the far end may have looked out on the gardens or on Saint Peter's Square; I did not take in the view, but sat down on a couch with gilded arms, into which I sank to a great depth. I presumed that this would be the proper place for me, with the archbishop in one of the two high and graceful chairs opposite. And I waited. There were no magazines to thumb through in this office, not even a Bible.

Soon enough, the scarlet-sashed archbishop, followed by a black-suited priest, entered through a door adjacent to the window. I arose, mumbled "Your Excellency," and Foreign Minister Tauran greeted me in English, to my relief, as I had feared that I would have to conduct the interview in His Excellency's native tongue and the traditional language of diplomacy. He chatted in a friendly manner for a few moments, asking about my accommodations in Rome and so on, and saying that he was pleased to be of any help he could with my book, in which he politely claimed to be very interested. He introduced his aide, Monsignor Luigi Gatti, a dark and suave gentleman, who greeted me in Italian. The archbishop's English was quite fluent, while graced with his accent of origin, which added to his manner of elegant sophistication. Something in his gestures, his unblinking and direct gaze, his precise diction, his slightly off-centre and ironic tone reminded me of someone. I could not think who that could be. As we took our seats, the name came to me.

It was Conor! The spitting image of him! Or, more precisely, as he was when I first knew him, in his early fifties, the hair still coal-black, plentiful and combed straight to one side; even the front teeth were the same as Conor's had been, with a slight space between them, before he replaced them with a bridge after a Protestant from the North knocked them out and a Catholic invited him to Tyrone "for a good Catholic beating". But the diction and the gestures truly marked the resemblance, which I can only term uncanny. That Conor loves reeling off French phrases ("Conor's French noises", Máire calls them) made the similarities all the stronger, as His Excellency sat in his chair with his hands draped languidly from the arms, just as Conor does, in the manner of a prince.

I must have been speechless, because I did not begin talking until I was conscious that the archbishop was staring at me, quizzically. At least, thank goodness, I refrained from saying, "You look just like . . . " or bursting out laughing. I began my well-rehearsed Major Question, struggling to get rid of the idea that I was actually talking to Conor, who for some reason that day was wearing a cassock and a golden crucifix.

The archbishop professed never to have heard about this alleged conversation between the pontiff and the Zionist in 1904, although he knew who Herzl was, all right. I added that after insisting on the Jews' conversion, His Holiness had said that if needed, the Church would send plenty of priests to the Holy Land to perform the baptisms. Archbishop Tauran found this prospect mildly amusing, but expressed a thoroughly Gallic scepticism of my account.

"Which pope was this?" he asked.

I had neglected to name the pontiff, for the simple reason that it had slipped my mind. Now I struggled to remember. Some Pius or other, surely . . . maybe not. Obviously the appearance of Conor had jumbled my memory.

"Benedict XV?" I ventured. "The year was 1904."

His Excellency conferred with Monsignor Gatti in muffled Italian. I had picked up enough of that language to gather that neither one of them was certain who had been pope in that year, a confusion I found surprising and reassuring. At length, the archbishop and the monsignor came to an agreement. Whoever had been pope at that time, His Excellency said, would never had said such a thing. Only political barriers had delayed Vatican formal recognition of Israel, which was always "recognised" by the Church. If anyone, it must have been a certain cardinal – I did not catch the name – with whom Herzl had conferred.

I pressed the matter of theological objections to the Jews' return. Was not the Diaspora perceived until recently as the Jews' punishment for denying Christ?

"These are theological questions," Archbishop Tauran said, very politely, but firmly. "As you know, in the Secretariat of State, we deal only with political matters."

Suddenly an appropriate French phrase entered my mind, as if sent to me miraculously through the ether. I rehearsed it briefly in my head, reminded myself to try to sound like Charles de Gaulle when I uttered it, and let fly:

"Ah well," I said, with my approximation of a Gallic shrug, *"Tout commence en mystique et finit en politique."*

"You said that very well," said the archbishop, smiling broadly.

"Péguy," I said.

"Yes, I know it."

We were on a different footing after that. By the time I took my leave, the archbishop and the monsignor, although they did not back down on the original question – I am sure they later found out that I was correct – promised me their full cooperation on further researches and wished me the best of luck, or Godspeed, I forget which.

As I passed through the square, always a pleasant thing to do, I thanked Conor for having come to my rescue with one of his favourite phrases, one that I have heard from him many times and read in his books: Péguy's aphorism that everything begins in the mystical and ends in the political, just as my discussion with the archbishop had done. As for Conor's premature reincarnation as a French archbishop, I could hardly wait to tell him about it and to hear what I was sure would be his rich interpretation of my paranormal Vatican experience.

For myself, I take the apparition as a sign that in the century that lies ahead, I mean the one that promises to be so full of information and devoid of philosophy, the only place left for a man like Conor, if there is another, will be the Vatican, with its heaps of books and manuscripts and other vestiges lovingly preserved, its many languages, even some Latin and classical Greek surviving. Perhaps, if he is truly what I thought he was, a palpable instance of metempsychosis, the young Jean-Louis Tauran, like a Julien Sorel, envisioned the Vatican as the only possible refuge for his kind, a fellow able to flourish at the intersection of politics and religion, diplomacy and metaphysics, with learning and style. There remains, of course, the problem of belief, not to speak of what to do about Madame de Renal . . . But I digress into vast complications. Thinking about Conor has that affect.

CHAPTER 6

MY SCHOLARLY AND SAGACIOUS FRIEND

THOMAS FLANAGAN

"'DOES MAN LEARN FROM HISTORY?' I ONCE ASKED A SCHOLARLY AND sagacious friend."

The question is asked in a novel of mine, *The Year of the French*, by one of the narrators, a Protestant clergyman named Broome. The Reverend Arthur Broome, MA Oxon, had been entrusted by his Church with the spiritual care of Killala, a coastal town in the west of Ireland. There, in August of 1798, exactly two hundred years ago, a French invasion fleet carrying a thousand infantrymen sailed into the harbour and ignited a long-delayed rebellion. It worked its disastrous course for a month before it was suppressed deep in Ireland's midlands, by which time thousands had been killed on both the rebel and loyalist sides. Broome is a loyalist, upon both nature and principle, but he is also a man of warm human sympathies and he grieves for the sufferings endured by them all. As he is setting forth his narrative, sometime in 1800, yet another foredoomed attempt is being made at a "permanent" solution to "the Irish question": this time by an Act of Union joining the two countries. This, so the novel's reader is to infer, has prompted the question which he put to his friend.

In fact, though, Broome is putting a question which I once put to my own scholarly and sagacious friend, Conor Cruise O'Brien. We were driving back to Dublin, in 1971, after having watched that year's Orange procession in Belfast. The procession, through its banners and music, its boisterous Lambeg drums, needlessly reminded the marchers themselves to "Remember 1690". William of Orange's victory at the Boyne River established, for several centuries, Protestant rule in Ireland. The crucial victory came not at the Boyne, but at Aughrim one year later, yet it is the Boyne which stands at the centre of the Orange imagination: William himself was in command there. His physically unimpressive figure, mounted on a fiery steed and strengthened and stiffened by the arts of iconography, dominates traditional Orange banners and gable-ends.

The North, Northern Ireland, the Six Counties – terms with crucial differences of meaning and affect – has become *a locus classicus* for the contention that certain unhappy places in the world never change, but repeat themselves over and over. Winston Churchill, in *The World Crisis*, gives to this view of history without change an expression so lapidary as to have become famous, if only for its rhetorical dexterity: "As the deluge subsides and the waters fall short we see the dreary steeples of Fermanagh and Tyrone emerging once again. The integrity of their quarrel is one of the few institutions that have remained unaltered in the cataclysm which has swept the world." Churchill himself, of course, had done his best to insure the permanence of that quarrel by helping to organise the partitioning of Ireland. To borrow a phrase from Conor, it is well to keep a suspecting glance on the historian.

As we talked in that darkening summer evening, we actually crossed the Boyne River. The crossing is just outside the town of Slane, and the river is wide there. The bridge is handsome. Set into the stone are lines written in memory of a poet who was executed for his role in the 1916 rebellion; they were written by another poet, a local young man who was himself to be killed a few months later serving with the British forces on the Western Front. The lettering was carved by a friend of mine, a stonecutter and a great storyteller. It is, as they say, a small country with a considerable history.

In my novel, I gave Conor's words to Mr Brome's scholarly and sagacious friend. Rather than dismissing the question with the scorn which it doubtless merited, he reflected on the matter and said at last: "No, I believe that we do not learn from history. But we can learn from historians." We will leave poor Mr Broome to ponder this Delphic utterance and return to the unriddling of it. It is Conor's habit to respond to any question, however meriting of scorn, if it is put to him in a spirit of serious inquiry. But it is also his habit, which he occasionally tries unsuccessfully to check, to add a dash of wit, or at least irony, whether fierce or, as here, gently mocking.

Years before Conor and I met I had been reading him, although in the earliest instance I did not know I was. In 1952 he published, under the pseudonym of "Donat O'Donnell" (a traditional practice of civil servants), *Maria Cross* a book of studies of certain modern Catholic novelists – Charles Péguy, Paul Claudel, Georges Bernanos, Graham Greene, Evelyn Waugh, Sean O'Faoláin, François Mauriac, Leon Bloy. In the final chapter "O'Donnell" writes that they share "an intuitive harmony of mystery and suffering, the reverberation, even at the oblique touch of a fingernail, of the great Catholic bell. However much we may disclaim the tie, we are all related, like Raymond and his father – through Maria Cross".

I had several reasons for admiring that book, which I read as a graduate student. Conor and I had something in common, I would later discover. We were both of us from Irish Catholic families, we had received Protestant educations and we ourselves were agnostics. But there were reasons more specifically literary. What was then called "New Criticism" held a dominant position in American academe. It held, to put the matter reductively, that the work of art was a "verbal icon", self-contained and self-protected. It was a mode of criticism in which I had been trained and which I respected, but it didn't suit me. "Donat O'Donnell" was writing the kind of essay to which I aspired, sensitive to tone and nuance, but insistent that literature, even poetry, was related to other large human concerns. Conor would later bring the same insistence to his examinations of writers and politics.

A few years passed and then one day the Irish critic Vivian Mercier and I met for lunch in the Columbia University Faculty Club. I was now a member of that faculty, and Vivian had reviewed, with generosity, a book of mine on Irish literature. In those days in New York it was not easy to find people outside of bars who wanted to talk about Irish literature, and I asked him about a brilliant book I had just read called *Parnell and His Party*, an almost unique example of modern historical methods brought to bear on a central topic of modern Irish history. A topic which, however central, had been left almost untouched by serious historians, although there did exist on the subject an abundant library of polemics, folktale and mythology.

I asked Vivian if he had heard of the book or its author, Conor Cruise O'Brien. Yes, indeed, he answered, with a complex and, for the moment, unreadable smile: they were close friends and had been roommates at Trinity College. Later I came to understand the smile's complexity. Vivian, a quiet, balanced, sensible man, had gone on to a respected academic career. Conor had had a vivid reputation at Trinity – as wit, writer, debater

– and then had gone on to the civil service, first in Finance and then in External Affairs. Several anecdotes of undergraduate life which Vivian recounted in an unusually spirited manner suggested an unusual sort of civil servant. Vivian assured me that Conor did very well at whatever he attempted, but he was describing a man with precisely the vigorous and impudent inquisitiveness about life and society which the civil service is intended to dampen.

Parnell and His Party remains one of the essential books of modern Irish history, a shrewd and clarifying study of the political party which Charles Stewart Parnell used, and had been used by, in shaping Ireland's political and, to some extent, its social identity. His career, stretching from the late 1870's to 1891, had been the great drama of Irish history between the tragicomic fiasco of the Fenians and the Rising of 1916. They were dramatic years, culminating in the sexual scandal which left him standing almost alone after the desertion of his Gladstonian allies and the most powerful elements within his own party. Conor halts his examination before the wild, bitter end of Parnell's life, amidst his furious, doomed attempt to recapture power, saying rightly that this is a subject not for history, but for literature.

And so it is, most memorably, perhaps, in the poetry of Yeats and the ferocious Christmas dinner scene in *A Portrait of the Artist*. But Conor, by concentrating on the dynamics of the party, upon the members considered one-by-one, with attention to their backgrounds, education, aspirations and relationship toward their leader, exposes the actual framework of political choice. O'Brien is not demythologising Parnell, but rather performing the historian's duty to place a legendary figure within the contingent world of circumstance, compromise, chance. And in doing so, he was working toward the establishment of a professional school of Irish history, as was his Trinity mentor, TW Moody. His, though, remains the most substantial and enduring product of that period, in part because of its sheer professionalism, its tracing of intricate political webbing, but for another reason as well, although one not easily demonstrated.

Conor's book maintains an (almost) unfaltering neutrality of tone and judgement, but he was dealing with a period of Irish history which still, even in the 1950s, held the passionate and partisan interest of many Irishmen. And it had for many, including Conor himself, great personal resonance as well. The Parnell drama reached its crisis in Committee Room Fifteen of the House of Commons, when the party split into uneven halves amidst rage, insult and grief. And one of the party members who refused to support Parnell was Conor's grandfather, David Sheehy. The drama of Irish politics, not merely the electoral nuts-and-bolts, lay in Conor's immediate background. (And, indeed, of modern Irish literature as well: his grandmother memorably appears, of course, in *Ulysses*, and his mother in "The Dead". His life has been an Irish paradox – at once extraordinary and representative.) First-rate prose, even when it is determinedly academic, has a music which sometimes can tell a story in apposition to its written words. *Parnell and His Party* is a fingernail scratching at the great bell of Ireland and Irishness and being Irish.

In particular, Conor evades, rather than resists, the glamour of the book's central figure. Of that glamour he was to write: "The elements that have gone to make up that myth are past counting. There is, first, Parnell's real greatness and the manner of it, with the residue of folklore that greatness leaves in the mind of a people." He was performing the curious task of demythologising a figure who still holds for him considerable mythological power.

* * *

Not too long after Vivian Mercier and I had that lunch, I moved from Columbia to Berkeley and opened the *San Francisco Chronicle* to discover a photograph of Conor on the front page. He was apparently taking part in a military operation in what had been the Congo; the photograph was blurred, but he seemed to be having a good time. As the world was discovering, he was a member of the Irish delegation to the United Nations and had been despatched by Hammarskjöld to the troubled province of Katanga. It seemed incredible that this should be the author of two scholarly books; it was as though he had leaped into outer space – as in a sense he had. It sealed my admiration. I have always had a callow admiration for writers who have had adventures in the real world – TE Lawrence, Malraux. As it happens, it is not an admiration which Conor shares, not for Lawrence and Malraux, at any rate. Katanga, of course, was one of the decisive events in his life, and as one of its consequences he resigned from the Irish diplomatic service.

When we became friends in Ireland almost ten years later, he had long been established as an intellectual of international repute, widely admired as a voice on the political and cultural left. That fame had begun with the Congo; his actions there were understood as a response to the efforts of Britain and Belgium, the lingering imperialist powers. Conor himself had defended this interpretation with extraordinary eloquence in *To Katanga and Back*, which is one of my favourites among his books. Jane Austen, in the history of England which she wrote as a schoolgirl, describes Charles I as "ever stalwart in his own defence", and in this regard Conor descends from the cavalier, rather than the roundhead, tradition. He brings great flair to his narrative, and the portraits of the principal characters suggest that he has studied his Waugh to telling effect. The title, of course, echoes the titles of countless books by Victorian explorers and thereby gently mocks both the explorers and himself. It should remind readers that they are in the hands of a stylist with an instinct for the arrangement of experience.

Beneath the skin of style and manner, of epigram and barbed description, a serious drama is being worked out between narrator and circumstance, and an alert moral, no less than political, intelligence is at play. He has always been aware, unlike some of his critics, of the gulf-like distance between the serious and the merely solemn. This distinction is vivid in the play, *Murderous Angels*, which later would be his imaginative return to the Congo. It centres upon the extraordinary characters of Dag Hammarskjöld and Patrice Lumumba, each carrying doom partly within himself, partly with the other man. It deliberately situates itself in the tense zone between comedy and tragedy, before History settles down to tragedy.

In the years following the Congo, Conor served as vice-chancellor of the University of Ghana, his role in the Congo having understandably won the admiration of Ghana's fickle ruler, Kwame Nkrumah. Those three years strengthened in various ways his sense of the importance to the world of academic freedom and freedom of inquiry. He and Máire, his wife, would later make vivid for me their affection for the landscape of West Africa and their far greater affection for its peoples. For four years after Ghana, from 1965 to 1969, he served as Albert Schweitzer Professor of the Humanities at New York University. He is a super teacher and director of studies, and the Henry James-era townhouse in which he and Máire lived became celebrated as a centre which joined the intellectual and the convivial. Máire, we may be certain, did as much as Conor to create that atmosphere. She is one of the most distinguished of modern poets in Irish, also has a background in politics and comes from a family which had a part to play in the foundation of the Irish state. Like Conor, she has her own, although different, awareness of the junctures and separations of politics and poetry. And she possesses a wit very different from Conor's, but equal to it in its swift and devastating accuracy.

In the New York years, through his university post, but more through his political and cultural essays and lectures, he was establishing himself more securely as a figure to be reckoned with, and in many ways a paradoxical one – both combative and cordial, witty and serious, conscious of the weight of moral authority which he carried and independent to the point, at times, of contrariness. If at times he seemed a whirling dervish in print, this was put down to his being Irish.

America during his New York years was going through a crisis of ideas and politics, and her intellectuals were under pressures of identity and choice more drastic than any, perhaps, since the Civil War. The Cold War and attitudes toward Soviet Communism, the steadily escalating war in Vietnam, the fight for civil rights and against segregation, the student movements in the universities were, at least within the universities, closely linked issues. And in all of them Conor made himself felt, taking part, with Máire, in anti-war demonstrations in New York and Washington – even getting arrested in the process – and evincing sympathy for student concerns. He thrived upon controversy, inevitably giving better than he got, as various Cold War ideologues discovered to their cost – "a smelly little ideology if ever there was one", as he succinctly put it in a letter to a friend.

The Conor who returned to Ireland in 1969 successfully contested for a seat in the Dáil as a member of the Labour Party. But that sentence is not phrased quite accurately. There has not been a year of his life when part of the time, even if sometimes only the summer months, has not been spent in Ireland. Home for him has been, since his early years as a civil servant and his first marriage, a comfortable site on the summit of Howth, with the sea seeming almost to spread out from it. It is a house which I would come to know well, visiting it with my family when they were in Ireland with me. Máire is the godmother to my two daughters, Ellen and Kate, and Kate, who this year gave birth to twins, has named one of them Conor. When in the country on my own I would soon enough appear at "Whitewater" with toothbrush and razor. Why we became firm friends so quickly is a mystery, as such things always are. I have but a single clue. In the early seventies I was helpful in Berkeley's decision to bring him there as a Regents Professor, and after his extraordinary lecture on Edmund Burke's "Little Platoon" a faculty wife said to me: "Your friend O'Brien and you have a bit in common. You tell jokes and try to say clever things, but when you are serious you are really quite interesting." She did not entirely intend it as a complement, but so I received it.

Conor has always had the knack, bordering on the uncanny, of living in style. I was once in London when he was editor of the *Observer*. I knew that he was living on a houseboat, with weekends back in Dublin, but for some reason assumed that it was moored somewhere near Gravesend, an abandoned hulk out of *Our Mutual Friend*. I should have known better.

The boat was moored in Chelsea, and the stateroom, if that is the proper term, was handsomely appointed, with framed posters of Turner's and Whistler's views of the Thames. Conor, his daughter Kate and I climbed up the stone steps into Chelsea and enjoyed a superb Italian dinner with superb Italian wine. Afterwards, we sat on the afterdeck, with some Irish whiskey, and looked along the river to where a summer evening darkened upon the Houses of Parliament. I found myself wondering how that scene would have looked a century earlier to a young Irish attorney just recently arrived as a Parnellite Member of Parliament. It was one of the germs out of which later grew a novel called *The Tenants of Time*. Conor was lecturing that night to Kate and myself, and to the dark, quiet Thames, upon the various cultural and proto-political enormities of the late-eighteenth century German writer, Johann Gottfried Herder. I had only a fuzzy recollection of Herder as an overall decent chap, as far as German Romantics went, keen to foster the cultures of small countries, and so forth. Not so, apparently. He was a spiritual child of Rousseau and one who lacked even the primitive virtue of filial loyalty: he had attacked Rousseau's – and Conor's – beloved French language. It seemed an unlikely subject for an evening on the Thames, but in those days, as I now can see, Conor was thinking through a number of his ideas, and in this task Herder had his part to play.

Conor's part in Irish life and politics after his return in 1969 is too well-known to need rehearsal. He served in the Dáil and in the Labour-Fine Gael government as Minister for Posts and Telegraphs. In the election of 1977 he lost his seat for what were essentially local issues, although the result was coloured by his increasingly unpopular, and increasingly implacable, attitude toward the crisis in Northern Ireland. In the Dáil, in his journalism and in books such as *States of Ireland* he attacked – and he continues to attack – the Irish Republican Army and its Sinn Féin spokesmen. Of his varied achievements and accomplishments, this is probably the one which is foremost in Irish minds. He has fought intemperately at times and would argue that this has been demanded by the seriousness of the situation.

Many of his oldest friends cannot follow him along that path, and at the moment I myself am one of them. Throughout the seventies and well into the eighties he was performing a very great service for the people of Ireland. It was his argument, copiously illustrated and furnished with a wealth of evidence, that the received, popular version of Irish history was a complicated and, ultimately, a sectarian myth. Moreover, it was a mythology which maintained its power well past the period of nation-building, through the years of the Free State and the bucolic de Valera years, always quietly at the service of political machines and a monolithic church. It survived as a chief cause of the wrenching apart of Northern society. The mythology of the Protestant community in the North, as made manifest in the B-Specials, Orange marches and the Reverend Ian Paisley, was equally noxious, he readily acknowledged, but he did so in what seemed to some a more cursory and less heart-felt way.

He was the foremost, the best-known and the most plain-spoken of what became known to the reading public as "the revisionist" school of Irish history. "Revisionism", however, has one meaning for historians and another one for outsiders. All history is in a sense revisionist, or else there would be no need for more than one book on any given subject. Fundamentalist Christians have long been advocates of this "One Book" theory. In Ireland professional historians and well-read people generally knew the shallowness of the received nationalist version. In casual conversation references to Red Hugh O'Donnell, or Napper Tandy or the gigantic inflation of Black and Tan defeats into the slaughter of battalions would be accompanied by a knowing roll of the eyes and some such expression as "So we must piously believe". The expression, however, is right on the money. Piety is too deep an emotion to be safely trifled with, however necessary the task. Revisionism can also be used for political and ideological reasons, and occasionally this charge too has been raised against Conor. It is true, but only in the sense that he is not seeking simply to describe the source and substance of nationalist belief, but drastically to modify it.

The problem, so it seems to this outsider, is that he does not at present realise how successfully he has performed his task. The Ireland of 1998 is not the Ireland of 1968 and much less, of course, is it the Ireland of 1798. Citizens, North and South, who voted "Yes" during the recent referendum did not heed the murmuring of Ancestral Voices. They were expressing their detestation of a dehumanising and apparently endless violence and their hope for a mutual accommodation between the peoples of this island. The people who voted "No" heard an Ancestral Voice right enough, the voice of the Reverend Ian Paisley and the language he carries forward from his dark conventicle. The ascription of historical causation is a notoriously tricky business, but I think that some day Conor's work of political education twenty years ago will seem even more impressive than it does today.

In the meantime, he has published his wise and brimming study of Edmund Burke. The resemblances between the two men has not escaped the attention of readers, beginning with Conor himself. They begin, and perhaps they return at the end, to an idea of Irishness. No previous scholar has been as resourceful as Conor in establishing, with its surround of land and history, Burke's specific Irish roots, and he has gone on to suggest ways in which those roots of sentiment and affiliation nourished unlikely aspects of Burke's mind and policy.

Conor is fond of quoting these lines from Burke: "To love the little platoon we belong to in society is the first (the germ as it were) of public affections." At the end of the acknowledgements page of *Ancestral Voices* Conor thanks those friends who helped him with the book and then all of his family. He adds: "I am sometimes asked whether I feel 'isolated', presumably because my views on things like *Ancestral Voices* are not everyone's cup of tea. I don't feel in the least isolated. I live and move in the best of company." He is speaking of his own little platoon. This occasionally wayward member remains a part of it.

IV

IRISH LITERATURE, HISTORY AND POLITICS

CHAPTER 7

YEATS AT FIFTY

ROY FOSTER

WHO OWNS WB YEATS' LIFE? IT SEEMS ODD TO POSE THE QUESTION MORE than half a century after his death, but for Irish people it still resonates. His huge international reputation is securely based on the mystery and grandeur of his late verse and the poignancy of his love-poetry, but he first came to fame as the exotically Celtic poet of a "new" nationalist Ireland: almost singlehanded, he made Irishness culturally fashionable. Spearheading a great cultural renaissance, he moved into his maturity as the voice of his country, memorialising her heroes, sitting as a Senator in her independent parliament, winning the Nobel Prize, dying full of years and honours.

Yet throughout his career he sustained an angry, quarrelsome, ambivalent relationship with much of Irish life; and for his first 50 years he lived more in England than Ireland. He was attacked in Ireland for the decadence, occultism and sensuality of his verse and the arrogant iconoclasm of his public utterances – and, indeed, his personal style. His reputation was violently fought over for years after he died, and much of this quarrel revolved around the issue of whether "England" or "Ireland" should claim him. Having completed the first volume of his biography, which takes him up to 1914, I am unsurprised by this. It would certainly not have surprised the poet himself. Nor was Yeats' potential for arousing controversy exhausted with his death in 1939. In the months immediately after his decease, attacks on him appeared in several Irish journals: he was "a poet of the Sewage School", "un-Irish and utterly exotic", who had been involved all his career in "a long war upon sacred things": and, at least as far as critics like Aodh de Blacam were concerned, these "sacred things" included nationalist politics as well as the Catholic Church.

By the time the Irish navy corvette sailed into Sligo harbour bearing his remains in 1948 these denunciations had died away, and he was acclaimed as the poet of the nation. But as late as 1965 the dedicatee of this present volume showed that Yeats' politics could still arouse passion. In fact, "Passion and Cunning" was the title of the seminal essay in which Conor Cruise O'Brien provocatively looked at the impulses behind the poet's political interventions, arguing for a consistent political impetus in Yeats' life and querying the accepted version of his political progress. Guided by the poet's brilliantly disingenuous *Autobiographies*, this had generally been seen as poetically revolutionary but politically ineffectual up to the attainment of effective national independence in the 1920s. Tutored by John O'Leary and entranced by Maud Gonne, the poet embraced Fenianism in the late 1880s and 1890s; though his generation "came down off their stilts" after 1900, he wrote *Cathleen Ní Houlihan*, despised the compromises of the parliamentarians and the flyblown rhetoric of superannuated Young Irelanders alike and was galvanized by 1916 into revolutionary poetry once more. When his country took her place among the nations of the earth, in Emmet's phrase, he could rightly claim his place as a founding father. If, in the 1930s, he went rather worryingly astray, this was seen as the prerogative of a Wild Old Wicked Man. In the end the poetry was what mattered – and that existed in another and purer world.

O'Brien's classic essay preferred to read politics as central throughout and particularly concentrated upon the developments behind Yeats' famous Senate speeches attacking the imposition of Catholic social teaching on Irish constitutional law; in a characteristically mordant – and hilarious – phrase, he remarked that this was the climax of a process whereby "the Protestant now reemerged with an audible sigh of relief; it had been stuffy in there, and getting stuffier". Class and tribal identifications stretched far back. O'Brien then argued forward to Yeats' embrace of anti-democratic politics in the 1930s, starting a hare that is still running hard. Despite several distinguished interventions in the chase, notably from Elizabeth Butler Cullingford, O'Brien's essay – after thirty-three years – still sets the pace and does so with commanding authority: though his closing speculations on Yeats' probable stance in the event of a Nazi victory must remain just that – speculation. For the purposes of considering where Yeats had arrived by his fiftieth year, what matters is

O'Brien's argument that Yeats' approach to nationalist politics was more analytical and calculating than usually allowed: and that his interrogation of conventional nationalism began much earlier on, at the time of Maud Gonne's marriage in 1903, but impelled by other changes of direction too.

Studying Yeats' life and thought from the turn of the century to 1914, I find myself in full agreement. Plays like *The King's Threshold* and *Where There Is Nothing* may be read as commentaries on the artist's relation to the politics of his day; he certainly abandoned his hopes of a revolutionary apocalypse after 1900 and avoided Fenian support-groups set up in the aftermath of the Boer War. Most of all, he opposed what he felt to be the version of a desired Irish culture advanced by Arthur Griffith's Sinn Féin movement from about 1905. And if the first half of Yeats' life pivots round one great emblematic confrontation, it is the row over JM Synge's play *The Playboy of the Western World* in 1907, when Yeats pitted himself and the Abbey Theatre against what he saw as know-nothing pietism and intolerance. The play's opponents are often represented as the outraged Dublin bourgeoisie; but Yeats identified them specifically as a Sinn Féin ramp – and said so.

In his essay of 1910, "JM Synge and the Ireland of his Time", which is a first instalment of autobiography masquerading as an elegy for his friend, who had died at the height of his powers in 1909, Yeats clearly constructed the arguments for a kind of nationalism which would be at once inclusive, imaginative and realistic. Griffith had described *The Playboy* as "a vile and inhuman story told in the foulest language we have ever listened to from a public platform . . . the production of a moral degenerate who has dishonoured the women of Ireland before all Europe". It was, in a word, un-Irish and anti-national. Yeats, in opposition, cited his own revolutionary record in Fenian organisations and accepted the directly political implications of *The Playboy* controversy, arguing (in a particularly sinewy and subtle way) that the nineteenth-century Young Ireland conventionalities no longer answered the questions of identity posed by modern Ireland. The invention of tradition, and "images for the affections", had done their work of confidence-building, and Irish national rhetoric must advance beyond chauvinism and defensiveness:

> Even if what one defends be true, an attitude of defence, a continual apology, whatever the cause, makes the mind barren because it kills intellectual innocence; that delight in what is unforeseen, and in the mere spectacle of the world, the mere drifting hither and thither that must come before all true thought and emotion. A zealous Irishman, especially if he

lives much out of Ireland, spends his time in a never-ending argument about Oliver Cromwell, the Danes, the penal laws, the rebellion of 1798, the famine, the Irish peasant, and ends by substituting a traditional casuistry for a country . . .

The modernity and relevance of this is arresting. Yet the question of contested possession continues to present itself. I am still haunted by the indiscreet but revealing reaction of one *soi-disant* Dublin intellectual when I referred to Yeats' background as a "marginalised Protestant": "How dare you say that – he was as Irish as I am." There are still those who think Protestant background negates "true" Irishness, even if they are mercifully thinner on the ground than they used to be. Though Yeats' immediate family were strong nationalists, his background was that of the declining Protestant bourgeoisie, civil servants and clerics rather than landowners, with roots stretching back to the centuries of dispossession and ascendancy. This was not only an inheritance he rediscovered in middle age; it conferred a burden which he carried from his youth, and in Ireland it would have been self-evident to anyone he met as soon as he opened his mouth. Much of his early life was spent trying to demonstrate to people that "marginalised Protestants" could be as Irish as anyone else – not always a popular case to make. To write his life is to venture into landmined territory, in terms of social history; and it is booby-trapped elsewhere too.

Perhaps this is why the project of his authorised biography itself carries a certain history. The idea was first mooted over 30 years ago by his family. Yeats himself expected a full biography: "a poet's life is an experiment in living", he wrote superbly, "and those that come afterwards have a right to know it". At the same time, however, he had taken fairly good care to dictate the form in which posterity would approach it. Joseph Hone's impressive *WB Yeats, 1865-1939* appeared in 1942 and was necessarily discreet. Richard Ellman's brilliant *The Man and the Masks* a few years later treated the life in terms of literary criticism, as did AN Jeffares' *Man and Poet*. What was needed, in the 1960s, was something more like Ellman's *Joyce* – linked to personal chronology and the history of the poet's times as well as to his work, and necessarily conceived on a large scale.

Thanks partly to the devoted guardianship of his wife, George, who had herself recently died, there was a great archive: partly dispersed in international collections, but substantially still in her son's and daughter's possession. Oliver Edwards had begun a scholarly biography and left only a couple of draft chapters. The great critic Denis Donoghue was asked to take on the task, but relinquished it after a few years, partly because of amicable disagreement over his wish to restrict access to family papers, which the Yeatses have generously always kept open to *bona fide* scholars, partly through pressure of other work. In any case, it was never going to be easy. Edwards went to interview the late Austin Clarke, a poet who had known Yeats and never liked him – and who himself considered writing a biography of the Titan. Watching this latest prospective biographer disappear out his gateway, Clarke remarked pessimistically to his son: "He'll never do it. He's too honest and he's *too nice.*"

Niceness apart, was it, in any case, a project for a literary critic – or for a historian? The answer came when in 1974 his successor was appointed – FSL Lyons, famous for learned but trenchant studies of Parnell and other late-nineteenth-century politicians and a monumental history of Ireland since the Famine. There was a brief furore among literary scholars at this invasion from a neighbouring discipline, more or less quelled by the *élan* with which Lyons began publishing and lecturing on Yeats. Ten years after beginning he sat down to write and almost immediately collapsed and died. When I was first approached about taking on the task in 1984 there was a certain *damnosa hereditas* about it, not helped by a cheerful woman I encountered at my first Yeatsian conference. "I wouldn't write about his life if I were you," she counselled. "A friend of mine did and Yeats tried to drown him when he was out swimming." The biographer's notebook was whipped out at once: was this at Rapallo in the 1920s? Cap d'Ail in the 1930s? Not at all, I was told scornfully: only last year at the Forty-Foot bathing-place in Dublin Bay. "Something grabbed at his leg and he knew it was Yeats." The old occultist could still, apparently, cast a long shadow.

The last decade has brought several strange encounters as well as warnings, veiled and aggressive, about earthbound historians passing in alien domains, whether literary or spiritual. It has also seen the appearance of the first three volumes of the *Collected Letters*, one of the most Herculean tasks in the history of modern editing, as well as the publication of Yeats' correspondence with Maud Gonne and a ramifying bibliography of book and articles (conservatively estimated at seven thousand items when I started, probably double that now).

Above all – and perhaps supplying the excuse for a historian taking on the task – there is the warp and weft of the revolutionary times in which Yeats lived his astonishing life. Born in 1865, he lived out his childhood and youth against a tapestry of failed insurrection, land agitation and the struggle for Home Rule waged by the magnetic figure of Parnell – whom

Yeats would later make an emblem for aristocratic, unmaterialistic Ireland. As a child he observed both his family, and the class whence they came, slipping down the ladder of social ascendancy, while a newly self-confident Catholic bourgeoisie began to assume the reins of authority. He was himself preternaturally certain about the course he would try to steer – most of all, that it must not resemble that of his father, John Butler Yeats, a charismatic but unsuccessful artist who never knew how to finish a painting. Dramatic closure would, by contrast, become a hallmark of his son's writing.

The Yeatses move to London during the poet's early childhood paralleled that of many others; it also happened at a time when, as George Bernard Shaw mordantly recalled, "every Irishman who felt that his business in life was on the higher planes of the cultural professions, felt that he must have a metropolitan domicile and an international culture: that is, he felt that his first business was to get out of Ireland". Yeats knew this, but he also knew the uncertainty of dislocation: though they returned to Dublin in the early 1880s, they were back in Hammersmith by 1887. The sharp pain of emigration suffuses his first novel, *John Sherman*. So does a background of genteel poverty and an atmosphere of psychological depression. Against this he arrived at the decision to "make poems on the familiar landscapes we love not the strange and rare and glittering scenes we wonder at – these latter are the landscape of Art, the *rouge* of nature". In a letter to Katherine Tynan he enclosed the first draft of "The Lake Isle of Innisfree":

> I will arise and go now and go to the island of Innis free
> And live in a dwelling of wattles of woven wattles and wood work
>   made,
> Nine been rows [*sic*] will I have there, a yellow hive for the honeybee
> And this old care shall fade.
> There from the dawn above me peace will come down dropping slow
> Dropping from the veils of the morning to where the household
>   cricket sings.
> And noontide there be all a glimmer, midnight be a purple glow
> And evening full of the linnets wings.

This version lacks the dramatic, personal intervention which closes the published poem: "While I stand on the roadway or on the pavements grey, /I hear it in the deep heart's core." But in his *Autobiographies* Yeats isolated the moment when he wrote "Innisfree" – in mid-December 1888, inspired by the same revelation he described in *John Sherman*, when a Strand window display suddenly transported him to the waters of Sligo. The power of association and memory which swept over him showed him that "personal utterance" might be a way out of cloudy rhetoric. Published in 1890, the poem achieved immediate success and still pursued him around the world, to his irritation, 40 years later.

It also forecast the way that he would come to query the uses of art and interrogate the relationship between life and literature. As outlined above, Yeats was involved in the revival of revolutionary separatism and then the cultural struggles around the new theatrical movement in the early years of this century. Into this he redirected his belief in ritual, his desire to educate an Irish public away from English materialism to intellectual independence, his ability to dominate committees and set up organisations. But politics proper (or improper) had a way of coming back at him. By the midpoint of his career, when my first volume ends, Ireland seemed to be moving towards Home Rule, while the European world lurched into war. In all these struggles Yeats was closely implicated, and they helped condition his life and work. His acute sense of social situation and perceived disadvantage is there from the beginning, as delicately honed as Proust's. ("We lived in a villa where the red bricks were made pretentious and vulgar with streaks of slate colour, and there seemed to be enemies everywhere.") An astute friend pointed out to me that by reading Yeats' life in this way, Freud is for practical purposes replaced by Foucault: not childhood trauma but social context and youthful power-struggles condition the later life. Another friend, only partly joking, took it further: for Yeats' life, the only analyst you need is Clausewitz. And Yeats certainly lived as if following the maxims of the great theorist of war. Time and again he defined his enemies, regrouped his forces, rallied an attack on a weak front and triumphantly snatched a victory. His early journalism, his struggles over the Abbey Theatre, his manifestos about intellectual freedom and the claims of nationalism, his tours of America: over and over the word "campaign" suggests itself.

This is true of his personal relationships too, notably his endless pursuit of Maud Gonne. At the outset of my researches I half expected to find that he used her as he did so many others, to provide a theme and a resource for his art. But studying his drafts, his horoscopes, most of all his letters to her, it is clear that from their first meeting he was, as he himself recalled, in a state where agony bordered on excitement – and he was utterly committed. Moreover, though they would come to violent political disagreement (she remained a revolutionary, he did not), his love would be continually recreated, "like the phoenix". She influenced nearly everything he did.

95

Strikingly, Yeats not only remained friends with most of his past lovers, he also relied heavily on mutually supportive friendships with women. This often involved an implicitly sexual element: extraordinarily attractive all his life, he had a way of lending himself out to the fantasies of others and then withholding himself while they stayed in thrall. This was true of his relationship with the English tea heiress, Annie Horniman, who founded the Abbey Theatre, and with several of the aristocratic hostesses who took him up in London drawing-rooms. An element of it may have even entered his relationship with Augusta Gregory, who meant immeasurably more to him than almost anyone else, and whose friendship sustained him through years of turmoil. With her, he embarked on the great enterprise of a national theatre, an emblem of Irish culture: a forum where "a mob would become a people". He visualised a cultural initiative which would try to be national but unpolitical: this priority distanced him from Gonne's revolutionary nationalism and, as we have seen, brought him into violent conflict with the nascent Sinn Féin movement, and it is symbolically associated with his attempt to assert a claim on the land through research into folklore and fairy belief. Here too he and Gregory met each other's needs.

Yeats' friends are a dazzling cast in themselves, and the theme of friendship is celebrated throughout his poetry and prose, often revolving around that emblematic figure of JM Synge. During Synge's lifetime, his relationship with Yeats was often uneasy: in their alliance over the Abbey Theatre, Synge often resented Yeats' dictatorial style, while Yeats felt Synge backed away from necessary conflicts with critics (often Sinn Féin nationalists) who felt that the putatively "national" theatre had been commandeered by a Protestant avant-garde. But in what mattered, he threw himself behind Synge. Though he must have resented his rival's ability to pack a theatre (audiences stayed away from Yeats' own plays in droves), in 1907 he fought the great battle of his early life over Synge's *Playboy of the Western World* – and won. After evenings when the audience rioted, and Yeats "stood there watching knowing well that I saw the dissolution of a school of patriotism that had held sway over my youth", he forced the play onto the repertoire; within a very few years it was quietly accepted. He had also brought the most troublesome actors to heel or forced them out. One of Lily's inimitable letters to their father puts it best, capturing the self-ironising humour which flashed out in private and made Yeats an entrancing companion:

The Abbey would cheer you up to see it. Motors, carriages and cabs in a string outside – Willy has won his fight – a hard fight. I asked him the other night how the company was getting on together. 'The usual quarrelling,' he said. 'But then,' said he, 'the founder of the Christian religion had the same trouble with his Company and had to invent parables to keep them in good humour.'

Like discipleship, friendship carried its dangers and tensions; Yeats was never more sharply observed than by those who had known him intimately and then quarrelled with him. One example was his art-school friend, the sage and mystic George Russell, whose letters observe his friend's progress to Olympus with a mixture of uncomprehending exasperation and astounded admiration, while also recording those summers at Coole Park with Lady Gregory.

A much more savage witness was George Moore, whose masterpiece of autobiography, *Hail and Farewell,* came out in horribly funny instalments in the years before the First World War. Even this adversity, however, was turned by Yeats (with Clausewitzian resourcefulness) to the purposes of art: responding with a series of poems about family pride and the first part of his autobiography. He knew what he was about. While the personal message of his poetry can be relocated and attributed to different personae, and episodes and encounters put through a prism which changes them, he was quarrying in himself for his art long before he meditated on the process in the great late poem "The Circus Animals' Desertion". He had defended Synge's artistic freedom with the ringing declaration that chauvinistic nationalism would inhibit "the imagination of highly cultivated men, who have begun that experimental digging in the deep pit of themselves, which can alone produce great literature". And here he was, as so often, covertly referring to himself as well. As early as 1900 he was complaining to Gregory that nationalist critics always saw what he did in terms of "heresy" against some supposedly agreed piety. And Gregory consoled him with the thought that the Catholic Church was hiding behind journalists like Griffith and DP Moran who attacked him as a heretic: but as the Gaelic revival educated "the masses" (Gregory's phrase), they would eventually throw off the shackles and "dare to praise you".

They never quite did. Resentment and even ridicule followed that ascent to Olympus, along with adulation. The private pain is always there, but Yeats' is a public life, layered on many levels; it could not be more different from that of, say, Eliot or Hardy or Larkin. Even as a little-known ex-art-student in the 1890s, experimenting with hashish and mescalin under the influence of Havelock Ellis, acquiring a beautiful married mistress who inspired his key love-poems of the mid-nineties and learning how to drop French names from Arthur Symons, he had a genius for publicity and for meeting (and impressing) some of the most interesting people of his time. From youthful encounters with Oscar Wilde and William Morris in the 1880s he proceeded to the *beau monde* of Edwardian England, where he dined with Asquith and weekended with the young Winston Churchill, but he never lost his taste for dramatic and *outré* company or his ability to juggle different worlds: he could deal with Aleister Crowley in the morning and Edmund Gosse in the evening. The professions of politician, dramatist, journalist, occultist jostle with the pastimes of lover, diner-out, traveller. He could draft a poem after breakfast, meet a journalist at lunchtime to plan a political initiative, attend an occultist society in the afternoon, dine out in the evening and then write several letters giving different angles on it all, according to his correspondent.

Money was always short – friends like Augusta Gregory or the homosexual aesthetes Ricketts and Shannon were astonished and slightly appalled at the rigours of his private life – but he never sacrificed style. Once he achieved freedom from his father's Bohemian household in Bedford Park, he lived in transit between his rooms near Euston Station, hired lodgings in Dublin, Lady Gregory's Galway house, Coole Park, and sorties to Maud Gonne in Paris and Normandy. Merely tracking his movements sets up interesting conjunctions and puts certain episodes and initiatives in different context. When he intervened in the public controversy over the foundation of the Gaelic League in 1893, it can be read as a covert appeal to Maud Gonne as well as a last salvo on his losing battle to capture a new nationalist publishing venture. His crucially important first visit to America in 1903-4 followed hard on the shock of Maud Gonne's marriage to a resolutely unmystical man of action, the republican activist John MacBride, and the trauma conditioned many of his radical pronouncements there. His first visit to Italy in 1907, which drastically affected his views on aesthetics and social relationships, should be seen against the controversy over Synge's *Playboy of the Western World* which had exploded just before his departure.

Nor should the role of his supernatural commitments be forgotten. The rituals of the Order of the Golden Dawn provided a sort of alternative university syllabus to discipline his autodidactic genius; "rectifying" horoscopes were cast to forecast outcomes of struggles and to make sense of past failures; any setback in love was accompanied by a surge in occultist activity. He used psychical research as do-it-yourself transactional analysis. From 1911 he was preoccupied by voices sounding through an assortment of shady mediums and by the revelations produced by the automatic writing of Bessie Radcliffe – years before his new wife would resort to the practice in order to rescue their disastrous honeymoon. He used Radcliffe's messages to supply guidance at difficult crossroads in his life. His compulsion to seek for patterns led him to produce some of the most disingenuous autobiographies in literature; they also impelled him to a poetry which both relies upon and conceals autobiographical impulse.

That autobiographical charge is often implicit. It is easy to forget that Yeats' first poetic attempts were verse dramas and that for ten vital years from about 1900 he was far more involved in writing plays than poetry. This made him an accomplished ventriloquist, adept at creating personae and throwing voices. But certain elements of his personal life kept coming through. The theme of family is always central. He knew he had to get away from his charming, didactic, talented father, hopeless as a provider but aggressively influential as a mentor; he constantly quarrelled with his sister Lolly, whose printing press produced the first version of most of his books from 1902 onwards; his relationship with his brother Jack, himself to emerge as a great artist, was never easy. But in the correspondence of his sister Lily, in his dependence on his saturnine uncle George Pollexfen, in his increasing fascination with his family traditions, we can trace a deep and sustaining influence.

The strain of family relationships was counterpointed by the eternal theme of love. Gonne's disastrous marriage in 1903 was one of the great upheavals of his life; her betrayal (as he saw it) was compounded by her commitment to a political creed in which he no longer believed and by her conversion to Catholicism, which contradicted the mystical and occult dedication he believed they shared.

Throughout this first half of his life, his yearning for Gonne never drove out other loves. They included Olivia Shakespear, Florence Farr and an obscure Irishwoman, Mabel Dickinson, who consoled him during the years 1908-13. Dickinson was an amateur actress and "medical masseuse", and their affair was kept secret from his friends; the relationship foundered when she pressed unwisely for marriage on the basis of a claimed pregnancy scare. The spurned lover herself went on to a respectable old age, marrying a barrister and dying in Devon in the 1960s; her influence remains in some poems and plays. But whenever he became involved with another woman, he simultaneously sought out Gonne once more, as if seeking reassurance that she would not, even now, be his. And it was when he had begun his affair with Dickinson that he and Gonne finally, if briefly, became lovers.

Yeats remained engaged with life, experiencing emotion (as Pound put it) from the centre, not the rim; he brought the same intensity to his work. The agonies with which he wrote a poem are well recorded in the manuscript drafts, with their savage scorings and scribblings, as well as in his work's myriad published versions; Russell and others could never understand why he kept on remaking things, never leaving well alone. The brilliant flourishes and glowing patina of his finished work conceal this; sometimes, in his more highly-worked love-poems, the bravura effects conceal something of the emotion too. This is why it is important for the biographer to quote work in the original form in which it was published, rather than the final version, often rearranged years (or decades) later. The revisions themselves have biographical importance, as when his relationship with Gonne more and more aggressively invades successive versions of "The Countess Cathleeen". And this is why the excisions in the drafts of some of his vital manifestos are worth reproducing; and why the draft of the idea for a lyric, never in the event completed, can show more poignantly than even (for instance) "Adam's Curse" the everyday pain of his unrequited love for Gonne in the early years of their relationship.

Work such as this shows how painfully the shimmering effects of his best verse were achieved and how hard he worked his passage. But at the point where my first volume ends, apprenticeship is over in magic and in much else. He is 49 and is finding his way to a new, pared-down authority in his literary voice, helped by his disciple and amanuensis, the young Ezra Pound – if not helped quite as much as Pound liked to claim. He thinks he has become distanced from radical Irish nationalism. He has brought his poetry directly into politics, intervening in public controversies by means of public poems on the editorial page of the *Irish Times* (prepared by lobbying leader writers behind the scenes).

Most of all he had returned, in his fiftieth year, to the politics of nationalism – but a very different nationalism from the Fenianism of the 1890s. When Conor Cruise O'Brien produced his commentary on Yeats' politics in 1965 he did not have access to certain letters and other material recording the poet's reactions to the Home Rule crisis and the Ulster impasses of 1912-14; and these add an intriguing dimension to the picture of passion, cunning and Protestant consciousness. In these years Yeats became, effectively, a spokesman for the Home Rule cause and even a defender of John Redmond's Irish Parliamentary Party. He did this in his own inimitable way. Particularly on speaking-tours in America, he allowed himself a certain amount of latitude: there he could say, for instance, that Home Rule was necessary "to educate Catholics mentally and Protestants emotionally". Even if he looked like part of the establishment now, he knew how to offend everyone impartially. In January 1912 he told Gregory that the chief danger to Home Rule came from extreme-Catholic claims and aggressive papal pronouncements; in fact, he was exactly wrong. The danger was coming from the diametrically opposite corner, in Ulster.

By April this was evident to Yeats as well, and he signed a public letter from Irish Protestants who supported Home Rule and deplored the claims of Unionist politicians that they feared for their future in a Home Rule Ireland. But he jibbed when he was asked by Stephen Gwynn to attend a Protestant Home Ruler meeting affirming faith in the tolerance of the Catholic Church:

> There is intolerance in Ireland, it is the shadow of belief everywhere and no priesthood of any church has lacked it. I would gladly have had my part in any declaration that the great majority of Irish Catholics are tolerant and easy, and that intolerance can be fought and crushed after Home Rule as it cannot be now . . .

When the wording of the resolution was changed he lent it his powerful support, and in a memorable speech looked back to his youthful nationalism and called for a national legislature to release Ireland's potential and draw back the best of its energies from England. In the process he produced a great image of Irish society as "a stagnant stream":

> where there drifts among the duck-weed, pieces of rotting wood, a dead dog or two, various rusty cans, and many old boots. Now, among the old boots drifting along there are a very objectionable pair, Catholic and Protestant bigotry. Some Irishmen object to one or another of these boots so much that they can think of nothing else, and yet we have merely to make the stream move again to sweep them out of sight . . . The best minds of Ireland have been tolerant from the beginning, priest and layman alike – it is the worst minds and the mediocre minds that make up that stagnant stream.

In 1914 Yeats was expecting a new Ireland; and he understood, as he told Gregory, that the future generations would see the past in terms of the autobiographies of their own era. So he began to write his memoirs. Approaching fifty, he was driven back to his beginnings. The result was *Reveries over Childhood and Youth*, a book originally entitled *Memory*

Harbour after his brother's painting of Rosses' Point in Sligo, which held all the Yeats children's most poignant memories. Spurred to autobiography by Moore and others, Yeats found himself repossessed by his childhood; but he wrote about it in the terms dictated by his life in 1914 and his expectations of a new political era, and it is all the more revealing for that. Loneliness flooded him, exacerbated by a recent quarrel with Gregory and the loss of Dickinson's consolations; he was deeply stung by Moore's portrait of him as a burnt-out writer taking refuge in snobbery and manipulation. Most of all, he wrote with elegiac passion about the world that had gone by him and the family and background which had passed through so many changes in the past half-century. The biographer can enclose the first half of his life, therefore, between two views of his childhood: the way it looked to others at the time and the way it looked to the poet as he faced fifty. Astrologer though he was, he could not foretell the future – which was to be in many ways even more astonishing than all he had made of his life up to then.

Those coming, unforeseen upheavals would seismically alter the political and social landscape of Ireland by the time of his death nearly a quarter of a century later. How near he really came to fascism in this later period is matter for a further volume. But already by 1914 the relationship of the man to his age was delineated. To end as we began – with the reactions to his death – that relationship is thoughtfully captured in an obituary written by Stephen Gwynn, who was familiar with Yeats both in literary and political circles from his youth and shared a similarly "marginalised Protestant" background. Gwynn's pronouncement also hints at some of the affinities presciently – and resonantly – drawn out by Conor Cruise O'Brien in his famous essay:

> First and last he was smashing idols in the market-place: at first, the cheap rhetoric of drum-beating ballads, false models in poetry; later, justifying work which his artistic sense approved as vital, while the crowd denounced it as 'an insult to Ireland'. First and last, he was a champion of freedom – but, above all, against the tyrannies of democracy. And in the end, the democracy which he never spared to resist and rebuke, marches, to its credit, behind his coffin.

CHAPTER 8

THE IRISH AND THE GREAT WAR: A CASE OF AMNESIA

KEVIN MYERS

IN 1979 I VISITED FOR THE FIRST TIME THE MEMORIAL GARDENS AT Islandbridge in Dublin. Designed by the great architect Lutyens, they were constructed by hand in the 1920s and 1930s to commemorate the "49,400" Irish dead of the Great War (the actual figure is, in fact, about 35,000). The gardens resembled a municipal dump. The great memorial stones were defaced with graffiti, old cars rusted and tinkers' ponies grazed on weeds where there had once been flower beds. The condition of those gardens said all that was needed about the state of Irish memory towards the thousands of Irishmen who had left these shores to lay their young bones in the battlefields of Europe.

The war was then over for sixty years: surely there must be many veterans still alive, or the families of veterans, who could tell me about the motives, feelings and popular mood which animated so many youngsters to go off to war? I wrote to every provincial and national newspaper in Ireland, some forty publications in all, seeking information from ex-servicemen or their families. I received just three replies, two from ex-soldiers and one from a woman in Carlow who had been engaged to one soldier who was killed and who married another. "I was wondering when somebody would ask about those men," she said. "They seem to have been forgotten." The paucity of replies suggests that not merely did the broader community forget: the veterans themselves, and their families, had entered into an informal community of silence about that time and their dead.

Such amnesia would no doubt have seemed inconceivable to Lieutenant-Colonel Jack Hunt of the Royal Dublin Fusiliers, who in 1917 was publicly canvassing opinions in Ireland about the nature of a future memorial to the Irish dead of the Great War. There is to modern ears a wondrously self-confident innocence about his enquiries, uttered as they were within the lingering political culture of the constitutional Irish Parliamentary Party which had dominated Irish politics for two generations. That party had finally achieved Home Rule in 1914, but it had been deferred until the war was ended; and the political situation had been thrown into confusion by the 1916 Rising. But to people like Hunt it must have seemed that events could be put back on track, something like the old order restored, and in the meantime what was essential was a proper memorial to the thousands of Irish dead who had, with unique generosity, volunteered for service in the War.

Alas for Hunt, and for the thousands of Irish soldiers like him, Ireland was undergoing a moral and political convulsion which was to cause a shutter to come down in the greater political psyche of the people. Vast events were to be lost on the far side of this shutter; while on the nearer side an obsessive and self-absorbed cameo – in part a mythicised version of the truth, in part complete fiction and in part a recognisable truth, all blended with a revolutionary vigour – came to dominate the consciousness of the political elite which was to take control of Irish nationalism and, more to the point, Irish historiography.

What was to lie invisible behind the shield was the extraordinary impact of the Great War on Ireland. Three Irish Divisions were raised, with as many Irishmen again serving in non-Irish units – in all, over 200,000 Irishmen saw service in the war. There could hardly have been an individual Irishman or woman who did not personally know somebody serving in the colours. Awareness of the war, of its battles and of Irish casualties, killed, wounded and captured, which must have exceeded 100,000, must have been a shared sensation throughout the island, causing an emotional commonality which filled both conversations and the newspapers of the time.

Jack Hunt was particularly suited for the task he had set for himself. A working class Dublin Catholic who had been commissioned from the ranks of the Dublin Fusiliers, in four meteoric years he moved from sergeant to acting Brigadier-General. He served for most of the war in the 16th (Irish) Division, which had recruited very heavily from the Irish Volunteers, the semi-paramilitary organisation which had been formed in response to the raising of the Ulster Volunteers to thwart all-Ireland Home Rule. When the Irish Parliamentary leader, John Redmond, declared the support of the Irish Volunteers for the British war-effort, a minority faction had split off in protest – and that minority was in due course to seize control not merely over events in Ireland, but over the collective memory of Irish nationalism as well.

John Redmond had intended the 16th Division to be the basis for the army of the independent Ireland which would emerge after war's ending – and it very much was the army of the existing political elite within Irish nationalist Ireland. Redmond's brother Willie, also a Member of Parliament, was serving in it and was to be killed on active service. Tom Kettle, one of the most eminent personalities in Dublin life (and, be it added, Conor Cruise O'Brien's uncle) had been MP for Tyrone. He too was killed in action. Other Home Rule MPs serving in the armed forces included John Esmonde, Stephen Gwynn and DD Sheehan, whose five sons also served.

Many of the 16th Division's officers who served alongside Hunt came from middle class, nationalist Ireland and they no doubt assumed, if only subconsciously, that they would be honoured in their own country for doing their duty, that they would be the political elite within the Ireland that was to come: their story, their world, would be the ones which Irish children in a free and independent country would learn about.

Such hopes were swept aside in the psychic convulsion which coursed through nationalist Ireland in the two years after the 1916 Rising. That convulsion was only in part caused by the Rising – there must have been pre-existing feelings, widespread, deeply felt but largely repressed or at least unspoken, that Ireland must not just be free and separate, but also *different*. Independence was in itself not sufficient; there must be a re-ordering of Irish life according to uniquely "Irish" values.

Such an aspiration had been the engine of the Gaelic revival, which had been a largely middle class and pacific cultural movement. The addition of a political and military agenda to that movement by the leaders of the 1916 Rising turned it into a revolutionary force which over time came to appeal to very large numbers of people who had hitherto felt themselves outside the workings of the political system. This was the Unconsulted Ireland, whose ambitions, hopes, dreams were barely articulated on the political stage by the Irish Parliamentary Party, which seemed content to build a British-style state with British political structures.

That conservative vision of the Irish future was swept aside by the revolutionary mixture of conspiratorial republicanism fuelled by a semi-racist view of Ireland: *saor agus Gaeilge, Gaeilge agus soar (free and Gaelic, Gaelic and free)*. The restoration of an aboriginal paradise, stolen by conquest, became the quest for political life in Ireland, and the language of politics in Ireland became obsessed with national pride and tribal identity rather than the conventional political issues of slicing the cake.

The Fianna Fáil victory of 1932 finally put the hands of Unconsulted Ireland on the levers of power and of the myth-making machine; but something of the direction that machine would take had become evident between 1919 and 1923, when the IRA murdered some 200 ex-servicemen in a campaign which has attracted remarkably little historical examination since. The period in question is so deeply disagreeable that it is hardly surprising that historians have shied away from its excesses; yet we can see in the conduct of the IRA and local councils at the time the very elements which were to become institutionalised in Irish life.

Across Ireland after 1919 Sinn Féin-dominated county councils either formally, as in Wexford, or more informally, as in Cork, adopted a policy of not giving employment to ex-soldiers. Their children were barred from county scholarships. Many became almost non-persons in many rural Irish communities, living in a condition of semi-boycott and often in one of permanent fear. Jack Moyney, the last surviving Irish Victoria Cross winner from the Great War, who had been decorated for extraordinary feats of courage in Flanders in 1917, told me that he was far more frightened during the War of Independence than during his war service.

Crowds of ex-soldiers found themselves wandering around Ireland looking for work; the IRA in response introduced informal ordinances against "tramps". In their captors' eyes, imprisoned tramps were instantly transformed into "spies", and their summary executions became almost casual affairs. Sometimes their bodies, often labelled "Spies and Traitors Beware", would be dumped; sometimes the corpses were simply buried and never found, their deaths never recorded. The degree of non-personage of these pitiful victims was such that up until recently no history of this period even mentioned this campaign of murder.

But total amnesia or marginalisation could not be achieved overnight. In 1922 more of the new poppy symbols which remembered the war dead were sold in Dublin than in Belfast. Even then, the very act of memorialising the war dead seemed to some to be an act of treachery, and throughout the 1920s there were clashes each November between ex-servicemen and republicans. Despite these clashes, the vitality of memory of a far greater suffering and sacrifice than had been experienced in Ireland's domestic wars remained unquenchable. But in the 1930s Eamon de Valera, the Taoiseach, used the threat of an IRA attack on marchers to pass public order acts which restricted public ceremonials and he repeatedly deferred the official opening of the Memorial Gardens at Islandbridge. Jack Hunt died, yet still the gardens were not opened. Finally, the outbreak of the Second World War gave de Valera an excuse not to open the gardens at all, and they began their ignominious journey towards ruin.

Their fate represented a suitable symbol of the memory of the Irish and the Great War. All public ceremonial and utterance were dedicated towards another vision, of the Ireland which had taken up arms against Britain, not that other and, in fact, larger Ireland which had worn the uniform of the Crown. When friends wished to erect in St Stephen's Green a bust of Tom Kettle, killed in action with the Royal Dublin Fusiliers on the Somme in 1916, the Office of Public Works permitted it only on condition that no mention was made of the circumstances or country of his death: his life was to be seen to end in a mysterious place called Ginchy, reason or whereabouts unknown.

In the North, memorialisation of the dead of the Great War was turned into a declaration of Britishness and loyalty, thereby driving nationalist Ireland further away from such memorialisation. In the Republic, honouring Remembrance Sunday came to be confined to Protestants, for whom it was a discreet, almost Masonically covert, statement of identity. This process was intensified during the Second World War, when again, despite Ireland's official neutrality, many thousands of Irishmen and women were serving in the British armed forces, but to whom no reference could be made in the Irish press owing to draconian censorship laws. Even death notices for Irish soldiers were censored, as too was news of the death camps when they were liberated by Allied soldiers. Ireland's public stance – as opposed to its private actions, which were pro-Allied – was of a priggish and fastidiously delicate moral equivalence, almost as if Ireland was above such worldly things as war.

Ex-soldiers had already ceased to speak of their own experiences in the Great War. Voices were silent; sons were not told about what fathers had done. Participation in the Great War came to be edited out of the lives of veterans such as the writer Liam O'Flaherty or the poet Thomas MacGreevy, curator of the National Gallery. Censorship, conscious or otherwise, became a way of thought, so that it was with no difficulty at all that the 1966 commemoration of the Easter Rising was able to avoid mentioning that the Rising had in large part been put down by Irish regiments under the command of their Irish officers, or that for every Irish insurgent in the GPO there were 200 Irish soldiers on the Western Front.

This elision of the truth did not just exist at a political or journalistic level; it was equally acute academically too. School textbooks simply made no mention of the fact that hundreds of thousands of Irishmen had freely participated in the Great War. My studies of Irish history at University College Dublin in the late 1960s were untroubled by any such knowledge. The first thesis on Irish involvement in the Great War, an MA by Martin Staunton (UCD), was not written until the mid-1980s, at about the same time that David Fitzpatrick began a class project at Trinity College on different aspects of how the war impacted Ireland. But even today, in 1998, eighty years after the war ended, there has never been a single question on the Leaving Certificate about the Irish involvement in the Great War.

The intellectual distortions required to continue this amnesia were not just subconscious. In the 1980s the British Legion attempted to broaden the base of public memory of the Irish dead and invited the President to attend its Remembrance Day service at St Patrick's Cathedral, which was attended annually by representatives of most embassies in Dublin, including those of West Germany and the Soviet Union, as well as by representatives of the Irish Army, out of military courtesy. The presidential invitation alerted the then Taoiseach, Charles Haughey, to the fact that the Irish Army was in the habit of being represented at this service. He instructed that the President should not attend and also ordered that the Army should no longer do so.

That year, however, the Army was represented at the annual service to commemorate the German dead of the Second World War at Glencree, County Wicklow, where German servicemen killed in or near Ireland during both World Wars (mostly pilots) are interred. Now, here was a pretty picture, indeed, a perverse and degrading version of a pettifogging, sanctimonious neutralism in which the dead of Nazi Germany were honoured, but the Irish dead of two world wars were studiously ignored.

This was disgusting and unsustainable, especially since the mood of nationalist Ireland was changing. A new brand of historical journalism had already emerged which spoke of the truths of Irish participation in the war, and this was made all the more topical by the 1987 IRA bomb attack on the Remembrance Sunday ceremony in Enniskillen, County Fermanagh. This atrocity, vile even amid a sea of vileness, served to confirm a growing sense that selective memorialisation marginalised and trivialised not merely the dead, but also those who remembered them, to the point where they had even become a legitimate target for terrorism.

In recent years, a broader sense of Irish identity, freed by the European dimensions of Irish life and separated in time from the obligatory obeisances of post-colonial political culture, has outgrown such sectarian and small-minded definitions. Irishness no longer seems dependent on anti-Britishness, and a grandfather's service with the Crown is no longer a matter of shame. In 1988, fifty years after they were completed, the Memorial Gardens at Islandbridge were restored and formally opened, and throughout the 1990s it has become an accepted norm that both the President and government ministers attend the Remembrance Sunday service at St Patrick's Cathedral. Ireland is finally facing its past, and Jack Hunt's task is done.

CHAPTER 9

"IN THE NAME OF GOD AND OF THE DEAD GENERATIONS": NATIONALISM AND REPUBLICANISM IN IRELAND

FRANK CALLANAN

THE VEXED TERMS "NATIONALISM" AND "REPUBLICANISM" ARE REPEATEDLY used as if they were binary constants in the history of modern Ireland. The motion of political history is conventionally situated in their rivalry, rather than in their internal mutations. This phenomenon is not limited to colloquial usage and is affirmed in the writing of history. Driven by literary convention, or expository convenience, narratives of Irish history are commonly organised around pendulum-like oscillations between physical force and parliamentary action. There are strikingly few attempts to elucidate critically their interrelationship. An honourable exception is Conor Cruise O'Brien's discursive review of Sean Cronin's *Irish Nationalism: A History of Its Roots and Ideology*, which is republished in *Passion and Cunning: Essays on Nationalism, Terrorism and Revolution* under the title "Ireland: The Shirt of Nessus".[1]

It is not simply an issue of distinguishing between nationalism and republicanism: each tends to be defined by reference to the other. Many would define nationalism as the moderate, or constitutional, expression of that of which republicanism is the extreme manifestation – and define republicanism conversely. If serviceable in ordinary political usage, such an interdefinition is historically crude. The reciprocity of the definitional scheme, moreover, dangerously posits the existence of an ineffable core of ethnicity interior to both nationalism and republicanism.

The terms seem, at times, to aspire to the condition of synonyms; at others, to relapse towards the harshly antonymic: they are feuding synonyms or antonyms which enjoy a curious *entente cordiale*. Likewise, to their adversaries, the relationship of nationalism to republicanism was that of Dr Jekyll to Mr Hyde. As the ambiguities are unceasingly displaced from one term to the other, the pursuit of definition becomes circular. The shifting usage of the terms nationalism and republicanism is the outcome of a continuing process of interdefinition. Rather than affronting these concepts directly, I propose to consider two disparate uses of the term "nationalist": the first in the historical context of the rise of Parnell; the second in the writings and rhetoric of Patrick Pearse.

* * *

One of the most intriguing sub-themes of the Special Commission (1888-90), which was established to enquire into the origin of the Pigott forgeries and, more generally, into allegations of Parnellite complicity in political violence, was a semantic contest over the meaning of the word nationalist. The initial, and for a time predominant, usage of the term nationalist had been to designate Fenians or separatists. It was, however, neither a canonical nor an exclusive meaning of the term. It was characteristic of Irish American adherents of Clan na Gael, the body established in 1867 to reunite the divided factions of the original Fenian Brotherhood, which had been founded by John O'Mahony in New York in 1858. This sense of the term was promoted particularly by John Devoy.

The usage of nationalist as a synonym for Fenian was not confined to the United States and achieved considerable currency in Ireland, notably in the latter half of the 1870s. There it was often used to distinguish Fenians from Federalists (a term which designated supporters of the Home Rule League of Isaac Butt, but which never quite caught on) or "Home Rulers" (an appellation applied equally to supporters of Butt and Parnell). Outside Irish America nationalist, in the sense of Fenian, was less-frequently encountered as a stand-alone term. The context, or a further qualifying objective, was generally relied on to make plain that this was the intended meaning. The usage survived into the mature phase of Parnellism chiefly in the term "advanced nationalist", indicating a Fenian or Fenian sympathiser. In practice, this compound term was more commonly used to refer to Fenians sympathetic to Parnell, or at least acquiescent in the forward movement of Parnellism. With the accompanying shift in the meaning of the term nationalist from Fenian to

Parnellite, the formulation advertised the comprehensive reach of the Parnellite coalition and subtly lent it unassailable patriotic legitimacy.

Parnell, if he did not disdain its Fenianesque resonance, was certainly not prepared to cede the term nationalist to Fenianism. The shift in the meaning of the term owed less to Parnellite revision than to appellative convenience, which was always a key determinant in the unfolding evolutionary usage and abuse of the terms nationalist and republican in Ireland. By the time of the hearings of the Special Commission, which took place between September 1888 and November 1889, the term nationalist overwhelmingly indicated in Ireland and (if to a slightly lesser extent) in England a member or supporter of the Irish Parliamentary Party.

At the Special Commission the counsel retained for *The Times* sought to revivify, and archaicise, the by then superseded use of the word nationalist to mean Fenian. The purpose was obvious: to taint Parnell by association with physical force, which was part of *The Times'* broader strategy of confounding Home Rulers, Fenians, dynamitards, Land League agitators and the diverse perpetrators of the agrarian outrages which were so compulsively totted up by Victorian statesmen to provide a measure of the efficacy of government policy or of Parnellite villainy. The Special Commission became in one of its aspects an enquiry into the political etymology of the term nationalist.

The Times' endeavour to resuscitate what was by then the largely historical and time-specific meaning of the term nationalist to designate Fenians was a somewhat contrived and lawyerly game. Among the counsel for *The Times*, the point was pursued especially by Sir Richard Webster KC (the Attorney General), Sir Henry James QC and by Stephen Ronan of the Irish bar. They allowed no opportunity to emphasise this peculiarity of usage to pass. They sought to compel Parnellite witnesses under cross-examination to confirm the usage of the term to mean "Fenian" or, if they did not compel them, to encourage them by the manner in which they put their questions.

Sir Charles Russell, who appeared with HH Asquith for Parnell, cited, in his speech opening the defence, a letter of May 1880 from the executive of the Irish Republican Brotherhood (IRB) condemning parliamentary involvement, which also referred to Fenians as "the Nationalists" and the "National Party". Russell somewhat apologetically interposed: "My Lords, at that date the name 'National Party' appears to have the meaning of a physical force party." Likewise, when quoting an account of events in 1878 provided two years later by Michael Davitt, the founder of the Irish

National Land League, he explained: "Nationalists, my Lord, at that time meant, in 1878, the physical force party, or principally so."[2]

While his client was untroubled by this former usage, Russell was evidently discomfited. His opponents seized on these remarks with barristerial theatricality to suggest that Russell had been compelled to make a damning concession, to the effect, as Stephen Ronan paraphrased it, that "the Nationalists in 1879 were the physical force men".[3]

Ronan's cross-examination of TP O'Connor – who as well as being a leading Parnellite was the author of what Ronan described as "a very elaborate history of the Parnell movement" – was representative. He put to O'Connor: "The Nationalists and Home Rulers in 1879 were different parties. Were not the Nationalists one lot and the Home Rulers another in 1879?" O'Connor sought to deflect the imposed nomenclature in his response: "I should say that in 1879 and 1878 certainly the large bodies of revolutionaries were entirely antagonistic to the Home Rule Party." At another point, with almost comical archness, Ronan asked: "Did you ever hear it suggested that the Fenians, who, I suppose, called themselves Nationalists, were in favour of crime or outrage?" Exasperated by the stilted usage, O'Connor had earlier objected: "You must know as well as I do that the term Nationalist would have very different meanings with very different bodies and different men."[4] Cross-examined by Webster, Davitt retorted: "Well, we might differ as to who are meant by the word 'Nationalists'. The Federalists – men who followed Mr Parnell – called themselves Nationalists, and always have; the extremists have been called Nationalists in years gone by."[5]

In a manner strikingly redolent of Richard Pigott, Captain WH O'Shea liked to posture as an admirer of those who frankly professed their allegiance to Fenianism. He rarely missed an opportunity to laud them for their forthrightness, their sense of honour and their freedom from the taint of low agrarianism. He sought thereby to posit a contrast with the pusillanimous duplicity he attributed to Parnell and his adherents. At the same time, he needed to be able to deny any knowing involvement with oath-bound Fenians. In his evidence to the Special Commission he referred to the Fenians variously as "Nationalists", "old Nationalists", "American nationalists" and "advanced Nationalists". He was cross-examined by Sir Charles Russell:

> Russell: You have spoken about your acquaintance with the advanced Nationalists or Fenian party in clear language . . . You say they were the old Nationalist party who were opposed to outrage?

O'Shea: Certainly.

Russell: Who went in for open revolt if they were able?

O'Shea: Yes, what they called the hillside men, the men who thought the day might come when they could fight their country's battle on the hill-side against the British forces, and in the meanwhile objected to all outrages.[6]

This answer brought the term "hillside men" into wider political currency and even led to Captain O'Shea being erroneously credited with its invention by some commentators in England.

The meaning of the term nationalist became a flashpoint in Webster's cross-examination of Parnell, because it touched directly on the very delicate issue of the political underpinnings of the "new departure", the term used to describe Fenian collaboration in the politico-agrarian movement under Parnellite auspices of the late 1870s.

Parnell had to tread a narrow path. He had not merely to discriminate sharply between the official Fenian opposition to all parliamentary movements, and the support of individual Fenians, but actually to rely on these contradictory phenomena in equal measure. Above all, he needed to repudiate any suggestion of a compact with Fenianism. He went so far as to propound a brazenly disingenuous definition of the "new departure" which eliminated the Fenians altogether: "My definition of the 'new departure' as far as I ever heard the expression in Ireland, if at all, is that it was a combination of the political with the agrarian movement."[7]

The relevant sequence of the Attorney General's cross-examination of the Irish leader ran as follows:

Webster: Then it is entirely erroneous to suggest that there was a combination of what I may call the secret and open movement, by which I mean the open Land league with a certain published policy of the secret movement, namely the Nationalists working together with the Land League: That is entirely a mistake?

Parnell: It is absolutely false.

Russell: When you use the word nationalist do you mean Fenian?

Webster: I really do not think there is any necessity for interruption. You heard Sir Charles Russell more than once say in his speech, in the years 1879 and 1880, Nationalist as distinguished from Home Rulers meant the physical force party?

Parnell: Nationalists as individuals have constantly taken action with reputed Nationalists in our movement.

Webster: I have a letter of your own I may tell you, but you agree with the statement made by Sir Charles Russell that Nationalists as opposed to Home Rulers, whether a party or not, meant the physical force party?

Parnell: Nationalists up to the date of the formation of the National League [1882] were understood to be men who believed in physical force.

Webster: I will not confound the term 'Nationalists' after the National League was founded, but I will refer to Nationalists in the sense you have referred to?

Parnell: But a great number of these men who had believed in physical force came into our movement and gave it a fair trial, believing that it would obtain benefit for Ireland by constitutional means, and I believe that their action was quite honest in the matter, and that they had no *arrière-pensée* of any sort.

Webster: Remember I have your distinct answer, that anything like a combination between the two parties you entirely repudiate?

Parnell: It is absolutely false, either in Ireland or in England, or in America, so far as I know. I believe to this day the physical force organisation has been consistently hostile to us since 1880.[8]

Parnell was subsequently cross-examined in relation to a speech he had made in the United States in January 1880, in which he said that when England was militarily defeated "the idea of the Irish Nationalists may be realised". This was a characteristically arch formulation: an assertion of the impracticality of recourse to arms couched in terms of an identification with Fenian tenets. Parnell unblushingly informed the Attorney General that he was using "the expression 'Irish Nationalist' in its broader sense as we apply it to ourselves today".[9]

In his speech in reply, Sir Henry James sought to harvest the meagre, though not altogether negligible, fruits of *The Times'* heavy play on the former usage of the term nationalist. Speaking of Davitt's visit to the United States in August 1878, he declared:

In order to construe the evidence that has been given, it is reasonable, I think, to note that at the time at which we are now speaking the word 'Nationalist' means 'Fenian'. Mr. Parnell explained the use of this term. Mr. Parnell said 'Nationalists' up to the date of the formation of the Land League were understood to be men who believed in physical force . . .[10]

While the report of the three Commissioners of 13 February 1890 picked up the use of the word nationalists to mean Fenians, it was in terms which followed the contemporary usage in cited documentary sources rather than in the sententious manner promoted by the counsel for *The Times*.[11]

There was a degree of underlying collusion in the semantics. If *The Times* was determined to maximise the seditious connotations of the word nationalist, Parnell was equally resolved to keep a firm grip on the rights to the term he had acquired. If it had some limited effect at the time in casting a penumbra of violence over Parnellism, the attempt by *The Times* to reinvest the term nationalism with a specifically Fenian connotation could not be maintained in the longer term. Unionist publicists, of course, continued to insist that the demand for Home Rule was objectively separatist in character, and that the avowed constitutionalism of the Irish party was at best naïve, at worst a sinister feint. Cartoonists continued to depict nationalist parliamentarians as bomb-wielding conspirators, although with the Parnell split the faction fight came to replace the terrorist conclave as the caricatural *mis-en-scène* of the Irish party.

It was not only on Irish history and politics that this definitional struggle left its mark. It was in relation to the Irish question that Britain had its primary and defining engagement with the concept of nationalism. The term nationalist in Britain was heavily laden with Irish resonances. In ordinary political and parliamentary usage, the term "Irish nationalist" was almost pleonastic in the period 1886-1918. The *Oxford English Dictionary*, likewise, offers as a general definition of a nationalist "one characterised by nationalist tendencies or sympathies" and a more specific meaning of "one who advocates the claims of Ireland to be an independent nation".

What in practice undercut the semantic adventurism of *The Times* at the Special Commission was the eclipse of Fenianism. That eclipse antedated, but was made manifest by, the rise of Parnell. Having completed the marginalisation of Fenianism as a political force, Parnell, at the Special Commission, appeared to write it out of history. This revisionism, which he adjudged necessary for the purposes of the Special Commission, was to prove less thoroughgoing than what was to follow under the auspices of Fenianism's successor republican movement.

* * *

In the burgeoning literature on nationalism there are, generally, two competing schools of theoreticians, sometimes designated as modernists and primordialists. The modernists assert that nationalism is a specifically modern phenomenon, at once a product (if not a pre-condition) of the modern and a reaction against it. The primordialists are more disposed to take at face value the pretensions of nationalism to the realisation of an ancient ethnicity, its assertion of a nationality anterior to the modern articulation of nationalism. I am not here concerned with this controversy, which in any case imperfectly fits the idiosyncrasies of Irish history. But the modernist emphasis on the ideological manipulation of history has considerable salience.[12]

The concept of an immemorial nation is common to Irish nationalism and republicanism. While the nationalist sense of history bore the heavy impress of myth, Fenians regarded the rhetoric of parliamentary nationalism as suspiciously sentimental and lacking in rigour: deprecations of parliamentary "spouting" were commonplace. With Pearse and his successors, this mistrust acquired hardened form. What the 1916 Proclamation referred to as Ireland's "old traditions of nationhood" required the ideological supplement of the idea of an unbroken and invariant republican tradition. This concept of revolutionary continuity owed something to the French model: the notion of an Irish republican continuity analogous to that of the French tradition is even more improbable than the substantive republican claim of fidelity to the principles of the French revolution itself.

The classic formulation of Pearse's concept of revolutionary continuity is contained in the 1916 Proclamation: "In every generation the Irish people have asserted their right to national freedom and sovereignty; six times during the past three hundred years they have asserted it in arms." There were, indeed, six incidents of armed rebellion, but the compression served to suggest that an identity of purpose united them. Pearse, revolutionary and schoolmaster, visionary and pedant, knew this to be a pretence and in both his capacities refrained from its explicit assertion.

I do not propose here to assess the republican claim to the legacy of the French revolution, which Conor Cruise O'Brien has searingly assessed in "Ireland: the Shirt of Nessus" and elsewhere,[13] but wish to consider the Fenian link in the Pearsean chain. For Pearse as an ideologue, the Fenians presented a considerable difficulty: Fenianism was a diverse and complex radical movement, which could not, save at its outer fringes, be defined in terms of a crude espousal of physical force.

His solution was commendably simple. He recognised and exploited the fact that, while the IRB provided a semblance of institutional continuity, Fenianism as a political movement was no longer extant. His rhetoric was premised on the demise of Fenianism. In his obituary to O'Donovan Rossa in August 1915 he wrote that he was "not the greatest man of the Fenian generation, but he was its most typical man". Quite apart from the fact that O'Donovan Rossa's views could hardly be considered typical, what was significant was the reference to the "Fenian generation". Pearse was drawing a line under the Fenians.[14]

While this ideological stratagem is rarely noticed, it is central to the celebrated conclusion of Pearse's oration at O'Donovan Rossa's graveside: "They think they have foreseen everything, they think they have provided against everything; but the fools, the fools, the fools, the fools! They have left us our Fenian dead, and while Ireland holds these graves, Ireland unfree shall never be at peace."[15] The rhetorical force was supplemented by a degree of revolutionary candour. The Fenians were dead, or at least defunct, and for Pearse most conveniently so. It was less a homage to the Fenian dead than a declaration of Pearse's intent to appropriate their legacy and mystique. In historical terms, it was to prove a more far-reaching emasculation than any they had suffered at the hands of Parnell.

Pearse had foreshadowed this theme in 1914. He wrote that as a boy he had journeyed through the Dublin mountains and afterwards told his grandfather that the Fenians were all dead: "I have gone through all the glens, and there was none drilling: they must be dead." He continued:

> And my naïve deduction was very nearly right. If the Fenians were not all dead, the Fenian spirit was dead, or almost dead. By the Fenian spirit, I mean not so much the spirit of the particular generation as that virile fighting faith which has been the salt of all the generations in Ireland unto this last.[16]

The reference to the "Fenian spirit" is a striking reversal of a rhetorical convention. Invocations of the "Fenian spirit" were something of a commonplace even among nationalist parliamentarians, at least when speaking in their constituencies in close proximity to polling day. These formulaic salutes to the "Fenian spirit" carried with them a tacit deprecation of the means to which Fenians were prepared, in principle, to resort. Pearse's purpose was quite different and marks a point of bifurcation in what was Pearse's very curious parallel development as a nationalist publicist and revolutionary ideologue. Pearse's vacuous lauding of the Fenian spirit – in eliding its complex ambiguity, its rootedness in the politics of its time – was intended to void Fenianism of its political substance.

While Fenians professed allegiance to an Irish republic, the occasions on which they avowed themselves "Republicans" *tout court* were conspicuously rare. This was attributable to their desire to avoid attracting the further opprobrium of the Catholic Church or the accusation of being unethnically doctrinaire. The entry of the word republican into general political currency awaited the 1916 Rising and its aftermath. With the Civil War it came to designate opponents of the Anglo-Irish Treaty. In contemporary politics it has come to refer virtually exclusively to Sinn Féin and the IRA.

Pearse not merely sedulously observed this terminological inhibition, but embraced it with conviction. He was careful throughout to designate himself a nationalist. In 1913 he looked to what he described as "the creation of a Gaelic party within the Home Rule Parliament, with a strong following behind it in the country".[17] Even in its constitutional manifestation, there was something a little chilling in Pearse's programme. Pearse's self-categorisation as a nationalist accurately reflected his own right-wing Catholic nationalist proclivities. Writing in the context of the Dublin lock-out, he asseverated: "I am nothing so new-fangled as a socialist or a syndicalist. I am old-fashioned enough to be a Catholic and a Nationalist."[18]

Even as Pearse came to oppose John Redmond's Irish party, he sought to supplant the word "Republican" with "Separatist". Citing the Irish republican lineage from Wolfe Tone, he wrote, in December 1915: "It thus appears that Ireland has been separatist up to the beginning of the generation that is now growing old. Separatism, in fact, is the nationalist position. Whenever an Irish leader has taken up a position different from the nationalist position he has been repudiated by the next generation".[19] Even where the word republican is most irresistibly suggested, it is refused by Pearse: "It will be conceded that Wolfe Tone is a Separatist. He is The Separatist." As late as March 1916 he was writing of Tone as "the intellectual ancestor of the whole modern movement of Irish nationalism".[20]

Of the Fenians, Pearse wrote almost apologetically: "It will be admitted that the Fenians were Separatists. They guarded themselves against future misrepresentation by calling themselves the Irish Republican Brotherhood." That is to say, the Fenians were, in the Pearsean canon, merely extreme nationalists. They did not harbour alarming secularist or Jacobin ideas and espoused the term republican as a fetish to ward off the taint of suspected pragmatism. In his capacity as a publicist, Pearse was seeking to allay the unease of Catholic nationalists. As an ideologue, he was ensuring that the republic to be proclaimed was his own creation. This statement is significant: it constitutes, from within their own tradition, a rebuttal of the pretensions of latter-day republicans to trace their ideological lineage to the French revolution.

The analogy with French republicanism favoured by republican apologists is instructive. In terms of the French republican tradition, Pearse is much closer (and he is very close indeed) to the reactionary nationalist right than to either of the classic strains of French republicanism: the left wing adherents of the revolutionary tradition; and the exceedingly pragmatic republican parliamentarians who elevated the idea of the secular state into a defining principle.[21]

In "Ireland: Shirt of Nessus", Conor Cruise O'Brien has argued that "Irish nationalism is not itself an ideology, but it has acquired an ideology: that of Irish republicanism". One could advance a less elegant alternative thesis to the effect that extreme nationalism was itself highly ideological and fed back into and fortified Irish republicanism. This is to posit an interactive cycle between the extremes of nationalism and republicanism. The regressively sectarian and chauvinistic disposition of reactionary exponents of nationalism in the late nineteenth and early twentieth centuries subverts the conventional perception that nationalism was invariably and in all respects less extreme than republicanism. Cruise O'Brien's argument rightly emphasises the cross-trafficking of Catholic nationalist values and republican ideology.

Was Pearse a republican or an ultra-nationalist? Pearse's (posthumous) capture of the term republican was so complete that the question seems almost whimsical. Breaking the circularity imposed by Pearse's lexical coup, it can plausibly be argued that Pearse was only a republican in the sense of the term he himself generated, and that he is more properly considered as a physical force nationalist. Pearse's own repeated characterisations of himself as a nationalist lend some support to this contention.

Pearse espoused, if he did not invent, a strain of nationalism of intense purity, whose incorruption was to be affirmed through blood sacrifice. This was a spectacular innovation, for which his effusively sentimental historical maunderings provided a cover. His holy simplicity was devised to render redundant both conventional nationalism and what remained of Fenianism. He offered an illusory, but highly alluring, resolution to the agonising over ends and means which had preoccupied constitutional nationalists and Fenians alike and which is integral to any scheme of political rationality in civil society. He sought not to mediate, but to transcend, the dichotomy between nationalism and republicanism.

He was more concerned with transposing nationalism to the plane of the sacral than with taking over a moribund and problematical republican tradition. That emphasis reflected his extraordinary ambitiousness as an ideologue. His efforts were directed far more to releasing the fervour of the larger Catholic nationalist constituency than to placing himself at the head of the tattered remnants of Fenianism. It is this which accounts for the force of his posthumous cult over the ensuing half-century and the continuing reach of his influence.[22]

The role assigned to Fenianism in Pearse's reductive scheme was that of a sacral conduit linking 1798 and 1848 with 1916.[23] The process of the occlusion of Fenianism has endured in our time. Neo-republican ideologues tend to disregard the Fenians as ineffectual and lacking in the requisite degree of revolutionary remorselessness. For liberals and many constitutional nationalists the savage nihilism of the Provisional IRA has cast a dark aftershadow over the Fenian readiness to countenance physical force.

In terms of historiography, the neglect of Fenianism owes much to its diversity and intractability as a movement. In its own time, Fenianism was an elusive phenomenon; as much a state of disaffection, a posture of defiance, as an organised movement.[24] The Fenian oath, as well as providing the requisite frisson of sedition, served to invest Fenianism with a semblance of the collective discipline and doctrinaire purpose in which it was, for the most part, conspicuously, and sometimes comically, lacking.[25] Fenianism was consigned to the semi-oblivion reserved for revolutionary movements which neither achieved their aims nor attained notoriety through the ferocity of sustained violence.

Fenianism's untidiness as a historical phenomenon rendered it resistant to assessment in terms of conventional narratives of history and politics in modern Ireland. The state of the historical art has not significantly progressed since TW Moody noted in 1967 the continuing exaggerated reliance on narratives and recollections of those who had been prominent Fenians. The tapestry of memoirs and published letters of commanding Fenian personalities, often highly individualistic, egotistical and quarrelsome, leaves one remarkably unenlightened as to what Fenianism was or was supposed to be. Moody concluded that much more intensive research was required before an adequate history of Fenianism could be written.[26] This represents the most gaping lacuna in the historiography of late-nineteenth-century Ireland. We know little about the less prominent

Fenian activists or its more passive sympathisers. The faces photographed in the police files formerly kept at Dublin Castle still belong to a lost anthropological realm, not yet annexed to historiography.

To state that the high Fenian doctrine of recourse to military engagement did not sanction physical force as practised by the Provisional IRA is a banal, though not a trivial, proposition. Avowed theoretical inhibitions in relation to the deployment of physical force have to be treated with very considerable circumspection and are unstable over time. In the case of the Fenians, these inhibitions, the product of historical circumstance, were as much strategic and prudential as ethical or moral. One also has to reckon with a marked tendency within Fenianism to close ranks over acts of violence which pushed out the frontiers of what was thenceforth considered legitimate. A substantial fringe of Fenianism was, moreover, less scrupulous in its choice of means and prepared to countenance or engage in a recourse to terrorist means (designated as "assassination" or "dynamite" strategies).[27]

These caveats do not remit the obligation to make and recognise distinctions. The disparities between Fenian doctrines of physical force, Pearse's concept of blood sacrifice and the pursuit of the Provisional IRA's engagement in the killing of civilians are too important to overlook. The spectacle of the acclamation of the Balcombe Street gang at the recent Sinn Féin conference in Dublin brought sharply into focus not just the issue of democratic politics versus the use physical force, but the relationship of the Provisional IRA to republicanism in Irish history. Recalling Yeats, one thought: Delirium, yes. Brave, no.

A deepened appreciation of the nature of Fenianism is necessary for an understanding of the process whereby an avowedly republican movement evolved in our own time into a populist, sectarian, political and paramilitary movement of the extreme right; and how an (at least theoretically) circumscribed doctrine of physical force was called upon to justify the murder of Irish Protestants.

The uses of the terms nationalist and republican have never been altogether fixed or exact, and have been determined by an intersection, shifting across time, between ideology and convenience of designation. In political usage in our time the word nationalist has increasingly come to refer to the Catholic minority in Northern Ireland or, in a broader usage, to the population of the Republic of Ireland in its relationship to that minority. In practise, the term is applied less and less frequently to the Republic of Ireland itself. This reflects, perhaps, less any waning of nationalist sentiment as the southern Irish state acquires a modern European cast than the fact that the term is aspirational and does not so readily suggest itself in relation to a realised statehood.

The issue of terminology remains acutely sensitive, even though the term nationalist has lost some of its former fluidity. In its internal Northern Irish usage it has denoted the Social and Democratic Labour Party (SDLP), in contrast to the republicans of the Provisional IRA and Sinn Féin. In a Pearsean *ricorso*, Sinn Féin has now rediscovered the merits of the term nationalism and sought to assert a claim to hegemonic status within it.[28] The odds do not favour the promotion of this shift of the interdefinition of republicans and nationalism. However rhetorically satisfying it may be to Sinn Féin, it is not a gambit which its publicists can afford to press too far, for it risks raising up against them the predominant usage of the term of nationalist since the time of Parnell's ascendancy to refer to constitutional and parliamentary action.

CHAPTER 10

MORE PAGES FROM AN IRISH MEMOIR

PATRICK LYNCH

These pages are from a diary recorded when I was Assistant to the Taoiseach. They refer to the repeal of the External Relations Act (1936) in 1948 and Ireland's withdrawal from the Commonwealth. Some contributions of John A Costello, Noel Browne, James Dillon, Seán MacBride and Patrick McGilligan to the Inter-Party Government are also discussed.

THE REPEAL OF THE EXTERNAL RELATIONS ACT (1936)

On 7 September 1948 – during an official visit to Canada, where he was the guest of the Governor General, Lord Alexander, and the Prime Minister, Mackenzie King – the Taoiseach, John A. Costello, told a press conference in Ottawa of the impending repeal of the External Relations Act(1936) and the emergence of Ireland as a republic outside the Commonwealth. He had already explained to the Canadian Bar Association why he found the Act unacceptable. He expected, nonetheless, to be questioned at the press conference about a report two days earlier in the Irish *Sunday Independent* stating that the Act was to be repealed.

I have described elsewhere the circumstances of that Ottawa announcement and have rejected suggestions that it was prompted by impulse or, in substance, lacked Government approval. The British archives, however, give a somewhat different version of these events. This is especially true of a series of reports from Lord Rugby (John Maffey), the British representative in Dublin. They consist, to a large extent, of uncritical anecdotal evidence construed to interpret the Taoiseach's announcement as an expression of his resentment of perceived discourtesies by the Canadian political establishment. Nevertheless, the diary I kept while I was Assistant to the Taoiseach – and travelled with him to Canada – leaves little doubt that the terms of his statement to the press were quite uninfluenced by personal considerations. At the same time, some recollections later attributed to the Taoiseach that seem to support Lord Rugby's interpretations do, indeed, require clarification.

On 16 August 1948, four days before Costello left for Canada, Rugby, proving himself a good prophet, reported to the Dominions Office: "As you know I have no doubt that it has been decided to repeal the External Relations Act. I expect this to happen soon after the reassembling of the Dáil in November." A few hours before the Taoiseach's press conference in Ottawa his Minister for External Affairs, Seán MacBride, attesting to the accuracy the British envoy's intuition, told Rugby (during a conversation in Dublin) that the "Government intended to do away with the External Relations Act . . . but that no definite time had been fixed for this step". Confirming his prediction made on 16 August, Rugby duly conveyed this message to Sir Eric Machtig, Permanent Secretary of the Dominions Office.

A great deal of discussion followed the Taoiseach's disclosure. For example, in a crucial submission to Whitehall, dated 30 September 1948, Rugby reported that MacBride had told him "in confidence that he himself had not changed course" – Costello had done that – "though he was strongly in favour of repealing the Act". In a remarkable breach of Cabinet confidentiality he added that he had not "brought up the matter in Cabinet. It had been brought up, strangely enough, by Fine Gael". Interestingly, MacBride is not reported as describing his own attitude during that Cabinet discussion, which clearly occurred before the Taoiseach had left for Canada.

On 21 December 1948 MacBride spoke again with Rugby, but in words different from those of the earlier conversation. MacBride now referred to the "surprise Mr Costello's sudden announcement had been to him and the other members of the Cabinet in Dublin". It was true, MacBride is said to have added, "that in their general line of policy they had a plan to get the Act removed, but they had no immediate intention of going ahead. They would have consulted [the British government] and certainly would not have come out with a statement likely to embarrass the Imperial Conference". MacBride did not, apparently, say whether he invoked this solicitude for the Imperial Conference when Fine Gael had "brought up" the matter in Cabinet. He was now distancing himself from the Taoiseach. He was telling Rugby, in effect, that while the Government had decided to repeal the Act, no details had been settled, and the Taoiseach's Canadian statement, although accurate in substance, had been unexpected.

During the same December meeting, Rugby asked MacBride whether "it were true that something had happened in the course of Mr Costello's visit to Canada to precipitate matters". The Irish Minister is reported as replying "that this was the clue to the whole business . . . " MacBride then supposedly reiterated the gist of an earlier message that Rugby had sent to London recounting a story he had heard from Seán T Ó Ceallaigh, the Irish President. According to Rugby's first report and his account of the more recent MacBride meeting, the President had asked John Costello about the cause of his sudden announcement in Canada; in reply, the Taoiseach said: "Because I was stung into it." It is unlikely, however, that the President questioned Costello in those intemperate terms or that a reply was expressed in such uncharacteristically sloppy words.

In the same vein, Rugby's dispatch errs elsewhere. He records President Ó Ceallaigh as saying that he had been told of Lord Alexander's invitation to the Taoiseach and Mrs Costello "to stay as [his] guests at Government House". If the Taoiseach made that statement during his conversation with Ó Ceallaigh his memory was at fault: there was no invitation. In June 1948 John Hearne, the Irish High Commissioner in Canada, had apprised Costello that visiting heads of government were normally invited to be guests of the Governor General, yet Costello replied "that I should prefer if arrangements could be made for our stay elsewhere".

Mr Costello, according to Rugby's December dispatch, also told President Ó Ceallaigh that "My wife and I could not fail to notice how the Alexanders ignored us when we first had an opportunity of meeting them . . . " Further, before dinner at Government House Costello asked John Hearne about the toasts, and was told that "there would be the toast to 'the King' followed by the toast to 'the President of Ireland'". Yet during dinner the "only toast given was that to 'the King' and this upset me. I mentioned this matter to Mackenzie King and he said that the External Relations Act surely covered [this protocol] so far as the Royal toast was concerned". Still, added Costello (according to Rugby):

There seemed to me to be no proper appreciation of our status. I was getting sore about things. I did not like the very pointed way in which a model trophy of one of the Derry guns used by King William's forces at the Siege of Derry at 1689 was put on the table in front of me at the

Government House dinner . . . I made the decision to cut through all this and I made the [press conference] statement . . .

On 1 December 1948 Rugby again wrote to London. He had now heard from a reliable source (probably the late Maurice Dockrell, TD) of "the Taoiseach's resentment at the absence of a toast to the President . . . " Since the Taoiseach must have known that Mackenzie King had been logically correct about the toast, the ambiguity of this situation might have acted as an indirect influence on his decision to repeal the External Relations Act. Nevertheless, Rugby's reports of his conversations with Seán MacBride and Seán T Ó Ceallaigh do not prove that Costello's Ottawa announcement was in any sense an emotional reaction instigated by real or imaginary Canadian affronts. His reply to questions at the Ottawa press conference was not a sudden outburst. Instead, his statement was a calculated response to speculation in the *Sunday Independent* that the Government had decided to repeal the External Relations Act. While preparing for the questions the previous day, John Hearne and I had urged him to make no comment on the newspaper story since he had not seen the full text. Indeed, I suggested that if pressed he could say that before the Dáil had recessed for the summer all of the parties were in favour of repealing the Act. Costello rejected our advice; he did not need to see the full text of the article to accept the accuracy of its conclusions. He seemed determined not to share with anyone responsibility for deciding to repeal the Act, a determination that was purely *political.* He told Hearne and me that he saw the merits of our arguments, but he was thinking on a different level; our arguments were not invalid, but irrelevant. Costello wanted to avoid the humiliation of supporting a bill introduced into the Dáil by an Independent Deputy, Peadar Cowan, who was contemplating just such a move; the Government would then be following where it should have led. His responses at the press conference were, therefore, part of a pragmatic domestic *political* process.

All this was far removed from the replica of Roaring Meg and the Governor General's lack of warmth. As time passed, however, these events added an element of drama to recollections that might have seemed prosaic if confined to an unexciting press conference. Gradually, Costello created a mythology that grew with repetition and, for some people, served as a substitute explanation for the reality of the press conference. The Taoiseach was, after all, an experienced constitutional lawyer. And he was unlikely to be decisively influenced on a great public issue by trivial

126

annoyances or even personal affronts, whatever their later utility as conversational material.

The bill to repeal the External Relations Act, the Republic of Ireland Act (1948), was circulated to the Cabinet by the Minister for External Affairs, Seán MacBride. The Taoiseach, however, assumed responsibility for guiding it through the Dáil and Seanad in order to demonstrate his proprietary interest in a legal measure that finally dispelled the constitutional infirmities and ambiguities he had described in his address to the Canadian Bar Association. We do not know whether he had considered if Ireland might become a republic inside, or in association with, the Commonwealth. Such a status could well have had attractions for the subtle and devious Seán MacBride. For John A Costello, however, the decision to leave the Commonwealth had to be unambiguous. He had discussed this formula with the Canadian Prime Minister, Mackenzie King, whose support – or at least whose understanding – he believed, rightly or wrongly, he had secured. He knew that King preferred accommodating different points of view and the avoidance of formal arrangements, rather than rigid definitions of Commonwealth relationships. He was also aware that King, a wily and complex politician, discerned Canadian advantages in the redefinition of Ireland's relationship with the Commonwealth, a process that concluded on Easter Monday in 1949, after which Ireland was officially described to be a republic.

THE INTER-PARTY GOVERNMENT, 1948-51
In the Inter-Party Government of 1948-51, Patrick McGilligan, the Minister for Finance, had the finest and most original mind, as sharp and penetrating as his wit. Never quite happy as Minister for Finance, he was disappointed when he was not offered the post of Attorney General after Cecil Lavery vacated it for the Supreme Court on 21 April 1950.

The most colourful member of the Government was the Minister for Agriculture, James Dillon, who had a splendid capacity for resounding rhetoric. He was unmatched as a speaker in the Dáil, with a gift for the apt phrase. Conservative in economics, he often sided with the Department of Finance, despite extravagant criticism of it from time to time. A master of hyperbole, he once objected to a fairly harmless proposal of mine that John Costello put forward by exclaiming: "Not that, Taoiseach; don't let's take to financial debauchery altogether."

My abiding memory of James Dillon was his attempt to convert Sir Stafford Cripps, Chancellor of the Exchequer in the Attlee Government, to capitalism. The occasion was an official dinner in London on a June evening in 1948 in the midst of trade talks between the two Governments. The Chancellor was toying with his vegetarian meal. James Dillon, enjoying something less austere, announced in stentorian tones over his burgundy:

> Chancellor, I was apprenticed to capitalism in the greatest department store in Chicago in the 1920s. When I returned to my modest business in the small Irish town of Ballaghadereen, I was determined ruthlessly to apply there the capitalist methods I had learnt in Chicago. I discovered that a competing shopkeeper was dispensing a free teapot with every five pounds of tea. When my customers arrived I said: 'No, I should be unfair if I sold you tea today. Go across the road and you will be given a free teapot with every five pounds of tea.' Chancellor, by mid-day my competitor had run out of tea pots; that's capitalism.

* * *

In the first Inter-Party Government Seán MacBride acquired a reputation as a responsible and respected Minister for External Affairs, even if his preoccupation with partition was excessive and added tedium to speeches on unrelated topics. He came to a department previously seen as an appendage of the Department of the Taoiseach and left it with a stature and status distinctively its own. He strengthened Iveagh House's position at the expense of the Department of Finance by securing for it a decisive part in the European Recovery Programme and in the allocation of Marshall Aid funds.

In response to worsening economic conditions, the British government devalued sterling on 18 September 1949. MacBride had long been predicting the imminence of this step, while simultaneously urging the repatriation of sterling assets. No doubt, the Department of Finance was fully aware of the approaching crisis, even if it was unwilling or unable to devise corrective measures. In any event, such measures could hardly have been effective in the short term. But MacBride was greatly dissatisfied when Ireland devalued its currency at the same rate as sterling. Referring to this parity link, he wrote in a memorandum to the Government: "The Government is deprived of any control of the finances of the nation; this is both intolerable and imprudent."

Shortly afterwards, on Saturday evening, 8 October 1949, I had a long talk with him. He was unhappy with the Government's general performance. Only Noel Browne, the Minister for Health, James Dillon and himself, he told me, were getting results. Dan Morrissey was not good enough for his job as Minister for Industry and Commerce. MacBride had no doubt of Patrick McGilligan's fine intelligence, but his apparently poor health prevented him from effectively directing the Department of Finance on broad policy issues; McGilligan was allowing his officials to make policy instead of carrying it out. Changes were needed at the top in that Department: MacBride had no faith in the Secretary, JJ McElligott, who, he said, was obstructing Government policy.

When I defended McElligott, MacBride replied that the Secretary had tried to influence American officials into providing Marshall Aid to Ireland in a manner at variance with the policy of the Department of External Affairs. He then told me that McGilligan had recently been said to be too ill for a Government meeting, yet two days later was well enough to attend the Arc de Triomphe race at Longchamps, outside Paris. He was totally dissatisfied with the inadequate attention paid by the Department of Finance and the Government to his copious memoranda on devaluation long before the sterling crisis. He blamed McGilligan for this, as well as the Taoiseach, whose knowledge and understanding of economic issues were inadequate. He said that he would have to leave the Government within two months unless there was a material improvement and the atmosphere ceased to be clouded by what he called Fine Gael conservatism.

MacBride dismissed with contempt a committee set up by the Government to examine the consequences of devaluation. He regarded it as a mere sop, most likely because of the Government's rejection of his own economic proposals. The results of the proposed committee, he said, would be a foregone conclusion, and he could already produce the two reports they were likely to submit. He did praise one potential member, George O'Brien, Professor of Economics at University College Dublin and a member of the Seanad, for being objective in his judgement of the intellectual poverty of the bank directors. MacBride saw no need to appoint, as McGilligan had suggested, Per Jacobsen, whose views he distrusted. Instead, he would rely on Professor Alfred O'Rahilly, President of University College Cork from 1943 to 1954. The committee, in MacBride's view, should have only one meeting and subsequently produce its recommendation. As it turned out, the Committee on Devaluation did not hold even that one meeting, perhaps because JJ McElligott had been even more devious than Seán MacBride suspected.

Later in our conversation MacBride explained his plans for a

Department of National Development to administer forestry, land drainage and housing programmes. When I raised serious objections to his proposals he suggested that I was acting as a civil servant. He would, he said, accept the Ministry himself if Sir John Esmonde replaced him in External Affairs. Nothing, alas, came of these suggestions.

* * *

On 5 November 1949 I saw George O'Brien. We discussed the proposed Committee on Devaluation. O'Brien said he had been seeing MacBride and felt that the committee would be very important. I was surprised when he told me he had been reading a book that MacBride had given him, *The Coming of Age of Wood*. George's taste in reading was certainly changing – from Proust and George Moore to the age of wood was a long and unexpected step.

George was genuinely pleased by the Minister's attentions, and I have no doubt that his reference to the benefits of afforestation – in a Seanad speech at the time – reflected Ministerial views. MacBride very effectively took advantage of O'Brien's long-standing grievance against the commercial banks; he did not know, however, the origin of this grievance: they had ignored him for membership on their boards. O'Brien, in fact, told me that he would have declined de Valera's invitation to be a member of the Banking Commission between 1934 and 1938 if he had not been urged by the Governor of the Bank of Ireland to accept the post so that the banks would have a member of the Commission whom they could trust as a friend! As our conversation developed, George made it abundantly clear that he was no longer the banker's friend. It became obvious that Seán MacBride, either by chance or design, had made an excellent choice when he selected George O'Brien as his Trojan horse for an attack on the banks. Toward the end of the evening George said that as a member of the proposed Committee on Devaluation he believed that the banks could be deservedly frightened by a threat of nationalisation and that their recent refusal to underwrite a loan to Dublin Corporation for housing had put them in an untenable position.

O'Brien had suggested to MacBride sometime earlier that as a reprisal the Bank of Ireland could be deprived of the Government Account, which could then be transferred to the Central Bank. He reminded MacBride that in 1924 the Minister for Finance, Ernest Blythe, had made this same threat when Sir John Keane had "persuaded" his co-directors to appoint him "permanent" Governor of the Bank of Ireland – and it worked. O'Brien also shared his opinion regarding several of the directors of the commercial banks: with the exception of Patrick Bourke, chief executive of the Provincial Bank of Ireland, and James Sweetman, a non-executive director of the Royal Bank of Ireland, "all were duds". He doubted if any of them, apart from these two, understood how banks could create credit. He regarded Lord Glenavy as vastly overrated in ability, especially by those who did not know him; I can vividly recall George's *coup de grace* on Glenavy: "he has a cynicism incongruous in an old man". How Seán MacBride must have loved it! No wonder he was now prepared to drop O'Rahilly from the Committee on Devaluation.

Toward the end of our discussion George told me that Bulmer Hobson – the renowned Irish patriot, author, recently-retired high-ranking official in the Revenue Commissioner's office and another possible member of the Committee – was just a predictable bore, but Alfred O'Rahilly was an intelligent, dangerous and disruptive crank. I recall the gleam in his eyes as he described O'Rahilly as a highly intelligent schoolboy, who was first in his class in every subject, but never grew up and had spent a resentful life behaving, acting and writing as if he had been deprived of a higher education. For good measure, before our meeting ended, he said that he believed that Joseph Brennan, the Governor of the Central Bank, and JJ McElligott had outlived their usefulness. His views on McElligott were decided by the intransigent attitude of the Department of Finance towards university finances during the previous twenty years. He was aware that Brennan's term of office as Governor of the Central Bank would expire in the new year and that MacBride would oppose a further term. He refused to be drawn about possible candidates for his replacement.

O'Brien saw the merit in many of MacBride's economic policies; indeed, he backed them so as to be in a position to dissuade MacBride of his more questionable views. With so many changes taking place all over Europe the time had come for realism and some compromise. The following day, Sunday, 6 November 1949, he wrote me a significant letter "to clarify" his thoughts. "I feel," he pointed out:

> that if [the Government] do not adopt a forward policy, they may suffer political damage. A little compromise with popular demands – even though based on ignorance – may be necessary to ward off worse evils. There is no doubt at all that the public have got hold of the ideas: (i) that our savings would be better invested at home than abroad; (ii) that the banks are standing in the way of progress. If the Government does not

recognise the existence of these developments [in] public opinion it will lose votes and may possibly lose power. In that case, the forward policy would be carried through by Fianna Fáil, with an orgy of waste, extravagance, dishonesty and graft.

To avoid this evil some compromise with financial orthodoxy is justified. The price is worth paying both from the political and the economic standpoint. The Government today are in the same position as the Irish unionists before the Treaty. The more enlightened unionists recognised the reality of the nationalist demand. They did not like it or agree with it, but they did not ignore it. Many of them were willing to go part of the way with it in the hope of satisfying it by a moderate measure of self-government. This was the attitude of the devolutionists in 1904. But they were prevented from doing anything by their own die-hards and by the officials in Dublin Castle. The result was the Rising, the Treaty and the Republic. A moderate concession to nationalist feeling would have prevented these developments.

There is an analogy between that situation and the situation of the Government today. The demand for some financial expansion is real and growing. It is wiser to placate it by some modest sop administered by the safe party in power than to resist it. Comparing 1904 and today, I would say that Dublin Castle is represented by the Central Bank and Sinn Fein by MacBride. If the Government give in unduly to the former they will hand the situation to the latter, who may ride away with wild and dangerous schemes. Surely the right thing to do is to go with him as far as is prudent rather than to break with him.

I have written this to clarify my own position. I do not want Alexis [FitzGerald] or anyone else to accuse me of inconsistency. I think a new situation has arisen that demands new policy. I am like Horace Plunkett, who, when I knew him, preferred the Union to Home Rule, but saw that the time had come to make some concession to nationalism to avoid worse things. The concession was not made and the (from his point of view) worse things came.

Seán MacBride may not have had a fully convinced convert, but he had brought George O'Brien quite a distance on the road to Damascus. Indeed, this letter is certainly evidence of MacBride's ability to persuade and of his part in the Government up to November 1949. In retrospect, I think this was the apogee of his influence. He had reduced the dominance of the Department of Finance and had enormously strengthened the position of the Department of External Affairs. I have quoted at length from this letter because it reveals the naïveté of George O'Brien: he had succumbed to the flattery of MacBride, who employed his charm of manner and subtlety of mind with insidious success. MacBride was quite consistent in pursuit of his objective. And he was only superficially contradictory in dismissing as myth the proposed Committee on

Devaluation, while simultaneously inflating its significance to George O'Brien, who believed that this phantom could become a national institution.

* * *

John Costello spoke to the annual dinner of the Institute of Bankers on Saturday evening, 19 November 1949. His address was a carefully considered statement of Government economic and financial policy expressed in Keynesian terms. After I had prepared the first draft I gave it to Alexis FitzGerald, Costello's adviser as well as his son-in-law, who discussed it in detail with the Taoiseach. The analysis was unambiguous: the chronic under-investment in the country had to be corrected; some foreign investment in sterling was necessary and valuable; gradual reinvestment of part of the balance in Ireland would redress past omissions by improving productive output at home, providing much-needed housing accommodation and improving health services; for these purposes a capital budget was required; and the current budget should be financed from taxation.

On Saturday afternoon, before a final rehearsal of the speech, I cleared every line with Patrick McGilligan. The Taoiseach did not expect that his speech would provide post-prandial relish for all of his audience. Still, the press reception was favourable, and some commentators saw it as the inauguration of a new and coherent economic policy. The Taoiseach had seized the initiative. From now on the humblest backbencher could compete with Seán MacBride by quoting from the speech or paraphrasing it. Keynes had come to Kinnegad.

On Monday morning, 21 November, I met JJ McElligott on the steps of Government Buildings as I was going to work. He asked about the speech to the bankers. When I admitted having had a hand in its preparation he admonished me in terms I have not forgotten: "Lynch, you are a young man with much to learn. One has to be very careful of politicians; the more they know, the more dangerous they are." We then went our different ways.

My next encounter with McElligott was on 24 April 1950. I had helped draft a speech that the Taoiseach was preparing for the Clonmel Chamber of Commerce. The drift of the speech followed the policies outlined in his address to the Institute of Bankers. It argued the case for a current budget financed from taxation and a capital budget as a mechanism for repatriation of sterling assets through a deliberately contrived deficit in the balance of payments. After reading a draft McElligott summoned me to his room. He had tried to stop the speech because he thought it was dangerous, but the Taoiseach had already left for Clonmel. McElligott told me that encouraging politicians to produce "things like that" was "the treason of the clerks". Further, to take seriously national income statistics, which he regarded as "mere guesses", was playing into the hands of politicians. "And they were all politicians," he added, "though de Valera had much of the statesman in him." He urged me to remember that the function of a civil servant was to restrain politicians from extravagant spending of taxpayers' money.

* * *

Towards the end of November 1950 the Taoiseach was becoming increasingly worried by the deterioration in relations between the Minister for Health, Dr Noel Browne, and the Irish Medical Association, which had recently rejected the Mother and Child Health scheme the Minister was developing. Even earlier, on 10 October 1950, James Staunton, the Bishop of Ferns and secretary to the Catholic hierarchy, had written to Costello to express the bishops' opposition to the plan. Staunton warned: "It is not sound social policy to impose a state medical service on the whole community on the pretext of relieving the necessitous ten percent from the so-called indignity of the means test." Moreover: "Education in regard to motherhood includes instruction in regard to sexual relations, chastity and marriage. The state has no competence to give instruction in such matters." Ominously, the medical profession and the Catholic hierarchy were now united against Browne.

On 23 November 1950 the Taoiseach told me that Dr Browne might resign from the Government and that Seán MacBride might follow him. Eventually, the drama was postponed because of rifts between the two Ministers, of which Costello was unaware at the time. My own feeling was that the Minister for Health was being rigid in his insistence on the avoidance of a means test in his Mother and Child Scheme. In practice, he could have achieved his objective without compromising his ideals by adopting a selective token payment or a system of insurance to meet the main objection of the hierarchy. The social environment of the late 1940s was very different from that of the hungry 1930s, when a means test could be a cruel and humanly degrading instrument. I believed that with flexibility of approach an acceptable solution could have been possible.

James Dillon tried on at least one occasion in my presence to persuade Dr Browne of the wise adage that "the best can be the enemy of the good". He urged Browne to be wary of challenging the bishops on matters of principle; he could not lose if he concentrated on practical arguments. He also reminded Browne of the success of Aneurin Bevan, the British Minister for Health, in cajoling the powerful medical lobby. Dillon, always to be relied on for a vivid phrase, ended this conversation in lofty tones: "Noel, my family has for generations often countered the thinking of the black brigade – and won." I doubt if Browne understood that Dillon was talking about the clergy.

The dreary exchanges between the Minister for Health and the hierarchy dragged on for another three months; John Charles McQuaid, the Archbishop of Dublin, repeatedly raised his objections with Browne, who, in turn, insisted that they were groundless. On Friday, 23 March 1951, the Taoiseach told me that he would not remain in a Government that put Browne's scheme into operation; moreover, he objected to it on principle. On the next day he confided in me that if Browne resigned he would take over the Department of Health himself and appoint Liam Cosgrave as Parliamentary Secretary.

Dr Browne resigned from the Government on 11 April 1951. The misunderstandings and misrepresentations about this affair have had unfortunate and enduring consequences. Many of the participants had little notion of what "Catholic social teaching" was, or whether there was even agreement among those competent to express their views. In the United Kingdom there had been no organised opposition to the welfare state or to the National Health Service. Dr Browne never questioned the right of the Catholic Church to decide on matters of "faith and morals". Most unfortunate of all, perhaps, was the Taoiseach being driven, out of desperation, to utter expressions in the Dáil that others could use to portray him as the leader of a confessional state.

The hierarchy had other objections to Noel Browne's proposed scheme. If, however, the provision requiring no means test had been omitted from the plan it is doubtful that they would have been too vigorously pressed. After all, Catholic social teaching had not been invoked in the past on behalf of members of the community compelled, through poverty, to avail themselves of the services of the bleak medical dispensary system or against well-off people who received children's allowances free of a means test. In any event, if the hierarchy had realised that confidential correspondence between its representatives and a member of the Government was going to be published, they would have expressed themselves with more intellectual rigour.

Noel Browne resigned from the Government, at the request of Seán MacBride, on 11 April 1951. Soon thereafter he published the correspondence on the whole affair. Two Independent deputies withdrew their support from the Government, which no longer commanded a majority in the Dáil, and a general election followed on 30 May 1951. As a result, the Inter-Party Government lost office.

CHAPTER 11

FOLLOWING CONOR

RUTH DUDLEY EDWARDS

I APOLOGISE FOR WRITING ABOUT MYSELF IN A BOOK COMPILED IN HONOUR of someone else, but this seems as good an opportunity as I'm likely to have to explain what circumstances led me to become a member of Conor Cruise O'Brien's Irish Praetorian Guard.

I was uncontroversial until 1977, when my biography of Patrick Pearse – *Patrick Pearse: The Triumph of Failure* – was published, and I found myself labelled a "revisionist". I had to ask my father, the Irish historian Robin Dudley Edwards, what the word meant. He explained that it was a term of abuse for those thought to be reacting to events in Northern Ireland by trying to undermine nationalists and nationalism. What was odd about that, from my point of view, was that by then I had been living in England for twelve years, and while I was deeply interested in what went on in Westminster, I was out of touch with Irish politics and not much better informed about Northern Ireland than anyone else who watched and flinched at the dreadful suffering being visited on ordinary people. I had never met, and had rarely read, Conor Cruise O'Brien and was slightly baffled when in reviewing my book he announced that his approval would be likely to form part of the "indictment" against me. Yet coming from a background even more pluralist than Conor's, I suppose it was only a matter of time before I followed him into the battle against violent republicanism.

* * *

My greatest inspiration was my paternal grandmother, born Bridget MacInerney in County Clare, a close relative of the only politicians in our family – the Fianna Fáil Lenihans, of whom my cousins Brian and Conor Lenihan and Mary O'Rourke are the present ornaments. My grandmother took off for London to become a nurse and there took up with a patient, Walter Edwards from Gloucestershire, who was from a mining family, but had acquired enough education to have a white-collar job. On his deathbed Walter told my father that he and Bridget were never able to marry, because although Walter and his wife, Ethel, had attempted to get a divorce, collusion had been proved and the divorce had been denied. (My father liked the idea of opening his reminiscences with the line: "They were always calling me a bastard and they were right.")

This had not deterred my redoubtable grandmother. She not only set up with him as his wife, but, being a thundering snob, insisted that he give her a name of which she could be proud. Thus well into his forties the poor chap was required to adopt his mother's maiden name and become Walter Dudley Edwards.

Grandmother took her common-law husband, a Methodist-turned-Quaker, to Dublin, where he got a clerical job in the civil service and Grandmother gave birth to two boys and took to suffragism and politics. He was a pacifist; she was a revolutionary and a virago. She hid guns in 1914, cheered on the 1916 Rebellion, sent her young sons into the Fianna and when they were, respectively, thirteen and eleven, instructed them to fight in the Civil War on the republican side. My father refused; his younger brother was sent home by the recruiting sergeant.

Nonetheless, Grandmother kept the flame of ideological purity alive: de Valera was never forgiven for moving into constitutional politics. She also remained an enthusiastic supporter of Mussolini and Hitler: when I asked her how she justified concentration camps, she explained that they were an invention of British propaganda. She died at 85 in the 1950s, still voting Sinn Féin. I owe her a lot. Because of her I have some understanding of uncompromising republicanism and the visceral loathing of the British that distinguishes even intelligent people in the IRA.

Grandfather Edwards was an interesting contrast. He died when I was two, but I always felt his influence, for my father, who couldn't stand his bullying mother, had loved his gentle father and had been greatly influenced by his interest in English literature and history. The way his strange background took hold of my father was to make him single-minded in the pursuit of historical truth. He spent his life trying to extricate Irish history from the trough of nationalist propaganda.

My maternal grandfather, James Florence O'Sullivan – known as Jim Flur – was head gamekeeper on the Leader estate in North Cork. Passionately interested in politics, he was a Home Ruler. Although he was highly intelligent, he couldn't read – he was probably dyslexic – but every day he demanded that the news be read to him. During the First World War, Grandfather absorbed every detail and in 1916, when the heir to the estate was killed in the trenches, Grandfather decided to go and exact vengeance from the Germans. At the age of 48 he lied about his age and joined the British Army, becoming what may well have been its only illiterate quartermaster.

Grandfather's absence was good news for his wife, Mary O'Sullivan, née Ford, because for the first time there was regular money coming in which her husband couldn't drink. My maternal grandparents were as badly matched as my paternal, for Jim Flur was bored and impatient with his gentle, dutiful and not very bright wife. She was not a political animal. During the Civil War, when Free State soldiers forced republicans to rebuild the nearby bridge that their forces had blown up, she used to trot out with tea for both sides. My mother once found she was hiding a gun for a republican. "Mother," she shouted. "Are you mad? You can be executed for doing that." "But what could I do?" Grandmother whimpered. "Sure wasn't it a neighbour's child asked me?" That story helped me later to understand why decent people give succour to terrorists.

My mother, who got herself to secondary school and teacher training college through scholarships, had a great affection for the Anglo-Irish, for her experience of them had been wholly benign. The gamekeeper's children had the freedom of the estate. "The barbed wire," my mother used to remark sourly, "did not go up until we got our freedom, the Anglo-Irish were driven out and the strong farmers took over." I grew up understanding quite a lot about the antipathy of the landless peasants to the acquisitive Irish farmer.

Much though my mother loved English literature, her deepest interest was in the Irish language, which she first heard when she was five. Having discovered her grandmother Ford was a native Irish speaker, she trotted off to her and begged to be taught Irish. "No, child," said her grandmother. "I wouldn't want to hold you back." But my mother was a persuasive child, so she was taught the language at her granny's knee. Later, as a mature student at University College Dublin, she – like her contemporary and friend, Máire Mhac an tSaoi – performed dazzlingly in Celtic Studies: when she died I learned that several people thought she was a native Irish speaker herself.

Presumably because of her upbringing, my mother not only thought well of Protestants, but regarded them as far more reliable, more honourable and honest than Catholics – though less fun. My father, being half Protestant, had a less romantic view, but he wanted Irish Protestants to have their proper place in Irish history – not to be represented as interlopers and foreigners who should accept the Catholic nationalist ethos or go home to wherever they had come from three, five or eight hundred years before. When doing his PhD at London University he acquired an important ally, the Northern Irish Quaker Theo Moody.

While Moody was at Queen's University Belfast – before he became a professor at Trinity College Dublin – he and my father developed a school of cross-border and cross-tribal history. The Irish Historical Society and its journal, *Irish Historical Studies*, were vital elements in encouraging the teaching and writing of unbiased and inclusive Irish history. The Conference of Irish Historians and its youth group, The Irish University History Students' Society, met at universities all over the country to talk history. Like rugby and show-jumping they were, and are, examples of that rare animal – the all-Ireland non-sectarian institution.

* * *

I first learned about religious differences when I went to school. I remember arriving home from school at five or so and my mother asking what I had done that day. "We threw stones at the proddywoddies from Green Lanes School," I said brightly. I can still see her horrified face and recall the feeling of surprise that she saw anything wrong in what I'd been introduced to as an enjoyable pastime. Now this was middle class Dublin, not West Belfast, and we didn't make a habit of it and, indeed, the practice never took hold because adult spoilsports forbade it, but that memory helps me understand something about the stone-throwing children in republican and loyalist ghettos.

Our doctors were a Protestant father and daughter, not just because they lived nearby, but, considering the view of the Roman Catholic Church on matters gynaecological, my mother thought it was useful insurance to have access to a Protestant hospital. And the Protestants who lived next door – two retired British Army captains married to two sisters – lived up to my mother's stereotypes. They were honest, decent, kind people with lots of stray animals. They mended our lawnmowers and came to our rescue when the lights fused. When our favourite member of the family died – Maureen Little, a woman of extraordinary sweetness of disposition – we committed a sin by going to the Protestant service.

As I grew up I realised that our family seemed pretty exotic compared to most of those I knew, and, of course, one played this exoticism down rather than up in those days. I don't suppose I told my friends that my grandfather had fought for Britain or that my mother's brother Jack had been in the Irish Guards. At my primary school, where all the subjects were taught through Irish, where one of the teachers was a cousin of Lord Haw Haw (the infamous Nazi sympathiser) and proud of it and where the dogmas of Irish nationalism were instilled in us alongside the catechism, it would have been courting trouble. And in my next school – a rather snobby convent – soldiers would have been regarded as common.

This rich religious and cultural mix was further complicated by my highly articulate and campaigning brother Owen's precocious socialism. Consider the household around the time of the 1954 election, when I was ten. Grandmother was upstairs in her eyrie, surrounded by republican and fascist icons and denouncing the traitor de Valera; Father was in his study reading the various party manifestos; Mother, who despised politicians, had announced that she was going to vote for that nice young independent who had told her no one else would vote for him; and the sixteen-year-old Owen was out campaigning for Noel Browne.

Irish politics was too complicated, too atavistic and too unprincipled for me, partly, I suspect, because my views such as they were had been inspired by a remorseless consumption of British fiction. My imagination had been fired by *Just William* and public school stories: I revered the stiff upper lip and, like Frank O'Connor, I got into trouble at school for owning up. I wanted to be a Girl Guide and have jolly japes, but since I didn't think the Catholic Girl Guides would be like my books and I couldn't join the Protestants, I didn't.

I was also seduced by PG Wodehouse and by country-house detective stories. I was in love with the ordered existence that seemed to be offered by English life. It was, I suppose, no accident that at sixteen I fell for Patrick Cosgrave, a very bright young man who had grown up in poverty on a council estate, had been educated by the Christian Brothers in their efficient, but brutal, manner, had a mother who was the stereotypical pious nationalist and whose reading had also made him anxious to hotfoot it out of Ireland to the tranquillity of croquet and vicars and dog-lovers and punting and afternoon tea. His heroes were Winston Churchill and the great Conservative Prime Minister Lord Salisbury.

Throughout our time at what was allegedly a non-denominational university, Patrick and I took great delight in flouting what we thought to be sectarian practices. We began a successful revolt in University College Dublin in the mid-sixties by continuing to read in the library while everyone else stood up to say the Angelus. We made friends with Trinity history students and debaters, who were, of course, almost all Protestant, for this was the period when the Archbishop of Dublin forbade Catholics to attend Trinity on pain of excommunication. When I look back, I think the Republic has a nerve to object to Ulster Protestants describing Home Rule as Rome Rule.

We visited Northern Ireland a few times for history conferences and a drama festival, but all I remember of the place was that everything was shut on Sunday, that it all seemed terribly forbidding and that it made one glad to get back to the South – Roman Catholic or no Roman Catholic Church – for at least in the South there was a lot of subversive fun. While, as a natural dissenter, I couldn't wait to leave the Republic, Northern Ireland seemed worse. I did not think I could bear the apparent joylessness and mean-spiritedness of the Northern Ireland ruling class and the angry intensity of its internal critics. Many of my generation in Dublin were fed up with northern nationalists who complained about their lot, but had unimaginable luxuries like free secondary education and university grants. Patrick, like the few other working class students, paid his own way through university by working in factories in England during summer holidays.

At twenty-one I left all the complexities of Ireland behind me when I married Patrick, moved to Cambridge and became involved in local Conservative politics, where the issues seemed simple. I was on the left, and Patrick increasingly on the right, and among the issues on which we fell out was Northern Ireland. For instance, I cried when I saw the television coverage of Bloody Sunday; he automatically took the side of the Paras. After we separated, Patrick went on to become a special adviser to Mrs Thatcher and a follower and biographer of Enoch Powell, while I became a political agnostic. We long ago made an agreement to preserve our friendship by never ever discussing Irish politics.

I was comfortably assimilated into English life, with good friends, interesting work and a passionate interest in British politics. After my divorce, I married an Englishman. By the late 1970s, having worked in the Post Office and the civil service, I thought I understood the British. Yet Ireland stayed with me. I kept in touch through family, friends and visits home. And my first book, *An Atlas of Irish History*, required me to do more concentrated reading and thinking about Ireland – including Northern Ireland – than I had done as an undergraduate. Sometimes during the worst of the Troubles I visited my friend Liam Hourican in Belfast, where he was the RTÉ correspondent, and I met politicians and journalists. I still vividly remember the horror of being there the day of the carnage in the Abercorn tea shop.

When a British publisher asked me to write a biography of Patrick Pearse I was delighted. I had always been interested in him, mainly because he was allegedly the greatest hero in Irish history, yet nobody seemed to know a damn thing about him. I think what I gained most from doing this book – apart from spending several months living again in Ireland – was an understanding of the nature of misguided idealism and the nobility of someone who sacrifices his whole life selflessly for a cause. I hate all the paramilitary groups – loyalist and republican – for the suffering and devastation they have caused, but, like Conor Cruise O'Brien, I have never denounced as monsters the kids who joined such organisations because in their ignorance they believed they were needed as saviours of their communities; it is the cynical and ruthless godfathers who deserve the blame and who have my undying enmity.

Having become fond of and rather sorry for Patrick Pearse and having tried hard to show that he was not a vacuous plaster saint, but a complicated human being, I was staggered by the resentment the book caused in certain nationalist circles. These attacks forced me to enter the debate on Northern Ireland: I had to examine my own attitudes in terms of contemporary politics and decide where I stood.

It took a long time and a great deal of thought, but eventually I came to accept Conor's view that the members of the Provisional IRA were absolutely correct in their claim to be successors of Pearse and his colleagues and that it was dishonest to deplore the Provos and defend the Irish Republican Brotherhood. It amazes me still that with my background and experience it should have taken so long for me to accept that the 1916 Rising was simply wrong, because in a democracy no group has any right to take it upon themselves to kill to bring about political change. Youthful indoctrination had gone very deep.

This was an early stage in confronting the beliefs of my own tribe; I have been involved in increasing conflict with it ever since. My nationalist critics, perhaps, do not understand how much time I've spent over the years trying to explain their point of view to the British, answering questions like: Why are the Irish so irrational? Why are they so damned sensitive? Why don't they trust us? Why at a conference at two in the morning does this chap who's always been terribly friendly accuse me of having masterminded the Famine? How can they vote for the rogue Charlie Haughey rather than that nice chap Garret FitzGerald? And so on and on. Yet it's easy briefing the British. However brutally frank one is, they take it well and can laugh at themselves. For, perforce, over many years they have tried to come to grips with many different civilisations and they strive earnestly to understand and make things better. Being short on imagination and long on reason, however, they often get things wrong.

Most Ulster unionists too are prepared to listen when I try to change their out-dated perceptions of the Republic, but recently my efforts have been seriously undermined by financial and clerical scandals and by the popularity among nationalists of people like Gerry Adams and Martin McGuiness, whom unionists see as their main tormentors over the past three decades.

But trying to explain the British or Ulster unionists to Irish nationalists – north or south – is a very different matter. I've lost count of the insults: I've sold out; I work for MI5; I work for MI6; I'm a lick-spittle to the British establishment; I've been cunningly manipulated by the security services; or, of course, I'm a neo-unionist, neo-loyalist or Orange apologist. Members of my tribe become irate about many of my views; they especially hate hearing me say that far from being cynical Machiavellis with a hidden agenda for Ireland (the view of Tim Pat Coogan and others with inferiority complexes), the British are always less interested in Ireland and less clever than the Irish think.

* * *

Meanwhile, my dual life – what you might call the twin-track approach to nationality – continued. On the British side, leaving the civil service to become a freelance writer brought me into a new world which widened my perspective. I wrote a biography of Victor Gollancz, an English publisher and public campaigner for socialism and pacifism who was neurotically hung-up about his Jewishness and got into even more trouble with his tribe than I do with mine. Then there was the history of *The Economist* (subtitled *The Pursuit of Reason*), which helped me to clarify such deficiencies of the British – particularly British intellectuals – as their frequent inability to grasp that there are bad people who are not susceptible to rational debate. I read many thousands of words from the 1930s written by people with Oxbridge firsts about how Herr Hitler was showing encouraging signs of statesmanship. My wariness about Sinn Féin increased.

Then there was *True Brits*, a book about the Foreign Office. I like the people in the Foreign Office, as I like those at *The Economist*, but they do persist in believing that every problem has a solution and in trying to make foreigners stop being silly and do things the rational, tolerant British way. But I admire them for their genuine desire to understand the other chap's point of view – something I spend my life doing for a living and for pleasure.

Simultaneously, I was becoming more and more involved with the island of Ireland. In 1980 I joined the committee of the British-Ireland Association, attended many political conferences, met the leading players and, in 1985, became the chairman of the new British Association of Irish Studies. Its members were mainly English, Scots, Welsh, Northern Irish and Irish academics and teachers interested in meeting the market demand in Britain for Irish politics, history, literature, drama and so on. After five years we had a tremendous faction fight in which a few Irish Catholics and one Northern Irish Protestant who shared atavistic anti-English sentiments played a rough and distinguished part in opposing what I considered to be the forces of reason, consensus, pluralism and good will. It was another great formative experience.

Initially, I had found northern nationalists friendlier and easier to get to know than their unionist counterparts. Also, though I have become very English in some ways, I remain very southern Irish in others, so the further reaches of Ulster Protestantism did not exactly attract me – too much frugality, discipline, narrowness and stubbornness. But having started out with the common perception that northern Protestants were a dour and dull lot, I came, through knowing individuals over the years, to appreciate deeply the great virtues of most them: the honesty; the tradition of dissent; straightforwardness; self-reliance; decency; and the warmth and generosity on offer when they trust you. And I went with an open mind to Orange parades, enjoyed them and resent the way in which they are ignorantly equated with bigotry.

"At least you know where you are with the buggers," was the feeling that first set me on the path to liking Ulster Protestants, followed by a delight in dealing with people who said exactly what they meant and who did not require one to employ a team of theologians to interpret their latest political pronouncement. As contact grew and trust developed, I began to appreciate the sheer passion that underlay the po-faced exteriors. Robert Greacen, a poet whom I greatly admire, is an Ulster Protestant who fled to Dublin and then to London. A few lines from his poem "Ulster" brilliantly sum up this aspect of his tribe:

> Ulster's soul is tense with beauty
> Wild, curtained beauty
> Bursting in fierce reticence.

I came to understand that although Ulster Protestants generally didn't have the other tribe's facility with words, their attachment to their country – call it Ireland, call it British-Ireland, call it the United Kingdom, call it Ulster or whatever – was as passionate as any nationalist's sense of Irishness, and I have been angry *for* them about the contemptuous way in which their culture and sense of identity is dismissed as misplaced, out of date and something which they must grow out of. I have made many friends in the Orange Order, I have come to enjoy their celebrations and, though I'm an atheist, I feel very comfortable at their services. There is no lack of people to make the case for Irish nationalism, but the unionists have had precious few sympathisers. So as I more and more tried to make their case, I found myself more and more coming into conflict with my own tribe, whose intolerance of dissent reminds me of the Dublin of the Archbishop McQuaid era.

My struggles towards pluralism are helped by living in London, where, apart from many of its native citizens, I have close friends from Australia, South Africa, India, Poland and, of course, Ireland. My friends' religions are just as various: the parents of my godchildren are Catholic, Presbyterian, Anglican and Jewish. But though I flourish in a multi-racial, secular world my Irish roots go deep and I know that the problem of the two tribes remains my problem. As does Robert Greacen – again – who, contemplating the sectarian horrors at home from the safety of London, ends his poem "Derry" with the poignant words:

Yet I who have gone away
To safe and easy exile,
Cannot just write them off
As simply ignorant thugs.

I, too, am involved in their crimes.

So I try to understand and I try to explain and mostly now I laugh at the insults. But I get angry about a lot of things: the fascist bully-boys on both sides; Sinn Féin's lies and manipulation; and the inexcusable hypocrisy of so many southern Irish Catholics who pretend to care about Northern Ireland but make no effort to understand the point of view of the majority there. On matters Northern Irish, Fianna Fáil, the political party with which I have my closest blood link, epitomises, with a few noble exceptions, those aspects of the Republic that madden me most: the pretence of seeming to care about that which you care not a damn and an absolute laziness of mind in refusing to face up to what is uncomfortable or difficult. That Conor Cruise O'Brien is so unpopular in Ireland is a direct reflection of that national failing. He relentlessly tells uncomfortable truths.

I did not follow Conor into membership of a unionist party, nor will I: I am neither nationalist nor unionist, just a democrat. And we disagreed tactically about the peace talks and the 1998 Good Friday Agreement. But I revere and honour him and am proud to be one of the small number of journalists who have defended his right to do and act as he has done: he has the same right to become a unionist as any unionist has to become a nationalist. Conor is a moral and an intellectual giant who, by employing the weapon of truth, has done more than anyone else to help peace and reconciliation in Northern Ireland.

CHAPTER 12

THE UNION AND THE ECONOMIC FUTURE
OF NORTHERN IRELAND

ROBERT MCCARTNEY

During the spring of 1998, the Northern Ireland Chamber of Commerce hosted a series of talks on the economic future of Northern Ireland. The Chamber of Commerce invited the leaders of all of the political parties in Ulster to outline their economic policies, especially in relation to the peace process and in the context of a possible political settlement. Other representatives also spoke, including the Minister for Northern Ireland, Mo Mowlam, the former British Prime Minister, John Major, and the Irish Taoiseach, Bertie Ahern. The following chapter is based on my own address to the Chamber of Commerce on 20 March 1998, which I delivered in my capacity as leader of the UK/Unionist Party; it also takes into account the signing of the peace agreement one month later. More to the point, I welcome this opportunity to honour Conor Cruise O'Brien, for I hold his friendship and principles in the highest regard.

THE PREVAILING VIEW OF THE LEADERS OF COMMERCE AND INDUSTRY IN Northern Ireland is that an end to terrorist violence is an absolute imperative. Yet it is an imperative which appears to be divorced from any concomitant public pledge to maintain the Union. What's more, the government of the United Kingdom has a shared understanding with pan-nationalism – arising out of the Hume-Adams dialogue of 1988-93 – regarding the long-term aims of the peace process: first, establish all-

Ireland political institutions, which are based on the Framework Documents of 1995 and are reflected in the recent political settlement; assign to them ever-greater cross-border responsibilities; and, finally, manage the gradual transition to Irish unity.

The leaders of the major business organisations in Northern Ireland have enhanced the credibility of this political strategy by supporting the development of a single-island economy. Since this economic model would ultimately require the formation of Ireland-wide macroeconomic planning committees and industrial policy institutions, it would eventually give rise to a functionally united Ireland. In fact, this Irish blueprint is largely predicated on the European plan for creating a politically united Europe. The distinction, however, is that while a substantial economic case can be made for a united Europe, a similar one cannot be formulated to justify a united Ireland. Nevertheless, business organisations in Northern Ireland have aligned themselves with a peace process that has discounted the economic benefits of the Union in favour of the economics of Irish unity and may, in effect, end the Union. The overriding question, therefore, is whether such a policy will ensure the future economic viability of Northern Ireland.

* * *

Is the political role sought by commerce to be confined to serving business and commercial interests alone? Colin Anderson, the president of the Northern Ireland Chamber of Commerce, seems to think so: several months before the peace agreement was signed he declared that "whatever settlement is reached (if any), the constitutional resolution must fit with the economic one".[1] The clear implication of this statement is that economic considerations must be paramount. Such interests, however, are not always compatible with the political wishes and values of Northern Ireland's citizens. In my view, if such a policy is pursued in the long-run it will alienate wide sections of the electorate and will paint the wrong picture of a business community dedicated to its own commercial interests. Moreover, when the policy seemingly adopted by business is questionable – not only on political, but even on economic grounds – the very influence which the business community seeks to exercise will become marginalised.

Only the foolish would deny the importance of commerce to the prosperity of ordinary people, but to subordinate other equally important issues, such as political allegiance, cultural identity and democracy, would be a mistake of major consequence. Men do not live by bread alone, nor do the essential welfare and liberty of a people depend only upon economic considerations – something which Rupurt Murdoch and Bill Gates have been made to remember in recent weeks.

Problems of commerce and politics are often very different and they do not easily lend themselves to the same solutions. The object of business is profit and, within the context of commerce, this is a very legitimate one. The businessman's bottom line is the size of the credit balance on the profit and loss account. He is answerable only to himself and to his shareholders. His only constraints are fiscal and social legislation tempered to his subjective view of commercial morality. His judgements are based upon an analysis of competitors, markets, cost efficiency and sales. His political concerns focus, for the most part, on policies that affect his business, whether they apply to investment opportunities, taxes, currency variations, interest rates or markets, to name but a few.

The rise of multinational corporations, economies of scale and global markets – all dedicated to greater commercial efficiency – have brought commerce and its interests into conflict with other principles and values considered important by the great majority of the electorate and with which its elected representatives must be concerned. The BSE crisis is a case in point. A balance must be struck between the economic distress of the beef industry and the safeguarding of public health, and this is, ultimately, not an economic decision, but a political one.

By the same token, the debate about European Monetary Union (EMU) is not solely about the economic benefits of entry. The main issue, which the British people will have to decide in a referendum, is whether the economic benefits to be gained by monetary union – even if they can, on balance, be proved – are worth the loss of national sovereignty and independent control of the national economy. The surrender of such control to a superior political institution will, in turn, result in the transfer of political sovereignty to a federated European super-state. Still, there are many in the upper reaches of industry and the world of finance who argue that whatever settlement is reached in Europe, the constitutional arrangement must fit the economic one. What is far from clear, however, is whether the supposed economic advantages of entry are worth the risks. It is in this general context that I wish to review some of the economic and political aspects of the settlement in Northern Ireland.

The terms of the Framework Documents of February 1995 and the Northern Ireland peace plan reveal the true aims of the British and Irish governments and the Social Democratic and Labour Party (SDLP). Their goals are similar to those of Europhiles who wish to see not only trade and economic union, but political union as well. In pursuit of their agenda they rely on the theory and method of functionalism. This process promotes the centralisation and unification of two or more independent sovereign states by situating them in an interlocking web of economic and financial institutions whose functions escalate from consultation to harmonisation to, finally, the executive administration of common policies in the cooperating states (often by anonymous officials unaccountable to the electorates in those states). The ultimate, albeit disguised, objective is that once effective functional and economic union have been completed, considerations of national sovereignty will become irrelevant, and political union will follow of its own accord.

In Ireland, as in Europe, an allegedly utilitarian economic programme – largely led by the two governments and the SDLP and given substance by certain elements in the business community – is masking a concealed agenda for political union. This project, however, has little or no support from professional economists; indeed, almost all of them, including the politically neutral, offer it little, if any, comfort.

The arguments against the economic viability of Irish unity ought to be well known, but have been suppressed, to a degree, for purposes of political expediency. Simply put, the Republic could not afford unity if it was required to maintain the social standards Northern Ireland now enjoys as part of the United Kingdom. Suggestions that the British fiscal transfer could be replaced by support from Europe or the Irish diaspora are the stuff of fairy tales. Equally improbable is the proposal for joint political authority, whereby each government contributes in proportion to its respective GDP, with Britain paying 95% of the cost for sharing 50% of the governance of Northern Ireland.[2] This is a very Irish solution to an Irish political problem. Realistically speaking, a thirty-two county Ireland offers no resolution to the problem of getting rid of the British while keeping their cash.

Of more immediate relevance to this gathering and, in particular, to the members of G7 (a local self-styled group of business leaders and trade union officials), is the case being made for economic integration at an all-Ireland level. The call for the creation of an island economy encapsulates this view. Sir George Quigley, chairman of the Ulster Bank, championed this blueprint in an influential paper, "Ireland: an Island Economy", delivered at the Annual Conference of the Confederation of Irish Industry on 28 February 1992. No sound economic interpretation, however, supports the conclusion that such a model will yield a significant material advantage, even when its alleged benefits are maximised. The argument that the border has led to the reduction of intra-island economic linkages (e.g., trade, financial services or company ownership and control) is highly questionable. Certainly, claims that greater North-South trade, anchored by the creation of a Belfast-Dublin business corridor, will generate 75,000 additional jobs have been proved to be gross exaggerations: the true figure may be a tenth of that.[3] North-South trade, after all, accounts for only 4-6% of Northern Ireland's GDP and has remained virtually static as a proportion of external sales from Northern Ireland during the 1990s.[4] There is no evidence, in short, that the benefits of an island economy would make any real difference to Northern Ireland's aggregate economic performance. Besides, the market mechanism itself should be capable of generating a greater level of all-Ireland economic cooperation: most of the potential gains can be exploited by links forged for purely commercial reasons. Political integration or the imposition of institutional political structures are therefore superfluous. Indeed, the insistence on such systems is politically motivated. Yet as Sir Charles Carter, former chairman of the Northern Ireland Economic Council, told the New Ireland Forum in 1984, the effects of island-wide political institutions "on unemployment would be equivalent to the products of nine bean rows on the Isle of Innisfree when set against a requirement of new jobs in the North by 2004 in the order of 200,000".

The simple truth is that neither the current level of trade between Northern Ireland and the Republic, nor whatever level may be reached in the future, can sustain the hype regularly appearing in the *CBI/IBEC Joint Business Council News* about the putative benefits that economic harmonisation and a Belfast-Dublin trade corridor will bring to Northern Ireland's economy. For example, between 1991 and 1996 sales from Northern Ireland to the Republic accounted for only 7-8% of the province's total sales and approximately 11% of its external sales.[5] It will be impossible to generate significant economic development in the future from such a low starting point. Moreover, between 1991 and 1996 there was no significant growth in export trade with the Republic as a proportion of either total external sales or total exports. The claim by the *CBI/IBEC Joint Business*

Council News that exports from Northern Ireland to the Republic grew by 62% between 1991 and 1996 ignores the fact that this increase involves a component still equal to only 7-8% of Northern Ireland's total sales, which themselves increased by over 60% in the same period.[6]

One of the attractions of the Republic for some Northern entrepreneurs is the Southern economic miracle, the so-called Celtic Tiger. While one cannot be dismissive of the substantial improvement in the Republic's economy in recent years, bust can follow boom, and all that glitters is certainly not gold. While economic growth has been very high, it has been growth from a very low level. Until recently, the Irish economy was one of the worst performers in Western Europe this century. The reasons for the recent growth surge are not entirely clear, but the experts offer four possible explanations. First, it is suggested that the recovery is export-led, based on the 1993 devaluation of the punt. Second, it is claimed that the Social Contract, which extends to the year 2000, secured industrial peace, led to wage restraint in the private sector, increased competitiveness and attracted inward investment. Third, it is European Union funding that has launched the Celtic Tiger into economic orbit. Fourth, the recovery has been driven by foreign capital from the multinational corporations rather than the strength of indigenous Irish industry, which remains very weak.

Those among you wedded to the idea of an island economy should give thought to the disturbing common factor linking these explanations. None of them possess any real durability or permanence, and the Irish government lacks control over most of them. Once the Republic joins EMU, devaluation as a means to aiding economic recovery is finished. The inflation rate, which must be less than 3% in order to meet the convergence criteria, may become a significant macroeconomic issue for the Republic within EMU due to an anticipated downward pressure on interest rates. Partnership 2000, by which wages in the private sector were restrained at the expense of government spending on public sector services, is unlikely to survive the millennium. Reliance on the foreign capital of multinationals, which themselves owe no national allegiance, is an uncertain foundation for the future. This is especially so in the context of the enlargement of the European Union, which will mean that foreign corporations can draw on low-paid, highly-skilled workers in the Czech Republic, Poland and Hungary. Enlargement also poses a serious threat to the current high levels of EU funding. Begging bowls for special economic assistance do not sit easily with claims that a country seeking such assistance is experiencing a raging economic miracle. To sum up, if Ireland's economy stumbles, the government's hands are tied: it cannot devalue the punt; it will not be able to count on substantial EU funding (even if a soft landing to ease withdrawal symptoms has been guaranteed); the restraints of the Social Contract may have disappeared and, with them, the multinationals in search of cheaper labour and a skilled work force in other parts of an enlarged EU.

The above may represent a worst case scenario, but closer all-Ireland integration, with the Republic in EMU and the UK outside of it, would be risk-taking of proportions unacceptable to a prudent businessman, particularly when the likely gains are relatively marginal. Indeed, Samuel Brittan of the *Financial Times*, one of the world's most respected commentators, has warned of the dangers of Ireland's rapid growth and doubts whether such high rates of expansion can be maintained: "The pressures are already showing up in asset price inflation, especially in the Dublin property market. Yet far from being able to raise interest rates in a pre-emptive move, the Irish Central Bank is having to prepare to reduce them as EMU membership looms." It is, of course, not just a matter of keeping inflation under 3% to meet the convergence criteria, but of holding it down thereafter to meet the stability requirements.

* * *

Let me now turn to a serious analysis of the absurd economic arguments advanced in this forum several weeks ago by John Hume, the leader of the SDLP.[7] On this occasion, economic proposals devoid of reality and substance were used to disguise a political agenda in favour of Irish unity. The economic myth of the island economy shared by some members of G7 was crystallised by Mr Hume. He offered two imperatives for Northern Ireland's economic future. First, that Northern Ireland must enter EMU as quickly as possible. Second, that Northern Ireland must associate with, or integrate into, the economy of the Republic.

Northern Ireland is a region of the United Kingdom, and there is simply no provision for a region being admitted into EMU while the sovereign state of which it is a part remains out of EMU. In any event, for Northern Ireland to enter EMU with the Republic would simply be buying into all of the problems which the Republic is going to face in the very near future. The key point here is that as a region within the EMU, and with the euro as its currency, the Republic, because of its significant trade with the United Kingdom (in the range of 30-40% of its GDP) will be vulnerable to both the depreciation and the appreciation of sterling against the euro within European Monetary Union. Why saddle Northern Ireland with this unnecessary economic burden? Further, Mr Hume's suggestion that Northern Ireland's position outside of EMU will affect trade relations with the rest of Europe or Ireland is groundless. The February issue of *Eurolink* clearly states that "the effects on cross-border trade and economic integration may be managed easily since a two-currency island, whether sterling-punt or sterling-euro, is already a reality".

Mr Hume's second point – Northern Ireland must associate or integrate with the economy of the Republic – is based on two assertions. First, that there is no other economy with whom we have more in common; second, that there is no other economy which is so willing to share with us. Neither of these arguments bear close scrutiny.

At present, trade links with the UK represent approximately 50% of Northern Ireland's external sales, while those with the Republic total 11%.[8] The fiscal transfer from Westminster ranges from £3.5 to £4 billion per year. Northern Ireland shares with the United Kingdom all of its institutional economic machinery. What the Northern Ireland economy shares with the Republic of Ireland is minuscule by comparison. With regard to the assertion that there is no other economy which is so willing to share with us, where is the evidence? We share with the rest of the United Kingdom its economic fortunes because we are an essential part of that sovereign state and as such enjoy all of the economic linkages and fiscal benefits that such a constitutional relationship naturally entails.

Those members of G7 who have bought into the island economy concept seem to have accepted the political thinking of Irish nationalism, that is to say, that a discrete geographical entity such as an island must have one economy, constitute one nation and be ruled by one government. It is the economics of map imaging and natural frontiers. The concept is as equally illogical and absurd as is its political counterpart. Mr Bertie Ahern, in a recent statement, declared that "any new settlement has to recognise the logic of Ireland as an economic entity". This statement is as devoid of economic validity as claims to natural frontiers are devoid of political realism.

* * *

In his paper, "Ireland: an Island Economy", Sir George Quigley firmly placed the idea of developing an all-Ireland economy on the political agenda. The Quigley economic perspective fitted into the political strategies of the so-called peace process and it has been especially employed to lend economic credibility to cross-border executive bodies, which are central to the recent political settlement. The use of economics to underpin a unificationist strategy has never been publicly challenged or repudiated by Sir George Quigley or by the leadership of the local Confederation of British Industry (CBI), the Institute of Directors or the Northern Ireland Chamber of Commerce, whose leaders are all in the vanguard of change. This represents, in my opinion, a combination of political naïveté and gross economic miscalculation, because the realisation of the unity objectives of the peace process and the settlement may destroy what is necessary for the viability of the business sector in Northern Ireland, namely, the Union.

Why do I say that the Union is the absolute basis for our future economic prosperity? I say so because there is no context outside of the United Kingdom within which Northern Ireland can sustain the robust rates of growth and the high levels of economic activity that its citizens desire. The island economy project envisages a range of economic harmonisation measures between Northern Ireland and the Republic in areas such as job promotion, tourism and farming and is underpinned by the development of the Belfast-Dublin corridor. The case for the latter is based on a gross exaggeration of anticipated trade and employment benefits that I have already mentioned. Nevertheless, nationalist politicians, particularly Albert Reynolds and the economic pundits of the SDLP, have employed the CBI's incredible claim that 75,000 new jobs will be created to underpin their political agendas, despite it being totally discredited by competent economic researchers. The use of the CBI's statistics by nationalist politicians is not merely a characteristic flight from economic reality, it also testifies to the high degree of intellectual dishonesty required by the lack of supporting evidence for the nationalist case. All of this was reflected in the empty economics of Mr. Hume's address, which provided a thin veneer for a very strong argument for political unification.

The economic future of Northern Ireland lies, as it always has, in its association with Britain as an integral part of the United Kingdom. For Northern Ireland's captains of industry to buy into the economics of Irish unity on the back of the uncertainties of European Monetary Union would be to risk the prosperity of one and a half million people for the financial gambles of a few. It would be to equate the possibilities of marginal gain with the probabilities of economic disaster and would, in the process, prejudice the constitutional wishes of the majority of our people.

V

THE CLASSICS, SHAKESPEARE, HISTORICAL CONSCIOUSNESS

CHAPTER 13

ABOUT LEARNING GREEK

DAVID GRENE

BY THE CIRCUMSTANCES OF MY LIFE – HISTORICALLY AND GEOGRAPHICALLY (between Ireland, very briefly Vienna and then mostly America), both in schooling and in teaching – I have lived through a tremendous change in the evaluation of Classical Studies in European culture, a subject to which I became committed, for seemingly trivial reasons, when I was eight to ten years old. I have thought this perhaps of sufficient general interest to write about it. Inevitably, as I look back, the general scope of the matter becomes crystallised in particular people, schoolmasters and university teachers – Irish or Austrian or American. These figures, whose personalities and special gifts deeply influenced the direction of my life, were themselves anchored in their moment of social estimate of the study of Greek and Latin.

One first observation on the last period of my real association with my alma mater, Trinity College Dublin, and the city itself. I was short of money and taught for two terms at Sandford Park, a private school in Dublin very near where I was born and lived until I went to study at Trinity. Apart from my regular work in Classics and English literature, I was asked to coach a boy (I believe his name was Morton) for Classical Sizarship. But in my class in English literature I saw a manifestly very bright and attractive lad who was studying for Sizarship in the newly-formed and esoteric combination of Irish and Latin. His name was Conor Cruise O'Brien. I suggested to the parents of Morton that if they didn't mind, I could take in Conor for the special sessions in Latin which I was giving their son. They were very pleased. And so began the lifelong friendship of Conor and myself, very broken by our different residences in our different countries and associations, but strikingly deep all the same. And on my side, at least, full of recognition and admiration.

The question of the study of Latin and Greek literature, and those who choose to study it, is, naturally, a very complicated matter. The old educational order which emerged from the sixteenth to the nineteenth centuries across the continent of Europe rested heavily on the instructional value of Classical literature in history, philosophy, literature and morality. This was especially the case in nineteenth-century Britain, where the Classics became a training ground for the governing-elite of the British Empire. It seems astonishing to me now that as late as my undergraduate days in the early 1930s the Indian civil service was stocked exclusively from candidates who had passed a single examination, a general paper and an interview. The civil service exam was really a repetition of the applicants' final Honours exam in their special subject at university. Classics was strongly favoured, and a very large number of those who went on to govern the Empire had received nearly everything that was important in their school and university education from Classical literature. After being passed for the Empire service the successful candidate spent a year or so at the government's expense learning a little law and whatever language seemed appropriate to where he was being sent. I distinctly remember dining, late in my undergraduate career, with a man who was the chief judicial authority in Burma only ten years after getting a first-class Honours degree in Classical Moderatorship, which I was to do myself a year later. The idea of employing someone for an important administrative position with almost no technical preparation is not one welcome to modern democratic governments today. But, by what evidence one can come by, the system seems to have worked surprisingly well. On a recent trip to India an admittedly casual observer like myself every day encountered strong praise – tinged with slight regret at its passing – for the general legal administration of British India. It was certainly not a system in which justice was *corrupted* in its court administration, although it was often ignorantly implemented. And the fact remains that the entire Indian legal system is based on that established by the Raj.

But the most remarkable feature of Classical training *in my time* was its obdurately philological character. This was much less so in France and Germany, where university professors paid much more than lip service to the content of Greek and Latin literature. Within such a specific context, our Irish professors certainly concerned themselves almost exclusively with the verbal and stylistic aspects of the languages studied (and the same was, as far as I can find out, largely true of much English education). In their publications these same interests took precedence. A few of these teachers and professors, I suppose, were a kind of barbarian, but not most of them. They felt that Classics in itself was something quite different from literature, philosophy or history. It was a study of a world of its own. I recently saw this very phrase in a speech by Professor Tom Mitchell, the present Provost of Trinity College Dublin; I know what he means and, in a certain way, I believe he is quite right. The greater philologists of the old order penetrated more than most scholars into the power of an imagination awakened by an endless attention to, and absorption of, the minutest aspects of words of well-known texts in Greek and Latin. These Classical texts are not exactly like those in modern languages, where contemporary usage is continually revising and rendering more exact our knowledge of the words and where there is always more literature coming into existence to modify one's understanding of what has already been read. The Greek and Latin classics, frozen in expression, are beyond further contemporary modification. There is a sense, of course, in which there is a line stretching from Homer through the Greek language of the fifth and fourth centuries to Koine, the language of the New Testament, and then to Byzantine and, finally, modern Greek. But Koine and the later forms of the language are not ancient Greek, even in the way in which Chaucer is subsumed into modern English.

There was also a deliberate circumscription of Greek texts, apparently for school books, going back to Hellenistic times. The selection continued and became the basis of the Classics when they were studied during the Renaissance. In the Renaissance the thought and the significance of the texts certainly mattered. But since the early nineteenth century, especially in Britain, the emphasis on the actual words and style has been predominant. A similar circumscription in Latin gives one Plautus and Terence, Lucretius, Cicero, Vergil, Ovid, Livy, Tacitus – all the way to Augustine. These two selected bodies of authors merged into a curious self-contained whole in the West, which has seen them in this light for hundreds of years. This entirety became, in effect, a series of contributions to a liturgy rather than a number of truly separate writers. Nowadays, there is a distinct effort to see the Classical projection as a field for comparative studies in anthropology or linguistic disciplines. But the period of Classical Studies between the nineteenth and early twentieth centuries knew very little of all this. Their attitude truly was towards a kind of liturgy, and liturgies achieve their effects by being learned (by heart if necessary) and forcing themselves into the obscurer parts of the mind and the emotions. There is necessarily a mysterious devotion about them. As a result, in the devotion, love and veneration of the actual words of the texts, something has come alive in the culture of the West that cannot, I think, be put totally to sleep or lost. That is what the old British civil service wanted of their applicants – a certain cast of mind.

After that was attained, the authorities thought it possible to fill that mind with various sorts of special aptitudes. But something imaginative of the greatest consequence came through the absorption of the liturgy and was the prime material out of which the useful elements would grow superimposed. The casualties were, as Gilbert Murray seems to have said, the many students who came to hate the subject because of the way it was taught and the manner in which it was examined; it constantly denied them the chance to see the books as a commentary on, or an extension of, their own kind of lives, as, in fact, modern literature seemed more fitted to do.

My own case is a mixed one. I am one of the last living products of the older training. There are times when I feel that my experience was fortunate, because I was a late developer and I doubt that in my early twenties I could have effectively dealt with the challenge to passion and mind in those Classical texts – all the matters that I now press on my American students' attention. I was, perhaps, better served by the relentless Talmudism of my teachers, as far as my future career went, than I would have been by what now appears to be a much more enlightened approach. At the end of eight years in school and four more undergraduate years in college I had come to know rather well, even if in a peculiar and, some people would say, distorted fashion, the languages and the texts of Greek and Latin literature. And the method in which I had been taught was to carry me on for scores of years afterwards when reading for my own advantage rather than thinking of my pupils. It has made a great difference to my translations and it has given substance to the freshness of my understanding of Greek and Latin that followed my starting anew at the University of Chicago and the Hutchins College. The old British model was on its deathbed anyhow. Willy-nilly, modern teachers of Classics have to give instruction much nearer in form to modern literature and history. One simple fact made this imperative, if nothing else. Clearly, it is no longer possible in modern schools to allow enough time to learn the two ancient languages to the complete exclusion of the hundreds of new subjects crowding for the pupils' attention. Still, on the whole, the present result is, it appears to me, fairly satisfactory. The texts of that ancient world are being used for the purpose inherent to all books: to make direct contact with their readers – and to change them. I am glad to believe that, perhaps, I do not make disgruntled as many students as the old system did. But I am heartily thankful for having lived inside it and witnessed the meaning of its mystery.

* * *

During my school days – from about eight to seventeen (kindergarten occupied the years from six to eight) – I attended two Dublin private schools. The first was St Stephen's Green School and the second St Andrew's. I was a student at the first for about seven years and the last for two – the years directly before entrance to the University of Dublin, Trinity College. I certainly learned a great deal of languages at St Andrew's and was well-taught. Yet I still do not think that much that formed my mind or intellectual interests would have happened but for one master in the first school. I can still see him, old (though not quite so old as I am now), with a red, round face and one slightly crossed eye, wearing very respectable grey suits. He had been retired from a provincial school, bigger than ours, some years before and when he came to Dublin he had been taken on as a cheap staff member at St Stephen's Green School. He was so excessively tender-hearted and so irresolute that he found it very hard to keep order in his class. When the boys made a row or were talking and inattentive, he was quick to put the offenders' names in the Detention Book, but almost always succumbed to their pleas before the end of the hour and rubbed their names out again. But give him a smaller number of impressionable boys and he was a different being – and his great passion was for Greek literature.

I remember he started us out on a book of elementary Greek readings which featured passages – a little modified and reduced in difficulty – by genuine ancient Greek authors. I should not even say "started", for he began, conscientiously, with the grammar, and we declined the declensions and the conjugations in a kind of chant. This lasted something less than two months, and we were then confronted with the book of readings. The grammar was still drilled into us coordinately with the

163

readings to make sure that we did not forget it. This was an entirely different method of instruction from what I had had in Latin, where the teachers kept us writing "sentences" in Latin, examined strictly for grammar and nothing else, for nearly two years before reading anything in the original language. I have no doubt about the superiority of the Dicky Wood system (that was his name) over my Latin learning. I suppose I am about as competent in the one language as the other now, but from those beginning years my *instinctive* response to the drift of the Greek periods and their meaning was much better than my rather wooden translation of the Latin. Dicky also started us reading the New Testament in Greek. We all knew lots of the New Testament (Authorised Version) by heart and we were absurdly proud of our ability to read the opening verses of St John's Gospel, with a not quite mistaken belief that we miraculously understood it as if without ever hearing it before.

In the second year Dicky had us read the *Alcestis* of Euripedes. (There were five of "us" in Greek; the others in our regular class, the Fourth, had chosen one of the two alternatives to Greek: German or drawing.) We were all made to take parts and dramatically read the lines, first in Greek and then in English; Dicky himself insisted on playing Alcestis. Our classroom for Greek was an unoccupied room in the huge old eighteenth-century house on St Stephen's Green (now demolished), unswept and usually unheated. I remember Dicky dying magnificently as Alcestis, flopping very naturally on the dusty floor, declaiming her dying speech. He knew Browning exceedingly well and Browning's version of *Alcestis* nearly by heart. It was Browning he usually recited when he came to give us the English version. We, of course, stumbled through with whatever simple translation we could manage. The bracketing of the strangely attractive and secret Greek with the excitement of the comprehensible and elegant Browning transported us – and in an elementary way the meaning of the Greek took hold despite our clumsy efforts to render it.

At this point Dicky also used to teach us English literature. He discussed all of his favourite books with his pupils and especially with me when I would walk part of the way home with him along Leeson Street. He had vivid and often unusual preferences in fiction. For instance, he was a great devotee of Walter Scott, and surprisingly both he and I chose *The Antiquary* before the others. After that I listed *The Heart of Midlothian* and he *Old Mortality*. He was always deep in nineteenth-century novels; I hardly ever heard him speak of Fielding or Smollet or Sterne – I suppose because in those twisted Puritanical days they would have been looked upon as undesirably coarse for the young. He knew and loved Dickens and Thackary, and especially Jane Austen and Charlotte Brontë, and he was strong on the connections of Charlotte's parson father with her stories of Ireland and, in particular, between those stories and Emily's *Wuthering Heights*. He passionately loved nineteenth-century poetry, especially Browning and Tennyson, but he stopped short of modernity in Yeats. One must remember that in the mid-1920s Yeats had not yet written what seem to me his greatest poems. I also remember once being brought up short by Dicky over a disagreement with me. I was about eleven years old and given to pretend to understand what I did not. In 1924 I saw *St Joan* and afterwards *Othello*. I ventured to say how both had moved me and how extraordinary the experience of *Othello* had been. Dicky said, rather hesitantly, "Don't you think it is a somewhat sordid story?"

I find it surprising, looking back, that even with Dicky's interest and influence as strong as it was in both Classical and modern areas – and rather more in literature than history or philosophy – I stuck resolutely to Greek rather than English literature as my area of concentration, for within a couple of years, from 13 to 15, those of us who expected to go on to university were already setting ourselves up to specialise in those subjects that suited us best. (This very early specialisation has been, and still is, one of the major differences between the English and the American systems of education.) After all, English was my native language; Greek and Latin I knew only imperfectly. Even the fragments of the two languages I had mastered were hard won and doubtfully grasped. The appreciation of literature in its elementary form, the passionate response to story or rhythm, with half-understood glimpses of "meaning" conveyed in them, were only partially present in my head in two foreign languages that were no longer evolving or in use and, therefore, in some sense dead. Yet I think my choice, if one could call such a slight inclination a choice, was not wrong. There is something in the process of learning Greek and Latin which baffles an immediate comprehension, which slows the response, but does not finally diminish the eventual depth of reception; often this does become associated with some vaguely deeper taste for literature, especially poetry, and leaves the curious being so disposed a Classicist rather than a scholar in English or, indeed, the other more accessible languages. I know that I owe more to Dicky for my love and knowledge of Greek and Latin than to anyone who ever taught me afterwards. Which would mean, if true – and I believe it is true – that the experience of a boy of ten to fifteen of a schoolteacher settled things for me in a way which could not be disturbed by far more qualified teachers later.

This was, perhaps, due somewhat to the nature of teacher and pupil. I was given to admire and follow someone idiosyncratic in authority, possessed by intense observable enthusiasm, but also someone vulnerable. Dicky, in turn, was hardly capable of sensibly discriminating between the enthusiasm of a child for a subject he himself so deeply cared for and the intelligent appreciation of someone much older. Many years later I learned that Dicky had been retired, a little prematurely, from his former schoolmastership because of a suspicion of pederasty. I certainly know that he never gave any overt, much less harassing, sign of it in relation to me or his other pupils at St Stephen's Green school. I do think it is possible that he felt, and awakened in his students, a depth of emotional attachment which may have originated in the side of his character that had caused him trouble in the past. Or, perhaps, the essential value of Dicky's teaching was the substantive experience of his rendering of the Euripidean play, which was quite unlike a merely didactic presentation

* * *

Ruthless and narrow-minded specialisation and constant emphasis on examinations started well before the end of secondary school. In the curriculum of my last two years of school science was not compulsory. I was interested to notice latterly that in his autobiography Bernard Knox – the writer of the two very best prefaces to the Homeric question: Fagel's *Iliad* and the same writer's *Odyssey* – mentions that in his secondary school (which was in England and better than mine) he also escaped any form of scientific instruction during his last two years. That this should have been so now seems almost impossible, but such are the facts. In Ireland, for those of us who were concentrating on Greek and Latin there was almost no mathematics either. We were being groomed for a very tough race, exactly like racehorses, and any activity which took time away from the main object was shelved. Similarly, those specialising in maths or science did not have to do any work in Classics. For most of us, our course, both in the first years in school and the four in college, was training for either the British civil service, teaching in a university or, in rare instances, in exceptionally highly-rated schools.

The men who taught Honours Classics in Trinity College had enough of the unusual and exotic to furnish a mysterious element to our education. They were nearly all of the recognisable British eccentric type, something grown much rarer since. There were five or six of them lecturing (or teaching as our tutors, if one preferred that title) and at least three of them – the seniors of the group – combined a well-deserved reputation for scholarship, backed up by a fair amount of scholarly publication, with a remoteness from ordinary life, manifest loneliness and, very notably, an inability to act, speak or dress like any ordinary member of their class or kind.

There was JG Smyly, one of the leading papyrologists of his day. Literary and other texts in Greek were preserved on papyrus for many hundreds of years before people came to use expensive calfskin and other materials. But papyrus was not very lasting, and most of what has come down to us is fragmentary. Indeed, many of the papyrus fragments are not literary at all. An unkind Classicist, vexed at the intrusion of the archaeolgists, once angrily discounted the value of learning from the contents of "thousands of washerwomen's bills in Egypt". Smyly and the two Oxford scholars Grenfell and Hunt had edited a huge body of this material, called the Tebtunis papyri. At the time I came to college Smyly was temporarily doing a job that he found slightly uncomfortable. The professor who was responsible for Indo-European Comparative Philology had died, and the exam paper in the subject, which was always a part of Scholarship in Classics – a very difficult and extensive exam in the middle of the Honours Classical course – had to be set by someone, and lectures given as a preliminary. Smyly was taken out of retirement for the purpose because of the enormous knowledge of rare Greek words which he had picked up from his readings in the papyri. These words tended to be useful for explaining the various shifts in sound and form in the evolution of the comparative philology process. Smyly certainly knew something about the theoretical side of comparative philology – mostly Meillet's seminal text of the mid-twenties, *Introduction à l'étude comparative des langues Indo-européennes* – but he made quite fascinating use of the rare words to illustrate Meillet. He made me feel a passionate, almost romantic, interest in comparative linguistics because of his own odd approach.

In the early 1930s Smyly looked like a photograph of a gentleman of the 1880s: stiff round collar, full morning dress and an immense head of white hair framing a face which suggested an old eagle. He was reputed to be a prince – or whatever the proper honorific title – in the order of the Masons; his presence was certainly steeped in aristocratic dignity. I remember the shock that ran through the class when he cited, as an example, the Greek word *epibda* from Pindar, which there means the consequences of over-indulgence in drinking. Smyly translated it for us as "You might say, ladies and gentlemen, the headache of the morning after". Somehow, everything was out of kilter – the pompous address (we were all about eighteen or nineteen), the formality of the words and the dress and the appeal to us in a colloquial reference which was intended, quite wrongly, to put us at ease. He was also a librarian of the College and a somewhat remiss librarian. His own main interests were in music and pornography, and books connected with these subjects were carefully attended to. I was told by his successor that he found boxes and boxes of volumes treating other subjects that had never been unpacked. He used to play the violin within hearing-distance of those of us who used the reading room of the Old Library, and to us he seemed to play extremely well.

There was George Mooney, who had just changed from being University Professor of Latin to the Regius Professorship of Greek. His main contributions during his Latin professorship were studies of two late *Greek* poets: uniquely valuable editions of Apollonius and the *Alexandra* of Lycophon. He celebrated his elevation to the chair of Greek (the senior of the two professorships) by editing Suetonius' *Lives of the Caesars*, an especially important Latin text. As a human being everything marked him as inaccessible. Extremely reserved and shy, his physical features were unusually off-putting. He had only one eye – the other had been lost, we were told, while hunting as a youth – and the single eye was unabashedly just that, without a shade or anything else. He had a husky sepulchral voice, which he used very little. His clothes were always in rags.

Mooney was a very severe examiner on texts, being notorious for setting extremely difficult "unseens" (passages which were not on the prescribed list of the author under study). On such an exam paper the difficulty was obvious and his marking niggardly. All that was clear and straightforward, however, and there were other examiners like him. But he also administered vivas (orals) in particular texts. On the Scholarship in Classics he had two vivas, one on the *Iliad* and the *Odyssey* and the other on Thucydides VII. He apparently assessed us by some private standard of his own which had little to do with the questions he asked. In any case, he used to examine in Scholarship every year and for some extraordinary reason asked the same questions on his viva. These questions were always quite particular, and as Scholarship was a very difficult exam, it was often taken by the same candidate two or three times before either getting it or giving up. Consequently, many students knew the exact questions that

Mooney was going to ask them. But evidently he early-on decided either that you had read the books thoroughly or that you had merely been told what his questions were. If the latter, he gave you three or four out of ten automatically. I remember sitting alongside of him on a desk as he glanced at me with his good eye. He said: "Lad, do you know the description of Olympus in the *Odyssey*?" I did know that this was one of Mooney's pet questions and had learned it by heart. There was an uncomfortable silence, which he broke by asking: "Do you know what word Homer uses for a worm?" (He made the keyword a distinct syllable – "wor-um".) This one I had not heard about, but fortunately remembered that there were two: one word for the worms that might have eaten Odysseus' bow, but didn't; the other for the "gleaming worms" that the gods had prevented from eating Hector's body. Mooney made a very slight movement and I knew that something had happened. He then asked me a number of detailed questions on reading, etc., and then quite unexpectedly made me talk about what I thought was the role of Laertes in the *Odyssey*, a discussion which he evidently enjoyed. "That will do, lad," he said, and it was over. He gave me eight marks out of a possible ten. I lost the other two, I think, for knowing the description of Olympus by heart.

Then there was Sir Robert Tate, knighted for his services as an interpreter to the forces during World War I. He had a DSO, so I assume he had also done some fighting. He apparently knew 10 to 15 modern languages along with his Greek, Latin and Hebrew. I have been told by his well-wishers, as well as their opposites, that he spoke all the modern languages with perfect correctness and an impeccable Anglo-Irish accent. He used to teach us how to write Greek and Latin prose and verse. He would, for instance, on a Tuesday give us a passage of any author from Milton to Wordsworth, or English prose, history or philosophy, and on the following Tuesday take up our version – in the case of poetry translated into whatever metre we deemed appropriate: hexametres for Milton; Ovidian or Tibullan elegiacs for Wordsworth. No one was compelled to hand up versions. I secretly believe that the very harsh criticism to which we were subjected by Sir Robert was partly designed to diminish the number of copies given to him to read. On the Thursday following he would enter the classroom and ostentatiously sit facing away from us and towards the window and lawn in the New Square. He would then catalogue our infelicities or downright blunders without attributing any of them directly by name to the unhappy listening faces, which would begin to redden. He would comment with something like this: "I say nothing about the poetry of this; it is too much to expect that you have enough feeling for English poetry to have any notion of how to render it in Greek or Latin, but at least you ought to know the simple rules of Latin and Greek metre." I remember once how I glowed with delight when he read my version through, saying nothing at first. He then remarked: "I don't say this is good, but it's not at all bad. But I don't like the last couplet; it has the wrong ring to it for Ovid." About three weeks later I was at a College dance and there was Sir Robert, a deservedly well-known dancer. During an intermission he walked over to me and quoted two lines from Ovid and said: "You see what I mean, my dear fellow; that's why your lines were wrong."

These three were, as I have said, a breed that has grown very scarce. Some time ago I had a conversation with a professor from Trinity College whom I had known since childhood days. He said that it had taken him a long time to realise that these eccentrics had been made so by suffering and frustration, and that was good for no one. I don't know; but I do know that each of these men made very notable written contributions to the exegetical and stylistic values of Classical literature. What is more, there is something special in being taught Classics by men whom you cannot possibly imagine as really like yourself when they were young. They come before you as part of the mystery that lies in their complete mastery of those long dead languages and their eerie power to jolt your imagination beyond almost anything that you can read in the more modern and, apparently, commonsensical literary criticism. It is true, of course, that they were dealing with works that themselves inflame the imagination; with Homer and Herodotus, with Thucydides and the tragedies, with Lucretius, Vergil and Tacitus. But it is sometimes better, I believe, if those who teach you do so from the heart of their own, perhaps, twisted personality rather than with the standardised presentation of new historical evidence or current theories of psychology or anthropology and even more so with new aesthetic standards of criticism. At any rate, there was some sort of inner harmony between the isolation and complexity of their personalities and their nearly magical way of understanding the texts and rendering them alive again in living linguistic detail.

* * *

Much of the political ambience of Trinity College was still tenaciously, and somewhat amusingly, backward. The Classical dons, Sir RW Tate and

Frank Godfrey, referred to one another – only half-humorously – as Major Tate and Captain Godfrey; they had, after all, served as officers in the Great War. This was a sentimental gesture, but one needs to remember that on 11 November every year we commemorated the thousands of Irishmen all over the country, and in our case the twelve or thirteen hundred students of Trinity College, who had died under the banners of the famous old Irish regiments: the South Irish Horse, the Dublin Fusiliers, etc. Forty thousand Irishmen died in that war fighting in the British Army in comparison with the mere handful of hundreds who died in the Rebellion of 1916 and the slightly larger number in the 1919-21 War of Independence.

A party around 1934 stands out in my memory. There was a group of 15 or 20 of us, including some faculty, e.g., Sir Robert (Major) Tate and also a young visiting German lecturer. We had all been drinking and later in the evening started singing national anthems. We sang our "new" national anthem – *Amhrán na bhFiann* (The Soldier's Song) – with a certain tipsy irreverence, and Sir Robert stood to his feet, though with a slight reluctance. After this we sang God Save the King, and Sir Robert clearly enjoyed that. But the most remarkable case was our German lecturer (remember, the date is 1934, early in the Hitler era). He had probably drunk more than all the rest of us, but when Deutschland Über Alles rang out he started to his feet, stood stramm and sang with all the seriousness of religious devotion. As the song ended, dear old Sir Robert approached the German and extended his hand, saying, "My dear fellow, if there had been more like you, the War would never have happened".

After I finished my last Honours exam in Classics in Trinity I had won what was called Studentship. This was a prize (if I correctly recollect) of £100 for a year together with the obligation to teach two Pass Courses in Classics. But the College also gave me a lectureship in Classics, tenable for three years, and this clearly marked me out as someone they thought of as a possible member of the staff or even as a Fellow with its lifetime association with the college.

I felt that I didn't really know what the Classics looked like in parts of the world other than Trinity and asked for a leave in March 1935 to study for some time in Germany. Since at this stage none of us wanted to spend a penny of money that could reach Nazi Germany, I asked my friend George Thomson, author of the best book I know on Greek lyrics, *Greek Lyric Metre* (written as part of his requirements for Tripos in Cambridge in 1929 and published by Cambridge University Press), where he thought

I should go. He and his Cambridge colleague (Adcock) suggested that I go to Vienna to study with Ludwig Radermacher.

I accepted their advice and lived in Vienna from March until December 1935. My impressions of the city were both good and ill; my view of Radermacher was wholly positive. He taught me how folklore could contribute to one's understanding of Greek comedy. I, in turn, made a real hit with him by reciting the verse sung by Irish boys on St Stephen's Day:

> The wren, the wren, the king of all birds,
> St Stephen's Day he was caught in the furze,
> And though he is little his fortune is great,
> So come out good people and give us a trate.

Nowadays, thank God, a mere representative of the wren is brought out. Still, Radermacher insisted that my performance supported his theory of Tier Masquerade, which showed how folklore indicates various examples of the assumption of the role of animals and birds in primitive rituals. He referred this to Greek comedy – *The Birds, The Frogs*, etc.

I have two other vivid recollections of my time with Professor Radermacher. I participated in his seminar on Longinus' *On the Sublime*, which was conducted in Latin, one of the very last sessions so managed on the continent, I am told. It was a revelation to me how in this setting speaking Latin, which all of us knew well, was hopelessly clumsy, if not impossible. However, I still think that an important dimension of the language is acquired by people who systematically speak Latin. For instance, my colleague in the Committee on Social Thought at the University of Chicago, David Tracy, greatly benefited from speaking Latin in Rome as a novice, even if the quality was sometimes of the order of the American cardinal who declared, in a conference, *"haec opinio non tenet aquam"* (this opinion won't hold water).

Otherwise, one last note on my recollections of Radermacher. He was a man who had read and thought at great depth about all sorts of authors of Classical commentaries, but had very little contact with the circumstances of the commentators. This, remember, was long before the era of peripatetic airborne professors in constant circulation. He referred, in a lecture, to Pickard *von* Cambridge, not knowing that the man's name was the specifically English absurdity of Pickard-Cambridge.

* * *

When I came back from Vienna I assumed that I was going to stay in Trinity College teaching Classics. That, indeed, was the intention of the college, which had generously sanctioned my travel to learn German and to study how Classics was taught on the continent. Now my real professional life was to begin, and I expected to remain in Trinity College until I retired, like so many of the other fellows and professors. These outlines had a reassuring feeling of ordinariness. I had always enjoyed myself there as a student, and if things had become a little duller and somewhat empty during the year I had finished my Honours degree, I was still eager to apply what I had learned in Vienna about Classical philology and the German system, of which Austria was a part. But what actually happened during the next six months changed everything.

I left Vienna at Christmas in 1935 and taught in the usual way at Trinity College in the spring of 1936. I then decided to go to Greece, stopping in Vienna again for a visit with the Brunswicks, a couple I knew well who lived on the Hasenauerstrasse. In late June Ruth Brunswick's father, Julian Mack, a very distinguished judge on the Circuit Court of Appeals in New York, came to Vienna to celebrate his birthday, and I was invited to the party.

Julian, who was a trustee of Harvard University, had been told by Provost Conant to look out for bright young academics during his visit to Europe. Accordingly, after some arranging I found myself offered a position in America. For several years Conant had been attracting the very cleverest young people to Harvard through a system of national scholarships which offered tuition exemptions and grants to promising students regardless of race, class and background. He felt, I think, that Harvard's complacency and stuffiness needed to be shaken up and he cordially believed that this was the way to do it. He certainly brought excellent students there who would never have been able to attend otherwise, as my own year of teaching at Harvard convinced me. But relief from the complacency and stuffiness proved harder to achieve, and I personally had no conviction that these were more than marginally punctured. In all my time in America, Harvard has been, to me at least, stuffy, unauthentically American and quite dull.

After I came to find Harvard disappointing I was going to return to Trinity College without any regret when, again, Julian Mack made a contribution to my life. He said: "Harvard isn't America, you know. Also, Harvard isn't American education either. What is happening in Chicago now seems to me much more interesting. If you like, I'll write Hutchins and see if he has anything he can give you." I had heard only a little about the academic revolution that Robert Hutchins was carrying out at the University of Chicago. However, I *had* very much enjoyed some aspects of America and certainly had a tremendous regard for some of the people I had gotten to know, so I told Julian that I would be very obliged if he wrote to Hutchins. A week or so later Julian wrote me, enclosing a single page of notepaper on which was written:

> Dear Julian,
> I am sending a dean
> to see Mr Grene.
>   As ever,
>   Bob.

Somehow, the absurdity of this note strongly prejudiced me in the writer's favour. A university president who would write like that, not just to an old friend, but a friend who was a respected federal judge, had to be someone special – and likeable. In the course of a month Dean McKeon from the University of Chicago interviewed me in New York. I was glad to have the opportunity to discuss with him a question that I had been thinking about ever since I had received the Trinity College appointment and had taken courses with Radermacher in Vienna: exactly how to teach Classical literature. The issue had recently become clearer to me. In a world where there was evidently less teaching of Classics in the universities and schools and where the huge expenditure of time on the two languages which was then expected from the students was no longer going to be possible, the old sort of philological training simply could not be the only methodology practised. Besides, during my own student years in Trinity College I had begun to wonder why we were never really asked to think seriously about what our Greek and Latin authors said to us; whether they were right or wrong; whether we enjoyed the poetry; whether we thought the history interesting or truthful; why, in fact, were we almost never required to know the meaning of what we read, but only the form in which it was written.

Ideally, one should be able to teach the languages adequately and at the same time discuss the contents of the books as one would books written in English and other modern languages. But this proves very difficult when students have not learned the two ancient languages (and I knew that ideally we ought to be learning Hebrew as well) to a sufficient level, such as the competency I had attained, for instance, by at the end of my undergraduate career. After all, I had started Latin at the age of 9 and

Greek at 10. That said, much of the elementary knowledge of ancient languages can be much more expeditiously and sensibly obtained when the student is more mature. But there is a limit to this. So I thought that it was necessary to do two things simultaneously. Students who were going to specialise in modern languages and literature ought, during their undergraduate career, to read much of the Classics in translation, and their teachers should teach Plato as part of European philosophy and Herodotus and Thucydides as part of western history, and so on. Then the students who were specialising in Classics should be taught Greek and Latin as well as their teachers could manage. Probably one-half of this, however, would have to be done in translation, the teaching itself being much like that which would be done for authors within broad divisions such as philosophy, history and drama. I was prepared to hear that this was a betrayal of true Classical study and education. Still, I thought that this objection was specious, and, indeed, if one could not make some such deal for Classics in modern university education we might as well fold our tents and depart.

I talked to Dean McKeon in this strain and he decided that I was the kind of man whom the new programme at Chicago needed. When I got there I found that this was largely true. The arrangement of the humanities and social sciences in the undergraduate school was very much along the lines I had sketched. In the end, I was offered a job as lecturer in the Division of the Humanities. My position allowed me to list a course in any department in the Division at the undergraduate or graduate level (though, as I was to find out, whether or not there would be any students for these unauthorised forays into higher learning was another problem altogether).

* * *

All of this transpired during my first year and a half in America. During my stint at Harvard, Julian had introduced me to his friend Felix Frankfurter and other members of the Law School faculty, including Henry Hart and his wife, Mary. Before settling in Chicago I travelled across America with the Harts. Not only the extraordinary extent of the country and its variety impressed me, but what DH Lawrence correctly described as its primitivism. The Cook City-Red Lodge Highway through the Rockies makes one imagine what a countryside that is totally without man is like, something that is very hard to find almost anywhere in

Europe. I lived in Berkeley most of the summer and saw something of university life there. I also saw a little of the west coast and Hollywood. All of this constituted a kind of extravaganza of what America could be for me. But when I took the train from San Francisco to Chicago in September 1937 – a trip on the old Challenger which lasted two days and three nights – I am proud to say that upon my arrival I recognised right off the solid face of a place where I could become someone decently, and yet excitedly, useful in my own right in a completely new way.

To win exams on Classical texts mostly on philological grounds was something respectable, but it told me little about myself. To teach those texts even to good students at Harvard who were interested in their literary, historical or philosophical meanings was worthwhile and an advance on Trinity College. But to be thrown into the fascinating chaos of the University of Chicago from 1937 to 1941, when you met some of the brightest students of 18 to 22 in the world, many of whom were New York and Chicago Jews and all earnestly asking what Aeschylus' and Sophocles' plays meant – in the same way as they posed the question about the works of Shakespeare, Ibsen and Shaw (all of whom were also studied in the College, i.e., the undergraduate period) – all of this was a challenge to me as a teacher that I had not experienced before. I was also teaching Greek as a language, of course, and after one year at the university I knew that I had found a significance in teaching that language that I was very proud to have a share in.

The University of Chicago already had a record of doing new things in a new way when Robert M Hutchins took over its management in 1929. I did not get there until 1937, when many of Hutchins' reforms had already been put into effect and some of the failures already admitted and dismissed. Therefore, I can only speak from personal knowledge of the years from 1937 until the outbreak of the war, the skeletal war years themselves and then the confused but intensely alive academic seasons from 1946 until Hutchins' departure in 1952, when the returned veterans contributed tremendous vitality to the campus and when the Committee on Social Thought (described below) was beginning to function as a proper independent entity. During the first two of these periods, I was mainly teaching in the undergraduate college and in the Greek Department; afterwards in the Committee on Social Thought.

Robert Hutchins was one year older than the century. He had driven an ambulance in the First World War and after earning his law degree from Yale became dean of Yale Law School in 1926. From there he came

176

to Chicago to take over the presidency when he was just thirty years old. It is said that when he was invited to visit Chicago in connection with "some" post he was sure that it was the deanship of the law school, which then was vacant. Only during the course of his interviews did he get an inkling of the truth and said afterwards that many of his answers to questions (offered on the premise that he was a candidate for the law school position) certainly must have sunk his chances for the presidency. Obviously, they did not.

Hutchins was a man who in his combination of talents would seem unlikely to have attained such important academic administrative posts so early in his life. He certainly was a great charmer, handsome, tall and noble in movement and gesture. But he was also sharply and fiercely witty and most unwilling to suffer fools gladly. It is hard for me to be just in dealing with the movement he initiated at the university. The ideas inherent in it were so deeply right, but sometimes too simplistic and too inflexible for application except by someone of consummate political skill and, therefore, probably by someone much older than thirty.

Briefly, Hutchins thought that the American university system had gone wrong in all sorts of ways, but notably so in doing away with a fixed and general education for undergraduates in favour of the permission granted by Dr Eliot, the president of Harvard, to put together any number of any courses that happened to interest young students. In his two wonderfully clever and amusing books – *The Higher Learning in America* and *No Friendly Voice* – he scarified American academia (with some allowance for caricature) as offering courses in hotel management and dishwashing, with no formal education at all. Specialisation between the ages of 16 and 20 or 18 and 22 deprived the country as a whole, he thought, of a society which had learned the great truths that man at different times had entertained about freedom and organisation, about God and natural law and causation in history. In the field of science he insisted, without neglecting the nuts and bolts of pragmatic science, on the importance of the general ideas on which scientific knowledge was based.

Such an undergraduate education, according to Hutchins, must be taught through original texts, not secondary books about the subject. Hobbes, Locke, Thomas Paine, *The Federalist* and Marx were what should be read in the social sciences. In humanities there were Shakespeare, Greek tragedy in translation, Tolstoy and Dostoevsky, but also very prominently Plato, Aristotle, Aquinas, Descartes, Hume, Hegel and Kant. History, as concerned the connections of these texts with one another or with other features of the times in which they appeared, was almost ignored. It was axiomatic that every great book can apprehended directly by anyone of proper intellectual gifts who takes it seriously and asks the basic questions of it. I still think this is the proper direction for undergraduate studies and, to a great degree, for much of graduate study also. But it did leave a great deal to be arranged in the matter of teaching and staffing.

* * *

I vividly remember the staff meetings of the revised college programme of 1939-46 – the Humanities Course – of which I was a member. There were ten or twelve of us, all teaching the same books to sections of the general course. Our individual teaching amounted to, perhaps, twenty or twenty-five students apiece. It was held that this necessitated the establishment of some common position on the books discussed, which required a chat at suitable intervals to establish what it was. What this meant in the time of Deans McKeon and Faust, two nominal champions of Hutchins' position, was a determined effort to chart the school's line on particular plays and novels. From the point of view of those who determined the interpretation of the books, there was no merit at all – in fact, the reverse – in having different views of each book explained to the students. This doctrine was presented as established truth. You could not, for instance, without instant rejection by the leaders of these supposedly informal chats, suggest that surely there was something peculiar in Aristotle's distinction between "simple" plays of a "spectacular" kind like *Prometheus Bound* and the "complex" plays like Sophocles' *Oedipus Rex* – and in the idea that Sophocles was, of course, superior. This way of handling the subject ignored not only the outstanding power of the *Prometheus* play, but its fascinating relation to the theological complexity of the *Oresteia* and its theology. Every play of every author was to be treated entirely on its own. There was no interest whatsoever in looking at the relation of one play to another by the same author. David Daiches and I were the sole, but very vocal, heretics. David went back to do intelligence work for the British during World War II, but he was already slated for removal from the college staff. I soldiered on for a couple of more years and got my dismissal notice from the college in 1945.

I spoke to Hutchins, who totally dissociated himself from my dismissal. He fascinatingly told me that in my first term in Chicago he had put a note in my file reading: "This man is not to be fired without consulting me." He spoke the truth, as always: the note is still in the records. Evidently, McKeon and Faust had not consulted him. He then asked me to join the newly-formed Committee on Social Thought. It was a new sort of graduate programme designed to deal with texts in humanities and social science, with enlightened aspirations towards PhDs of a "larger" character than the average doctorate. We were committed to very strict standards in the students we admitted, awarded our own PhDs, relied heavily on tutorials and allowed our students the run of the university for such courses as they wanted to prepare them for their final exams, while constantly treating them as "junior colleagues". It was the creation of Hutchins, John Nef, Robert Redfield and Frank Knight. It was in expression very idealistic as to our intellectual objectives – and it still is. I also think that it makes a very fair attempt at really teaching in the light of this idealism. I think that there is some common mark on most of our students, and not a bad one, by the time they finish. The unifying idea was that the teaching members of the Committee should be specialists of a high order in particular subjects, but that we all distrusted a strictly technical specialisation in the education of our students. I have now been associated with the institution for close to fifty years and it is the only educational institution I know that is small enough to live by its principles.

A rather important aspect of the Committee was initiated by Otto Simson, author of *Sacred Fortress*, and myself, namely, that the first three years of each student's work with the Committee were to be devoted to ten or twelve significant texts in philosophy, history and "imaginative literature" from ancient, medieval and modern life, and each student's written reflections on the texts were crucial. Each student then took an exam on these "fundamental texts" and, in the light of the results, went on to work on a PhD in some special aspect of learning.

There has been just enough oddity in the Committee's creation by Hutchins and Nef, and in its continuation thereafter under various blessedly lucky administrations (lucky for us, I mean), to ensure that we are not regarded as properly responsible in the sense of an ordinary department. Sometimes we do not get an appointment when we want one, but no one tells us that it is the "sort of appointment" that the university does not approve. In its early days the Committee on Social Thought consisted nearly exclusively of young men who had had trouble with their conventional professional departments – Shils, myself, Otto Simson. Yves

Simon – our sole philosopher, a Thomist – was constantly deplored as inappropriate by most of the critics who viewed Hutchins' courses with fixed Classical texts as authoritative. Hence, Simon, as a neo-Aristotleian critic and a Catholic, was typical and unfortunate. Yet perhaps, on the whole, we did well enough to satisfy our champions.

* * *

Robert Hutchins was no dictator, contrary to the charges constantly levelled against him. He couldn't be one while working inside of the American academic system at the University of Chicago. He also was not a dictator primarily because he didn't like the very idea of authoritarianism. But the two salient features of his "reign" were, first, that he thought that there was a right and a wrong way to think about the questions that the western world had repeatedly set itself from the Classical age to the twentieth century. And, second, he was not a good judge of choosing men to implement an educational programme that grew out of this central belief. He despised the relativism of those who talked of the difference in how philosophic problems *looked* at different historical moments. He had very strong feelings about his favourite literary texts, but, perhaps, too often because the objective truth of the author's vision in the poem, play or novel seemed to affirm his own. He had less of a gift for admiring the size and power of a vision with which he ultimately disagreed. He had almost none for letting the truth or untruth, as it appeared to him, live in some limbo of non-decision until time and experience crystallised his final judgement. His belief in logic and his lawyer's skill at elucidating it very often proved a disadvantage. It undermined the latent ambiguities in his mind, which were richer than the brilliance of his direct conclusions and their expression.

He was also a man of exceptional bravery. He defended our university against the Broyles Commission, which was created by the state of Illinois to impose moral, political and social standards (of *their* choosing) as the criteria for the retention and advancement of professors at the university. When one state legislator named Walgreen attacked Hutchins for having a history department where his own daughter was taught Marxism, Hutchins, with his natural bonhomie, induced Walgreen to endow a series of lectures on democratic institutions. "I am delighted to have all controversial subjects debated in the university," he said, "but I will not have any of them dropped or discriminated against except on *strictly intellectual* grounds." It was on his interpretation of intellectual grounds that Hutchins was most vulnerable. There was always something too simplistic in the logic he applied to the criteria that determined what was discardable or not.

In the difficult financial times still persisting during the late 1930s Hutchins froze all appointments at the university, but he cut only one salary – his own – and that by 50%. He was utterly indifferent to ordinary conventional distinctions of rank and position. He showed me every sort of kindness and generosity in tolerating my arguments and the troubles into which they led me when I was an instructor and he was president of the university. He remained unaffected by my violent dissent from his friends and agents. He was capable of the most personal and amusing criticism irrespective of whether it might embarrass the recipient. For a time the Committee on Social Thought published a journal, *Measure*, which Otto Simson edited and the rest of us participated in. I remember one day when we were discussing a paper for possible publication and I criticised it. I believe I had used the word "bloke". Hutchins responded: "David, I wish you would try to talk with any tolerable vocabulary. You use words like an Indian that are clearly English literary slang of 50 years ago. You use expressions which, God help you, you think are American. As a background you have an Irish psychological dialect all your own." How many friends could one find to be so funny, so truthful and so disconcerting in public?

There was some celebration shortly after the end of World War II – I cannot now remember what it was – but it involved a large assembly of university staff with Hutchins in the centre shaking hands with everyone. This he did with a certain mechanical dignity and total personal withdrawal. I came in with Marjorie, my first wife; we had driven in from the Illinois farm where we had lived since 1940. Hutchins never varied his monotonous "How do you do?" save for a second when he looked into the middle distance and said to no one in particular: "You see, even the country people are here. Look at their boots." This sense of phrase, utterly reckless in its kindness or propriety, but somehow quite without malice, was very much his own. I remember his description of a distinguished Irish minister, of whom someone said: "He is like a Shakespearean actor." He corrected: "Yes, like a third-rate Shakespearean actor." He was, unfortunately, deadly accurate – most of Hutchins' *bon mots* tended to be – but also deadly quotable.

In or about 1948-49 he had formidable rows with the faculty. I forget

181

the particular occasion now, but the background was a serious proposition put forward by him regarding the government of the university. He suggested that the president of the university should, like a British prime minister, have a term of four to six years which would at any moment be terminable by a vote of no confidence. But also there should be only one title in the university – "member of the teaching staff" – and salaries would be adjustable in terms of need rather than the existing system of rank. Thus a needy and married assistant professor could, by the decision of the university committee appointed for the examination of such cases, come out earning more than a celibate or wealthy full professor. This kind of thing made him intolerable to much of the faculty, although, interestingly enough, mostly the senior faculty. Furthermore, I am afraid these propositions were not realistic. But they were pure Hutchins and only the most extreme and logical extension of his best educational policy.

The senior faculty of the university finally presented the trustees with a memorandum characterising Hutchins' administration as dictatorial and directed against the proper faculty participation in the government of the university. Within days the junior staff, including myself, sent another memorandum to the trustees expressing total disagreement. We cited what Hutchins had done for the staff in the matter of the Broyles Commission: how he refused to allow the state legislators to come to our private university and "investigate" us on the charge of communism; the hundred and one ways he had defended us against slanders by the state, the city, the media; how he had overcome his own repugnance to the atom bomb project so as to allow its prosecution within the university, because he felt it his patriotic duty to do so. These, we said, were very far from the acts of a dictator nor did they show sympathy with what dictatorship had come to mean in our time. I am very glad to say that we received an entirely generous and sympathetic answer from the trustees, and the senior faculty's attack was received with a cold acknowledgement coupled with some doubts about the accuracy or relevance of its main evidence.

But Hutchins was very hurt by the whole episode and he began to think of leaving. I saw him upon my return from a six-month sabbatical in Europe in 1950-51 when the news of his resignation was already public. I asked him why he had done it, and he said: "There is really nothing I can bring to fulfilment here any more. I have raised opposition all around. If I stay on, I am afraid that one day I will wake up to find myself the grand old man of the Midway. I don't want that." It is possible to find this comment of his frivolous. I don't. He passionately wanted to be *doing* something in which he believed. He had neither the patience nor, indeed, the insight to see when some of his previous plans were still leading to good results. There is no doubt whatsoever that the basic assumption of his Chicago plan – that undergraduates should study great original texts instead of secondary redactions – took hold of the American undergraduate experience and has never let go. The modern wave of enthusiasm for other than western texts may not be a blessing to education, but it certainly has a seriousness that the old potted commentaries dealing with vague, unsustainable historical and philosophical positions did not.

I am very sure that Hutchins was by far the greatest educational theorist I have ever known who was in a position to do something practical to turn his theories into actuality. He did a great deal; he also brought to the job a temperament almost congenitally unfitted to do more. I wonder sometimes if this wasn't inevitable. Without his intense idealism and without his human incapacity to suffer fools gladly and, unfortunately, to suffer those who irritated him by being cautious and unreceptive, I doubt he would have carried with him the enthusiasm of the entire junior faculty of the university between 1937 and 1952. I am only speaking of the years of which I have personal knowledge. He did kindle that enthusiasm among us and we were always on his side. He would generously tolerate differences of opinion among us as to the wisdom of what he did. He would do no such thing for anyone he felt belonged to those who were his enemies. That seems to be a very serious flaw in anyone who by the nature of his position must be, at least partially, a politician.

I am very proud of our last interchange. I wrote a little book of essays, *Reality and the Heroic Pattern*, more than twenty-five years ago now. The essays dealt with the last plays of Sophocles, Shakespeare and Ibsen. I dedicated it to RM Hutchins and the university "which he did so much to build" and sent him a copy. I got an answer, a couple of lines as his letters so often were: "What you have to say or to write always stirs my thoughts to life."

* * *

As I read what I have written about Chicago during this crucial era of the thirties and forties, I feel that in many significant ways it does not do justice to Hutchins. He made an extraordinary contribution to establishing a general programme in literature and social science as the most significant aspect of undergraduate training. The present day college lives on in a form not widely different from what he envisaged, much less different, indeed, than what was carried out in his name by Faust and McKeon. The programme has also been widely imitated throughout the United States.

Finally, I will most sincerely claim that I have never seen better students and have never enjoyed teaching as much as in the Division of Humanities, the Humanities Course (1939-46) and in the Committee on Social Thought. The great contributions of Hutchins – the emphasis on original texts, the encouragement of an independent mindset in students, the freshness and originality of the atmosphere at its best – were, indeed, invaluable and they were undeniably and characteristically his. Whatever was undesirable was the result either of dissension between Hutchins and the departments or his ill luck or ill judgement in the choice of his agents of change.

CHAPTER 14

POLITICS AS PSYCHOLOGY AS POLITICS:
A READING OF *MACBETH*[1]

DEIRDRE LEVINSON

AS THE SCATTERED NOBILITY OF SCOTLAND, EMBOLDENED BY THE APPROACH of the English power under Malcolm, assemble to join forces with it, Caithness – significantly making his first appearance in the play at the latter end of it – exhorts Lennox to prepare to shed his last drop of blood in their country's defence. "Or so much as it needs", replies the chicken-hearted Lennox, voicing the underside of his fellow-thane's grandiloquence with the craven self-interest which, with the single exception of Macduff, is the hallmark of the entire Scottish nobility. "Thy kingdom's pearl", Macduff calls them, without apparent irony, as they hail Malcolm king of Scotland. With such pearl, Malcolm might well ask, who needs paste? These are the self-same thanes who, within hours of discovering the murder of Duncan, forswearing – in accordance with their general preference for disowning knowledge[2] – their avowed intent "To know it further", named Macbeth king of Scotland. Thus, the first of the items on the agenda the politic Malcolm announces in his inaugural address to the thanes at the play's finale takes the form of a ritual act signifying the transformation of their character. In the presence of Macbeth's severed head he renames them:

> Henceforth be Earls; the first that ever Scotland
> In such an honour nam'd.

Malcolm has no illusions about the treacherous nature of the thanes he

185

inherits along with the crown. He learnt that lesson effectively the morning after his father's murder, to the frustration of Macbeth's many plausible agents duly commissioned to reel him in. But neither does he cherish illusions about the nature of his father's reign that gave treason such scope. The victorious young king who has commanded his army in person is a far cry from the infirm old king who owes the successful outcome of his war to deputies. As his father's constant attendant in that war, serving, indeed, as the eyes of the myopic old king, Malcolm observes at first hand the frantic extremes he resorts to at its conclusion. Duncan is walking on eggs; his kingdom is barely unified, his kingship barely pulled out of the fire. The defeat of the rebels notwithstanding, their violent threat to his rule has evidently exacerbated his unconscious ambivalence about his fitness to rule (a trait common to Shakespeare's usurped kings). Hence his hectic show of omnipotence in ordering the summary execution of Cawdor, in flagrant disregard of due process and on evidence as flimsy as the grounds for his former "absolute trust". And hence too, at the other extreme – as if it were not his royal prerogative to reserve the choicest title in his gift for his eldest, Malcolm; as if he feels the title of Cawdor insufficient reward for his salvaged kingship – the devious lengths to which he goes to propitiate Macbeth, professing to owe him "more than all can pay", yet not him exclusively, Banquo too, "That hast no less deserv'd". Immediately upon which, in the presence of those "whose places are the nearest", he names Malcolm as his successor.

Such a plethora of double-talk from the king's own mouth, such raising and dashing of hopes, such giving with one hand, taking away with the other, this is the ideal stuff for the prescient witches to turn to commodity. As we know, they are having a field day.

At this point – for Malcolm has yet to mature – only the witches, hovering like an opportunistic disease "through the fog and filthy air" of Duncan's Scotland, are aware of how crucially the tremulous Duncan has contributed to his country's imminent ruin. His thanes see no fault in him as they see none in themselves. Quite overlooking their active collaboration in Macbeth's ascendancy, they "pine" for the day when they "may again . . . / Do faithful homage" (as they did at Duncan's, then at Macbeth's, coronation) "and receive free honours" (free as Duncan's appropriation of Cawdor's title to honour Macbeth). They and Duncan are mirror-images of each other, the aged king and the loose confederation of insubordinate chieftains under his flaccid command alike holdovers of an obsolescent power-structure. Their Scotland – so readily to be given over to a reign of terror recalling in its savagery "th'olden time,/ Ere humane statute purg'd the gentle weal" – is still in its barbarous age, the habitation of witches, a land pervasively befogged, where nothing is clear, its laws indeterminate, the succession itself so ill-defined – hereditary, or elective, or both – as virtually to ensure that the throne is up for grabs.

Though Macbeth and Banquo are competitors for the throne from the first, Macbeth, who fleeces his peasants at home as avidly as he butchers his opponents in battle, is by far the better equipped of the two to do the needful, and by far the readier to do it. As the witches know, in his spectacular defence of Duncan's sovereignty – his "personal venture" against the rebels, the "self-comparisons" with which he confronts the invading Norway – his covert intent is to crush these assorted contestants for the prize he has marked out as his own. That is why "the day of success" is the day the timely witches appoint for their meeting with him. Evil in the imagination of his heart, he has so long and so freely indulged his fantasy of murderous usurpation that the witches have only to hail him "King hereafter" to actualise his elliptical thought "whose murder yet is but fantastical" (with the emphasis on "yet"). The thought is not new to his lady either. As appears from her volcanic response to his studiedly inflammatory letter, and more particularly from her outrage at his eleventh-hour demurral –

> What beast was't then,
> That made you break this enterprise to me?
> . . . Nor time, nor place
> Did then adhere, and yet you would make both –

this enterprise has long been their pillow-talk. This is what they have been living for.

As ignorant of Macbeth's nature as she is of her own, Lady Macbeth fears in him the same impediments to the golden round, the same vulnerability in his moral, as in her physical, nature. But, in fact, as we see from the first, when Ross brings him the title of Cawdor, Macbeth has so contrived to dissociate his conscience from his consciousness that he recognises his guilt in his surfacing intention only by the effect of its image upon his senses. It is his affronted senses, involuntarily doing the punitive work of his conscience, that bring his guilt home to him when the time comes. His conscious mind, long since licensed to entertain itself with regicidal fantasies, harbours no moral imperatives. He diligently itemises the moral prohibitions against his imminent assassination of Duncan, but only under the heading of "when 'tis done". His sumptuous imagination, notwithstanding its spectacular capacity to body forth the whole Christian cosmos with all its exalted properties, only masks the moral vacuum at his centre. Thus, electrifyingly as his imagination, projecting (like its proprietor, always a jump ahead) the consequences of his impending crime, pictures for him Duncan's clamorous innocence uniting heaven and earth in his cause –

> his virtues
> Will plead like angels, trumpet-tongu'd, against
> The deep damnation of his taking-off;
> And Pity, like a naked new-born babe,
> Striding the blast, or heaven's Cherubins, hors'd
> Upon the sightless couriers of the air,
> Shall blow the horrid deed in every eye,
> That tears shall drown the wind –

this amounts to no more than his fear of retribution – not in the life to come, which he has already expressed his willingness to "jump", but "here", in this one.

Lady Macbeth is the active, Banquo the passive, accomplice of Macbeth in the murder of Duncan. No sooner have the witches all-hailed their man than Banquo (though not without first adverting pointedly to Macbeth's telltale perturbation) demands their equal attention. The essential components of Banquo's character are encapsulated here in his long-range, narrow-eyed rivalry with his "noble partner" – immediately apparent in his concern to know specifically "which grain will grow, and which will not" – and in the sanctimony with which he habitually conceals his corruptibility from himself – "Speak then to me, who neither beg, nor fear,/ Your favours nor your hate".

With Duncan's murder still in the works, Macbeth refrains from apprising his wife of the dynastic prophecy to Banquo, though the unappeasable sense of incompleteness at the core of his being (the magnetic focus of the "imperfect speakers") already has him scheduling Banquo next-in-line for the kill. First things first, however, to ensure his accession he needs the compliance, tacit as may be, of this reverend thane. Instantly apprehending, on his instant elevation to the title of Cawdor, that Banquo's hopes ride on his tails, he urges him, as they resume their interrupted way towards the king, to "Think upon what hath chanc'd", the better to prepare for a frank exchange of confidences, "The Interim having weigh'd it".

But Macbeth knows no interims. Not until he is on his murderous way to the sleeping king, whom Banquo has just seen to bed, do the two, their paths crossing in the starless dark, have a private word again. Meanwhile, Banquo has, indeed, as agreed ("Very gladly"), been thinking upon what hath chanced, but to such bedevilling effect that now – as his self-deceiving sanctimony proves no substitute for inner restraint – "the cursed thoughts" surfacing in dreams he seems to recognise as wish-fulfilments make him afraid to sleep, afraid even of footsteps in the dark on his way to bed ("Give me my sword./ Who's there?"). That it is he, nonetheless, who broaches the subject –

> I dreamt last night of the three Weird Sisters:
> To you they have show'd some truth –

that he now uncritically designates as "some truth" what he so very recently imputed to the long-range malignity of "The instruments of Darkness" is a measure of his progressive capitulation to his dynastic fantasy as it is likewise a measure of the unbridgeable gulf it has fixed between him and those "merciful Powers" he unavailingly appealed to just a moment earlier.

Macbeth, over-extended as he is at this point, postpones discussion of "that business" (a euphemism he otherwise reserves for his prospective murders), but, never one to miss a trick, doesn't fail at the same time to capitalise on the moment with an offer Banquo can't refuse:

> If you shall cleave to my consent, when 'tis,
> It shall make honour for you.

So the two of them cut a deal: Banquo, while discreetly hedging his bets with a prolonged curtsy to the pieties, tacitly agrees to lend his countenance to Macbeth's usurpation, "when 'tis", in the prospect of due enlargement from the royal bounty. This interpretation of their cryptic interchange is borne out by the course of Banquo's actions subsequent to the discovery of Duncan's murder the following morning.

Momentarily sickened by the evil news, first imploring Macduff to contradict himself, as is his own familiar practise, "And say, it is not so", Banquo thereafter refrains from comment till, duly heedful of Macbeth – by now in desperate plight, both feet in his mouth – he calls for the unclothed assembly to disband, "And when we have our naked frailties hid,/ That suffer in exposure" (as he puts it, with a glance at Macbeth), to reconvene to investigate the crime. With which, drawing copiously on his unfailing resources of cant, he proceeds to announce, to general acclaim, his exemplary position on the regicide:

In the great hand of God I stand; and thence
Against the undivulg'd pretence I fight
Of treasonous malice.

It is not, however, as shortly appears, the great hand of God, but the
bloody hand of Macbeth he is standing in; thence, far from investigating
the treason, let alone fighting it, he, with the rest of those "That would
make good of bad" at his heel, names Macbeth king that very day.

The next time we see Banquo – his preferment delivered as promised,
mainstay of the king's council, "chief guest" at the forthcoming royal
banquet – he is in the palace soliloquising, unceremoniously addressing
himself in fantasy to the newly-crowned Macbeth. He starts off with a
reproving wag of the finger at the regicide he has so promptly legitimised:

Though hast it now, King, Cawdor, Glamis, all,
As the Weird Women promis'd; and, I fear,
Thou play'dst most foully for't.

With which he summarily changes course, for the matter, not the manner,
of Macbeth's attaining the crown is Banquo's vital concern. As his dynastic
hopes soar commensurably with Macbeth's ascendancy, he now sees his
way clear to realising his consuming desire for parity with the man to
whom he has so unvaryingly played second fiddle. "Yet it was said,/ It
should not stand in thy posterity": not sticking to doctor what was actually
said to sweeten his triumph, he proceeds to calculate the likely fulfilment
of his hopes on the model of the now complete fulfilment of the promises
to Macbeth:

If there come truth from them
(As upon thee, Macbeth, their speeches shine),
Why, by the verities on thee made good,
May they not be my oracles as well,
And set me up in hope?

So his initial view of their provenance ("What! can the Devil speak true?")
is now completely reversed, "The instruments of Darkness" transformed
into instruments of light, "oracles", their utterances to luminescent truths,
"verities" sanctified in their fulfilment; and the crime to which Macbeth
owes his success, as it is equally the crime to which Banquo owes the
blossoming of his hopes, disavowed. With this it is clear that his
maturating corruption is now full-blown.

While Banquo has lost no time in transferring his allegiance from Duncan to Duncan's murderer –

> Let your Highness
> Command upon me, to the which my duties
> Are with a most indissoluble tie
> For ever knit –

his Highness too has lost none in lining up his equally dutiful hit-men ("We shall, my Lord,/ Perform what you command us"). Inevitably, Macbeth's reign is to be a reign of terror, his "cause of State" a cut-throat obstacle race in pursuit of that safety, the attainment of which – like his father's title ("By Sinel's death I know I am Thane of Glamis") – for him, from the first, necessarily incurs a death. Macbeth's pathological insecurity, his inveterate sense of himself as an incomplete man (unrecompensed by the titles he didn't kill for), is the genesis of all his crimes. The engulfing fear he brings with him to the throne, however ("To be thus is nothing, but to be safely thus"), is the immediate consequence of his murder of Duncan. His imagination has proved to be an unreliable ally of his evil will, acting upon his desire as much drink, according to the Porter, acts upon lechery: "it sets him on, and it takes him off". If it set him on in the form of the hallucinated dagger he is later to claim "led" him to Duncan, it set him off with a vengeance once the deed was done. His concentrated experience then, under the onslaught of his revolted senses, of unprecedentedly inescapable guilt and unbearable terror of that guilt necessitated a radical operation on his consciousness: "To know my deed, 'twere best not know myself." That "myself" is his guilt: he is to disown the knowledge, not of his deed (shortly to be repeated), but of the guilt belonging to its doer. With this policy he ascends the throne.

Accordingly, in the hours preceding Banquo's assassination, he variously accounts (to himself, to the hired assassins, to his wife) for its necessity on the grounds that Banquo is threatening his safety – that very safety he had thought to ensure by way of murdering Duncan "to gain our peace", to achieve the "greatness" that would have made him perfect, had not Banquo, intimidating the witches (so his argument runs), commandeered for his own "seeds" the succession they had meant for Macbeth's, thereby robbing his portion of all its efficacy, leaving him with nothing to show for his defiled mind, envenomed peace, forfeited soul, but "a fruitless crown", "a barren sceptre". Banquo, in effect, has rendered him sterile. He thus imputes to Banquo both the unconscious cause and the disowned consequence of his regicide, identifying himself ("our innocent self") with the murdered and usurped old king, Banquo – his notional assailant ("every minute of his being thrusts/ Against my near'st of life") – with the old king's murderous usurper.

But Macbeth's guilt will not be so cheated. No sooner is he apprised of the news (brought right into the banquet-hall, where it belongs) of Banquo's dispatch "With twenty trenched gashes on his head", than his hapless imagination, sparked by this graphic particular, proceeds to perform as if bidden ("Would he were here!"), its projective function before his appalled eyes. Even so, this time he "dare look on that/ Which might appal the Devil"; his eye is no longer "the eye of childhood" it was in the hour of his first murder ("Look on't again I dare not"). Terrorised to madness as he is again by the image of his guilt – this time in public – and compelled as he is by the image of the murdered Banquo to experience as a reality the malevolence (the threat to his safety, his manhood, his throne) he imputed to the living Banquo, he nevertheless dares defy it, challenge it, indignantly protest this new order of resurrected murdered men who "push us from our stools".

The party is barely over before he has the foolproof cure for his ailment literally at hand: an accelerated course of murder ("For mine own good") guaranteed to immunise him to fear by "hard use" and, at the same time, to preclude any further imaging of his deeds ("Which must be acted, ere they may be scann'd") by short-circuiting the dangerous interval between the "strange things" in his head and their enactment. Reinforced by the shows the witches lay on for him the next morning in the same hour as word comes of Macduff's flight to England, this resolve proves appropriate for his purposes: "I have almost forgot the taste of fears," as he says in response to the cry announcing his wife's death, which he lacks the wherewithal to mourn. Now that he has "supp'd full with horrors", his erstwhile frenzy has given place to a monstrous ennui, all tomorrows indistinguishable from all yesterdays, his leached vision of the utter aridity of his own life encompassing all life as his death-wish encompasses the whole "estate o' th' world". The unsleeping scourge of Scotland, "aweary of the sun", wants to take it all down with him as he goes into battle companionless against the invading army of ten thousand warlike men abundantly augmented by his own deserters.

It is Macbeth's fate, inscribed in his psyche, to suffer in this life, consciously and to the full, the retribution he initially wishfully consigned to the after-life. He thus consciously suffers, in this last phase of his life,

192

the ultimate state of the damned (to which, according to Dante, the souls of those fixed in the ice of the ninth circle often fall before their bodies die), forever isolated by his relentless self-dehumanisation from the human fellowship he knows he "must not look to have". It is his sustained consciousness of his remorseless mind's agony, in its icebound as in its fevered season, the merciless exactness with which he unfailingly gives it voice, that enforces our identification with him, beyond his massacre of the innocents at Fife, to the end.

The regeneration of Scotland is first signalled by Macduff's flight to the English court for that purpose. How limited that regeneration is to be, however, is more pointedly signalled by the scene at Fife, in which the character of this saviour of Scotland – what manner of a man is he in leaving his family undefended "in a place/ From whence himself does fly" – is submitted to critical inquiry by his wife and one of his babes. What the ubiquitous Ross, himself poised for flight, prefers to call wisdom, the erect and plain-speaking Lady Macduff calls madness, cowardice, betrayal, which prompts the little boy – who, in the matter of manliness ("He has kill'd me, mother:/ Run away I pray you!"), has much to teach his father and every man in this play – to raise the pivotal questions: "Was my father a traitor, mother?" and "What is a traitor?" Though both wife and son, closing ranks against the murderers' denunciation ("He's a traitor"), defend Macduff's character literally to the death, his betrayal, while distinguished in kind from his fellow-thanes', nonetheless relegates this impeccable patriot to "the bill/ That writes them all alike".

Meanwhile, the political credentials of the fugitive husband and father, put to Malcolm's battery of tests, are not found wanting. Exploding at last under his racking cross-examination – "Thy royal father/ Was a most sainted king" – he anathematises Malcolm as a prince of the blood who "does blaspheme his breed". Here, Macduff, though fooled literally to a fare-three-well, puts his finger on Malcolm's innermost secret, for, under cover of claiming an appetite for evil so egregious that beside it "black Macbeth/ Will seem as pure as snow", Malcolm has involuntarily acted out the oedipal core of his wish to dissociate himself from his father. Otherwise, his feelings about him never break cover. In fact, from the time of his reappearance in the play in Act IV, though it is evident in all his proceedings how studiously he has reflected in his sojourn at the miracle-healing King Edward's court upon his father's insalubrious reign, Malcolm never mentions his father at all. His oblique glance, by way of explaining himself to Macduff, at Duncan's negative example – "modest wisdom plucks me/ From over-credulous haste" – is as close as he comes to voicing his message that, Duncan's blood though he be, he is nothing allied to Duncan's disorders. But Macduff's canonisation of the bumbling old king is not therefore unwelcome to Malcolm's ears. His piety is integral to his fierce passion to restore his suffering country to legitimate rule, and this passion – so all-consuming as to eclipse his more urgent familial obligations – is the perfect complement of Malcolm's calculated measures to achieving that end. Malcolm has already mobilised the army from England in advance of Macduff's hotfoot arrival there for that purpose: "Now we'll together." As he everywhere demonstrates in this scene, not least in his readiness to capitalise on Macduff's appalling bereavement, his success is a foregone conclusion.

Malcolm comes to the throne alone in his knowledge that in the old order the terrorised thanes have yearned for (as in Ross's idle wish to have things return "To what they were before"; as in the "wholesome days" of that Scotland of Macduff's idealised memory) lay the cause of Scotland's ruin. His renaming of the thanes in his inaugural address to them thus signifies, beyond its ritual function, his introduction of a new order no less sharply distinguished from his father's than from the tyranny it gave rise to. Nevertheless, Malcolm's bright new order bears the stamp of the same old pernicious stereotype, the same old dehumanising idea of manhood writ large in Macbeth's and Lady Macbeth's pathology. Indeed, Malcolm, exhorting the desolated Macduff to "Dispute it like a man", duplicates the very tones of Lady Macduff in her prime. "But I must also feel like a man", Macduff protests out of his heart's blood. Even so, he is to betray his moment of truth a moment later. As he submitted his heart's affections ("He wants the natural touch") to the urgency of the time, he now, forbearing to "play the woman" with his eyes, submits the fullness of his mourning likewise to the time's demands, much to Malcolm's relief ("This tune goes manly"). Thus, while the rampant disease afflicting Scotland's body politic is killed with Macbeth, its chronic disease of the heart (though by no means exclusively Scotland's heart, as Old Siward chillingly demonstrates), as it looks to be enshrined in Malcolm's new order, casts a long shadow on Scotland's future.

CHAPTER 15

POLITE LETTERS AND CLIO'S FASHIONS

JOHN LUKACS

MY TITLE DERIVES, IN PART, FROM MY READING OF THE EXCELLENT bicentennial history of the Royal Irish Academy.[1] "Polite Literature" was one of the sections of the Academy at its beginning. Indeed, its charter of incorporation defined the purpose of the Academy as "promoting the study of science, polite literature and antiquities".[2] The Chancellor of the University of Dublin, Professor WB Stanford, in his excellent chapter devoted to the history of that section, was elegantly apologetic about this. "Polite," he wrote, "obviously carried associations with a standard of elegance and refinement suitable for an Academy that was intended to be a 'select society of gentlemen'. But it would not be long before the era of dilettantism and amateurism in literary and linguistic scholarship would come into disrepute."[3] To which I now add that a similar, and perhaps analogous, development had occurred not only within literary, but also historical, scholarship. I further read that during the nineteenth century "historical topics became commoner" in the Transactions and Proceedings of the Academy; and then, in 1901, the Academy changed the title of the section from "Polite Literature and Antiquities" to "Archaeology, Linguistics and Literature". As Professor Stanford wrote, this showed a kind of demotion of "literature to a third place, but still, rather curiously, subsuming history under either Literature or Archaeology, despite the pleas of Bury and others that it was essentially a science".[4]

Now, the purpose of my discourse is to propose that there is no longer any reason to be apologetic about the phrase Polite Literature or, as I put it in my title, Polite Letters. I chose this title for my discourse not because of a *captatio benevolentiae* and not out of a wish to make some kind of a sly or arch reference to a phrase sodden with antiquated charm. To the contrary: my argument is that near the end of the twentieth century that phrase may be more timely than we are accustomed to think; that what is antiquated and corroded is the insistence of JB Bury and others (stated by Bury in the very first year of this century) that history is essentially *a science*; that when, at the end of the eighteenth century, the gentlemen of the Royal Irish Academy inclined to consider literature and history together they were not altogether wrong. What has happened, after two centuries, is that the relative hierarchy within their alliance has changed. It is not history that is a part of literature, but it is literature that shows signs of becoming a part of history, in a new and broader sense of that word, in the sense that history is more than a discipline: it is – or, more precisely, it has become – a form of thought.

Everything has its history, including history. A distinct historical consciousness – as distinct from historical existence, and then from historical thinking – may be said to have arisen only three or four hundred years ago in Western Europe and England. Consequently, during the eighteenth century the appetite of all kinds of readers for all kinds of history rose. So, during the last three centuries we may discern the following large developments. In the eighteenth century history was seen as literature. In the nineteenth century, largely (though not exclusively) because of the solid achievements of German scholarship, history was seen as a science – a development that reached England and Ireland more slowly and more hesitantly than elsewhere (which is why at the end of that century Bury's insistence that history was a science was already outdated). We must consider too that the word "science" in that century had a more spacious meaning than it has acquired since. It was somewhat akin to the German *Wissenschaft*, meaning both science and knowledge (the word "scientist", in English, appears only in the second half of the nineteenth century). Thus during two centuries history advanced from literature to science. And what about the twentieth century, near the end of which we now live, whereby we have the opportunity for a certain retrospect? About it we cannot make such a general statement. It seems, rather, that we are in the presence of two, essentially conflicting, different and divergent tendencies. One still dominant tendency is to consider history as social science. The other is to consider history as a form of thought.

196

The consideration of history as a social science has sprung from several sources. The main one of these has been the general reluctance of academic historians to relinquish the prestige that the scientific notion of history brought to their profession – and thus to themselves. That was not only the result of the general acceptance, by 1914, of the PhD degree conferred upon historians throughout the world. It corresponded (and it still corresponds) to a general belief among the peoples of the world (a belief that had not existed a century earlier) to the effect that the historian is but another scientific specialist, that is, a professionally accredited scientific student of records. That such a narrow concept of the historian reduces him, in effect, to that of an archivist (as it reduces too the view of the past to merely that of the recorded, and not of the remembered, past) has not been recognised. (Nor has it been recognised that there is no difference between a source and a "historical" source, or between a document and a "historical" document.) Gradually during this century a slight, because inadequate, variant of the older nineteenth-century concept of history as a science gained acceptance: the notion that, well, if history is not quite like a science it is surely a social science of a certain kind. I say "inadequate" because most historians were fain to recognise the essential difference that men such as Dilthey had proposed as early as 1875, namely, the difference between *Naturwissenschaften* and *Geisteswissenschaften*, issuing from the comprehension that man's knowledge of man is essentially different from his knowledge of other, less complex organisms and matters. This is so not only because of the complexity of the human being, but because, perhaps especially in the case of history, the observer and the observed belong to the same species. As a consequence, not only the subjects of historical knowledge, but the very conditions, indeed, the nature of that knowledge itself, differ from the so-called natural sciences. Throughout the twentieth century we may observe evidences of a lamentable split-mindedness among many historians who will nod at criticisms of historical determinism as if those were truisms; and yet they go on writing and teaching history as if history *were* determined.

Another reason for the acceptance of history as a social science has been a more honourable one. One hundred years ago it was largely taken for granted what the English historian JR Seeley, the Regius Professor of Modern History at Cambridge, wrote: "history is past politics and politics present history". This was not very different from the standard nineteenth-century view as expressed, for example, by Droysen, who said that "the statesman is the historian in practice", or by Ranke, who saw history as concerned mainly with the life and the relations of states. Yet with the development of universal literacy and modern mass democracy it was already evident that a restriction of historical study to politics resulted in too narrow a scope; that history of governments and their relations, no matter how decisive and important, cannot but consider the history of the governed; that, in other words, the history of states must, on occasion, become both broadened and deepened by contemplating the history of peoples, including conditions of their everyday lives. With all due respect to the important achievements of the French *Annales* school, beginning shortly before the First World War, allow me to say that their recognition of this need was – or should have been – already a foregone conclusion at the time. What Oscar Wilde said about some men "who pursue the obvious with the enthusiasm of a short-sighted detective" must not be applied to those French social and intellectual historians of the *Annales* school such as Lucien Febvre or Marc Bloch, whose work, in retrospect, not only deserves our respect, but is worthy of emulation. But the pursuit of what seems to be intellectually fashionable and professionally profitable amounts to a temptation to which many scholars are, alas, not immune. The results are all around us, ranging from the huge confections of Monsieur Fernand Braudel, to the often unreadable and sometimes even ludicrous publications of specialists. On the one hand, we are faced with the boundless, and senseless, pretensions of someone like Braudel to the effect that what he had attempted, and achieved, is the *total* history of a place and of a period. On the other hand, we are faced with a disintegration of the discipline of history, through its implicit disregard of the political thread that, no matter how roughly, had once bound and still binds together the history of nations. This disintegration has created not only specialised "fields" such as social history and economic history and intellectual history, but such "fields" as black history and women's history – pursued, alas, by ambitious men and women who seem to be rather less interested in the history of their people, and sometimes not even in that of their subjects, than in the prospect of their standing in the academy: that is, not in history, but historianship. The verminous fads of Quantification and Psychohistory are only extreme examples of the social-scientific attitude, with its wrongheaded practices of a thoughtless borrowing and adaptation not only of the methodology and the language of the natural sciences, but of the questionable terminology of Freudian psychoanalysis (about which another Viennese once wrote that it is the disease of which it pretends to be the cure). Thus *corruptio pessimi pessima*; but even for the *optimi* the acceptance of history as a social science has resulted in something that might appear as a more sophisticated and up-to-date way of dealing with history, whereas it is hardly more than a retrospective (and therefore hopelessly shortsighted) kind of sociology.

* * *

The alternative to this devolution, I propose, is the recognition of history as a form of thought – indeed, as a dominant form of thought in the twentieth century, consequent to the evolution of our historical consciousness during the last three hundred years; to a gradual evolution of our minds that in the very long run may be more profound than the discovery of the scientific method three hundred years ago. The phrase "history as a form of thought" is essentially epistemological. It suggests an historical philosophy that is the very opposite of a philosophy of history. It recognises the futility of attempts to define universal laws or patterns for the knowledgeability of history. It issues from the recognition of the historicity of knowledge and – this is important – of language. Thus it may be said that implicit in the recognition of history as a form of thought lies the recognition that "facts" of history are merely so-called, since they are neither hard, nor distinctly isolable; that no fact exists by itself, but that its meaning depends on its association with other facts; that facts are not separable from the words in which they are expressed; that the statement of every fact depends on its purposes; that history is not only written, but spoken and taught and remembered in words and, moreover, in words that are not those of a scientific terminology, but words of the common and everyday language; indeed, that words themselves are not merely the symbols of *things*, but that they are symbols of *meanings* – meanings that in themselves have been formed by history.

Now, unlike the social-scientific school (if that is what it is), those who see history in this way do not coalesce into a school of thought. But they, often tucked away in the oddest places, have their great forerunners, historians such as Tocqueville, Burckhardt, Huizinga, in whose published works, lectures and letters we find recognitions and elaborations of what I have tried to summarise above. Space does not allow for a detailed account of the pedigree of this alternative recognition of what history consists of.

But I shall briefly turn to Jakob Burckhardt for two reasons. The first is the indisputable recognition that he was the founder of what we may call cultural history, something that is truer than are any pretensions to "total history", since what Burckhardt achieved was the historical representation of both the cultural forms and the modes of thinking of a certain place and time, often (though not always and not necessarily) expressed in its art. My second purpose in citing Burckhardt is to draw attention to the wisdom inherent in the humility of his purpose. "I never dreamed of training scholars and disciples in the narrower sense," he wrote in a letter:

> but only wanted to make every member of the audience feel and know that everyone may and must appropriate those aspects of the past that appeal to him personally, and that there can be happiness in so doing . . . Furthermore, we must understand that when we try to immerse ourselves wholly in the reading of a classic, only *we alone* can find what is important *for us*. No reference work in the world, with its quotes, can replace that chemical bonding that mysteriously occurs when a phrase found by ourselves illuminates something in our mind, crystallising itself into a real piece of spiritual property that is ours . . . We are unscientific [*unwissenschaftlich*] and have no particular method, at least not the one professed by others.[5]

This conception, I once wrote, is something very different from amateurism as well as from subjectivism. With all of his stoic contemplation of the world, Burckhardt maintained his high faith in the potentiality of the human spirit:

> The spearhead of all culture is a miracle of mind, namely, speech, whose source, independently of the particular people and the particular language, is in the soul; otherwise, no deaf mute could be taught to speak and to understand speech. Such teaching is explicable only if there is in the soul an intimate and responsive urge to clothe thought in words.[6]

To which I should add: to *complete* thought in words; for speech is not only the clothing, but also the completion, of thought. Thus when speaking about cultural history we cannot avoid the relationship of history to language. And there are few places in the world where the consideration of that relationship is more appropriate than Ireland.

* * *

During a visit to Ireland several years ago, I found Professor FSL Lyons' important and thoughtful book, *Culture and Anarchy in Ireland, 1890-1939*. Professor Lyons' thesis is that – contrary to what Matthew Arnold had set forth – culture might not be a unifying, but a destructive force, leading to anarchy; that political problems may be the results of cultural problems; that in Ireland, surely since 1916, there was a failure "to find political solutions for problems which in reality are much more complex", because these problems are cultural, in the broadest sense of the word.[7] Now allow this foreigner to essay his comments about this important thesis.

What Professor Lyons said in this first chapter of his very valuable work is applicable not only to Ireland, but to most of the world. What he calls "culture" may be something that I might prefer to describe as "national characteristics" or "national tendencies", though I am aware that the two things are not quite the same. To put it in simpler and rougher terms: contrary to the lucubrations of Marxists and all kinds of social scientists, it is painfully evident that the main historical and political force in this world, even now, has little to do with economics. It is nationalism; and nationalism, a sense of nationality, national characteristics, national consciousness are cultural, not material, factors.

Our problem lies with a definition of "culture". I think that Matthew Arnold thought of culture and employed the term in a more narrow and aesthetic sense than we are wont to do. This is what TS Eliot implied when he found a certain "thinness" in Arnold's essay.[8] Lyons mentioned this in his crucial first chapter. But I think that Lyons was wrong when he wrote that there was "a prelapsarian innocence" in what Arnold wrote in the 1860s, because at that time (I quote Lyons) "the social sciences were still in their infancy. There were no social anthropologists or social psychologists to compel him to explain himself more intelligibly".[9] I think that Lyons, who was a first-class historian and not an academic votary of social science, gave here too much credit to the latter. In my opinion, the shortcoming of Arnold's old-fashioned essay consists in an unwitting philistinism of his own. He thought too much about art and aesthetics, and not enough about language and truth, almost like his American confrere, Emerson, who said that "the corruption of man is followed by the corruption of language", whereas it is arguable that the reverse sequence is true. To me, it seems that while one side – and a very important side – of Professor Lyons' thesis is correct, there is another side of which he was widely aware, but the importance of which he saw differently from this foreign observer: this is the tremendous asset of Ireland (and of Ireland's prestige in the world) that have been the results of the presence and of the effect of Irish genius on the literature of the English language.

Professor Lyons says somewhere that with the spreading of English and the shrinking of Gaelic during the nineteenth century "the marketplace" was bound to triumph over a remnant in the folk museum. Yet when Daniel O'Connell admitted that he did not mind the gradual disappearance of Gaelic – "I am sufficiently utilitarian not to regret its gradual passing"[10] – this was, I propose, a utilitarianism entirely different from the contemporary utilitarianism across the Irish Sea, that of poor Cobden, who wrote around the same time that he "advocated nothing but what is agreeable to the highest behests of Christianity – to buy in the cheapest market and to sell in the dearest". No: to my mind, Professor Lyons' "marketplace" was not the *mot juste*. The source and the driving force of that high mastery of the English language by Irish writers and thinkers and poets has not been utility, but attraction; not calculation, but affection, the affection that a master has not only for his tool, but for the scope and purpose of his work. To paraphrase Yeats: how can you separate the painting from the paint?

I should like briefly to refer to my native country, Hungary, because of the appositeness of a certain chapter of its history to that of Ireland at a particular time. Between 1867 and 1914 (it is uncanny how the limits of that period, from Butt to Redmond, correspond to the very same years of Hungarian history, from Deák to Tisza) many leading minds in Ireland (especially Griffith) saw in the home rule that had been secured by Hungary from Austria a reasonable and propitious model for Ireland. We also know, in retrospect, how this did not come about; and that many of its ideas proved to be illusory and outdated. Yet on a cultural – and not merely political – level (and, in terms of a *longue durée* much more meaningful than those enunciated by Braudel) some things happened that proved immensely beneficial in the long run. I am not only thinking of the sudden and extraordinary flourishing of literature and of the arts around the turn of the century, in Ireland as well as in Hungary, a flourishing that was not overcast by the pale neuroticism so evident in other cultural capitals of Europe at the time (as, for example, in Vienna and even in the London of the Yellow Book Nineties). I am thinking of a development that has been insufficiently recognised in Hungary even now. This was the extraordinary assimilation of German-speaking people in Hungary into Hungarian culture. Extraordinary indeed: because, with hardly any exceptions, this was the single such instance in Central and Eastern Europe at the time. For the German minorities before, say, 1865 their assimilation into what they saw as inferior and peasant-like peoples was unthinkable and – in more than one sense of the word – unspeakable. And yet in Hungary it happened: less because of political pressures than because of the Germans' recognition of the increasingly obvious qualities and merits of the native culture of the land where they lived. What I see here is a similarity – though not a parallel – between that Hungarian development and the identification of the Anglo-Irish with Ireland. And this would not have happened if, in the early twentieth century, the main demotic language of Ireland had not been English.

It is true, as Professor Lyons wrote, that the tragedy of the Anglo-Irish "was that, hesitating as they did between two worlds, they could never be fully accepted by either. To the English they came increasingly to seem an anachronism, to the Irish they remain an excrescence". I am not happy with that word "excrescence".[11] Or perhaps I am – not in the pejorative sense of it – because excrescence means an outgrowth; because excrescence is, after all, an organic function; and I happen to believe that much of Anglo-Irish, and also Irish-English, literature had a function more alive, and more enduring, than the sometimes bloodless appearances of Bloomsbury on the once robust tree of English letters. In this respect, I am thinking not only of world-wide celebrated writers of Irish origin such as Joyce or Shaw, but of representations such as *The Real Charlotte*, that small masterpiece which not only all lovers of English prose, but historians – and not merely historians of the Anglo-Irish – may ignore only to their loss. And I think I know that the mastery of the prose is inseparable from the deep-seated Irish loyalties of someone like Edith Somerville, who, born in the Ionian Islands, remained an Irish patriot through the most terrible and tragic years of the Troubles, probably aware of the condition of which Horace once wrote: *"patriae quis exsul se quoque fugit"* – an exile flees not only his country, but himself. Indeed, Professor Lyons himself wrote about "the man or woman in whom love of place transcended divisions based on origins, religion, or politics".[12]

* * *

"Love of place"– a phrase and reality that now makes me return to another, more recent, definition of culture: the celebrated – but senseless – one by CP Snow.[13] His thesis of the "Two Cultures" is alarmingly simple. There is a humanistic culture and a scientific one, and the solution is obvious: the humanists should know the Second Law of Thermodynamics and the scientists the *Areopagitica*. That such achievements may result in an aviary of stuffed owls should be obvious. The owl of Minerva, the Greeks told us, flies only at dusk; but *Snow's* owl will not fly. Less obvious, but more important, is the present condition: for, if there are two cultures in our world the division between them is not vertical, but horizontal. For the first time in the history of mankind there *is* a global, and therefore international, culture; a culture whose evident examples are airports that all over the world are alike; a culture whose most evident expression is a computerised and bureaucratic business language, a pseudo-scientific jargon artificially glued (not grafted) onto something that resembles Anglo-American. Yet next to – or, rather, beneath – this international language there are the national languages and cultures that are seldom translated and translatable, reflecting not only how people of different nations speak, but also how they live: not in their offices, not at their computers, not from nine to five, but after five, within their families and in their homes. In this respect, we may discern that, as this century proceeds, all *great* literature, prose as well as poetry, remains deeply national. There is no such thing as an international poem; and if there is such a thing as an international poet, he ought to be greeted – and kept – inside the waiting-lounges of airports, where he truly belongs.

But I wish to go beyond this evident recognition of the increasing presence of two cultures to propose that, in reality, there may be only one culture. The evolution of consciousness, perhaps especially in the western world, is now such that every man and woman among us is a walking cultural historian. Or, in other terms: all of us are historians by nature, while we are scientists only by choice. We must admit that history is *not* a science and can never be one: because its very unpredictability issues from the complexity of human nature, whereby the mechanical causality on which all technology and Newtonian physics depend does not apply to the history of human beings. Thus history cannot be studied scientifically – while (and this is what I mean by history being a form of thought) science can be studied historically. While history is not part of science, it is science that is part of history: because first came nature, then came man, and only then came the science of nature. It is exhilarating, at least to me, to know that this common sense truth has been confirmed by the recognitions of the greatest physicist of the twentieth century, Werner Heisenberg, who not only stated the fundamental condition of indeterminacy and uncertainty within the existence of the smallest particles of matter, but who also recognised the impossibility of separating the observer from the matter observed – whereby the epistemological recognition of man's own limitations ensues. The true scientific method can no longer assume that it deals with objects or subjects wholly apart from ourselves. To the contrary: it must take into account the process and the purpose of the observation itself – together with the inevitable limitations and suggestions of the human mind and of language. That this opens the way from the Cartesian dualism to a new, chastened, monistic view of the universe has been my conviction for a long time.

* * *

And so, nearing my conclusion, I now return to the relationship of polite letters and history. On the one hand, we are in the presence of a profound crisis in the study of history that is only partially due to the narrow-minded attraction of many of its practitioners toward something like a social science. Another element of the crisis is the inflation of materials, including records, with which the modern historian must deal. In the past, the historian was plagued by the fragmentary and insufficient survival of records. When dealing with the history of the last one hundred years (and sometimes not only with those) the problem of the historian has become the very opposite. An overwhelming mass of material threatens to suffocate him. The existence of this new condition calls (or should have called) for a drastic revision of the canons of historical research and scholarship (and perhaps of the training of future historians too). That this has not yet happened is a sorry reflection on the wanting vision and dedication of the professional historians' guild. On the other hand, we are in the presence of a growing appetite for history on the part of many people and portions of societies who in the past were hardly interested in it – a fundamental and important phenomenon which few historians have, as yet, recognised. The evidences of this burgeoning interest in history are so protean that even a superficial sketching of them would require a substantial lecture on its own. Of course appetites can be badly fed; and an interest in history, indeed, the knowledge of history, can be damnably misused. We have had enough evidence of that during the last two hundred years. But that appetite is there: and its very existence proves, at least to me, the continuing evolution of historical consciousness.

Two centuries ago it was historical consciousness and interest in history that brought about the historical novel. But I think that we must go further than that – especially in this discourse dealing with the relationship of letters with history (or with history as a form of thought).

My point is that every novel is a historical novel; and that the appearance of the novel, as a new literary form, was – like professional history – part and parcel of the same development. For a long time the novel was – and still is – seen as a new, prosaic form of the epic. Yet the novel and the epic, as Ortega y Gasset wrote in 1914:

> are precisely poles apart. The theme of the epic is the past as such: it speaks to us about a world which was and which is no longer, of a mythical age whose antiquity is not a past in the same sense as any remote historical time . . . The epic past is not *our* past. Our past is thinkable as having been the present once, but the epic past eludes identification with any possible present . . . [14]

It is not a remembered past (history is that), "but an *ideal* past".

Consider how, coming out of history, the novel grew with history. Consider, for example, not Walter Scott, but the preface with which his contemporary, Jane Austen, began *Northanger Abbey* in 1816:

> This little work was finished in 1803, and intended for immediate publication. It was disposed of to a bookseller, it was even advertised, and why the business proceeded no further, the author has never been able to learn . . . But with this, neither the author nor the public have any other concern than as some observation upon parts of the work which thirteen years have made comparatively obsolete. The public are entreated to bear in mind that thirteen years have passed since it was finished, many more since it was begun, and that during that period, places, manners, books and opinions have undergone considerable changes.

It is unnecessary to press the point: Jane Austen's concern was decidedly, evidently historical. Now consider what Thomas Hardy wrote eighty years later:

> Conscientious fiction alone it is which can excite a reflecting and abiding interest in the minds of thoughtful readers of mature age, who are weary of puerile inventions and famishing for accuracy; who consider that in representations of the world, the passions ought to be proportioned as in the world itself. This is the interest which was excited in the minds of the Athenians by their immortal tragedies, and in the minds of Londoners at the first performances of the finer plays three hundred years ago . . . [15]

Another eighty years later it is my conviction that *conscientious history* has come to replace the desideratum which Hardy stated as *conscientious fiction*. It is history which can excite a reflecting and abiding interest in the minds of thoughtful readers of mature age, who are weary (and how weary we are!) of puerile inventions and famishing for truth.

I say "truth" because I shall venture to go further than Thomas Hardy. In the first place, I claim to detect the gradual absorption of the novel (indeed, of perhaps all polite letters) by history, not at all in the form of the historical novel, but through something else, indeed, by its opposite. In the second place, I venture to see in conscientious history, as well as in what Hardy called conscientious fiction, more than the far from ignoble attempts to present a mirror of real life; I see in their purpose something not very different from what had once impelled Thucydides to write his first history: the purpose of reducing untruth.

Someone once said that women are torn between the desire to be dressed and to be undressed. This is a half-truth. Culture is not nakedness, but it is not frippery either. Like all the other Muses, Clio is an inspiration of consciousness. To speak of Clio's subconscious exhibits a stupidity that borders on the obscene. A Clio stripped of her spiritual garments is no longer a Muse; and a Clio adorned with fashionable frippery is merely an antique frump. And this is worthy of our special attention now, when we must consider that the Muses, as Hesiod told us, were the daughters of Zeus and Mnemosyne, the incarnation of memory; and when Calliope and Melpomene, the personifications of epic and tragedy, may be witnessing their sister Clio's beneficent ascent in rank.

The reduction of untruth cannot be served by an inadequately retrospective and abstract sociologisation, no matter how profitable that may be within the airless circles of professional historians straining to impress and write only for other professional historians. Allow me to paraphrase Yeats for the last time: Out of our colleges we have come; small minds, stuffy rooms; small hatreds, little art. That is one choice. The other is to recognise the truth inherent in Veronica Wedgwood's polite little formulation: "History is an art – like all the other sciences." For memory is an art, too: truly the mother of all arts.

VI

BURKE, TOCQUEVILLE, IRELAND, AMERICA

CHAPTER 16

"BURKE'S POLITICAL TESTAMENT": THOMAS HUSSEY AND THE IRISH DIRECTORY

DÁIRE KEOGH

I

EDMUND BURKE'S LETTER OF 9 DECEMBER 1796 TO REVEREND THOMAS Hussey, president of the Catholic seminary at Maynooth, has been described by Conor Cruise O'Brien as "Burke's political testament with regard to Ireland".[1] While some might dispute such an appellation, few can deny the significance of this missive. For at once we are forced to confront the paradox of Burke: his opposition to reform in England, while advocating a radical reordering of society in Ireland. At the same time, this letter, which is reprinted in full following this introduction, reflects his alarm at Ireland's rapid descent into anarchy. He partially attributed the deteriorating conditions in Ireland to the influence of the French Revolution, what Hussey called the "French Disease", the spread of Jacobin ideas that also inspired the formation of the radical Society of United Irishmen. Still, Burke identified a more sinister element propelling Ireland towards rebellion: the machinations of those whom he considered to be the real Jacobins in the country – the leaders of the Protestant Ascendancy. Burke eyed these unfolding events in his native land from his adopted home in England, but, as his letter to Hussey makes clear, this vantage point did not blur his vision.

II

From as early as 1779 Thomas Hussey was counted amongst Burke's most intimate friends.[2] As chaplain to the Spanish embassy in London, Hussey, a native of County Meath, was at the heart of a lively political and intellectual circle which included the Duke of Portland, Lord Chatham, the younger Pitt, Charles James Fox and Dr Johnson.[3] These social connections gave rise to various opportunities for Hussey. During the American Revolutionary War, a secret embassy under the leadership of Richard Cumberland, Secretary of the Board of Trade, was sent to Spain in an effort to break the Franco-Spanish alliance. At the special request of King George III, Dr Hussey joined the delegation and, despite its failure, he made an impression in the Spanish Court.[4]

But while Hussey rose to the top echelon of British society (in 1792 he was admitted a fellow of the Royal Society of London) he was despised by some. Just as John Wilkes, who represented Middlesex in parliament, had claimed that Burke's oratory "stank of whiskey and potatoes", William Drennan, the Belfast Presbyterian United Irishman, dismissed the "native broadness and vulgarity" of Hussey's brogue, finding it "strange that someone of the most ancient strain of Ireland and in foreign courts all his life should smack so strongly of the bogtrotter".[5]

Undeterred, Hussey immersed himself in the affairs of the Catholics of England and Ireland. In 1790 he was requested to represent the Committee of English Catholics in Rome in an effort to defuse the crisis produced by their "Protestation", namely, their declaration of Catholic civil and religious principles which contained a repudiation of papal authority.[6] In spite of his commitment to the Catholic cause, Hussey declined this invitation. Nonetheless, exhibiting what Burke called "a very rare union . . . of the enlightened statesman with the ecclesiastic", he argued that full Catholic emancipation was not only desirable, but essential.[7] In 1790, as the prospect of conflict between Great Britain and revolutionary France loomed on the horizon, Hussey wrote to Edmund Burke's son, Richard, asserting that "should these kingdoms be involved in a war, a further toleration of the Catholics of Ireland will become unavoidable".[8] It was absurd, he argued, to wait until necessity compelled what true policy should offer voluntarily:

Hitherto, the Catholics of that country have proceeded with proper deference and submission to the laws, in their application for redress . . . Sublimated, however, as men's minds are by the French Disease . . . one cannot foresee what a continuation of oppressive laws may work upon the minds of the people; and those of Irish Catholics are much altered within my own memory and they will not in future bear the lash of tyranny and oppression which I have seen inflicted upon them, without resisting or even complaining.

Such arguments reflected the unity of sentiment which existed between Hussey and Edmund Burke. As the decade progressed their relationship deepened, and the priest eventually became his principal Irish correspondent.

III

The bulk of Burke's writings on Ireland constitute a concerted attack against the Protestant Ascendancy. While the Glorious Revolution of 1688 had restored the Constitution in England, in Ireland it had proved an unmitigated disaster for Catholics. The Revolution facilitated the establishment of a sectarian Protestant state buttressed by the provisions of the penal laws, which, in Burke's own words, had "divided the nation into two distinct bodies". "One of these bodies was to possess *all* the franchises, *all* the property, *all* the education: the other was to be composed of drawers of water and cutters of turf for them."[9] Burke attacked not only the injustice of the system, but its folly. The laws had failed to destroy Catholicism in Ireland, they had impoverished the island and were the root cause of the problems of government. The solution lay in gradual reform and the removal of the penal disabilities; such advances would be dependant upon the good will of Irish Protestants and the English, but Burke constantly urged Irish Catholics to assert the justice of their case and to maintain pressure for reform.[10] When conditions demanded it, however, Burke counselled a more subtle approach. In 1779, for instance, the British government seemed disposed to playing the Catholic Card in order to counterbalance Irish Protestant sympathy for the American War of Independence, so Burke urged Catholics to keep themselves quiet, to show themselves dutiful to the crown.[11] Such clear-headed advice demonstrates Burke's political shrewdness, his steady grasp of the need to correlate tactics to circumstances.

In the 1790s Burke's principal concern was the spread of Jacobinism; in Ireland this crusade was intimately related to his assault upon the Protestant Ascendancy, which he believed lay at the heart of Irish Catholic disaffection. Hussey's writing reflects similar sentiments. More important, as Burke's principal Irish correspondent, the cleric's alarming reports on the condition of Ireland fuelled Burke's anxiety. Hussey sent one such warning in February 1795 when the Irish parliamentarian Henry Grattan introduced a Catholic Relief Bill into the Irish House of Commons (a legislative body that possessed limited powers and was dominated by a

Protestant Ascendancy membership). Hussey urged Burke to impress upon the British government that Grattan's measure, which proposed the abolition of the bar against Catholics sitting in parliament, in reality involved "another awful one – whether they mean to retain Ireland or abdicate it to a French government, or to a revolutionary system of its own intention".[12]

The recall one month later of the esteemed Viceroy of Ireland, Lord Fitzwilliam, his replacement by the Earl of Camden (John Jeffreys Pratt) and the consequent defeat of the Relief Bill astonished Hussey, who had recently arrived in Ireland to assist in the establishment of a proposed Catholic seminary. "How in the name of God," he asked Burke, "can the spirit of this nation bear [that] the most popular and virtuous viceroy that ever came to this country should be removed?"[13] He continued, with reference to the Irish House of Commons:

> The people begin to view the interference of the British cabinet in a hostile light . . . They will wish for a separation from Great Britain and the contemptible light in which they will view their own parliament will induce them to lay it in the dust and to erect a convention on the French scale in its place.

This was the defining moment in the political development of the 1790s.[14] Ireland was poised on the brink of civil war, constitutional reform channels were blocked and the new viceroy, the Earl of Camden, arrived with specific instructions to "rally the friends of the Protestant interest".[15]

Hussey intended to return to England, but remained in Ireland at the request of the Duke of Portland, the Home Secretary, to ensure the progress of the Catholic seminary, duly established at Maynooth in County Kildare. Hussey's satisfaction at being appointed the first president of the College was unquestionable: in November 1796 he assured Burke that Maynooth was his "favourite spot, this *punctum saliens* of the salvation of Ireland from Jacobinism and anarchy".[16]

Yet Hussey's position became more complicated in August 1796 when Pope Pius VI granted him vicarial authority over the King's forces in Ireland. William Pitt, by now the Chief Minister in the British cabinet, knew Hussey to be a staunch anti-Jacobin and confirmed this appointment in the belief that he would help stamp out disaffection in the ranks.[17] Following his appointment, Hussey began to seek redress for what he regarded as a gross injustice: the practice of forcing Catholic soldiers to attend Protestant services. This problem was not new, but it had become more acute in 1793 when the government established a second-line militia force (the Irish Militia), the rank and file of which were predominantly Catholic. The issue came to a head in 1795 with the case of Private James Hyland of the Irish Light Dragoons, who had been sentenced by a court martial at Carrick-on-Suir to 200 lashes for refusing, on the advice of his confessor, to attend Protestant services. Hussey complained to Burke about Hyland's treatment and also raised the question with Lord Fitzwilliam, whom he urged to issue a proclamation against such practices. Burke, in turn, warned Fitzwilliam that the French revolutionary war against religion could only benefit from a civil war in Ireland.[18]

In the autumn of 1796 there were further reports that the men of the Irish militia regiments stationed at Ardfinnan Camp in County Tipperary were being compelled to attend Protestant services. Hussey attempted in vain to meet the viceroy or his secretary; both, he informed Burke in November, "were too busy settling their bargains with the orators of College Green" (the Protestant parliamentarians in Dublin) to afford him a meeting.[19] This alienation from Dublin Castle, the seat of the British administration in Ireland, alarmed Hussey, particularly as recent approaches from several military corps prompted him to describe for Burke the dire alternatives now facing Irish Catholics: "the two evils of oppression, or Jacobinism". If the consequences of the latter choice were alarming, the causes were clear. Hussey placed responsibility for the disturbed state of Ireland at the door of the so-called "junto", the coterie of Ascendancy jobbers who surrounded the viceroy at the Castle:

> How little does His Majesty suspect, that those upon whom he heaps honours, and powers here, are his greatest enemies and the very men who are Jacobinising the country! They are urging these cursed sentiments throughout the country under the name of United Irishmen, this evil is extending beyond imagination . . . I am terrified at what I foresee regarding my own unfortunate country. To pass by parliament, and break the connection with Great Britain, is I am informed the plan of the United Irishmen. The wretches never consider that their grievances are not from England but from a junto of their own countrymen.

It was actually this dire warning from Hussey in November 1796 that prompted Burke's letter of 9 December – what Conor Cruise O'Brien calls "Burke's political testament with regard to Ireland".[20] It is, indeed, an extraordinary missive which openly expresses Burke's sympathy for the rebellious Irish Catholics.[21]

At the heart of all of Burke's great crusades was his opposition to the abuse of power. How then was he to respond to Hussey's image of the Catholic soldier, "with down cast head, and arms, whipped like a quadruped to a hostile church, by a little Tyrranizing Officer"?[22] This ill-treatment of Catholic soldiers roused Burke's emotions as had the judicial murder of Fr Nicholas Sheehy at Clonmel in 1766. On that occasion he gathered material to write about the case – just as Voltaire had exposed the murder of Calas in France.[23] In December 1796 Burke expressed his anger in his extended letter to Hussey and granted him permission to "shew [it] to all those (and they are but very few) who may be disposed to think well of my opinion".

Motivated by his disgust at the spectre of a soldier called to church "not by the bell, but by the whip", Burke initiated a renewed assault on his favourite enemy, the Protestant Ascendancy. In 1767 Burke had attributed the "rottenness of the country . . . to the ill policy of government towards the body of the subjects there" – referring, of course, to the deleterious effects of the penal laws.[24] By the late 1790s circumstances had changed somewhat. It is true that the bulk of the penal laws had been removed, but the manner in which Catholic relief had been imposed by London upon an unwilling Irish parliament deprived these measures of conciliatory effects in Ireland. For example, the response to the Relief Act of 1793, which extended the forty shilling county franchise to Catholics, reflected the frustration of both parties – the Protestant Ascendancy and the Catholic citizenry. John Foster, a pillar of the Ascendancy, was convinced that the Relief Act would only whet the appetite of Catholics for further reform (more than this, it was an admission of the justice of the Catholic cause). It was vain, he said, "to imagine that admission to the elective franchise does not draw with it the right of representation".[25] Theobald Wolfe Tone, the legendary leader of the United Irishmen, aptly described Catholic anger when he declared that if they deserved what had been granted, they also deserved that which had been withheld.[26] Similarly, Lord Fitzwilliam's great plan to bind Irish Catholics to "their" state had failed; they remained, according to Burke, "public Enemies" within society and were subjected to numerous informal impediments which replaced the crumbling penal laws.[27]

As the 1790s progressed the forces of reaction at the disposal of the state – regular forces, militia and yeomanry – proved insufficient in the face of revolutionary threats from Defenders (the shadowy Catholic secret society), the United Irishmen and their French allies.[28] Consequently, starting with the Carhampton campaign in north Leinster and Connacht in the summer of 1795, the Dublin Castle administration increasingly abandoned normal legal restraints, adopting instead measures which the French Terrorists had applied with such effect in the Vendée. This illegal campaign, described by Camden as "a salutary system of severity", was retrospectively excused by the terms of an Indemnity Act (1796), while the tactics were enshrined in law by an accompanying Insurrection Act.[29] At an unofficial level, the Orange Order (Burke's "Zealots in Armagh" in his letter to Hussey) inflicted horrors upon Catholics of mid-Ulster which James Coigly, the Armagh priest, compared to the "tyranny of Robespierre".[30] There was, however, no recourse to justice. Increasingly, Catholic Defenderism became the only restraint upon the Protestant Ascendancy since, as one victim concluded, "every magistrate in Ulster, but one or two, was an Orangeman".[31]

Such contingencies, Burke told Hussey in his December 1796 testament, presented Catholic subjects with the "desperate alternative between a thankless acquiescence under grievous Oppression, or a refuge in Jacobinism with all its horrors and all its crimes" (thus echoing the priest's own words).[32] Burke understood the attraction of the latter, but had no doubt about its destructive potential in Ireland. It was, indeed, more dangerous than continental Jacobinism, which was "Speculative in character" – "the very levity of character which produces it may extinguish it". Irish Jacobinism, on the other hand, arising from spurned loyalty, was a more intransigent phenomenon.[33] Still, since growing Catholic frustration could not be ignored, Burke warned Hussey of the dangers of preaching passivity to an "irritated people" – thus revealing once again his sensitivity to particular political circumstances.

Burke was equally alarmed at the nature of government in Ireland. Throughout the eighteenth-century the problem of political management had dogged successive administrations. Some stability had been achieved in the late 1760s by the replacement of the undertaker system with resident viceroys,[34] but the so-called "Constitution of 1782" had made the problem of management more acute, because it had extended the powers of the Irish parliament. What's more, the constitutional safeguards afforded by Poynings' Law and the Declaratory Act were now gone. As Burke put it in his epistle to Hussey, the English Government had "farmed out Ireland, without the reservation of a pepper Corn rent in Power or influence".[35] In this way, Ireland's Catholics were deprived of the protection previously afforded by the "superintendency of the British parliament". Burke lamented: "If the people of Ireland were to be flayed alive by the predominant faction it would be the most critical of all attempts so much as to discuss the Subject in any public Assembly upon this side of the water."[36] Catholics were prey to the "junto", the die-hards of the Ascendancy, Ireland's "Directory", which centred on John Beresford, John Fitzgibbon and John Foster, who were now working from within the Castle administration, not from without, as had been the case in Burke's earlier crusades.[37] Such considerations clearly illustrated the desirability of an union of the kingdoms; not a Protestant union, but one which would admit emancipated Catholics to the British state. Significantly, in the course of the Union debates three years later, in 1799, Thomas Hussey welcomed this proposal, declaring his preference for "a union with the Beys and Mamelukes of Egypt to that of being under the iron rod of the Mamelukes of Ireland".[38]

V

In retrospect, Conor Cruise O'Brien's description of Burke's missive as his "political testament with regard to Ireland" is justified. Certainly, Burke's letter "To Unknown" written two months later addresses the many ills of Ireland, the reckless policy of the government and the injustice of the penal laws, but this correspondence lacks the vigour of his earlier assault.[39] The contrasts between the two are immediate. The former is addressed to his most intimate confidential correspondent, Hussey, who within months would administer spiritually to him in his last illness.[40] The latter document, which O'Brien believes might be marked "for beginners", is directed to an acquaintance, a contemporary of his son, Richard, and contains a more superficial analysis of Ireland.[41]

While composing the December letter, which he dictated from his home in England, Burke was conscious of his imminent demise; in this sense, he *believed* this would be his testament and may have anticipated its publication. His mental powers had begun to decline, but the urgency of his task produced a rally which mirrored the vigour and ability of his prime. The consistency of his argument is immediately apparent – if the impact of the "French Disease" had introduced a "stridency and anger" into Burke's writings of the mid-1790s, his critical condition in December 1796 produced a red-hot assault on the Irish establishment.[42] Burke adopts a sarcastic tone to disparage the Dublin Castle junto, "the little wise men of the West", "snakes, whose primum Mobile is their Belly".

In Burke's view the threat to the security of the kingdom came not from the United Irishmen or the Defenders, but from this junto *within* the Castle. From this intellectual position Burke produced an ironic parody, one which measures the "victories" of the Ascendancy against the accomplishments of its allies in Europe: the pathetic "Glories of the Night expeditions in surprizing the Cabin fortresses in Louth and Meath" – the harsh, illegal measures employed to suppress Defenderism in South Ulster and North Leinster – are sardonically compared with the substantial achievements of the "Zealous Protestant Buonoparté" on the Plains of Lombardy. The cabal, Burke believed, were the real Jacobins of Ireland, the arrogant zealots of the Ascendancy who had abandoned the rule of law and violated the "compact of human Society" in their "Western Crusade against Popery". Yet, in the spirit of the Nagles, his revered Catholic cousins of the Blackwater Valley, Burke urged Catholics to be assertive: not to imitate the Jacobinism of their oppressors, but rather to steer a middle course. "There is nothing," he concluded, "which will not yield to perseverance and method."

EDMUND BURKE TO THE REV THOMAS HUSSEY [*post* 9 December 1796][43]

My dear Sir

This morning I received your Letter of the 30th of November from Maynooth. I dictate my answer from my Couch, on which I am obliged to lie for a good part of the Day. I cannot conceal from you, much less can I conceal from myself, that, in all probability I am not long for this world. Indeed things are in such a Situation independantly of the Domestic wound that I never could have less reason for regret in quitting the world than at this moment; and my End will be, by several, as little regretted.

I have no difficulty at all in communicating to you or, if it were of any use to mankind at large, my sentiments and feelings on the dismal state of things in Ireland; but I find it difficult indeed to give you the advice you are pleased to ask, as to your own conduct in your very critical Situation.

You state, what has long been but too obvious, that it seems the unfortunate policy of the Hour, to put to the far largest portion of the Kings Subjects in Ireland, the desperate alternative, between a thankless acquiescence under grievous Oppression, or a refuge in Jacobinisin with all its horrors and all its crimes. You prefer the former dismal part of the choice. There is no doubt but that you would have reasons if the election of one of these Evils was at all a security against the other. But they are things very alliable and as closely connected as cause and effect. That Jacobinism, which is Speculative in its Origin, and which arises from Wantonness and fullness of bread, may possibly be kept under by firmness and prudence. The very levity of character which produces it may extinguish it; but the Jacobinism which arises from Penury and irritation, from scorned loyalty, and rejected Allegiance, has much deeper roots. They take their nourishment from the bottom of human Nature and the unalterable constitution of things, and not from humour and caprice or the opinions of the Day about privileges and Liberties. These roots will be shot into the Depths of Hell, and will at last raise up their proud Tops to Heaven itself. This radical evil may baffle the attempts of Heads much wiser than those are, who in the petulance and riot of their drunken power are neither ashamed nor afraid to insult and provoke those whom it is their duty and ought to be their glory to cherish and protect.

So then the little wise men of the West, with every hazard of this Evil, are resolved to persevere in their manly and well timed resolution of a War, against Popery. In the principle and in all the proceedings it is perfectly suitable to their character. They begin this last series of their Offensive Operations by laying traps for the consciences of poor Foot-Soldiers. They call these wretches to their Church (empty of a Volonteer congregation) not by the Bell, but by the whip. This Ecclesiastic military discipline is happily taken up, in order to form an Army of well scourged Papists into a firm Phalanx for the support of the Protestant Religion. I wish them Joy of this their valuable discovery in Theology, Politicks and the Art military. Fashion governs the World; and it is the fashion in the great French Empire of Pure and perfect Protestantism, as well as in the little busy medling Province of servile imitators that apes, at an humble distance, the Tone of its Capital, to make a Crusade against you poor Catholicks. But whatever may be thought in Ireland of its share of a War against the Pope in that outlying part of Europe, the Zealous Protestant Buonoparté has given his late Holiness far more deadly blows in the center of his own power and in the nearest seats of his influence, than the Irish Directory can arrogate to itself within its own Jurisdiction from the utmost efforts of its political and military skill. I have my doubts, (they may perhaps arise from my ignorance) whether the Glories of the Night expeditions in surprizing the Cabin fortresses in Louth and Meathe[44] or whether the Slaughter and expulsion of the Catholic Weavers by another set of Zealots in Armagh,[45] or even the proud trophies of the late potatoe Field in that County,[46] are quite to be compared to the Protestant Victories on the Plains of Lombardy; or to the possession of the Fiat of Bologna,[47] or to the approaching Sack of Rome where even now the Protestant Commissaries give the Law. In all this Business great Britain, to us merely Secular politicians, makes no great figure; but let the glory of great Britain shift for itself as it may. All is well, provided Popery is crushed.

This War against Popery furnishes me with a Clue that leads me out of a Maze of perplexed politicks, which without it I could not in the least understand. I now can account for the whole. Lord Malmsbury[48] is sent to prostrate the dignity of the English Monarchy at Paris, that an Irish Popish common Soldier may be whipt in to give an appearance of habitation to a deserted protestant Church in Ireland. Thus we balance the account. Defeat and dishonor abroad; Oppression at Home – We sneak to the Regicides, but we boldly trample upon our poor fellow Citizens. But all is for the Protestant Cause.

The same ruling principle explains the Rest. We have abdicated the Crown of Corsica, which had been newly soldered to the Crown of Great Britain and to the Crown of Ireland, lest the British Diadem should look too like the Popes triple Crown.[49] We have ran away from the People of Corsica, and abandonned them without Capitulation of any kind; in favour of those of them who might be our friends. But then, it was for their having capitulated with us, for Popery, as a part of their Constitution. We make amends for our Sins by our Repentance, and for our Apostacy from Protestantism by a breach of faith with popery. We have fled, overspread with dirt and ashes but with hardly enough of Sack Cloath to cover our nakedness. We recollected that this Island, (together with its Yews and its other salubrious productions) had given birth to the illustrious Champion of the Protestant World Buonoparté – It was therefore not fit (to use the favorite French expression) that the Cradle of this religious Hero should be polluted by the feet of the British Renegade Slaves, who had stipulated to support Popery in that Island whilst his friends and fellow Missionaries are so gloriously employed in extirpating it in another – Our policy is growing every day into more and more consistency. We have shewed our broad back to the Mediterrenian. We have abandoned too the very hope of an alliance in Italy. We have relinquished the Levant to the Jacobins. We have considered our Trade as nothing – Our policy and our honor went along with it; but all these objects were well sacrificed to remove the very suspicion of giving any assistance to that Abomination, the Pope, in his insolent attempts to resist a truly protestant power resolved to humble the Papal Tiara, and to prevent his pardons and his dispensations from being any longer the standing terror of the wise and virtuous Directory of Ireland; who cannot sit down with any tolerable comfort to an innocent little Job, whilst his Bulls are thundering thro' the world. I ought to suppose that the arrival of General Hoche is eagerly expected in Ireland;[50] for He, too, is a most zealous Protestant; and he has given proof of it by the studied cruelties and insults by which He put to death the old Bishop of Dol;[51] whom, (but from the mortal fear I am in lest the suspicion of Popery should attach upon me) I should call a glorious martyr and should class him among the most venerable prelates that have appeared in this Century. It is to be feared however, that the Zealots will be disappointed in their pious hopes by the Season of the Year, and the bad condition of the Jacobin Navy, which may hinder him this Winter from giving his Brother Protestants in Ireland his kind assistance in accomplishing with you what the other friend of the cause, Buonoparté, is doing in Italy; and what the Masters of these two pious Men the Protestant Directory of France, have so thoroughly accomplished in that the most Popish, but unluckily whilst popish the [most] cultivated, the most populous and the most flourishing of all Countries the austrian Netherlands.

When I consider the narrowness of the views and the total want of human wisdom displayed in our Western Crusade against Popery, it is impossible to speak of it but with every mark of contempt and scorn – yet one cannot help shuddering with horror when one contemplates the terrible consequences that are frequently the results of craft united with Folly – placed in an unnatural elevation. Such ever win be the issue of things, when the mean vices attempt to mimick the grand passions. – Great men will never do great mischief but for some great End. For this they must be in a state of inflammation and in a manner out of themselves – Among the nobler Animals whose blood is hot, the bite is never poisonous, except when the Creature is mad; but in the cold blooded reptile race, whose poison is exalted by the Chemistry of their icy complexion, their venom is the result of their health, and of the perfection of their Nature – Woe to the Country in which such snakes, whose primum, Mobile is their Belly, obtain wings and from Serpents become dragons. It is not that these people want natural Talents and even a good

222

cultivation; on the contrary, they are the sharpest and most sagacious of mankind in the things to which they apply – But having wasted their faculties upon base and unworthy objects, in any thing of a higher order, they are far below the common rate of two legged animals.

I have nothing more to say, just now, upon the Directory in Ireland which indeed is alone worth any mention at all. As to the Half Dozen, (or half score as it may be) of Gentlemen, who, under various names of authority, are sent from hence to be the subordinate agents of that low order of beings, I consider them as wholly out of the question – Their virtues or their vices; their ability or their Weakness, are matters of no sort of consideration. You feel the thing very rightly – all the evils of Ireland originate within itself. That unwise body, the United Irishmen, have had the folly to represent those Evils as owing to this Country, when in truth its chief guilt is in its total neglect, its utter oblivion, its shameful indifference and its entire ignorance, of Ireland and of every thing that relates to it, and not in any oppressive disposition towards that unknown region. No such disposition exists. English Government has farmed out Ireland, without the reservation of a pepper Corn rent in Power or influence, publick or individual, to the little narrow Faction that Domineers there. Thro' that alone they see, feel, hear, or understand, any thing relative to that Kingdom; nor do they any way interfere that I know of, except in giving their countenance and the sanction of their Names to whatever is done by that *Junto*.

Ireland has derived some advantage from its independance on the Parliament of this Kingdom; or rather it did derive advantage from the arrangements that were made at the time of the establishment of that Independance.[52] But human blessings are mixed; and I cannot but think, that even these great blessings were bought dearly enough, when along with the weight of the authority, they have totally lost all Benefit from the superintendancy of the British Parliament. Our Pride is succeded by fear. It is little less than a breach of Order, even to mention Ireland in the House of Commons of Great Britain. If the people of Ireland were to be flayed alive by the predominant faction it would be the most critical of all attempts so much as to discuss the Subject in any public Assembly upon this side of the Water. If such a faction should by its folly or iniquity or both, provoke disturbances in Ireland, the force paid by this Kingdom would infallibly be employed to repress them. This would be right enough, if our public Councils here at the same time possessed and employed the means of enquiry into the merits of that cause in which their blood and treasure were so laid out. By a strange inversion of the order of things not only the largest part of the Natives of Ireland are thus annihilated; but the Parliament of Great Britain itself is rendered no better than an instrument in the hands of an Irish faction – This is ascendancy with a Witness! In what all this will end it is not impossible to conjecture; tho' the exact time of the accomplishment cannot be [fixed] with the same certainty as you may calculate an Eclipse.

As to your particular conduct it has undoubtedly been that of a good and faithfal Subject, and of a man of integrity and honor – You went to Ireland this last time, as you did the first time, at the express desire of the English Minister of that Department[53] and at the request of the Lord Lieutenant himself.[54] You were fully aware of the Difficulties that would attend your Mission; and I was equally sensible of them – Yet you consented, and I advised, that you should obey the voice of what we considered as indispensible duty. We regarded as the great Evil of the time the growth of Jacobinism, and we were very well assured that from a variety of causes no part of these Countries were more favorable to the growth and progress of that Evil than our unfortunate Country. I considered it as a tolerably good omen, that Government would do nothing further to foment and provoke the Jacobin malady, that they called upon you, a strenuous and steady Royalist, and an enlightened and exemplary Clergyman; A man of birth and respectable connexions in the Country; a man well informed and conversant in State Affairs, and in the general Politicks of the several Courts of Europe, and intimately and personnally habituated in some of those Courts. I regretted indeed that the Ministry which had my most earnest good wishes declined to make any sort of use of the reiterated information you had given them of the designs of their Enemies, and had taken no notice of the noble and disinterested Offers, which thro' me, were made for employing you to save Italy and Spain to the British Alliance. But this being past and Spain and Italy lost I was in hopes, that they were resolved to put themselves in the right at home by calling upon you that they would leave on their part no cause or pretext for Jacobinism except in the seditious disposition of Individuals; but I now see that instead of profiting by your advice and services, they will not so much as take the least notice of your written representations or permit you to have access to them on the part of those whom it was your Business to reconcile to Government as well as to conciliate Government towards them. Having rejected your services as a friend of Government, and in some sort in its employment, they will not even permit to you the natural expression of those sentiments which every man of sense and honesty must feel, and which every plain and sincere man must speak upon this vile plan of abusing Military discipline and perverting it into an instrument of religious persecution. You remember with what indignation I heard of the scourging of the Soldier at Carrick[55] for adhering to his religious Opinions – It was at the time when Lord FitzWilliam[56] went to take possession of a short lived Government in Ireland – Breves et infaustos populi Hiberni amores.[57] He could not live long in power because he was a true Patriot, a true friend of both Countries a steady resister of Jacobinism in every part of the World. On this occasion he was not of my Opinion. He thought, indeed that the Sufferer ought to be relieved and discharged and I think he was so:[58] But as to punishments to be inflicted on the Offender, he thought more lenient measures comprehended in a general plan to prevent such Evils in future, would be the better course. My Judgement, such as it was, had been, that punishment ought to attach so far as the Laws permitted, upon every evil action of subordinate power as it arose. That such acts ought at least to be marked with the displeasure of Govermnent because general remedies are uncertain in their Operation when obtained, and that it is a matter of great uncertainty whether they can be obtained at all. For a time his appeared to be the better Opinion. Even after He was cruelly torn from the embraces of the people of Ireland, when the Militia and other Troops were encamped, (if I recollect rightly, at Loughlinstown) you yourself with the knowledge and acquiescence of the suceeding Government publickly performed your function to the Catholicks then in Service.[59] I believe too that all the Irish who had composed the foreign Corps taken into British pay had their regular Chaplains.[60] But we see that things are returning fast to their old corrupted Channels. There they will continue to flow.

If any material Evil had been stated to have arisen from this Liberty that is, if Sedition Mutiny, or disobedience of any kind to Command, had been taught in their Chappels, there might have been a reason for not only forcing the Soldiers into Churches where better doctrines were taught, but for punishing the Teachers of disobedience and Sedition, – But I have never heard of any such Complaint. It is a part therefore of the Systematic illtreatment of Catholicks – This System never will be abandonned as long as it brings advantage to those who adopt it – If the Country enjoys a momentary quiet it is pleaded as an argument in favour of the good effect of wholesome rigours – If, on the Contrary, the Country (grows) more discontented; and if riots and disorders multiply, new Arguments are furnished for giving a vigorous support to the authority of the Directory on account of the rebellious disposition of the people. So long therefore as disorders in the Country become pretexts for adding to the power and emolument of an odious junto, means will be found to keep one part of it or other in a perpetual state of confusion and disorder. This is the old traditionary policy of that sort of men. The discontents which under them break out among the people become tenure by which they hold their situation.

I do not deny, that in these Contests the people however oppressed are frequently much to blame, whether provoked to their excesses or not, undoubtedly the Law ought to look to nothing but the Offence and to punish it. The redress of grievances is not less necessary than the punishment of disorders; but it is of another resort. In punishing however, the Law ought to be the only rule – If it is not of sufficient force, a force, consistent with its general principles, ought to be added to it. The first duty of a State is to provide for its own conservation. Until that point is secured it can preserve and protect nothing else; but, if possible, it has a greater interest in acting according to strict Law, than even the Subject himself. For if the people see, that the Law is violated to crush them they will certainly despise the Law, They on their part will be easily Led to violate it whenever they can, by all the means in their power. Except in cases of direct War, whenever Government abandons Law, it proclaims Anarchy.

I am well aware, (if I cared one farthing for the few Days I have to live, whether the vain breath of men blow hot or cold about me) that they who censure any Oppressive proceeding of Government are exciting the people to Sedition and revolt. If there be no oppression it is very true or if there be nothing more than the lapses, which will happen to human infirmity at all times and in the exercise of all power, such complaints would be wicked indeed – These lapses are exceptions implied: an allowance for which is a part of the understood covenant by which Power is delegated by fallible men to other men that are not infallible; but whenever a hostile spirit on the part of Government is shewn the Question assumes another form. – This is no casual Errour, no lapse, no sudden surprise. Nor [is] it a question of civil or political Liberty. What contemptible stuff it is to say, that a Man who is lashed to Church against his conscience would not discover that the whip is painful, or that He had a conscience to be violated, unless I told him so? Would not a penitent Offender confessing his Offence, lamenting it, and expiating it by his

226

blood, when denied the consolation of Religion at his last moments, feel it as no injury to himself or that the rest of the world would feel so horrible and impious an oppression with no indignation, unless I happened to say it ought to be reckoned amongst the most barbarous acts of our barbarous time. Would the people consider their being taken out of their beds and transported from their family and friends to be an equitable and legal and charitable proceeding, unless I should say that it was a violation of justice, and a dissolution, 'pro tanto', of the very compact of human Society? If a House of Parliament whose Essence it is to be the Guardian of the Laws, and a Simpathetic protector of the rights of the people (and eminently so of the most defenceless) should not only countenance but applaud this very violation of all Law, and refuse even to examine into the Grounds of the necessity upon the allegation of which Law was so violated, would this be taken for a tender Solicitude for the welfare of the poor, and a true proof of the representative Capacity of the House of Commons, unless I should happen to say (what I do say) that the House had not done its duty either in preserving the sacred rules of Law or in justifying the woeful and humiliating privilege of necessity. They may indemnify and reward others.[61] They might contrive, if I was within their grasp, to punish me, or if they thought it worth while to stigmatize me by their censures; but who will indemnify them for the disgrace of such an Act? Who will save them from the censures of Posterity? What act of Oblivion will cover them from the wakeful memory, from the Notices and issues of the Grand remembrancer, the God within? Would it pass with the people, who suffer from the abuse of lawful power when at the same time they suffer from the use of lawless violence of Jacobins amongst themselves that Government had done its duty and acted leniently in not animadverting on one of those Acts of violence? If I did not tell them, that the lenity with which Government passes by the Crimes and oppressions of a favourite faction, was itself guilty of the most atrocious of all Cruelties. If a Parliament should hear a declamation, attributing the Sufferings of those who are destroyed by these riotous proceedings to their misconduct and then to make them self-felonious, and should en effet refuse an enquiry into the fact, is no inference to be drawn from thence, unless I tell men in high places, that these proceedings taken together form not only an encouragement to the abuse of Power, but to riot, sedition, and a rebellious Spirit which sooner or later will turn upon those that encourage it?

I say little of the business of the Potatoe field, because I am not yet acquainted with the particulars. If any persons were found in arms against the King., whether in a field of Potatoes, or of Flax, or of Turnips, they ought to be attacked by a military Power, and brought to condign Punishment by course of Law – If the County in which the Rebellion was raised, was not in a temper fit for the execution of justice, a Law ought to be made, such as was made with regard to Scotland on the Suppression of the rebellion of 45 to hang the Delinquents.[62] There could be no difficulty in convicting men who were found 'flagrante delicto'. But I hear nothing of all this. No Law, no tryal, no punishment commensurate to Rebellion; nor of a known proportion to any lesser delinquency, nor any discrimination of the more or the less guilty. Shall you and I find fault with the proceedings of France, and be totally indifferent to the proceedings of Directories at home. You and I hate Jacobinism as we hate the Gates of Hell – Why? Because it is a System of oppression. What can make us in love with oppression because the Syllables Jacobin are not put before the *ism*. When the very same things are done under the *ism* preceded by any other Name in the Directory of Ireland.

I have told you, at a great length for a Letter, very shortly for the Subject and for my feelings on it, my sentiments of the scene in which you have been called to act, – on being consulted you advized Sufferers to quiet and submission; and giving Government full credit for an attention to its duties you held out, as an inducement to that submission, some sort of hope of redress. You tryed what your reasons and your credit could do to effect it. In consequence of this piece of Service to Government you have been excluded from all communication with the Castle; and perhaps you may thank yourself that you are not in Newgate. You have done a little more than in your circumstances I should have done. You are indeed very excusable from your motive; but it is very dangerous to hold out to an irritated people Any hopes that we are not pretty sure of being able to realize. The Doctrine of Passive obedience as a Doctrine, it is unquestionably right to teach; but to go beyond that, is a sort of deceit; and the people who are provoked by their Oppressors do not readily forgive their friends, if whilst the first persecutes and the others appear to deceive them. These friends lose all power of being serviceable to that Government in whose favor they have taken an illconsidered Step. Therefore my Opinion is, that untill the Castle shall shew a greater disposition to listen to its true friends than hitherto it has done, it would not be right in you any further to obtrude your services. In the mean time upon any new Application from the Catholics you ought to let them know simply and candidly how you stand.

The Duke of P[ortlan]d sent you to Ireland from a situation in this Country of advantage, and comfort to yourself and of no small utility to others. You explained to him in the clearest manner the conduct you were resolved to hold. I do not know that your writing to him will be of the least advantage – I rather think not; yet I am far from sure, that you do not Owe it to him, and to yourself to represent to his Grace the matters which, in substance, you have stated to me.

If any thing else should occur to me I shall, as you wish it, communicate my thoughts to you. In the mean time, I shall be happy to hear from you as often as you find it convenient. You never can neglect the great object of which you are so justly fond; and let me beg of you not to let slip out of your mind the Idea of the auxiliary studies and acquirements, which I recommended to you to add to the merely professional pursuits of your young Clergy; and above all, I hope that you will use the whole of your influence among the Catholics to persuade them to a greater indifference about the Political Objects which at present they have in view. It is not but that I am aware of their importance; or wish them to be abandond. But that they would follow opportunities and not to attempt to force any thing. I doubt whether the priveleges they now seek or have lately sought are compassable. The Struggle would, I am afraid only lead to some of Those very disorders which are made pretexts for further Oppression of the oppressed. I wish the leading people amongst them would give the most Systematic attention to prevent a frequent communication with their adversaries. There are a part of them proud, insulting, capricious, and tyrannical. These of Course will keep them at a distance. There are others of a seditious Temper who would make them at first the instruments and in the End the Victims of their factious Temper and purposes. Those that steer a middle course are truly respectable but they are very few. Your friends ought to avoid all imitation of the Vices of their proud Lords. To many of these they are themselves sufficiently disposed. I should therefore recommend to the middle ranks of that description in which I include not only all merchants but all farmers and tradesmen, that they would change as much as possible those expensive modes of living and that dissipation to which our Countrymen in general are so much addicted. It does not at all become men in a State of persecution. They ought to conform themselves to the circumstances of a people whom Government is resolved not to consider as upon a par with their fellow Subjects. Favour they will have none. They must aim at other rescources to make themselves independent in fact before they aim at a nominal independence. Depend upon it, that with half the privileges of the others, joined to a different System of manners they would grow to a degree of importance to which, without it, no privileges could raise them; much less any intrigues or factious practices. I know very well, that such a discipline among so numerous a people is not easily introduced; but I am sure it is not impossible – If I had youth and strength, I would go myself over to Ireland to work on that plan, so certain I am, that the well being of all descriptions in the Kingdom, as well as of themselves depends upon a reformation among the Catholicks. The work will be very slow in its operation but it is certain in its effect. There is nothing which will not yield to perseverance and method. Adieu! My dear Sir – you have full liberty to shew this Letter to all those (and they are but very few) who may be disposed to think well of my Opinions. I did not care, so far as regards myself, whether it was read on the change; but with regard to you more reserve may be proper – But that you will best judge.

CHAPTER 17

A "VANQUISHED ARISTOCRAT" IN DEMOCRATIC AMERICA: ALEXIS DE TOCQUEVILLE

JOHN PATRICK DIGGINS

A STUDENT AND TEACHER OF AMERICAN HISTORY HAS A STRANGE, YET familiar, experience reading the many-sided thoughts of Alexis de Tocqueville, particularly when dealing with the subject of aristocracy in writings that presage the coming of modern democracy. One feels one's self back in early American history, oscillating between two supposedly conflicting political universes: the enduring world of Jeffersonian liberalism and the lost world of Hamiltonian conservatism. In some respects, Tocqueville straddled the two worlds when he recognised the inevitability of democracy and, at the same time, continued to value the indispensability of aristocracy. The older culture of aristocracy provided liberty, stability and responsibility; the newer culture of democracy promised freedom, equality and opportunity. The last thing Tocqueville wanted to do, he tells us in his *Memoir*, was to be forced to choose between the two. Of contemporaries speculating on his political position, he remarked:

> They ascribe to me alternatively aristocratic and democratic prejudices . . .
> But my birth, as it happened, made it easy for me to guard against both
> . . . When I entered life, aristocracy was dead and democracy was yet
> unborn. My instinct, therefore, could not lead me blindly to one or to the
> other . . . Balanced between the past and the future, with no natural
> instinctive attractions towards either, I could without effort look quietly
> on each side of the question.[1]

231

All politics involves preference and choice, and the alternatives facing Tocqueville seemed to be either government by the best or government by the people; either the upholding of wisdom and honour or the pursuit of wealth and happiness; either the elevation of excellence in culture or the energy and dynamism in commerce; either, in a word, virtue or interest. Observing Tocqueville grappling with two alternative political systems, each with conflicting values, one is reminded of F Scott Fitzgerald's remark that the ability to hold in the mind two "contradictory ideas" and still function rationally is the test of a "first-rate intelligence". [2]

Another first-rate European intelligence who wrote about America was Edmund Burke, the subject of Conor Cruise O'Brien's magisterial *The Great Melody: A Thematic Biography and Commented Anthology of Edmund Burke*. Burke's great speech, *On Conciliation with America*, had once been on the syllabus of the American school curriculum from 1898 to 1933, O'Brien reminds us. Today Burke is no more read in high school history courses than is Tocqueville. Neither author was cited in Ronald Reagan's presidential inaugural. Instead, Americans heard their president-elect rhapsodise about Thomas Paine, the nemesis of both Burke and Tocqueville, the influential pamphleteer who espoused France's bloody revolution.

Tocqueville and Burke saw an emergent America as inevitable and representative of something new in politics, a regime that was breaking free of the past. Both thinkers recognised that older classical politics, particularly ancient republicanism, or what is called in scholarship today "civic humanism", had nothing to do with the new world in the making across the Atlantic. In ways that presage the later pragmatism of John Dewey and the neo-pragmatism of Jurgen Habemas, the Frenchman and Irishman alike recognised that human action arises from need based on circumstance and not from some abstract theory based on conviction.

Calculations about what we might gain or lose, Burke advised, "are the *cords of man*. Man acts from adequate motives relative to his interest, and not on metaphysical speculations". Tocqueville described such behaviour as "enlightened self-interest" or "self-interest rightly understood", which he hoped would be restrained enough so that an inevitable materialism in America might be "virtuous" rather than "pernicious". Although Burke wrote about America more than a half-century earlier than Tocqueville, he anticipated that America would develop without a philosophy of government or a theory of the state. Writing in the era of Jacksonian democracy, Tocqueville saw America's suspicion of government stemming from Jeffersonian localism and individualism. Much earlier Burke discerned a distrust of power in general in the American political psyche, which two centuries later became a central theme in Bernard Bailyn's *The Ideological Origins of the American Revolution*. The paranoid suspicion and jealousy that Bailyn uncovered in the colonial pamphlet literature had already been detected by Burke in his famous speech on conciliation. In most countries, Burke observed, people wait to "judge of an ill principle in government only by actual grievance; here", he continued, referring to America, "they anticipate the evil, and judge of the pressure of the grievance by the badness of the principle. They augur mistrust of government at a distance, and snuff the approach of tyranny in every tainted breeze".[3]

Both Burke and Tocqueville recognised that commerce, rather than politics, would determine America's future and both wondered about a rising political culture reluctant to submit to political authority. But here the perspectives of Burke and Tocqueville diverge in significant ways. Burke's hope for modern society resided in the idea of an organic continuity among the living, the dead and those yet to be born. Although Burke recognised the advent of the bourgeois era, in the French Revolution, as we shall see, he defended the age of chivalry and raged against the disorders of modern life. Tocqueville, in contrast, saw all remnants of organic order lost to the forces of modernisation, and in America, especially, the ravages of time erased all traces of the past. Where Burke valued integration, Tocqueville saw everywhere in the modern world only atomisation. And both thinkers had different thoughts about aristocracy.

Tocqueville's attitudes toward aristocracy intertwined with his early life. Born in 1805 into a royalist, aristocratic background, he remembered his family barely surviving the Jacobin terror of the 1790s. His father, Comte Herve de Tocqueville, woke up one morning to see in the mirror that his hair had turned completely white; his mother, Louise-Madelene, suffered migraines and fell into melancholy; numerous friends and relatives were taken off to the scaffolds. Years after the Revolution and Napoleon's reign, Alexis entered government service as a junior magistrate during the monarchical restoration. But a few years later the Revolution of 1830 erupted. While his family would support the newly formed Orleanist monarchy, Tocqueville had lost what he called his last "vestige of hereditary affection" for the whole Bourbon regime. In a letter to a friend written in the midst of the tumultuous "July days", Tocqueville wrote: "All of this – the bloodshed in Paris, the shouts of alarm – haunt me relentlessly, and as for the Bourbons, they have behaved like cowards and do not deserve a thousandth part of the blood that has been spilled over their cause."[4]

Disgusted with France's monarchical traditions, dreading the prospect of what might replace them, Tocqueville decided to take a trip to the United States with his friend, Gustav de Beaumont, a trip that had been on his mind for some time. In a letter written several years after he returned, Tocqueville told Louis de Kergolay that he had been thinking about America for more than ten years and that the proposal to write about the "penitentiary system was an excuse; I used it as a passport that would allow me to go everywhere in the United States". Why the curiosity about America?

> I am as profoundly convinced as one can be of anything in this world that we are irresistibly drawn by our laws and our mores toward an almost complete equality of social conditions. Once social conditions are equal, I no longer see any intermediary stage between a democratic government (and by the word democratic I mean not a republic, but a state of society in which everyone, to a greater or lesser degree, takes part in the political process) and the unchecked rule of one man. I don't doubt for a moment that the time will arrive at one or the other.[5]

Karl Marx observed that the advanced countries of the world would offer the less developed countries a glimpse of their future, a key to what they would become. In 1831, the year of Tocqueville's visit, America was by no means an advanced country with respect to economic development; yet Tocqueville had something else in mind. The American people are "not only the most enlightened, but (something I place well above that advantage) they are the people whose practical political education is the most advanced".[6] Advanced toward what? Does Tocqueville mean it in a positive or negative sense? "This whole book," Tocqueville tells us in the introduction to *Democracy in America*, "has been written under the impulse of a kind of religious dread inspired by contemplation of this irresistible revolution advancing century by century over every obstacle and even now going forward amid the ruins it has itself created."[7] If the eventual equalisation of social conditions could possibly lead to the "unchecked rule of one man", what class would that despot represent?

It may be the case that the kind of revolution Tocqueville dreaded as the tragic fate of the western world was due not to a democracy that sought to be born, but to an aristocracy that refused to die. Scholars have noted how Tocqueville often equates democracy and revolution. In democratic countries, he wrote:

> it is always to be feared that revolutionary instincts, calmed and regularised, but not extinguished, may gradually be transformed into governmental practices and administrative habits. Hence I know of no country in which revolutions are more dangerous than in a democracy, because apart from the accidental and ephemeral ills which they are ever bound to entail, there is always the danger of their becoming permanent and, one may almost say, eternal.[8]

A genuine revolution presupposes conflict and class antagonism, a revolution aiming to transform social relations. In an American democracy, where, as Tocqueville emphasised, people share a solid core of common interests and values, against whom would Americans be revolting? Tocqueville's brilliant insights about America led to in our time what is known as the "consensus" interpretation of American history. As long as Americans consent to consensus, it is difficult to see the danger of a radical revolution, which would mean, as Ernest Gellner has pointed out, that people have the capacity and willingness to give up being who they are to become something other than they are.[9] A people could rise up against a class alien to itself without risking its identity. Historically, that class has been the aristocracy in one form or another, and in America it had no real form or substance.

In America democracy preceded industrial capitalism, rendering unlikely the rise of a revolutionary proletariat on the left and, as we shall see, leaving Tocqueville wondering whether an aristocracy might rise out of the manufacturing sector to constitute a conservative threat from the right. It was as though political philosophy ran up against the American environment and, stopping to scratch its head, slumped into a question mark. America confounds the socialist and the classical republican alike. Neither Marx nor Machiavelli made it across the Atlantic, and thus the missing actors in the theatre of American history were the revolutionary workers and the virtuous citizens, components whose absence meant that America would have to get along without class consciousness from below and civic duty from above. Tocqueville was the first to see that in America one could no more hope to forge a radical revolution than one could expect to sustain a conservative tradition. But curiously, in the passage above, he seems to have put aside those features of America which rendered the New World different, unique, exceptional, as he describes the same "laws" driving both France and America toward equality of social conditions. If the forces of democracy were to triumph in France, as they had in America, could a mass democracy endure without an elite aristocracy?

* * *

The title of Tocqueville's famous book is bare, austere, noncommittal, and its author is as haunted by the silent movement of power as are today's poststructuralists. Tocqueville is, as well, almost as sceptical as they are of the Enlightenment. While the poststructuralists obsess about surveillance, discipline, control and domination, Tocqueville meditates on people and their souls. Unlike the poststructuralists, Tocqueville has a subject, and the subject is angst-ridden democratic man (now that women are fully in politics, they get to share the angst). We are familiar with the dangers of democracy in a post-aristocratic condition: an individualism that leads to self-interest and a withdrawal from public life; an egalitarianism that leads everyone to see themselves in the same condition to the point of succumbing to conformity and possible "democratic despotism"; and a tendency toward state centralisation as a result of people demanding the elimination of privilege, while requesting their own private benefits. Although Tocqueville came from a Catholic background, his worries are strikingly close to the seventeenth-century Calvinist, John Winthrop. Both saw that equality isolates the individual from the community as people turn inward upon themselves, unable to resist the pursuit of wealth and comfort as social relations become the sphere of ambition and envy. As did Winthrop, Tocqueville feared that the loss of moral authority meant the ascendancy of a new source of sovereignty in society itself. And America was a society without an aristocracy, with neither a nobility of the living nor a nobility of the dead.

Not exactly. Among the first persons Tocqueville met in America were Chancellor James Kent and Albert Gallatin: the famous jurist and author of the learned *Commentaries on American Law*; and the Geneva-born statesman, who earlier had served as Thomas Jefferson's Treasury Secretary. To the historian Henry Adams, Gallatin stood in American history as the supreme example of aristocratic virtue, a government advisor who could fuse together a politics of circumstance and a politics of principle. But Gallatin remained a rarity in American history, and later in the nineteenth-century Adams would look upon American politics as little more than "the systematic organisation of hatreds".[10]

Where, then, could any possible remains of aristocracy be found in America?

Tocqueville never took the trouble to look for aristocracy in the one institution where it was supposed to take up residence: the US Senate. John Adams wrote volumes arguing why superior men of knowledge and talent should be in the upper house, where they would be isolated from members of the lower – and hence constrained from manipulating their inferiors – and where they would be so observed and kept under a close watch that America could check their vices, while exploiting their wisdom. Unlike Alexander Hamilton, Adams did not trust the "rich, well-born, and able", but he remained absolutely convinced that America would, like the Old World, have an aristocracy. The only question was whether it would be "natural", as Jefferson hoped, or "artificial", as Adams feared.

Did Tocqueville himself see the slightest possibility of an aristocracy emerging in America? Below is a conversation he had with a member of the Livingston family, which had reigned in New York in the pre-evolutionary era as a kind of gentry aristocracy. Tocqueville asked Livingston why America lacked a class that would concern itself with culture and "intellectual questions":

[Livingston:] Chiefly because of the law of inheritance. When I was young I remembered the country peopled by rich landowners who lived on their estates as the English gentry do, and who used their minds, and had, too, a sense of tradition in their thoughts and manners. Then there was distinction in the behaviour and turn of mind of one class in the nation. The law making shares equal has worked continually to break up fortunes and form them anew; our former standards and conceptions have been lost and this process goes on from day to day. Land changes hands incredibly quickly, nobody has time to strike root in one place, and everybody must turn to some practical work to keep up the position his father held. Almost all families disappear after the second or third generation.

[Tocqueville:] Is there anything analogous to the influence, patronage, of large landholders?

[Livingston:] No, only individual merit counts here.

[Tocqueville:] How do the wealthy classes put up with such a state of affairs?

[Livingston:] They put up with it as something inevitable since there is nothing whatsoever to be done about it.

[Tocqueville:] But is there, nonetheless, some resentment between them and the common people?

237

[Livingston:] None. All classes joined together in the Revolution. Afterwards, the strength of Democracy was so paramount that no one attempted to struggle against it. Generally speaking, the people show no distaste for electing the very rich or well-educated.[11]

Such conversations could only reinforce Tocqueville's conviction that politics would turn less on the forms of government than on the conditions of society. The *ancien régime* depended on a nobility rooted in the soil; aristocracies are territorial and only land ownership, as opposed to trade and commerce, can assure family continuity. Such feudal or even post-feudal conditions never took root in America, hence "all classes joined together in the Revolution".

Tocqueville does note that in the colonial period the South had an aristocracy, or at least a class, with such proclivities. There were "rich landowners in that part of the country", to be sure. "But their influence was not exactly aristocratic, in the sense in which the word is used in Europe, for they had no privileges, and the use of slaves meant they had no tenants and, consequently, no patronage."[12] Yet in the North as well as the South it was, Tocqueville remarks, the ranks of the upper classes that provided the best leaders of the American Revolution.

But the Revolution itself did not give birth to democracy. "It was the law of inheritance which caused the final advance of equality", Tocqueville noted, and he wondered why "ancient and modern writers have not attributed greater importance to the laws of inheritance and their effect on the progress of human affairs". Such laws can make or break an aristocracy. With primogeniture the family expresses itself in its land, "perpetuating its name, origin, glory, power, and virtue". But when the law ordains dividing up property, land no longer represents the family, and its members are more interested in selling their shares than preserving their heritage. With the rise of commercial society wealth replaces land as the medium of value, and what once was to be perpetuated is now circulated with such rapidity that classes rise only to disappear, and land becomes little more than real estate speculation.

* * *

Curiously, one place where Tocqueville saw traces of aristocracy had little to do with land as private ownership. The traveller discovered such traces in the environment of the Native American Indians. Tocqueville happened

238

to be in America at the time controversy erupted over the removal of the Cherokees from their land in Georgia. He criticised the dispossession of a tribe that had its own written language and a "fairly stable form of government". But observing other tribes without a sense of property or productivity left him distressed. "The natives of North America consider labour not only an evil, but also a disgrace, and their pride fights against civilisation almost as obstinately as their laziness." Tocqueville feared that Indians lacked the very Protestant work ethic that was transforming America. "No Indian in his bark hut is so wretched that he does not entertain a proud conception of his personal worth; he considers the cares of industry degrading occupations; he compares the cultivator to the ox plowing a furrow and regards all our crafts as merely the labour of slaves."

Although some historians like to believe that white Europeans projected their cultural assumptions and saw in Indians what they expected to see, Tocqueville was genuinely surprised by what he came upon. "How odd it is that the ancient prejudices of Europe should reappear, not only among the European populations on the coast, but in the forests of the New World."[13] That the Old World's aristocratic prejudices against labour should crop up in the woods of America saddened Tocqueville. What would be the fate of a people who, like the old European aristocracy, saw itself as too proud and noble to stoop to labour, clung to hunting and warfare and had no identity other than ancestral memory?

Aristocracy had always been historical and associated with a past that had been rural and originally feudal. But for a moment Tocqueville wondered whether a new environment might produce a new type of aristocracy. In the chapter titled "How An Aristocracy May Be Created By Industry", we encounter thoughts that ought to give Marxists some sleepless nights. The division of labour is not going to resolve itself through the dialectical struggle of opposites, with workers succeeding capitalists, as in Marx, or with the slave replacing the master, as in Hegel. In his "Economic and Philosophic Manuscript of 1844" Marx thought otherwise, convincing himself, and many of the sixties generation to boot, that somehow workers could work their way out of the very conditions of alienation that they had worked themselves into. "This new formulation of the problem," Marx wrote in reference to labour as both alienating and redeeming, "already contains its solution." All development, transformation, and even progress itself, entail contradiction, and thus "the overcoming (*Aufhebung*) of self-alienation follows the same course as self-alienation".[14]

With Tocqueville, however, workers are going nowhere as long as they remain at the same task, and such a predicament could only distress a writer who praised the extent to which work itself was admired in America everywhere outside the South. In explaining the "roundabout way industry may in turn lead men back to aristocracy", Tocqueville discusses the specialisation of labour and the reduced cost of production when workers are engaged in large scale operations. "There is nothing in the world of politics that deserve the lawgivers' attention more than these two new axioms of industrial science", advised Tocqueville, who proceeded to explain that the capitalist class advances to the detriment of the working class, that labour itself cannot overcome human alienation and that those who manage and administer will become powerful, while those who make and produce will sink to the level of a brute. As the worker devotes himself more and more to a single detail of production, he loses all capacity to think beyond a "singular dexterity" and takes on fixed, monotonous habits he can never shake off. Simultaneously, the employer turns his attention to larger endeavours requiring knowledge, science and imagination:

> Thus, at the same time that industrial science constantly lowers the standing of the working class, it raises that of the masters.
>
> While the workman confines his intelligence, more and more studying one single detail, the master daily embraces a vast field in his vision, and his mind expands as fast as the other's contracts. Soon the latter will need no more than bodily strength without intelligence, while to succeed the former need science and almost genius. The former becomes more and more like the administrator of a huge empire, the latter more like a brute.
>
> So there is no resemblance between master and workman, and daily they become more different. There is no connection, except that between the first and last links in a long chain. Each occupies a place made for him, from which he does not move. One is in a state of constant, narrow, and necessary dependence on the other and seems to have been born to obey, as the other was to command.
>
> What is this, if not an aristocracy?

This "manufacturing aristocracy" rising among us is the harshest and most remorseless the world has seen in its treatment of workers and yet, at the same time, it "is one of the most restrained and least dangerous". The rich, Tocqueville assures readers, have no common association among each other, and while wealthy manufacturers may exploit workers, they cannot rule over them in a free labour environment, where workers can take a hike and walk off the job.

Could wealth itself, whatever its form, constitute an aristocracy? Tocqueville fails to address this issue directly, perhaps because he saw wealth as volatile and passing from one person to the next with such rapidity that a class could not be permanently formed around it. Tocqueville's description of America would have been a nightmare to Edmund Burke, who insisted that men belonged to a fixed social standing, which by no means should be eroded by money or equality. Tocqueville also believed that work itself came to be so honoured in democratic society that a stratum whose status was based on wealth alone, without any sense of civic responsibility, would command little authority. Tocqueville, of course, was analysing pre-industrial America. In post-Civil War industrial America Henry Adams and Thorstein Veblen saw things differently, with wealth openly buying political power, as though the Senate was up for sale, and with a new leisure class enjoying its idle, non-productive status, while work itself lost the esteem it once held and somehow came to be stigmatised as "irksome".[15]

* * *

If aristocracy could find a home anywhere in America it would not be in the economic sphere, but in the political. Following the classical tradition, Tocqueville looked to political and civil associations as activities that nourished human excellence and, while he saw Montesquieu's idea of virtue as self-renunciation as antiquated, he believed that some semblance of aristocracy could be reconstituted if democratic man saw the weakness in his own self-image of individual self-sufficiency:

> I firmly believe that no new aristocracy can be established in the world. But I believe that ordinary citizens, by associating with one another, can become prosperous, influential, and strong – in a word, aristocrats. In this manner one might obtain several of the greatest political advantages of aristocracy without its injustices and dangers. A political, industrial, commercial, or even scientific or literary association is an enlightened and powerful citizen, which cannot be made to bow down at will and cannot be subjected in obscurity to the heel of oppression, and which, by defending its private rights against the exigencies of power, preserves the liberties of all.[16]

It might be noted that Tocqueville uttered such thoughts in 1835, a year or so before the New England Transcendentalists came on the scene with an entirely different message: Politics means "cunning", and a life involving reciprocal associations is a life of "quiet desperation" in which the self is strangled by society.

But Tocqueville saw association as liberating rather than suffocating, and nowhere more so than in the legal and juridical sector. Tocqueville believed that lawyers provided the last remnant of an aristocratic element that enabled democracy to withstand its worst features. Lawyers share the aristocrat's preference for order and procedure, equate regularity with legality, have scorn for the popular sentiments of the crowd, distrust the arbitrary and the unprecedented and respect what is old. Tocqueville believed that legal affairs involving rights and justice compelled people to engage one another, and he looked to the jury system as an institution enabling the common man to learn the lessons of justice and responsibility by trying to arrive at independent, objective judgement. The bail system, however, represented a lingering aristocratic privilege that allowed the rich to stay out of jail. "Yet," Tocqueville adds, "in America, it is the poor who make the laws, and usually they reserve the greatest benefits of society for themselves."[17]

At the level of government, it would be facile to suggest that Tocqueville saw the aristocrat serving on behalf of virtue, while the democratic looked only to interest. Tocqueville so defined, and redefined, interest as "enlightened", "well-understood", "a sort of refined and intelligent selfishness" and other such expressions that he appeared to be trying desperately to save virtue from its fate in commercial society.[18] In the corridors of government, Tocqueville did indicate that the aristocratic politician was more capable of considering the public good and the long range benefits to society, while the democratic politician responded to the electorate and its interminable demands. But if the aristocrat can afford to be proud, the democratic cannot afford to be poor. Those born into wealth and abundance are almost indifferent to their possessions, concerned, as John Stuart Mill put it, not with:

> le but de la vie, but une maniere de vivre. An aristocracy, when put to the proof, has in general shown a wonderful facility in enduring the loss of riches . . . but to those who have chased riches laboriously for half their lives, to lose it is the loss of all; une vie manquee; a disappointment greater than can be endured.[19]

Thus in the halls of Congress one finds the same characteristic American unease about wealth and status on the part of those politicians who cannot distinguish the welfare of the country from their own needs

242

and desires. Classical political thought promised to discipline desire; with the aristocrat replaced by the democrat, desire demands to be fulfilled, and the desire to acquire only increases the fear of loss. "The very equality which enables each citizen to sustain great hopes makes all citizens equally weak," wrote Tocqueville. "It limits their strength on all sides at the same time as it allows their desires to spread." The literary scholar Réne Gerard took that and other passages of Tocqueville to suggest that while the aristocrat is secure in his identity, the democrat is plagued by a vanity born of unfulfilled, acquisitive instincts. "The vanity of the *ancien régime* was gay, unconcerned and frivolous; the vanity of the nineteenth century is sad and suspicious; it has a terrible fear of ridicule. 'Envy, jealously and impotent hatred' are the accompaniment of internal mediation."[20]

One could say in the light of the above observation that the difference between Tocqueville and Burke is the difference between the nineteenth and the eighteenth centuries. When Burke wrote about aristocracy in *Reflections on the Revolution in France*, he had in mind an *ancien régime* that was confident about itself and responsible toward society. In *The Old Regime and the French Revolution*, written more than a half-century later, Tocqueville criticises Burke for his adoration of aristocracy and hints that the author of *Reflections* needed to reflect more on the difference between a responsible English aristocracy and a French aristocracy lacking in *noblesse oblige*. Burke looked to aristocracy as the only class capable of despising danger in pursuit of honour (also the dream of Alexander Hamilton), but such a class had been lost to French history, and America entirely lacked the aristocratic virtue of disinterestedness born of aristocratic security.

Aside from the question of aristocracy, however, Tocqueville agreed with Burke about the importance of religion in history and politics and he was even more emphatic in agreeing about the nature of liberty as organic and continuous. Even though the American Revolution was made in the name of natural rights, such rights were scarcely recent incantations, as in revolutionary France, but long rooted in an English love for liberty. In France, Tocqueville observed in thoughts that Burke would have cheered, the idea of liberty was born overnight; in America it derived from age-old habits and customs as well as the rule of law.

* * *

While Tocqueville hoped that law, politics and civil associations might save the American character from its angst-driven self, and that the residues of aristocracy might mitigate the defects of democracy driven by irrational desires unresponsive to reason, *The Federalist* authors, and John Adams in particular, had a different take on the nature of government and on human nature itself. Hamilton could agree with Tocqueville about the primacy of law, and Madison somewhat presaged the Frenchman's fear of the "tyranny of the majority" when he warned against the danger of "overbearing" popular factions. But Hamilton saw law as an instrument of nationalism that would help consolidate the nation-state, while Tocqueville grew nervous at the thought of centralisation; and whereas Madison saw democracy as a threat to property, Tocqueville took pains to explain why property would be safe in a democratic republic where everyone outside of the South valued land, free labour and the expectation of making money. For some strange reason, the framers failed to see what Tocqueville and Max Weber later saw: that an early Puritanism endowed America with a viable Protestant work ethic that would hold property in respect. Missing that perspective, the framers structured the Constitution on the premise that America would, indeed, experience the class conflicts of the Old World. As Louis Hartz put it in his brilliant, if profoundly despairing, *The Liberal Tradition in America*, "the Founding Fathers devised a scheme to deal with conflict that could only survive in a land of solidarity. The truth is, their conclusions were 'right' only because their premises were wrong".[21]

A number of scholars wish to demonstrate the influence *The Federalist* had on Tocqueville.[22] Certainly the influence was true in regard to the idea of federalism, but it should be noted that Tocqueville rejected the institutional premises of the Constitution when he questioned the idea of a "balanced" or "mixed" government. The framers assumed such devices were necessary to balance class against class. "I have always considered what is called a mixed government to be a chimera," wrote Tocqueville. "Eighteenth-century England, which has been especially cited as an example of this type of government, was an essentially aristocratic state." Those who looked to England, as did America, are mistaken:

> The mistake is due to those who, constantly seeing the interests of the great in conflict with those of the people, have thought only about the struggle and have not paid attention to the result thereof, which was more important. When a society does have a mixed government, that is to say, one equally shared between contrary principles, either a revolution breaks out or that society breaks up.[23]

The framers looked to a "mixed" government because they foresaw America replicating the class structures of the Old World, and John Adams, in particular, believed America would have its own aristocracy. Adams insisted there would always be differences of merit and abilities, and what constituted aristocracy would not be privilege, but certain "talents", particularly reputation, personal images, intelligence, charisma – in short, whatever gave some persons advantages over others. The key was "influence", the ability to command the votes of others. Jefferson would agree with Adams that aristocracy could be defined as the rule of the influential, but he wanted to see it as "natural", based solely on talent and virtue. Every aristocracy, Adams replied, was based on talents. But "Education, Wealth, Strength, Beauty, Stature, Birth, Marriage, graceful Attributes and Motions, Gait, Air, Complexion, Physiognomy" were talents, and to the extent any of these influenced others made the possessor of that attribute an aristocrat, an "artificial" one, to be sure.[24]

"You judge democracy," François Guizot wrote Tocqueville in 1835, "like an aristocrat who has been vanquished, and is convinced that his conqueror is right."[25] John Adams could not have agreed more. Tocqueville wondered about the future of an American democracy enduring without the guidance of an enlightened, responsible aristocracy. Adams saw aristocracy burdened with the same vanity and universal depravity that inhabits the soul of every sinner, whatever class or status. Good Calvinist that he was, he instructed Americans on why they should trust no one, not the one, the few or the many, neither monarchy, aristocracy nor democracy. All have tendencies to usurp the rights of others; hence all must be controlled. Long before the poststructuralists of our times, Adams was the true "master of suspicion".

* * *

A student of history cannot conclude a paper on Tocqueville's juxtaposition of aristocracy to democracy without a word on how to handle this theme in regard to the study of history. In the chapter titled "Some Characteristics Peculiar to Historians in Democratic Centuries", Tocqueville offers an analysis rich in irony and one that might help explain what has happened in the academic world today. Historians writing in aristocratic settings generally attribute what has happened to the forceful and personal, the "will and character of particular men", and they have their eye out for slight occurrences, and even accidents, as

245

possible causes of "the greatest revolutions". Historians who live in democratic environments, in contrast, ignore the role of individuals and great leaders and make "general causes responsible for the smallest particular events". The reason for these differences is that the aristocrat looks upon history as a theatre where leading actors control the whole play; he is interested in unravelling individual motives, since the aristocratic historian assumes that the behaviour of the larger crowd can be traced back to "one man's act". In a democracy, however, individuals exist separate from one another and do not appear to have any influence over others as society seems to go its own way. In periods of equality, in contrast to aristocratic ages, causes remain remote, "infinitely more various, better hidden, more complex, less powerful, and hence less easy to sort out and trace, whereas the historian of an aristocratic age has simply to analyse the particular action of one man or of a few men amid the general mass of events". The democratic predilection for general causes becomes attractive precisely because it consoles "mediocre" minds to the point that they cease caring about them and instead turn to surrogates. The historian, "lost in a labyrinth, unable clearly to see or to explain individual influences, he ends by denying that they exist. He prefers to talk about the nature of races, the physical character of the country, or the spirit of civilisation".

Tocqueville himself believed that in a democratic culture general causes explain more and particular influences less, and the opposite case applies in aristocratic ages. But this dichotomy is not what troubles him. "Those who write in democratic ages have another tendency that is more dangerous." Namely:

Once the trace of the influence of individuals on the nation has been lost, we are often left with the sight of the world moving without anyone moving it. As it becomes extremely difficult to discern and analyse why the reasons which, acting separately on the will of each citizen, concur in the end to produce movement in the whole mass, one is tempted to believe that this movement is not voluntary and that societies unconsciously obey some superior dominating force.

A democratic culture may prize freedom, but its approach to history could lead its people to "depend either on an inflexible providence or on a kind of blind fatality" that presumes a fixed destiny. Democratic cultures prefer necessity to contingency, since it is easier to believe what happened simply happened than it is to ponder why things did not turn out differently. To Tocqueville democratic history leads to intellectual laziness, an acceptance of the given and the curtailment of wonder and curiosity. In contrast:

> in reading historians of aristocratic ages, those of antiquity in particular, it would seem that in order to be master of his fate and to govern his fellows a man need only be master of himself. Perusing the histories written nowadays, one would suppose that man had no power, neither over himself nor over his surroundings. Classical historians taught how to command; those of our own time teach next to nothing but how to obey.[26]

The eyes blink! That "societies unconsciously obey some superior dominating force", that "we are left with the sight of a world moving without anyone moving it", that "man had no power, neither over himself nor over his surroundings" – what is this cryptic cosmos, but the world of Michel Foucault and poststructuralism![27] Perhaps Tocqueville provides the clue to why postructuralism, with its maddening effects without causes, history without agency and power without reason or purpose caught on in a democratic America, which settles for simplicity, and not in more aristocratic France, with its richer sensibility for complexity. "The doctrine of fatality", observed Tocqueville, "so attractive to those who write history in democratic periods", lets scholar off the hook by providing them "with a few mighty reasons to extricate them from the most difficult part of their task, and while indulging their incapacity or laziness, gives them a reputation for profundity".[28]

I would like to think that Monsieur Alexis de Tocqueville would take Herr Friedrich Nietzsche's advice. The best "medicine" that can be "effective against an excess of historical education", Nietzsche wrote, particularly an education that undertakes "constructions of a world process" and does so with a "misleading owlish seriousness", is to "parody" it.[29]

VII

AFRICAN ART, EDUCATION
AND POLITICS

CHAPTER 18

THE ARTS OF AFRICA

K ANTHONY APPIAH

Tenabea nyinaa nse.
(All dwelling places are not alike.)
– Asante proverb

I

I LEARNED ABOUT ART GROWING UP IN MY HOMETOWN, KUMASI, THE
capital of Asante, an old Akan kingdom at the heart of the new republic
of Ghana. There were paintings and drawings on our walls; there were
sculptures and pots, in wood and ivory and earthenware and brass; and
there were art books in the bookcases. But above all, my mother collected
Asante goldweights: small figures or geometrical shapes, cast in brass,
usually from wax originals, that had been used for weighing gold dust
when it was our currency (as it was well into this century). The figurative
goldweights are wonderfully expressive: they depict people and animals,
plants and tools, weapons and domestic utensils, often in arrangements
that will remind an Asante who looks at them of a familiar proverb. And
the abstract geometrical weights, their surfaces decorated with patterns,
sometimes use the *adinkra* symbols, which are found as well on Akan
stools and funeral cloths. Each of them has a name – Gye Nyame, for
example – and a meaning – in this case, the power of God. There is no
established correlation between what one of these miniature brass
sculptures looks like and what it weighs: each person knew his or her own

collection. In short, the goldweights of West Africa are richly embedded in significance; and a representative sample of them was on display at the Guggenheim Museum during the summer of 1996 in the exhibition "Africa: The Art of a Continent".

The show had begun at the Royal Academy in London in 1995, as part of a celebration of African cultures, and the catalogue, produced for both installations, contains most of the pieces that were shown in both places, along with a few that did not travel to New York; the Guggenheim then supplemented the full catalogue with one subtitled *One Hundred Works of Power and Beauty*, which reflected the addition at the Guggenheim of major pieces from American collections.[1]

* * *

The Akan goldweights in the main catalogue were shown in both places. I knew they would be there from the moment I first heard the show was being planned, because I knew that Tom Phillips, the member of the Royal Academy who curated the show, was an avid collector, and another avid collector – my mother – had corresponded with him. The pieces he chose covered, as I say, the whole range of the genre. There were some of the earliest geometric weights, used from the fifteenth century in the northward trade of gold across the Sahel, their surfaces inscribed with such familiar simple shapes as the inverted swastika and with less familiar designs that put me in mind of Klee; and there were also the better-known human figures, which seem to have been created first in the seventeenth century, as the trade turned to the new European partners on the Guinea coast. Among the figures were: a couple *in flagrante* (probably from the eighteenth century); a slightly earlier palm wine tapper, seated by a felled palm tree, gathering in a bowl the sap whose fermentation will soon make good drinking; and a nineteenth-century horseman, spear held boldly aloft, his mount caparisoned in curlicues of bronze. I also recognised a figure, familiar from many exemplars in my mother's collection, of a woman carrying both a child on her back and a heavy load on her head, representing the proverb *"Obaa sima na ne ba hye n'akyiria, osoa nnooma"* (If the hardworking woman has a child on her back, she also carries a load).

There were fish and elephants and birds, household objects, farming implements and weapons of war and, finally, the direct castings of seeds, leaves, insects and other natural objects, that – along with the weighing scales (which were also represented) and the odd seed or scrap of metal or cloth – would have filled out a collection of goldweights a hundred years ago. These goldweights – none of them more than a couple of inches tall – leave an impressive record of five centuries of West African material life.

My favourite piece, I think, is a beautifully patinated weight in my mother's collection, one that belongs to a common genre representing two crocodiles with a shared stomach. This figure evokes the proverb *"Funtumfunafu ne Denkyemfunafu baanu yafunu ye yafunkoro; nanso woredidi a na woreko no, na firi atwimenemude ntira."* It means, roughly: Stomachs mixed up, crocodiles' stomachs mixed up, they both have one stomach, but when they eat they fight because of the sweetness of swallowing. The meaning of the proverb, which expresses one of the dilemmas of family life, is that while the acquisitions of each family member benefit the whole family (there is only one stomach), the pleasure of enjoyment is an individual thing (the food has to get into the stomach through one of the mouths).

* * * *

Anyone who has handled a decent number of weights – and, like so much else in the show, they cried out from the museums vitrines to be touched – will have noticed quite often among these elegant objects, so obviously crafted with great skill and care, one that has a lump of unworked metal stuffed into a crevice in a way that seems completely to destroy its aesthetic unity; or, sometimes, a well-made figure has a limb crudely hacked off. These amputations and excrescences are there because, after all, a weight is a weight: and if it doesn't weigh the right amount, it can't serve its function. If a goldweight, however finely crafted, has the wrong mass, then something needs to be added (or chopped off) to bring it to its proper size.

Because of this, you can learn a great deal of history by weighing a collection. The weights correspond to an extraordinary mixture of weighing systems, from the earliest Islamic system – one based, so the Guggenheims' catalogue informs us, on "a *mitqhal* of gold dust (about 4.5 grams or a sixth of an Islamic ounce)" – through those based on the Portuguese ounce of the fifteenth century to the Dutch troy ounce from 1600 on. By the nineteenth century a complex system of about sixty units, reflecting this long history of different trading partners, was in use. And every one of these pieces, however exquisite, was there to correspond to one of those units.

There is thus an extremely elaborate cultural code expressed in these miniature sculptures; and with the patina that comes from age and human handling, and the exquisite detail produced in the lost-wax process by which they were made, many of them have an obvious aesthetic appeal. It doesn't take long to recognise that the goldweights of Asante differ from those of other Akan societies: Fante (in Southern Ghana) or Baule (in Ivory Coast), say. (There is a kind of Baule figure, for example, whose head is almost spherical; the heads of Asante figures tend to be flatter and more elongated.) Nor is it hard to recognise stylistic change over the centuries. There are histories of taste written in these objects, if only we could read them. (May we assume, for example, that the growth of figurative weights reflected, to some degree, the turn from trade with Moslem cultures, less friendly to human representation, toward trade with the Portuguese, with their taste for the human figure?) Goldweights, in sum, have many of the features that we expect of works of art. In Ashanti itself, they were appreciated for their appeal to the eye, or for the proverbial traditions they engaged. But in the end, as I say, they were weights: and their job was to tell you the value of the gold dust in the weighing pan.

* * *

The best of the Asante goldweights are among the splendours of African creativity. But they were not the product of a culture that valued these objects as art. Their decorative elegance was something prized and aimed for, of course; but it was an ornament, an embellishment, on an object that served a utilitarian function. It is clear that some people – chiefs among them, but also the richest commoners – had particularly fine collections of weights, and that, in using them in trade, they advertised their wealth at the same time by displaying the superior craftsmanship of their possessions. Perhaps once, when the weights were still being used, people knew the names of those who made them best; but no one now knows the names of the great casters of goldweights from the past. Still, to insist upon my point, in appreciation and collecting these weights as art we are doing something new with them, something that their makers and the men and women who paid them did not do.

The goldweight tradition is also very particular. The use of figurative and abstract weights, made in brass by the lost-wax process, is not widespread in West Africa, let alone Africa more generally. Outside the Akan region of Ghana and Ivory Coast there are, so far as I am aware, no traditions that have produced objects that could be mistaken for Akan goldweights. They are African, because the Akan cultures are in Africa: but these traditions are local and while they reflect the complex cultural and economic exchanges between, say, Asante and the Islamic traders of the Sahel, or between Baule culture and the European trade of the coast (and thus reflect currents of life wider than those of the societies in which they were made), it would be a mistake to see them as capturing the essence of the vast gamut of African creativity.

Particularity and locality are to be found too in African masks, the form with which African "tribal" art is most widely identified – in large measure, of course, because of the emblematic (and, for all I know, apocryphal) encounter between Picasso and the mask he saw at the Trocadéro museum in Paris in 1907. Anyone who has looked at collections of masks from Western and Central Africa will tell you that you can soon learn to recognise roughly where most of them come from: the traditions of each society in masking, even those that have influenced and been influenced by neighbouring traditions, are still quite recognisably distinct; as are the roles masks play in the different forms of performance, where they have their fullest life.

Indeed, what makes something a mask, I am tempted to say, is that we see it as a mask. Consider the Dan, Mano and the Weinon masks, wooden masks from Liberia, five to ten inches tall, two dozen of which are to be found in the catalogue. They look, of course, like something you could wear to a (slightly eerie) Venetian ball, though they're mostly too small to cover an adult's face. But in these cultures they weren't used that way at all. They were, as one learns from the catalogue, to be kept hidden, "destined for personal protection or enhancement". At the initiation rites of certain Dan secret societies, the path to the gathering place was strewn with these small masks, and initiates had to pay to have them removed; at circumcisions the knife blade might be wiped on a small mask; a tray of masks could represent the benevolent spirits of a region; they might be installed on personal altars. They are, in fact, small representations of a human face: what is done with them, what they are *for*, can be enormously various.

Yet elsewhere in the region, in other forest cultures – Yoruba and Igbo, for example, in Nigeria – masks *are* worn in public, in masquerades, where the wearer comes to represent a god or an ancestor through possession and the donning of the mask (a practice familiar to many western readers from the account of it in Chinua Achebe's *Things Fall Apart*). So the mask we see, still in the museum, once lived on the face or rode on the shoulders

255

of a man who was standing in for a spirit. But masquerades with masks can be pure entertainment too as they are in the Guro dances of Ivory Coast: and there are three Guro masks in the catalogue – one of an elderly man, and one of young woman, the third unidentified – that were made to be worn in inter-village dance competitions.

The point here is simple enough: Africa's creative traditions are both various and particular. You will no more capture the essence of Africa's arts in a single tradition than you can grasp the meaning of European art by examining Tuscan painting of the fifteenth century. And what goes for art goes, even more, for life. Africa's forms of life are too diverse to capture in a single ideal type. An understanding of our goldweights requires that you know something not of African, but of Akan, life: the generalities about African life are, by and large, human generalities.

So we might as well face up to the obvious problem: neither Africa nor art – the two animating principles of the show the Royal Academy originated and the Guggenheim exhibited – played a role as ideas in the creation of the objects in that spectacular show.

* * * *

Take, first, "Africa": through the long ages of human cultural life there and, more particularly, in the half-dozen or so millennia since the construction of the first great architectural monuments of the Nile Valley, most people in the continent have lived in societies that defined both self and other by ties of blood or power. It would never have occurred to most of the Africans in this long history to think that they belonged to a larger human group, were defined by a shared relationship to the African continent: a hundred years ago it would not have occurred to anyone in my hometown. Only recently has the idea of Africa come to figure importantly in the thinking of many Africans and those that took up this idea got it, by and large, from European culture.

The Europeans who colonised the continent thought of sub-Saharan Africa as a single place, in large part because they thought of it as the home of a single – Negro – race. (That is why, when we speak of Africans, black people come to mind: despite the fact that lighter-skinned North Africans – Arabs, Berbers, Moors – are unequivocally inhabitants of continental Africa.) In the European imagination the cultures and societies of sub-Saharan Africa formed a single continuum, reflecting an underlying racial unity, which expressed itself in the "savage rhythms" of African music, the "sensuality" of African dance, the "primitive vigour" of sculpture and masks from what they called the "Dark Continent".

As intellectuals in Africa came to think of themselves, for the first time, as members of a Negro race – and as Africans – they drew not only on this general western conception, but also on the ideas of African-American intellectuals (Alexander Crummel, EW Blyden, WEB Du Bois), who had been taught to understand themselves as Negroes in the context of the New World system of racial domination, the consequence of slavery. In the New World, where so many dark-skinned people had been brought together from Africa and deprived of the specific cultural knowledge and traditions of their ancestors, the common experience of the Middle Passage and of enslavement bonded together people whose ancestors had lived very diverse styles of life, hundreds, sometimes thousands, of miles apart. In the New World – in Brazil, or Cuba or the United States – people of diverse African ancestries, bound together in each place by a shared language, might end up experiencing themselves as a unity.

But in Africa itself the great diversity of societies and cultural forms was not homogenised by the slave trade. Over the last millennium, as Islam spread across North Africa and into West Africa and down the East African littoral; over the last few centuries, as Christianity came (with its multiple inflections) in the footsteps of European trade and colonisation; over the last century, as colonial empires bound African societies increasingly tightly into the new global economic system and into the modern order of nation-states; over the last decades, as the global spread of radio and television and the record and film industries has reached its tentacles into villages and towns all over Africa – throughout this time there have, of course, been enormous forces bringing the experiences of African societies closer together. But despite all these forces, the central cultural fact of African life, in my judgement, remains not the sameness of Africa's cultures, but their enormous diversity.

This should not be surprising. We are speaking of a continent of hundreds of millions of people. We are talking of hundreds of languages. A thousand years ago Christianity in Ethiopia was older than it is now anywhere south of the equator; Islam was settled in Egypt and beginning to move into a period of dominance in the Sahel; and a majority of Africans worshipped the thousands of gods whose posterity remains in shrines all over the continent. Long before Charlemagne was crowned, the ancestors of the San people in Southern Africa were living – as many continued to live until a hundred years ago – free of rulers, in small nomadic family groups; but African kingship in Egypt was millennia old. When the American republic began there were matrilineal kingdoms in Asante and patrilineal kingdoms in Yorubaland; there were female regiments in Dahomey, and high-born Hausa women living in enclosed Moslem households in Kano in what is now upper Nigeria; cats were food for the Mossi in West Africa and taboo for the Asante; and the range of clothing across the continent included most of the forms of dress (and undress) that the human species has known. Religious diversity, political diversity, diversity in clothing and cuisine: Africa has enough cultural diversity to satisfy the wildest multiculturalist.

* * *

But the fact is that the legacy of the old European way of thinking, which sees Africa as united, as the home of the Negro, makes it natural for us, here in the West, to expect there to be a shared African essence; and the tradition makes us equally likely to expect that this essence will show itself in the unity of African art. In this older way of thinking, after all, all the arts everywhere expressed the common genius of a people. (This is one reason why so many of the objects collected by Europeans in Africa during the last two centuries are labelled not with the name of a maker, but with the name of a "tribe": an ethnic group whose shared conceptions these masks or bronzes or shrine-figures were thought to express.) But as one could see as one made one's way through the show at the Guggenheim, it would take an eye completely blind to the particular to reduce this magnificent miscellany to the expression of the spirit of a singular, coherent, African nature.

I have remarked, already, on the diversity of masks (and I did so mentioning only West African examples). But wandering among the installations in London and New York, one saw the magnificent brass plaques of Benin, with their representations of warriors and monarchs; Nubian incense burners in copper; lapis lazuli figurines from Egypt; Luba healing-figures from Zaire. In the installation at the Royal Academy there was a marvellous wall of wooden headrests, beautifully patinated, their burnished surfaces echoing the panelling of the room and with an elegance of design that would have been at home at the Museum of Modern Art. These were used as pillows and came from several cultures of Southern Africa (a region of intense cultural cross-fertilisation); but the Zulu headrests and Tsonga headrests fell into distinctive patterns, and the

Ethiopian headrests in the neighbouring room were different from the Somali headrests, and neither of these East African styles could be mistaken for those of Southern Africa.

What unites the show's pieces as African, to put it simply, is not a shared nature, not the shared character of the cultures from which they came, but our ideas of Africa: ideas which, as I have said, have now come to be important for many Africans – and thus are now African ideas too.

II

Let us now explore, for a moment, the second side of the difficulty I have been describing: the fact that what unites these objects from Africa as art is our concept of art as well. There is no old word in most of the thousand or so languages still spoken in Africa that adequately translates the word "art". This too is not surprising once you think about it: there is, after all, no word in seventeenth-century English (or, no doubt, in seventeenth-century Cantonese or Sanskrit) that carries exactly that burden of meaning, either. The ways we think of "art" now in the West (and the many places in the world where people have taken up this western idea) began to take something like their modern shape in the European Enlightenment. And it is no longer helpful to try to explain what art has come to be for us by offering a definition; in an age in which, as John Wisdom liked to say, "every day in every way, we are getting meta and meta", the art world has denizens whose work is to challenge every definition of art, to push us beyond every boundary, to stand outside and move beyond every attempt to fix art's meaning. Any definition of art now is a provocation and it is likely to meet the response: Here, I have made (or found) this thing that does not meet your definition and I dare you to say it is not art.

Still, we have received ideas about art and about artists: and my point is that most of these ideas were not part of the cultural baggage of the people who made the objects that we see in shows like the Guggenheim's, in western museum exhibitions of African "tribal" art. For example: since the nineteenth century especially, we have made an important distinction between the fine and the decorative arts, and we have come increasingly to think of fine art as "art for art's sake". We have come, that is, increasingly to see art as something we must assess by criteria that are intrinsic to the arts, by what we call aesthetic standards. We know art can serve a political or a moral or even a commercial purpose: but to see something as art is to evaluate it in ways that go beyond asking whether it serves these "extrinsic" purposes. Many of the objects shown at the Guggenheim, on the other hand, had primary functions that were, by our standards, non-aesthetic, and would have been assessed, first and foremost, by their ability to achieve those functions.

Take, for example, perhaps the best-known form of Kongo art: an *nkisi nkondi*. *Minkisi* (the plural of *nkisi*) are rituals for dealing with problems or achieving one's ambitions. In the course of these rituals Kongo people make use of various materials, among them carved figures with medicines sealed in their bellies, figures that are known, derivatively, as an *nkisi* too. An *nkisi nkondi* (the latter word means hunter) was aimed at chasing down wrongdoers, from oath-breakers to thieves to witches. On the surface of an *nkisi nkondo* there are often symbolic reminders of its function (one marvellous one in the show, from the Tervuren museum in Belgium, had a hunter's net wrapped around its legs). Part of what is most striking about these wooden figures is that they are covered with scores of iron nails or blades, pieces of metal that were embedded in them in the course of the ritual. To these pieces of metal, bits of cloth or hair might also be attached – the hair, say, of a stolen animal – in order to point the *nkisi* in the right direction.

The extraordinary visual impact of these figures, covered, porcupine-like, with these jagged metal extrusions, is thus the result of the process of using them. For those who did so, even for those who made the carefully carved miniatures that are often attached to their surfaces, the hunting of evil is what they were for. However evocative we find them, the fundamental test of an *nkisi* was that it should work. By contrast, something about our attitude to art is captured by the incomprehension we would feel for someone who looked at a painting and said: "It's profoundly evocative, of course, but what is it for?"

* * *

Nothing I have said is inconsistent with the recognition that masks and *minkisi* and goldweights were made by people who had notions of form that the object needed to meet if it was to be judged a well-made artefact; nor do I deny that notions of pleasing the eye existed in pre-colonial Africa and were applied to some of the objects – the gold jewellery, decorated doors and silk cloths, for example – in the Guggenheim show. The work of African art historians has unearthed a whole ethnography of such notions. The late Sylvia Boone, for example, tells us, in her *Radiance from the Waters*, how the members of the Mende Sande Society, a women's organisation in Sierra Leone, assess a mask for use in their rituals: "For a mask to be accepted by the Sande Society, it must first and foremost be beautiful, enchantingly beautiful in Sande eyes." This means that it should meet a whole range of formal criteria. It must have a smooth surface and be sharply and delicately cut. It should be properly made, with a "full, striated neck, small face with closed mouth, lowered eyes, large forehead, plaited hairdo – all symmetrical and balanced, carved in wood and dyed deep black".[2] (The Sande mask in the show was, by these standards, imperfect: it lacked the full neck.) Finally, it must be comfortable: for it exists to be worn by dancing women, and if it is uncomfortable it is "*nyande gbaméi* – useless, empty, beauty".[3]

Sylvia Boone translated the word *nyande* here as "beauty", which is, in the context, a fine translation. But this might mislead someone who does not know that, as Boone says earlier, its "exact meaning . . . can vary but will be found in the cluster of 'beautiful, good, kind, nice'".[4] (The same is true of *fé*, the word in Asante-Twi, my father's language, that you would translate as "beautiful": it is a word used to describe attractive people, ethical behaviour and good manners.) There are words like this in many languages, in Africa and elsewhere; in classical Greek, for example, there is καλοκαγαθια (kalokagathia). It is certainly not a word that suggests, as "beauty" does, a focus on how things appear to the eye and the ear. That focus reflects the tying together of art and sensation that is implicit in the very word "aesthetic". (We still keep the trace of the Greek meaning of the root "to perceive" in our word "anaesthetic": something that deprives you of sensation.) The thought that there is a certain class of artefacts – of works of art – that are primarily to be assessed by their appeal to our senses is one of the elements of that Enlightenment invention, the notion of the aesthetic, which begins the modern western idea of art. Many of the objects in the Guggenheim show, by contrast, were evaluated, like the *nkisi*, for what they did rather than how they struck the (educated) human eye.

* * *

If African art was not made by people who thought of themselves as Africans; if it was not made as art; if it reflects, collectively, no unitary African aesthetic vision; can we not still profit from the assemblage of remarkable objects we find in western collections of African art?

What, after all, does it matter that this pair of concepts – *Africa, art* – was not used by those who made these objects? They are still African; they

261

are still works of art. Maybe what unites them as African is our decision to see them together, as the products of a single continent; maybe it is we, and not their makers, who have chosen to treat these diverse objects as art. But the Guggenheim exhibition was also *our* show – it was constructed for us now, in Europe and America. It might be anything from mildly amusing to rigorously instructive to speculate what the creators of the objects celebrated in London and New York would make of our assemblage. (Consider: some of these works had religious meanings for their makers, were conceived of as bearers of invisible powers; some, on the other hand, were in use in everyday life.) But *our* first task, as responsible exhibition-goers, was to decide what *we* would do with these things, how we were to think of them.

In presenting these objects as art objects, the curators of the exhibition invited us to look at them in a certain way, to evaluate them in the manner we call "aesthetic". This means that we were invited to look at their form, their craftsmanship, the ideas they evoke, to attend to them in the way we have learned to attend in art museums. (It is hard to say more exactly what is involved here – at least in a brief compass – but most adults who go regularly to exhibitions of painting and sculpture will have practised a certain kind of attention and found it worthwhile; and if they haven't, it is hard to see why they should keep going.) So what's important isn't whether or not they are art or were art for their makers: what matters is that we are invited to treat them as art, and that the curators assure us that engaging our aesthetic attention will be rewarding. (That these assurances were warranted could be seen on the faces of the crowds in London and New York.)

We can also accept that, because the objects were selected as coming form an entire continent, there is no guarantee of what they will share, no certainty about how these objects will respond to each other. Provided you did not expect to discover in the creations a reflection of an underlying African artistic unity, an engagement with the whole exhibition could be more than the sum of the unrelated experiences of each separate object, or each separate group of objects, from a common culture. How these individual experiences added up depended, of course, as much as anything else, on the viewer, which is as it should be. But there are questions that might have guided a reading of this show and, in closing, I would like to suggest a few of mine.

* * *

First, the exhibition decisively established that anyone with half an eye can honour the artistry of Africa, a continent whose creativity has been denigrated by some and sentimentalised by others, but rarely taken seriously. I have been arguing that to take these African artworks seriously does not require us to take them as their makers took them. (If that were so, we should, no doubt, be limited to religious evaluations of Western European art of the High Middle Ages.) And one other way to take them seriously would be to reflect through them on how the enormous temporal and spatial range of human creativity exemplified in the exhibition has been adapted in our culture over the last few centuries to an interpretation of Africa as the home of people incapable of civilisation.

What does it teach us about the past of western culture that it has had such great difficulty learning to respect many of the artworks in the Guggenheim show because they were African? Many of these objects come from European collections and were assembled as curiosities or as puzzles or as scientific data: they were undoubtedly appreciated – loved even – by many of the persons who gathered them. But they have rarely lived at the heart of our aesthetic consciousness; and when they have, it has often been with astonishing condescension. Ladislas Szesci told readers of Nancy Cunard's *Negro* (a work published in 1934 in celebration of black creativity) that "the Negroes have been able to create works of art because of their innate purity and primitiveness. They can be as a prism, without any intentional preoccupation, and succeed in rendering their vision with certitude and without any imposition of exterior motive".[5] It is part of the history of *our* culture – something that bears reflection as we travel among these African artefacts – that half a century ago this was an obvious way of speaking up for African art.

What (more hopefully, perhaps) does it tell us about our cultural present that the shows at the Royal Academy and the Guggenheim brought together, for the first time, so many, so marvellous African artefacts not as ethnographic data, not as mere curiosities, but for the particular from of respectful attention we accord to art? How, in fact, may we interpret the exhibition itself as part of the history of our western culture: a moment in the complex encounter of Europe and her descendant cultures with Africa and hers? This is a question that everyone who visited this exhibition was equipped to reflect on: all of us can dredge up a common sense that we have picked up about Africa and we can test that common sense against these uncommon objects.

I saw "Africa: The Art of a Continent" for the first time at the Royal Academy. I flew to London for the weekend and spent a day among the treasures. By a mixture of luck and planning I was able to meet up with an assortment of my kin; and so I began in the morning, going around with my sister (who lives with her Norwegian husband in Namibia), her eldest son, my eldest Nigerian nephew, and an English aunt and cousin. My sister and I have grown up with goldweights; my Nigerian nephew often has seen the treasures of Benin in the national museum in Lagos; my Norwegian-Namibian nephew knows well the artefacts of Southern Africa, including the cave drawings and the ivory *omakipa* from Namibia; but for my English aunt much of the show was entirely unfamiliar. The youngest of us was not yet a teenager, the oldest was entitled to the discount for "old age pensioners" (a term more precise than "seniors", our American euphemism). It is a measure of the show's power that all of us in this disparate group of people, drawn together by my family's all-too-apparent xenophilia, found the exhibition both exhilarating and exasperating.

My sister (with her sense of what was lost to the gallery visitors who did not know, as she did, the place of goldweights and of *omakipa* in the lives of those who made them) felt the labels were too perfunctory. (What is one to do with *Nkisi nkondo, Kongo, Zaire, before 1878, wood, cord, iron, cloth?*) My aunt, on the other hand, was entranced by the look of so many unfamiliar things: they engaged her senses, they surprised her . . . and there were too many of them.

I agreed with them both. There *was* too much to see; the labels *were* too cryptic; some of them, I fear, *were*, as we happened to know, plain wrong. But the consensus over lunch was that the show was wonderful; and what made it wonderful was that the eye could linger with pleasure on the forms, the shapes and the surfaces, the patination and the pigment, and engage each object with whatever we happened to know of its materials, its history, its origin. In short, we found ourselves responding naturally to these African artefacts as art; which, when all is said and done, was all that Tom Phillips, the curator, and the Academy, had invited us to do.[6]

CHAPTER 19

CONOR CRUISE O'BRIEN: A LEGON PERSPECTIVE

ALEXANDER KWAPONG

IT IS WELL-KNOWN THAT AFRICA HAS PLAYED A SIGNIFICANT, IF NOT formative, role in Conor Cruise O'Brien's personal life as well as in the evolution of his work as a writer, political activist and one of Ireland's leading men of public affairs. Yet before his journey to the Congo in 1961 Conor had never actually set foot on African soil south of the Sahara. His direct knowledge of Africa, and Africans, had been derived from his work with the Irish foreign service, especially at the United Nations, where he came into close contact with representatives of the growing Afro-Asian bloc. Before then, Conor's historical, political and literary focus had been mainly Irish and European. It was the Congo that transformed him from the gifted historian of Parnell and the pseudonymous "Donat O'Donnell" (the author of *Maria Cross*) into the "serious . . . work-artist" Conor Cruise O'Brien, the creator of *To Katanga and Back: A UN Case History*.[1]

It was in that "electric marvel" (in Donald Harman Akenson's wonderful phrase) that the genius of Conor as an author in his own right first burst forth. Things have never been the same since. *To Katanga and Back* laid the foundation for the major works that followed during his middle years. Brilliantly written with passion (and cunning?) after his explosive resignations from the Irish diplomatic service and the United Nations, *To Katanga and Back* proved to be no ephemeral, nor merely personal, apologia. It quickly attained the status of an African classic and has stood the test of time – over three and one-half decades – since its first publication in 1962. On reading it again today, one is more than ever convinced that it should be required reading for both Africans and non-Africans alike who wish to make any sense out of the historical reality and colonial perspectives that lie behind today's tragic post-independence conflicts in Central Africa and the Congo of Mobutu and Kabila – crises with which the United Nations still continues to grapple.

Conor himself has admitted that until his Congo experience he had led "a relatively isolated and also limited middle class life and that it was in the Congo that he was pushed in at the deep end, as it were".[2] He claims that one of the reasons why Dag Hammarskjöld, the UN Secretary General, chose him as his representative to enforce the Security Council's resolution to bring the secession of Katanga to an end was because he had gained a reputation for being "the radical member of the Irish delegation who wore his mandatory anti-colonialism rather more aggressively than was prudent".[3] Here, one may also recall the ironic self-portrait he paints of an off-stage autobiographical character in his play *Murderous Angles*, a trouble-maker destined to make all hell break loose: "Clever. Bumptious. Talks too much. The British say he's a Communist, but they just mean that he's Irish. He likes to hobnob with Africans and Asians, and behaves a bit like one. He would just love himself as a kind of anti-imperialist pro-consul."[4]

* * *

If the Congo imbroglio marked an important watershed in Conor's life, the three years he spent as vice-chancellor of the University of Ghana (1962 to 1965) were no less important with regard to both his general relationship with Africa and his later career. Yet the Ghana period is not as well-known as it ought to be. It is often overshadowed by the interest he took in, say, the conflicts in Biafra and Southern Africa or his more recent, highly courageous, controversial defiance of the academic boycott imposed against South African universities on the eve of the apartheid regime's collapse.

Perhaps Conor's Ghanaian experience remains shrouded in mist because he unconsciously kept a promise made during a farewell party given in his honour by the staff and students of the University of Ghana in June 1965. To the disappointment of his numerous friends and admirers who had hoped that he would write such a book, and probably to the relief of his critics who feared that he might actually do so, Conor promised that upon leaving Accra he would not write a sequel to *To*

Katanga and Back. Because Conor kept his word, and instead contented himself with a series of newspaper articles, magazine essays and book reviews about wider political developments in Africa (including Ghana from time to time), there is neither sufficient awareness nor comprehension of the enormous and timely contribution that he made to the University of Ghana and higher education in Africa generally.

Until Donald Akenson's excellent biography filled in the gaps and told the story of Conor's stewardship of Ghana's premier university, the part his Ghanaian experience played in the unfolding of his genius – as an intellectual, literary critic, anti-apartheid activist and liberal defender of freedom – remained greatly under-appreciated. This relative ignorance about his work in Ghana, and especially his relationship with President Kwame Nkrumah, has led some even to question Conor's democratic credentials during his stay in the country: recently, one Irish journalist erroneously described him as "a devoted servant of the late Kwame Nkrumah of Ghana, whom many sincere people would characterise as a despot".[5] There were, no doubt, a number of expatriates in Ghana at the time who may be rightly characterised as "devoted servants" of Nkrumah, but Conor certainly was not one of them.

I had the good fortune to work closely with Conor during his stay in Ghana and later became his successor as vice-chancellor. I believe that it is valuable to throw further light on Conor's tenure at Legon (the actual location of the campus, just outside of Accra), for these years constitute a genuine milestone for both Conor and the university upon which he left such an indelible imprint. Conor lived in Ghana for only three years, but this was, after all, the longest stretch of time that he resided on the African continent. What's more, this was an exciting era of drama and high expectations for African colonial emancipation and freedom. And Ghana, as the first colony to gain its political independence, was the focal point of change in Black Africa.

The political, intellectual and emotional forces that Conor experienced during those heady times in the history of Ghana are, I believe, a key understanding the strong African dimension to his writing. The Ghanaian experience was a significant part of the transformation that "pushed him in even deeper at the deep end", reinforcing and intensifying his "mandatory anti-colonialism". It gave to his work a long-term direction and focus that can be discerned in his two principal preoccupations as a writer during this period. One of these preoccupations was with the conflicting concepts of the United Nations and, in this regard, his fight against neo-colonialism. The other was his defence of freedom in all of its forms, but especially his campaign for political and intellectual freedom, a battle he has continually waged on many fronts: in the academy, the political arena and on the printed page.

* * *

After Ghana gained its independence in 1957 Kwame Nkrumah rapidly emerged as the foremost exponent of the burgeoning, radical anti-imperialism sweeping across the Southern Hemisphere and also as a spearhead for the pan-African freedom and unity movement gathering momentum in the wake of Harold Macmillan's "winds of change" speech in 1960. In 1962 Nkrumah, in his capacity as chancellor of the University of Ghana, offered Conor the vice-chancellor's post. This was not an unusual move, for at the time a strong mutual affinity between the two men clearly existed. Conor admired Nkrumah for his vigorous opposition to apartheid in South Africa. He even admits that Nkrumah's analysis of the dire situation in the Congo, enunciated during a speech to the UN General Assembly in September 1960, deeply influenced his own approach to the crisis. Conversely, during the height of the fighting in Elisabethville one year later, Nkrumah, having come to respect Conor's outspoken stand against British and Belgian neo-colonialism in Katanga, publicly expressed concern for his personal safety. In addition, *To Katanga and Back* was read with great interest in Ghana.

The University of Ghana to which Conor and his wife, Máire, came in 1962 was a young, fourteen-year-old institution in a crisis of transition. It was first established as the University College of the Gold Coast in 1948. It was one of several post-war university colleges established by the British in Africa, Asia and the Caribbean, all of which were affiliated to the University of London. The bulk of these institutions had been established with grants from British Colonial Development and Welfare funds, but the University College of the Gold Coast was distinctive in being a genuinely nationally-funded project.

It is important to emphasise the national ownership of this new institution, the pride the people of Ghana felt for it and their insistence that it should be nothing but the best of universities. Originally, the British had proposed only one university college, located at Ibadan in Nigeria, to serve the whole of West Africa, but the people of the Gold Coast had demanded and obtained one of their own. This was built, equipped and sustained with generous financial resources provided by the colony's rich gold and cocoa economy. Remarkably, within a decade (which, incidentally, coincided with the last decade of the Gold Coast's own transformation into independent Ghana), a beautifully-landscaped, earthquake-proofed residential college campus had been created at Legon. A first-rate teaching and research faculty comprising an expatriate majority and a growing Ghanaian minority – all with international academic credentials – had been assembled. And a small, but steady, stream of graduates was being produced and then absorbed by the public and private sectors of the country, thereby providing some of the high-level manpower necessary for the nation's smooth transition to independence.

The college was fortunate to have as its founding Principal Mr David Balme, a distinguished Cambridge Classical philosophy scholar, Aristotelian expert and Royal Air Force ace during World War II who turned out to be a remarkable institution-builder. During his nine-year tenure, Balme succeeded in creating not only a university second-to-none in Africa and beyond, but one with a special style and character patterned after the Oxbridge residential system, complete with tutorials, academic gowns, high tables and Latin grace before meals. One decade later these traditional trappings had given way to a more mundane style, but it is important neither to mistake these outward, archaic forms of academic ritual – essentially a matter of style – for the substance of Balme's vision of a university nor to belittle his enduring achievement of laying solid academic foundations for university education in Ghana. Balme articulated his vision during the inauguration of Legon Hall (the first permanent hall of residence) in 1953:

> I was instructed to plan a university of 5,000 students. It will be many years before the secondary schools will support so large a university, though in terms of the total population and the work to be done, the figure is not unreasonable. Universities are never complete until they are dead. This university must be part of the country's growth, growing with it, responding to its needs, reflecting the development of its genius.

As the subsequent history of the university has confirmed, such a vision has served the university, and the nation, well.

Balme's successor, Dr RH Stoughton, Professor of Agriculture from Reading University, was less fortunate. He faced several problems during his short, three-year term, most generated by the rapid pace of political change. Relations between the university and the state, for instance, were inflamed by the circumstances surrounding the passage from university college status with links to London to an autonomous institution located in a newly-independent nation. On one occasion an international academic advisory commission recommended that the contracts of existing staff members should not be terminated during the transition period, yet the government ignored this advice by refusing to renew the contracts of six faculty members (five were expatriates and the sixth, a Ghanaian who was the school's highly competent academic registrar, was discriminated against on political grounds). This action demoralised the faculty and precipitated a serious crisis that persisted throughout most of 1961.[6] It still festered in October of that year when the University of Ghana was formally inaugurated under a new charter and President Nkrumah became chancellor – not only of the Legon campus, but of universities in Kumasi and the Cape Coast as well.

* * *

Well-aware of this background, and especially the strained relations between the state and the university, Conor Cruise O'Brien agreed to assume the vice-chancellorship *only after* satisfying for himself, during an exploratory visit undertaken with Máire, that he would be welcomed not just by Nkrumah, but by the university faculty also. Conor, after all, had no wish to appear as a political appointee "imposed by the state on an unwilling university or to be caught in a cross-fire similar to what [he] had encountered in Katanga".[7]

When Conor and Máire visited Legon in February 1962 I was on a sabbatical at Princeton University and cannot, therefore, claim to have been one of the senior staff members who encouraged him to become vice-chancellor. Yet the rest of the faculty were relieved to find that someone suitable had been proposed for the vacant post. Conor's appointment, as it turned out, was a masterstroke of genius – and one that Nkrumah himself could hardly have anticipated. His unique combination of assets – an international high-profile, political clout, his *bona fides* as an anti-imperialist, his scholarly and intellectual brilliance and, above all, his fearless integrity – quickly demonstrated to staff and students alike that he was the right man for the right occasion. It is, indeed, no exaggeration to say that at the end of his tenure his numerous admirers in the university and country at large considered him to be a kind of *homo ex machina* who had not only saved the institution from irreparable damage, but ensured that it would evolve into a great university.

I returned to Legon in September, just as Conor took up his appointment. Soon thereafter the faculty elected me to the posts of pro-vice-chancellor and dean of arts – the first Ghanaian to hold these positions. In these capacities it was my good fortune to work closely with Conor for the next three years. I saw him on a daily basis and came to know him as well as anyone on the Legon campus. As pro-vice-chancellor it was my responsibility to provide the vice-chancellor not only with administrative and academic support, but to give him the loyalty and critical advice, especially in matters requiring local knowledge and institutional memory, that he was entitled to expect from his colleague. In the process, we soon became firm friends.

* * *

The first year of Conor's tenure was a honeymoon period between the university and the Nkrumah government, and a harmonious official and personal relationship developed between Conor, Máire and the president. Signs of this rapport included occasional exclusive dinners at the vice-chancellor's lodge, Nkrumah's informal consultations with Conor on several foreign policy issues, including the Congo, and Conor's occasional ghost-writing of speeches for the president. Generally, Conor appeared to have the chancellor's ear on matters concerning the university. But equally important, Conor swiftly secured his academic base by asserting his intellectual and moral leadership within the university and by placing his policy cards face-up on the table. In his initial meeting with the university's academic board, for example, he explained the two basic principles which would govern his tenure of office: developing the role of the university in a newly-independent country; and the sanctity of academic freedom.

With regard to the first guideline, Conor pointed out that as great as the university's services to Ghana had been so far, it had been rather slow to adapt itself to vital changes in the environment, that is, the milieu of national independence. This delay had given rise to friction and mutual distrust and had led to the "brusque transition". He therefore urged the university to develop a relationship of continuing dialogue with the state that would favour "a steady, healthy and undisturbed expansion of the university's work: an expansion in which the *university itself will be setting the pace*" (my emphasis). And he reminded his listeners that informal discussions he had held with staff members demonstrated that "there was a great determination among Ghanaians and expatriates alike in the university to serve Ghana – and through Ghana, Africa – in all the many ways in which a university can contribute to developing countries".[8]

On the second issue – the nature and conditions of academic freedom – Conor delivered a classic exposition that strongly resonated with his audience and was, in fact, prophetic. "Speaking purely pragmatically," he argued:

> a university, in any large sense of the word, cannot flourish in . . . conditions [of extra-academic surveillance and interference] and the defence of academic freedom in that sense is a necessity of university life. *If academic freedom in that sense were ever to be assailed here, it should be my duty as vice-chancellor to defend it by all means in my power, and I should do so* (my emphasis).

And he added, somewhat optimistically: "But I have no reason whatsoever to believe that this basic freedom is under attack or is likely to become so." Demonstrating his feel for nuance, he rejected the opinion held by some that:

> a university, even if financially dependent on the state – as this university is – has the right, or even the duty, to ignore the views of the state as regards, for example, the number of students which should be accepted for higher education, or the categories of graduates which the country most needs. On the contrary, the university must argue and defend its own viewpoint . . . Academic freedom, in the central, pragmatic sense, is a flag well-worth fighting for [and] that is all the more reason for not unfurling it without good and sufficient cause.[9]

This well-received address to the academic board was aimed at the university community in the first instance, but it also served notice to the state authorities and the wider public in Ghana of the kinds of policies that Conor intended to pursue. Within months he successfully reinforced his aims by convincing Nkrumah to publicly announce, during a graduation dinner in February 1963, that the state would scrupulously respect academic freedom in all of the universities throughout the country. In fact, he read, without any substantial modification, a statement drafted by Conor. In the light of the use that Conor later made of this passage in his unanticipated battles with Nkrumah, it merits attention. "We know that the objectives of a university cannot be achieved without scrupulous respect for academic freedom," the chancellor rhapsodised:

272

for without academic freedom there can be no university. Teachers must be free to teach their subjects without any concern [other] than to convey to their students the truth as faithfully as they know it. Scholars must be free to pursue the truth and to publish the results of their researches without fear, for true scholarship fears nothing.[10]

Later, Nkrumah assented to having his speech reprinted in the *Vice-Chancellor's Annual Report* (1963); it also featured prominently in Conor's address one year later during the height of a crisis that was soon to break out. With foresight, Conor had set a rhetorical trap – and later sprung it to defend the university.

* * *

Indeed, despite its auspicious start, the last two years of Conor's tenure descended into days of mounting turmoil. A detailed account of these events is available elsewhere,[11] but the following summary, as seen from my own "ringside" view, will prove helpful. Three inter-related issues gave rise to the crisis: the establishment of a medical school; indigenous disenchantment with the law faculty; and the sudden demand that all students enroll in a course in political indoctrination masquerading as a citizenship-training programme. A common denominator linking these matters – and worsening relations between the state and the university – was a growing anti-Americanism now manifest within the government and its puppet organisation, the Convention People's Party. Adding fuel to the fire was the creeping centralisation of political power in the person of Nkrumah – now addressed by the Akan appellation "Osagyefo", meaning "redeemer" or "mighty warrior" – who wished to transform the country from a *de facto* into a *de jure* one-party African socialist state. The university was one of the few institutions where party activists were thin on the ground, and this imbalance needed to be redressed.

As a result, Nkrumah's cabinet scotched Conor's nearly-completed design for a medical school on the ideological grounds that it was over-dependent on American financial backing – a form of neo-colonialism, in other words. Conor ruefully remarked: "this isn't changing horses in mid-stream; it amounts to shooting your horse under you just as you reach the opposite bank". More to the point, this sudden change of policy marked the beginning of Conor's real disenchantment with Osagyefo's dispensation, a sentiment that intensified when Nkrumah instructed Conor to dismiss all expatriate members of the law faculty (including

Burnett Harvey, the dean of the law school who was on a two-year secondment from the University of Michigan). Conor refused to carry out this request, just as he blocked the establishment of a "citizenship training programme" (with the complete support of the faculty, all of whom admired his skilful, Fabian tactics). Obviously, Conor was animated by the spirit of the university's motto: *Integri Procedamus* – Integrity with Progress.

Nevertheless, external events weighed heavily on the campus. They interacted with internal pressures to bring the crisis to a boil. In December 1963 a panel of judges ruled that three party officials on trial for treason were innocent, but Nkrumah overturned the acquittal, dismissed the judges and ordered the rearrest and retrial of the defendants. Conor, who was in Geneva recruiting faculty for the medical school, immediately issued a statement to the International Commission of Jurists condemning Nkrumah's actions: he had acted, he explained, in his capacity as vice-chancellor of a university with a law school. Upon his return to Ghana he wrote to Nkrumah seeking a meeting, but was denied access to the chancellor for virtually the remainder of his term of office.

Similar episodes rapidly followed in January 1964. A popular referendum approved Nkrumah's plan to turn Ghana into a one-party state; a police bodyguard attempted to assassinate him; two members of the university faculty were arrested, one of whom was later deported. The final bombshell exploded when the security forces demanded that Conor dismiss four members of the university staff for allegedly subversive activities and later deported six expatriate lecturers, including Professor Schuster, an African-American who had arrived in Ghana only two weeks previously.

In response to this systematic harassment of the faculty, several student groups planned a demonstration, but this provoked a massive, pre-emptive invasion of the Legon campus by thousands of noisy, placard-bearing activists from the Convention People's Party on 7 February, the very day the government deported the members of the faculty. The registrar, Kofi Edzii, and I tried to contain the crowd, while Conor dashed off to Flagstaff House, the residence of the president, to protest to the secretary of the cabinet. Fortunately, the university students heeded Conor's earlier plea for calm, so clashes with the protesters did not ensue.

In the midst of this sombre atmosphere Conor delivered an address to the University Congregation on 14 March. It is one of the greatest, most eloquent speeches the University of Ghana has ever heard. The air was electric; the community and, indeed, the country had awaited Conor's response to the recent *evenements* and they were not disappointed. Quietly, but with controlled, deadly lucidity, Conor summoned forth a work of art, a paean in defence of academic and universal freedoms. It was true, he asserted, that:

> The values to which we adhere have nothing in common with colonialism or with any other system of oppression, nor have they anything in common with neo-colonialism or any other system of deceit. They are forces of their nature hostile to such systems as colonialism and neo-colonialism, and they have served to bring about the downfall of the first system and the exposure of the second. Respect for truth; intellectual courage in the pursuit of truth; moral courage in the telling of truth – these are the qualities of a real, of a living university. Since the days of Socrates in Greece and Mencius in China these values have been asserted, and have been attacked. None of us, alas, is Socrates or Mencius – and philosophy seems to have fallen on evil days – but no member of an academy can forget, without being unfaithful to his calling, how Socrates lived and how he died . . . These are not European values; they are universal values. Mencius taught in China very much in the same spirit as Socrates taught in Greece . . . In Europe, and in America, these values have had at least as many enemies as defenders, as the names of Dr Goebbels and Senator McCarthy remind us.
>
> This ancient continent of Africa, which gave the world one of its first and richest civilisations, has the right to share in and contribute to the universal intellectual heritage which we associate with Socrates and Mencius. The University has the duty, not only to transmit intact that heritage, but to provide intellectual conditions in which a modern African genius can make his own fresh and unpredictable contribution to the development of the human mind. We are here to provide, in Yeats' phrase: . . . *not what they would /But the right twigs for an eagle's nest.*

This speech sums up the essence of Conor's achievement in preserving for posterity a vision which has inspired later generations. And in retrospect, Conor's tenure as vice-chancellor of the University of Ghana, which ended in 1965, was not a transient interlude in the history of the school. *Au contraire*, Conor's brilliant, timely and dogged defence of the twin principles of academic freedom and university autonomy, on the one hand, and his strong demonstration of the university's relevance to the development needs of the nation, on the other, ensured that the premier educational institution in Ghana emerged intact from the grave crisis it faced and matured into the great *African* university first envisioned by its founders.

I wish to close, however, with a few personal reflections. My most vivid memories of Conor are of his extraordinary intellectual creativity, epitomised by the rich and unceasing stream of literary criticism, book reviews and essays that he poured out to various magazines and journals. At the same time, he conscientiously attended to the daily routine of a very busy vice-chancellor – endless academic committees, correspondence and administrative duties – while taking the trouble to meet with and entertain staff, students and various personalities outside of the university. Towering above these memories is my recollection of the brilliant epistolary campaign that he successfully waged against Nkrumah when he was denied access to him. As pro-vice-chancellor I was privileged to see the many literary gems he penned to the president in response to the latter's copious demands. But above all, I remember my great appreciation when Conor shared with me the draft manuscript of his great essay on the politics of Yeats, "Passion and Cunning". He wrote this seminal piece at Abetifi, a retreat in the hilly country of Kwahu, some eighty miles from Accra, to which he and Máire had retired during a lull in the battle in February 1964.

Finally, the support, love and comfort that Máire gave to Conor was tremendously significant. She sustained him during his three years at Legon, and she is fondly remembered by their many friends here in Ghana as an essential part of the memorable contribution that Conor made to the development and preservation of the University of Ghana.

CHAPTER 20

CONOR CRUISE O'BRIEN AT THE
UNIVERSITY OF CAPE TOWN:
THE GREAT CACOPHONY

DAVID WELSH

IT IS NECESSARY TO BEGIN THIS CONTRIBUTION WITH AN EXPLANATION: I appear in it rather more than would usually be considered appropriate in a *Festschrift*. It is unavoidable, however, since I was one of the principal actors in the drama that surrounded Conor's visit to my university.

As (then) head of the Department of Political Studies at the University of Cape Town (UCT), I had invited Conor to be a visiting professor and to deliver a course of lectures to undergraduate students in the fourth quarter of 1986. Conor had visited South Africa in 1985 and delivered two lectures in the Department. It was soon after this visit that he wrote a seminal article, "What Can Become of South Africa?" in the *Atlantic Monthly*.[1] The article was a wonderful mix of acute reportage and deep historical knowledge. Conor put forward these propositions to the South Africans he met: "The maintenance of the status quo is impossible. Reforms acceptable both to the white electorate and to politicised blacks are impossible. Revolution is impossible."

The propositions gave rise to considerable debate in South Africa. Implicitly, Conor had identified the stalemate whose making was then well advanced. It would take that rare conjunction of outstanding leaders, FW de Klerk and Nelson Mandela, to recognise that unless the stalemate were broken, and negotiations initiated, South Africa's low-intensity war might become a high-intensity one.

277

South Africa in 1986 did not look a hopeful society. Much of the 1980s featured turmoil and violence. State President PW Botha had made a number of important reforms, but, like Gorbachev, he was unable fully to liberate himself from the apartheid paradigm. Tension was felt in every institution in the country, not least in the universities, where a rising generation of black activists, hardened by a decade of resistance, were flexing their muscles. The state of emergency that was extended in 1986 to the entire country was a powerful instrument of coercion that resulted in the detention of thousands of the state's opponents, but at the cost of heightening their anger and determination.

It was into this cauldron that Conor and his son Patrick came in September 1986, at my invitation. He was to teach the second segment of a course called Siege Societies – which comprised a comparison of South Africa, Israel and Northern Ireland – to a class of approximately 100 students.

Most of Conor's class were white, middle class English-speakers, probably of a generally liberal outlook. The University of Cape Town is a venerable institution that traces its origins back to 1829, when the South African College was established. Full university status was achieved in 1918. The admission of non-white students proceeded slowly in the inter-war years and accelerated slightly after 1945. Most were Coloured ("mixed-race"). By 1959, when apartheid was applied to those universities that, in principle, admitted students of all races, the percentage of students who were other than white was four. The euphemistically-named Extension of University Education Act of 1959 debarred non-white students from attending "white" universities except by permit from the relevant government department. Such permits were granted only in cases where the study course a student wished to take was not offered by the university college (also established in terms of the 1959 legislation) appropriate to the student's race or ethnic group. Thus three institutions (including Fort Hare University College, which had been established in 1916) served Africans of different ethno-linguistic clusters; one, located in Durban, served Indians; and another, located in Cape Town, served the Coloured community. All five operated under tight official control.

The so-called "open" universities of Cape Town and the Witwatersrand, Johannesburg, regarded the 1959 legislation as a serious violation of university autonomy and protested vigorously before and after the legislation's enactment. Both had become strongholds of liberal thought in the 1950s and had broadened their protest to encompass the entire range of apartheid policies. By the late 1970s student organisations, like the elected Student Representative Councils and the inter-university National Union of South African Students (NUSAS), were fast shifting beyond the traditional liberal values that had underpinned university protest. Varieties of Marxism sprouted as student activists joined "the struggle". In the 1980s it was not uncommon for more conservative white citizens of Cape Town, apprehensive about the influences to which their student offspring were being exposed, to refer to UCT as "the Kremlin on the hill". Increasingly also white student radicals sought to make common cause with the banned African National Congress (ANC) and, after its formation in 1983, the United Democratic Front, which soon became little more than an internal surrogate of the ANC. It is highly likely that an active branch of the South African Communist Party flourished secretly on the campus.

Another development was also profoundly shaping the student body: the permit system, which restricted the number of non-white students granted admission into UCT, was rapidly breaking down. Legislation enacted in 1983 requiring universities to enforce racial "quotas" in their admissions was not enforced in the face of vigorous protest. In short, the barriers to the admission of non-white students were falling: by 1986 UCT's student body of over 12,000 included 439 Africans, 1295 Coloureds and 299 Indians, i.e., over fifteen percent of the total.[2] Although they were a minority, and by no means all or even most were activists, their presence on the campus brought a new dimension to student politics. In the turbulent 1980s it was not possible to divorce life as a student on the (relatively) tranquil campus of UCT from life in the besieged townships in which these students lived.

On the whole, the University of Cape Town's record of protest against apartheid was a creditable one, notwithstanding occasional carping criticism that it was "ritualised" or merely "formal". Many members of the teaching staff shared their students' views; many were *engagé* scholars, whose writings embodied far-reaching critiques of apartheid; and some, along with student leaders, had been "banned" under the notorious Suppression of Communism Act and thus forced out of the university. The university's leadership found itself in an ongoing dilemma: it opposed the draconian legislation that infringed upon university autonomy and academic freedom, but, simultaneously, it sought to maintain at least some semblance of institutional neutrality. It supported the right of students to protest, but only within the bounds of legality. Successive vice-chancellors gained considerable experience in defusing potential confrontations between student demonstrators and the police or making representations to obtain the release of those arrested.

In 1986 the vice-chancellor was Dr Stuart Saunders,[3] a physician by training and a liberal by conviction. He was broadly sympathetic to the students' cause, but he did not wish to see his institution destroyed by major confrontations with the state. Shortly before Conor's arrival, Saunders had been part of a combined delegation from the University of Cape Town and the University of the Western Cape that had visited the ANC at its exile headquarters in Lusaka, Zambia. The opening address at the meeting was delivered by Professor HJ Simons, formerly one of UCT's leading scholars, who had been banned from teaching in 1965 and thereafter left the country. At the time he headed the ANC's education desk. The ensuing discussions were cordial, and Saunders was pleased to hear of the high regard in which ANC officials held UCT and their hopes for the role it could play in a post-apartheid South Africa. But they disagreed on an important issue that was to become the principal bone of contention of Conor's visit: the academic boycott. The ANC believed that white South Africa should be isolated in every possible way: economically (implying sanctions), politically, intellectually and in international sport. By 1986 the academic boycott, driven principally by British academics, was beginning to have an impact on the four "historically white" English-medium universities. Applications from abroad for posts dwindled (though poor university salaries in South Africa were also a factor); invitations to British scholars to act as external examiners were increasingly being refused; fewer foreign scholars were prepared to make even brief trips to South Africa through fear of incurring their colleagues' displeasure; and South African scholars found it more and more difficult to attend overseas conferences or even to have their papers published in foreign journals.

Publicity for the academic boycott reached a climax with the decision of the organisers to "disinvite" South African delegates to the World Archaeological Congress, held in Southampton from 1-7 September 1986. The act of "disinvitation" had occurred exactly one year before, in September 1985, thus allowing a full year for public debate prior to Conor's departure for South Africa in September 1986.

Conor entered the debate in Britain with characteristic trenchancy, arguing that while he supported economic sanctions, he opposed the academic boycott. In a speech at the meeting where the fuse was lit (see below), Conor said of the academic boycott:

> its impact on the apartheid regime would be nil, but the inroads it was making on academic freedom and freedom of expression were very serious

indeed. These values would be vital to a non-racial South Africa and to other free societies. What was being conducted in South Africa under the banner of an academic boycott seemed to be a sort of creeping form of the Cultural Revolution, which had wrecked the universities of China and which the China of today repudiated with abhorrence.[4]

The first three or so weeks of Conor's visit went off smoothly. Many in his class appreciated that they were hearing one of the great minds of the western world, which, of course, was precisely why I had invited him. I entirely shared Conor's views on the folly of the academic boycott, believing that it would achieve little, further impoverish our already isolated universities and perhaps even please the government, which was never keen on "undesirable" foreign influences in the universities.

It seems that the impetus to wreck Conor's tour came from Ireland and Britain and was readily supported by local ANC-aligned sources. In an interview after the events, the president of the Students' Representative Council, Carla Sutherland, quite openly acknowledged this:

> There was a huge row even before he [Conor] had left Ireland. After he had arrived in South Africa, the Anti-Apartheid Movement and the National Union of Students of England [sic] directed a request to NUSAS and the Azanian Students' Organisation [a radical black movement] that the 'issue' against him should be 'taken further'. There was also pressure on the University of Cape Town.[5]

It was subsequently revealed, to Ms Sutherland's embarrassment, that she had endorsed a request by the Political Studies Department to an internal university body, the Students' Visiting Lecturers Organisation, to provide some of the funding for Conor's visit.

Another contribution to wrecking the lecture series came from an altogether different quarter: the notorious Security Police. For years before the Security Police had infiltrated student organisations, spied on lecturers and listened in on their classes. They also employed *agents provocateur* to incite students to engage in illegal activities (not difficult in South Africa's circumstances) or to inflame conflict situations (which occurred often), so that the ever-vigilant Security Police could burnish its reputation as essential custodians of the racial order. One Danie Cronjé, who took a prominent part in the demonstrations against Conor (including attacking the Campus Control officials with a studded belt), later confessed to his role as a police informer and *agent provocateur*.

The actual events that led to the termination of Conor's lectures need only be described briefly. They began on 2 October 1986 when Conor was conned into what he had understood to be a debate, which was arranged by the Social Sciences Students Council (a body dominated by radicals). It turned out to be what Conor called "an organised grilling", led by Patrick Bulger, then a student, now political editor of the (Johannesburg) *Star*, one of the leading English-language dailies. Tempers, including Conor's, rose. This was, no doubt, the organisers' intention. Irritated by the transparent attempt to put him off his stroke, Conor grew angrier and called the academic boycott "Mickey Mouse stuff" and described "alternative" education programmes run by militant activists as propaganda. But he did not lose his temper and he did *not* say (as the University of Cape Town's Commission of Enquiry subsequently claimed, solely on the basis of hearsay evidence) that "I was insulting and condescending. I did not follow my own standards. I was guilty of an error of judgement".[6] Still, the unflattering references to the academic boycott and the alternative programmes gave the radicals the stick they needed.

Thereafter, tensions rose and the pace of events accelerated. Protests were held against Conor's presence on the campus, including a march on the vice-chancellor's office demanding to know why the Azanian Students' Organisation had not been consulted prior to the invitation being extended to Conor. Plans were later made to disrupt a lecture that Conor was due to give on the evening of 7 October to the Institute of Jewish Studies. The university authorities, knowing of the plot, invoked the so-called "special rules", designed a few years earlier to protect the right of visiting speakers to be heard. (They were colloquially known as the "Buthelezi rules", after Mangosuthu Buthelezi, the Inkatha leader and a frequent target of militants, had been denied the right to deliver a lecture in August 1984.) Essentially, the special rules were an honest effort by the university to safeguard freedom of expression in an unpromising context, wherein it was threatened by both left and right. In practice, the rules meant little more than students being required to show their registration cards to gain admission. The right of dissenters to protest was specifically protected, provided that their actions neither infringed disciplinary rules nor violated the rights of those who had extended the invitation to the visiting speaker.

The special rules counted for little on 7 October. Conor delivered a much-truncated lecture amidst a hubbub of protest from nearly 200 students who had been locked out of the lecture theatre. At approximately 8:30 pm – just as the vice-chancellor, who had taken the chair, was adjourning the meeting – the students forced their way through the front doors and streamed into the theatre. Conor was spirited out by a side door.

Much the same happened the following day when Conor attempted to give his normal, scheduled lecture to his Political Studies class. Radical students broke through a human chain formed by 12 Campus Control officers guarding the building and poured into the lecture hall. Again, Conor, who remained cool, was whisked out a side entrance, guided upstairs, ushered into my wife's car and rushed off the campus. Although the protesters denied any violent intent, and UCT's subsequent Commission of Enquiry played down the potential for injury, it was the opinion of many of Conor's students that he had been in real danger of serious assault had the protesters been able to corner him.

After this episode the campus was in uproar. An *ad hoc* committee formed by anti-Conor students (never more than a few hundred) ensured that the temperature remained high. An ANC pamphlet circulated at the time urged students to "Boycott Foreign Academics". Part of it read:

> The presence of reactionary academics like Connor [sic] Cruise O'Brien at UCT exposes the real position of UCT in relation to our struggle for liberation. For too long, universities have pretended to be islands of democracy and non-racialism in the ocean of Apartheid. This is not entirely correct. The universities remain white controlled. How many administrators, professors and Council members are from the ranks of the oppressed? How does the university serve the needs of the working people? When does the university consult with popular organisations to build people's education? Yes, NUSAS and the UCT and UWC [University of the Western Cape] administrations have consulted with the African National Congress, which is a step in the right direction. But the university staff and students still have to show through action that they are not part of Apartheid tyranny but are for people's power. Importing foreign academics does not assist our struggle.[7]

The pamphlet provided revealing insights into the ANC's views on universities, not only during the anti-apartheid campaign, but, very likely, after liberation as well. They were seen in essentially instrumentalist terms, with little room for either autonomy or neutrality. Likewise, they were "sites of struggle", which, historically, has seldom been good for the health of universities so enmeshed. Students opposed to the academic boycott issued a rival leaflet which pointed to the baneful consequences of (even greater) isolation, saying: "If you are concerned about the future of this university and the quality of your education, then take every opportunity to show your opposition to the foolhardiness of deliberate academic self-isolation."[8]

After the break-up of Conor's lectures it was clear that it was unsafe for him to remain on campus, let alone finish his course, which, in any case, was almost over. He and Dr Saunders acquiesced in terminating the course, Saunders saying that they had jointly agreed that Conor would leave if "his continuing to lecture on campus was a source of disruption and could cause danger to life and limb".[9] Unhappily, this was true. There was, to my deep chagrin and to UCT's embarrassment, no alternative. It showed how fragile and vulnerable universities are in the face of even small, but militant, groups determined to hold an institution to ransom.

Saunders was in an invidious position: he was roundly opposed to the academic boycott; he greatly admired Conor's writings over the years; yet he faced other constraints. First, he could not call in the police to maintain "law and order": it was a long-standing practice not to do so, since this would have appeared to align UCT with the principal instrument of state repression. By the same token, Campus Control, although efficient, was too small to hold the line, especially if militants from the nearby University of the Western Cape (the self-proclaimed "intellectual home of the left") were bussed onto the UCT campus to join the protests. More pressing than these weighty factors, however, was the imminent start of the end-of-year examination season. Disruption of the examinations was a serious possibility, whose consequences would be grave.

Both the University Council and the Senate (consisting largely of faculty) passed resolutions condemning the events. In particular, both bodies rejected "in the strongest possible terms any actions aimed at further curtailing academic freedom".[10] Both bodies supported Dr Saunders' view that a Commission of Enquiry be established to examine what had happened and how such events could be prevented in the future. Essentially, it was a move aimed at defusing a volatile situation. Thus was born the (du Plessis) *Commission of Enquiry into the Events which occurred on the campus of the University of Cape Town on 7 and 8 October 1986*. Its members were Dr DJ du Plessis (an academic surgeon and a former vice-chancellor of the University of the Witwatersrand), Advocate Arthur Chaskalson, SC (a leading public interest barrister, who had defended many accused in political trials) and Advocate Ismail Mahomed, SC (also a prominent defence counsel in many political trials). It is worth mentioning that Chaskalson is now President of the Constitutional Court and Mahomed is Chief Justice of South Africa.[11] Clearly, the latter two members were chosen to ensure that the Commission enjoyed credibility in more radical circles. Even so, NUSAS, the SRC and AZASO declined to be officially represented at the Commission's hearings on the grounds that they had not been consulted about the appointment and terms of reference of the Commission.

284

The Commission completed its labours on 18 December 1986, in the middle of the university's long summer vacation. Its report was submitted to the University Council, which met in special session on 12 January 1987. Despite serious criticisms of the report's lack of objectivity, notably by Dr Frank Bradlow, an art historian and long-serving member of the Council, the Council resolved to accept the "main thrust of the recommendations made by the Commission" and to reaffirm its commitment to upholding the freedom of the university and "the right of any academic, subject to the normal rights of the heads of departments, faculties and Senate, to invite any person to take part in an academic programme . . ."[12]

The key phrase in all of this was the "main thrust of the recommendations". It enabled the Council to evade passing judgement on some of the Commission's principal findings, which it knew to be incorrect – and several members believed to be seriously biased. If it was a ploy, which I suspected, I was determined not to let it succeed.

The vice-chancellor declined to give me access to the report until 20 January 1987. When I read it I was appalled. I immediately did two things: resign as head of department and issue a press statement. My press release described the report as:

> one-sided, flawed and shoddy. In major respects, its reading of the evidence is faulty, while crucial pieces are ignored. I resent in particular the Commission's unfairness to Dr O'Brien, whose alleged personality characteristics and motivations are subjected to an analysis to which Dr O'Brien has had no opportunity to reply. The Commission evinces little recognition of his stature as a scholar and it accepts too easily specious evidence which claims that he came to UCT for ulterior, non-academic reasons. Dr O'Brien is a friend of mine and I take full responsibility for inviting him – yet I was not asked a single question by the Commission about his personality or about the reasons for my inviting him or his accepting. It is perhaps indicative of the Commission's approach [I should have said 'provincialism'] that they even spell his name incorrectly [throughout the report he is called 'Connor'].[13]

The errors made by the Commission and the faultiness of its judgements are too numerous to list, let alone analyse comprehensively. Still, its most egregious blunders merit attention. First, Conor's massive achievements as a scholar are hardly acknowledged. Instead, he is portrayed as a "political activist who, over the years, has evoked considerable controversy in political circles".[14] Furthermore, he was described not only a political activist, but also "a person endowed with what appears to be a colourful and volatile personality, not easily able to

285

maintain academic detachment under conditions of emotional stress and excitement".[15] This was an amazing finding, falling just short of a slur on alleged Irish ethnic characteristics. It made no allowance for Conor's having been set up for a supposed debate nor the jeering and sneering to which he was subjected. To compound the insult, the report imputed hearsay evidence to him, quoting him as apologising for being "guilty of an error of judgement" – all of which Conor denied.[16] Some balance might have been achieved had the Commission assayed an attempt to portray the alleged personality characteristics of his leading detractors. I called them "little fascists of the left", which, in retrospect, was far too mild.

Secondly, I was blamed, obliquely (the commission did not appear to have the courage of its convictions roundly to criticise me), for the "wisdom" of inviting Conor.[17] I rejected this with the contempt that it deserved. I was also blamed for not having the "special rules" invoked, which was absurd on two levels: the university authorities were well aware of the impending crisis, especially after the Institute of Jewish Studies lecture (mentioned above); but also because the common understanding of these rules was that they were intended to apply to "one-off" talks given by outside speakers, not relatively long-term visitors like Conor, whose course had, in any case, been approved by the Senate.

Thirdly, the Commission deliberately appeared to overlook critical evidence. The most serious instance of this was its failure to pay heed to Carla Sutherland's admission that outside pressure had played a part in stirring the pot (see above). The Commission was given access to all press clippings covering the period, and their attention was specifically drawn to her comment by my faculty colleague, Hermann Giliomee, when he gave oral evidence. How does one explain this omission of evidence that was important to any assessment of the causes? A Nelsonian blind eye because it might have complicated a concerted attempt to whitewash the disrupters and blame the victims (principally Conor and me)? Or, more charitably, oversight? I do not know.

A telling comment was made by Frank Bradlow: that the Commission "failed to deal with the most essential issue aroused by the O'Brien incident, namely, who is to run the University, a small group of dissident students whether they be right-wing students or left-wing students, or the executive [of UCT] and academic staff and administration?"[18] I was also unable to understand why the University Council was so reluctant to repudiate the Commission's findings on Conor's alleged personality traits and my negligence. I was angry about the latter, but far angrier about the defamatory remarks made about my friend, who was justifiably annoyed about such animadversions. I spent a lot of time over the next few months trying to secure a repudiation, even suggesting to Dr Saunders that he fly to Dublin and personally apologise to Conor. It was all in vain.

It was not until 21 April 1987 that some measure of justice could be done. This was at an extremely rancorous Senate meeting. A relatively uncontroversial motion, proposed by one of the deputy vice-chancellors, John Reid, acknowledged that the invitation to Conor had been extended "for academic reasons only". The fireworks began when I, seconded by my colleague, Robert Schrire, proposed that the Senate reject those findings of the Commission's report which concerned Conor personally and express to him its apology for any damage that was done to his reputation.

I made a fiery speech, extracts from which I now quote (at Conor's express request):

I would have hoped for a motion that rejected this report outright: it is a shoddy effort, unworthy of association with UCT, and incapable of being used as a basis for reconciliation . . .

I remind Senate that we are not dealing with some hick from the bogs of Ireland, but a world-class scholar. [I then listed some of Conor's literary achievements.] But even were he a hick, it would not excuse the Commission's handling of him; even less the Council's crass dealing with the issue.

The report is a classic case of blaming the victim . . . Hardly less extraordinary – and, I might add, unforgivable – is UCT's failure to ensure that Dr O'Brien had received a copy of the report before its release to the Press . . . [I then quoted Conor:] 'The first I heard about it was on radio and in the newspapers. I feel pretty shabbily treated in not being given a warning, and I'm surprised at such behaviour on the part of a very respectable university.' So were many of us [at UCT] . . .

I invited him, and I could have told the Commission exactly why I had done so . . . I certainly had in mind no thought other than giving our students the opportunity to hear one of the great minds of our time. Yet I was not asked about this. It is hardly necessary to add that the Commission ignores completely the [highly favourable] reaction of Dr O'Brien's class to his course and to the debacle whereby it was terminated [which they deplored].

It is not good enough for the UCT Council to take refuge in the statement that it accepts the 'main thrust' of the recommendations. That, frankly, is an evasion which has brought UCT into disrepute. If the Council, for reasons that I find inexplicable, finds it impossible to bring itself to make a formal apology, then it behoves Senate to do so. I too wish to heal wounds, but of one thing I am certain: you cannot heal wounds by ignoring the real injustice done to individuals.[19]

287

After lengthy and acrimonious debate a slightly amended version of the motion was accepted by 59 votes to 9, with 22 abstentions. I was delighted to hear from a colleague that after the meeting a senior official of UCT was overheard to say that mine "was the most disgraceful speech he had ever heard in Senate". I could not have wished for a better accolade!

So, was it a storm in a far-off teacup, with little universal or durable significance? Or did the whole episode give an indication not only of the temper of the times in South Africa, but also of the regard in which a future ANC government might hold freedoms, in general, and academic freedom, in particular? The ANC would no doubt argue that the academic boycott was necessary in the context of the times (although Conor's prediction that its effect on apartheid would be nil was exactly right), but now that liberation has been achieved freedoms are secure. Indeed, the South African Constitution of 1996 specifically protects "academic freedom and freedom of scientific research" as a component of freedom of expression.

It takes considerable optimism, however, to suppose that the Bill of Rights has taken root in the infertile soil of what is still a deeply divided society. It would also be premature to believe that the rights of visiting speakers and their campus audiences are secure. Few South African universities are sufficiently free from a high degree of political partisanship that a speaker with "incorrect" views would be allowed a fair hearing. I have doubts, for example, whether Mangosuthu Buthelezi or FW de Klerk would escape the wrath of militants at UCT, even in today's ostensibly democratic times.

Academic freedom is never complete and it cannot be turned on and off in accordance with the supposed dictates of the times. As I have argued elsewhere, "academic freedom is a particular subset of wider human freedoms: if you like, it is civil liberty in an academic context. As such, it most certainly embraces freedom of speech, subject, of course, to the rules of scholarly debate and the general criteria of academic civility".[20] At the same time, the habits of disruption and intolerance are hard to break. Conor thus spoke prophetic words after leaving the University of Cape Town in 1986:

> I believe that free debate is serving the community in the long term and it is very important to the future of South Africa that the universities should be intact when the change to a society with non-racial institutions comes. To let radical students decide who should teach and who should not is destroying the university from within.[21]

I can only say Amen.

VIII

THE UNITED NATIONS
AND THE MIDDLE EAST

CHAPTER 21

ENCOUNTERS

GIDEON RAFAEL

UNTIL THE ADMISSION OF IRELAND INTO THE UNITED NATIONS IN 1955 THE representatives of Israel were seated, by the rigour of alphabetic order, between Iraq and Lebanon. Since, in the view of these Arab delegates, the state of Israel did not exist, they ignored the presence of its representatives. Conor Cruise O'Brien, Ireland's first delegate on the Special Political Committee, has commented that his seating between Israel and Iraq greatly "relieved each of them of an extremely uncongenial neighbour".[1] Conor turned out to be a good-humoured companion of mine as we rafted through the roaring cascades of UN oratory.

The representative of Iraq, Fadil al-Jamali, was rather strict in his ostracism. His Lebanese colleague, Charles Malik, a Greek Orthodox, and a man of friendly disposition inclined to philosophical musings, was more lenient in the application of the social ban. The Iraqi delegate, who tried to avoid me when passing the ashtray to his Lebanese colleague – yes, at that time delegates still smoked in public meetings – usually transferred it behind my back in an exercise demanding a measure of severe bodily contortion which he apparently was ready to suffer for the sake of the cause.

Charles Malik, however, occasionally turned to me, much to the dismay of his Iraqi colleagues, and very courteously asked me to point out to him the part of the relevant document the committee was discussing. Observers were divided in their interpretation of his approaches. Some thought they were the aberrations of an absent-minded professor; others

291

attributed them to the good manners of a well-educated diplomat. Be that as it may, over the course of the years Ambassador Malik (who later became Lebanon's Foreign Minister) increasingly disregarded the Arab sound barrier. To be sure, we continued our controversies in plenary and committee sessions, yet we conducted searching conversations on the future of Israeli-Arab relations in the delegates' lounge.

In August 1953 the *New York Times* reported that I had been appointed to a new post in Jerusalem to "prepare specific plans for some of Israel's disputes with the Arabs, against the day when agreement seems near. Israeli sources said that the Foreign Ministry wanted to be ready for the time when an Israeli-Arab peace became a reality".[2] The day the story appeared Charles Malik came up to me in the delegates' lounge, his face beaming. "My heartiest congratulations on your new appointment," he exclaimed, pumping my hand, much to the consternation of his Arab colleagues. "You are a lucky man to have landed, so early in your career, a nice and quiet lifetime job."

A few years later, before the outbreak of the Six-Day War, Malik published a well-argued analysis of the future of Arab-Israel relations in a noted Arab periodical. He argued that in view of Israel's scientific and technological advancement, and its special relationship with the United States, the Arabs could not defeat Israel in battle. The conflict, he asserted, could only be settled by peaceful means.

In July 1982, at the height of Israel's military intervention in Lebanon, I visited the battle zone. The Israeli forces were deployed on the heights dominating Beirut. Their command post was not far from the presidential palace. The Foreign Ministry in Jerusalem had instructed its liaison official with the armed forces to arrange a meeting between myself and Charles Malik, who had retired to his native village in the vicinity. Indeed, Malik had passed along word that he looked forward, with pleasure, to meeting his "old friend".

At the appointed hour, however, Israeli artillery and air forces began a fullblast bombardment of Beirut, barring movement in any direction. The liaison official had to cancel our meeting. Malik regretted this outcome, especially the cause which had frustrated our reunion. Charles Malik died a few years later. His "old friend", though meanwhile retired, still hopes to see the accomplishment of "his lifetime job".

* * *

Fadil al-Jamali, the representative of Iraq, never became an "old friend". He religiously observed the ban against speaking with me throughout all the years of his tenure. But once, in the heat of a debate, he slipped. Since Israel did not exist he would never address its representatives, in customary UN style, as "the distinguished delegate of . . . " Instead, he would use all kinds of circumlocutions. During one debate, having exhausted his stock of substitutes, Ambassador al-Jamali hurled his verbal assault against a "Mr Gideon", accusing him of all the sins of Israel. The committee chairman, visibly amused by al-Jamali's comical innovation, and apparently afraid that the debate might degenerate into another verbal slugging match, adjourned the meeting for lunch – an enticing proposition, always enjoying common assent.

Feeling that al-Jamali's diatribe addressed to a "Mr Gideon" was a gratuitous occasion to make light of his idiosyncrasy, I asked for the floor. The chairman, referring to the committee's decision to adjourn, refused my request. But there is always a last resort in parliamentary procedure: the ominous point of order, one of the most abused circumventions of orderly conduct.

Ignoring the dismay of the chairman and the impatience of my colleagues, I said: "I greatly appreciate the distinguished representative of Iraq addressing me by my first name. I would like to see in it the beginning of a rapprochement, foreboding a new relationship. However, I feel that the vehemence of his tirade against the country I am privileged to represent contradicts somehow the intimacy of addressing its representative by his first name. To foster the bonds of neighbourliness, I wish to introduce myself to him." Then, with a polite bow, I presented myself: "Gideon Rafael, representative of Israel." My slightly perplexed neighbour responded with a faint smile, while the members of the committee, animated and relieved, quickly adjourned.

A few years later Ambassador Fadil al-Jamali, who by then had been named the last Foreign Minister in the pro-western government of Nurit Said, fell victim to the military coup which overthrew the Iraqi monarchy and its administration. On 14 July 1958 the insurgents, under the command of Brigadier Abd al-Karim Qassem, the leader of the revolution, murdered King Faysal and his family. Prime Minister Nuri Said was slaughtered by a mob while trying to escape; the frenzied crowd dragged his mutilated body through the streets of Baghdad.

Al-Jamali was condemned to death by the so-called Court of the Revolution. Conor Cruise O'Brien tells us in his book, *The Siege: The Saga of Israel and Zionism*, that when the General Assembly convened in September 1958, two months after the Baghdad coup, O'Brien "asked his new neighbour, the head of the new Iraqi delegation on the committee, whether he had any news of his predecessor [Fadil al-Jamali]. Without moving a muscle, and with his gaze firmly directed into space, my new neighbour pronounced the single word: 'Hanged'".[3] This statement was apparently based more on wishful thinking than actual fact. Fadil al-Jamali, though having been condemned to death, had had his sentence commuted. And, being married to a German lady, he and his wife were permitted to emigrate to her country.

In 1967 I met one of Ambassador al-Jamali's successors, Adnan Pachachi, a scion of a distinguished pre-revolutionary Iraqi family. We had known each other from sight, but as "uncongenial neighbours" at the United Nations had never exchanged a word. In April 1967, with the clouds of war gathering in the Middle East, my government entrusted me with a special mission to Moscow. My task was to clarify, at the highest available level, the dangerous situation in the Middle East and explain that the Israeli government sought to avoid a military confrontation. We felt that the Soviet policy of one-sided political and military support of the Arab side, however, was increasing tensions in the region.

Travelling to Moscow with my daughter in an Austrian airliner, which we had boarded in Vienna, I discovered a familiar travel companion. The man seated on my right at the United Nations was on board: Adnan Pachachi, by then the Foreign Minister of Iraq, was also Moscow-bound. Apart from the destination, we had nothing in common. Although he glanced from time to time in my direction, he displayed remarkable self-control in suppressing his obvious curiosity about the reasons for our joint flight and separate missions to Moscow.

Andrei Gromyko was waiting at the steps of the plane to greet his Iraqi counterpart. Pouring rain and the apprehension that I might descend into the midst of the reception festivities shortened the proceedings to a brief handshake and deprived Pachachi of his well-deserved bear hug. He was swiftly whisked away. To be on the safe side, Soviet protocol allowed a decent interval to elapse before we were invited to disembark.

SECRETARIES GENERAL

In the course of more than twenty years representing Israel in various capacities in the United Nations, I enjoyed close working relationships and personal friendships with three Secretaries General: Trygve Lie, Dag

Hammarskjöld and U Thant. I worked with them in times of crisis – the on-going Arab-Israel conflict always provided ample opportunities – and shared their confidences and anxieties when they suffered personal attacks or political intrigues.

On this personal level, I remember encounters with Trygve Lie at the height of the McCarthy witch-hunts, when he was accused of having fostered the infestation of the Secretariat with communists and Soviet agents. After a harassing FBI investigation had driven one of his closest colleagues, the legal adviser of the United Nations, Professor Abe Feller, to commit suicide, I encountered Lie in a state of utter despondency. He was lamenting his helplessness in the face of the persecution of members of his staff, which was conducted by organs of the United States government. These same forces were also waging a personal defamation campaign against him. Unable to protect the United Nations, he said he had no alternative but to resign. And so he did.

Our political contacts with Trygve Lie were more cheerful, by far. One late Sunday afternoon in January 1949 he called my Israeli diplomatic colleague, Arthur Lourie, who was the Consul-General in New York, and requested him to travel immediately to his residence in Forest Hills. Lourie asked me to accompany him. We suspected that the reason for the urgency of his summons was the shooting down by the Israel defence forces of three or four RAF spitfires on a reconnaissance mission over the war zone in the southern part of Israel. The fighting against the invading Egyptian forces had not yet been concluded by an armistice agreement. The incident aroused furore in Britain; simultaneously, in other countries it evoked admiration for the prowess of Israel's fledgling air force.

Lie received us with a sombre mien, quite different from his usual jovial countenance. With a commanding gesture to sit down, he said: "The British Ambassador to the United Nations, Sir Alexander Cadogan, presented me today with a strong protest and stern warning to the government of Israel, claiming that its armed forces had attacked a number of RAF planes flying over Palestine. Her Majesty's Government felt bound to warn the government of Israel of the grave consequences of its action. In the absence of diplomatic relations between Britain and Israel, the Ambassador had asked the Secretary General to transmit the note to the Israeli mission at the United Nations."

Handing over the paper to Arthur Lourie, Trygve Lie asked for details about the incident. We told him the little we knew at that hour and promised to get back to him as soon as we had received a full report. At that point, Lie, leaning back in his armchair, visibly satisfied at having acquitted himself of an unpleasant duty, resumed his amiable mien, excusing himself for the informality of his attire. His stout figure, dressed in a hunter's costume, made him look like Wotan in Wagner's Valhalla.

"As you see me here, I just came back from a hunting trip," he continued. "Half a day I stood in a swamp, up to here," he said, pointing to his voluminous waistline, "and didn't bag a single bird, and you fellows manage to shoot down on a Sunday morning a couple of British fighter planes. Wow, that's something." Then, reaching for the decanter, regaling us with excellent whiskey, and with an amused grin, he raised his glass to toast Israel.

Of the "grave consequences" threatened in the British note, the only concrete result was a stormy debate in the House of Commons, where the opposition accused the government of being foolish for refusing to establish diplomatic relations with the state of Israel instead of following the example set by the United States, the Soviet Union and numerous other governments from the four corners of the world. A few weeks after the parliamentary debate Her Majesty's Government appointed its first Ambassador to Israel.

DAG HAMMARSKJÖLD

The relations between Trygve Lie's successor, Dag Hammarskjöld, and Israel were less placid and, on occasion, rather strained. One particularly delicate period comes to mind: the negotiations between the Secretary General and the delegation of Israel in the aftermath of the Sinai-Suez campaign in 1956. Hammarskjöld considered the joint Franco-British-Israeli operation a flagrant violation of the United Nations Charter. A vast majority of the members of the organisation who followed the lead of the Eisenhower administration and the Soviet government supported his view and his subsequent actions. Instantly, after the outbreak of hostilities, the Security Council had imposed an immediate cease-fire and ordered the withdrawal of foreign forces from Egyptian territory. France and Britain succumbed to Washington's pressure without much hesitation. Israel, however, tried to hold on to Sinai and Gaza as long as possible or at least until the Canadian-initiated United Nation Emergency Force had been deployed there.

Abba Eban, Israel's Ambassador to both the United States and the United Nations, headed our negotiating team. He discussed the relevant issues with Secretary of State John Foster Dulles in Washington and with

Secretary General Hammarskjöld in New York. The going at both places was not easy at all. It was particularly difficult in New York, where Hammarskjöld opposed any concessions to Israel, such as guarantees against the reinstitution of the Egyptian blockade at Sharm el-Sheikh and the recurrence of raids against Israel from the Gaza area. With tenacity, and while tiring and exasperating the Secretary General in the process, we defended every inch of our position against the United Nations bulldozer. Whenever Hammarskjöld felt he required added weight to break an impasse in the talks he activated the General Assembly, which dutifully supplied him with more ammunition.

While the talks in the Secretary General's office were dragging on inconclusively, Golda Meir followed them with growing anxiety from her hotel suite at the Savoy Plaza. It was the first time she had attended the General Assembly as Israel's Foreign Minister, having recently replaced Moshe Sharett, who resigned because of his opposition to the planned Sinai Campaign. At a particularly difficult point in the negotiations Golda decided to join us. It was one of those late-night sessions necessitated by the full daytime schedule of the participants. She was determined to take the Secretary General to task for his callous disregard of Israel's dilemma. She did not mince her words nor spare Hammarskjöld personal reproach.

Hammarskjöld was normally a patient, but tense, listener. Yet with every new cadence of Golda's indictment he became more and more fidgety, until he lost his self-control. With his face flushing red, he interrupted her icily: "Why are you so bitter, madam?"

His words hit Golda like a stone. For a moment she was stunned, but rallied quickly. "Because I am anguished by the thought of the bitter fate awaiting our people if we are deprived of our capacity to defend ourselves," answered Golda with a heavy heart, but a much softer voice. The exchange did not alter anything of substance, except that from now on Golda accorded Hammarskjöld a prominent and lasting place on her list of *personae non gratae*.

* * *

My personal relations with Dag Hammarskjöld, however, were not affected by our differences on the Sinai Campaign and other aspects of the Arab-Israel conflict. His personality was fascinating. His wide intellectual scope was impressive. His personal sensitivity, convictions and civility were put to severe tests in the rough and tumble world of strife and cynicism dominating the United Nations. Circumstances compelled him to navigate between Scylla and Charybdis.

I met Dag Hammarskjöld for the last time in the spring of 1961. He was in a sombre mood. A long and stormy session of the General Assembly, which had been attended by a formidable array of heads of state, had just concluded. This was the session, in fact, where Nikita Khrushchev pounded the desk with his shoe and the president of the Assembly – Freddy Boland, Ireland's Permanent Representative to the United Nations – broke his gavel while trying to restore order. More ominously, earlier in the Assembly session the representatives of the Soviet bloc had launched an all-out attack on the Secretary General, demanding that he resign and be replaced by a troika.

When the session resumed in March 1961, after adjourning the preceding December, it soon became apparent that the Soviet fury against Dag Hammarskjöld had not abated. Andrei Gromyko, the Russian Foreign Minister, led the assault. On one deplorable occasion, while he was being called an accomplice to the murder of Patrice Lumumba in the Congo, Hammarskjöld sat in his seat to the Assembly President's right, as silent and as serene as a statue, without wincing even once.

When I entered his office high above the East River soon afterwards, Hammarskjöld greeted me with his customary courtesy. Still, he looked tired. His drawn expression showed the strain of a six-month effort to steer a fractious General Assembly through roaring rapids to a safe haven. As always, we sat down in one corner of his large office.

"Well, this was a rough session," he began. "I'm glad it's over, but so much remains to be done. Ralph Bunche told me that you were worried about the deterioration of manners and parliamentary procedure in the United Nations."

I nodded, remarking that my ambassadorial assignment to Brussels had prevented my attendance at the last three sessions. I also expressed my astonishment and distress at the vulgar political language that was being employed, and even tolerated, in the supreme international forum. I added that it seemed to me the United Nations was high in principle, but low in practice. Hammarskjöld's face lit up.

"You're right," he said, "something should be done to improve the parliamentary conduct of the UN. The increase in membership alone calls for some streamlining of procedures."

I agreed.

Hammarskjöld leaned forward and continued: "But if this troika proposal were to be adopted, the work of the United Nations would come to a halt; the whole organisation might even disintegrate."

I reminded him that our delegation opposed the idea of replacing the Secretary General with a three-man directorate. I jokingly added that from what we had experienced, the United Nations was adequately and effectively represented by a single Secretary General. Our long exchanges in the wake of the Sinai Campaign had convinced us that he did not need two additional colleagues to be able to pursue his aims.

He corrected me: "The aims of the United Nations."

I said: "I wonder. Many things have happened during the last four years to vindicate our position. But, of course, we are still too close to the events for an objective assessment. Let future historians decide who did what and why."

Hammarskjöld returned to the troika proposal: "I wonder why the Soviets are pushing it so hard, for it has no chance of being adopted. After all, I am their main target. What they want is to oust me. I am their *bête noire*, because they believe that I frustrated their plan to gain power and influence in the Congo."

After I expressed my admiration for the way he had countered the offensive against him, Hammarskjöld continued: "I don't think the Soviets have sufficient political strength to force my resignation. Not only do the western powers support me, most of the non-aligned countries also stand behind me. As long as I have such backing I feel strong enough to carry on." He paused and closed his eyes. Then in a low, soft voice, as if speaking to himself, he said: "Yes, political support – that's all right – and Soviet opposition is understandable. After all, they did the same thing to Trygve Lie. Any man in my position has to expect opposition. But whether I have the strength to bear their vulgarity I just don't know." I tried to change the subject, but Hammarskjöld returned to his point: "I tell you the only thing that really worries me is that this vulgarity may prove intolerable."

Our talk reverted to the Congo. Hammarskjöld spoke of the course of action he planned. He asked my opinion of certain individuals there and the position of certain countries on the question, mentioning my visits to the Congo and my assignment in Belgium. But our conversation had lost its momentum. Hammarskjöld's anxieties brooded over it.

I got up to take my leave. He shook my hand firmly and asked me to remember him to a number of friends in Israel. As I reached the door I turned around. Hammarskjöld was standing in the middle of the room, his legs apart, his hands behind his back. He raised his head and said, as if reciting lines from a Classical drama: "Here I work and try to do what I believe to be my duty. But suddenly I feel that strange beasts are lurking in the shadows around me. From which direction will they charge? I look over there, but they come at me from here."

I was stunned. There stood the Secretary General of the United Nations, like a character out of Shakespeare, voicing the tribulations of the high and noble. I felt deep concern and could only say: "*Au revoir* until September."

But in September, in the dark African night, death claimed a man who could bear the fiercest political attack without flinching, but whose armour was not proof against the slings and arrows of vulgarity.

U THANT

Secretary General U Thant's spiritual world, his beliefs and, I dare say, his superstitions were entirely different from those of his European predecessors. He was a mild mannered man, courteous to the extreme. His natural restraint, bordering on introversion, prevented him from seeking publicity when he came into international prominence as a candidate to succeed Dag Hammarskjöld.

As representatives of two very friendly countries, Burma and Israel, we maintained close working relations. Regardless of Dag Hammarskjöld's tragic death, the Soviet government continued to vigorously pursue their troika proposal, which produced a complete deadlock in the search for a new Secretary General.

By chance or design, a member of the Secretariat told me one day that Andrei Gromyko – during a conversation with a high UN official when Hammarskjöld was still in office and while the Soviet Union was still pressing its troika demand – mentioned the name of U Thant as a possible compromise candidate for the post of Secretary General. Yet since the western countries had not the slightest inclination to replace the incumbent, no one had pursued the hint. After Hammarskjöld's death I inquired, in a casual talk with Valery Zorin, the Soviet Union's UN representative, whether U Thant would still be acceptable to his government as a compromise candidate. Zorin answered with a question: "Would the Americans support him?" I said I had no idea. "Then go and ask them," commanded Zorin.

Instead, I decided to ask U Thant whether he was available. He questioned me intensely about the details of my conversation with Zorin, particularly the date and exact hour of our meeting, which he noted in his diary. Then, without committing himself, he suggested that I follow Zorin's advice.

I did and met with Adlai Stevenson, the Permanent Representative of the United States. The news surprised him. He was rather sceptical about Soviet intentions and the professional ability of U Thant, but promised to check the idea with Washington. The next day he called and suggested that I advise Zorin to contact his American colleague. I informed U Thant accordingly, who again asked for every little detail of my talks with Stevenson, especially the exact hour and the location where they had taken place. After delivering the American message to Ambassador Zorin I ended my role as go-between, leaving the deal making to the powers-in-being.

After U Thant's election I told the story to a friend, who knew U Thant intimately. I asked him to explain to me the reason for U Thant's meticulous listing of the date and exact hour of my conversations. My friend was astonished about my ignorance. "Don't you know," he said, "that U Thant always consults his horoscope before taking any decision?"

In 1967 U Thant came under strong criticism for having mismanaged the crisis preceding the Six-Day War. His critics claimed that by dealing more forcefully with the situation on the eve of the war he could have prevented its outbreak. I found it unfair to saddle U Thant with the major responsibility for the course of events. Addressing the Security Council, I said: "U Thant tried to do his best. The war was not his fault." Who else's fault was it then? Probably his horoscope's.

POSTSCRIPT

On the twenty-fifth anniversary of the Six-Day War the State Department sponsored a conference in Washington, during which prominent participants in the 1967 crisis – Israelis, Arabs, Russians, Americans, UN officials – gathered to reexamine the steps and missteps that led to the war. One of those who attended was George Tomeh, Syria's UN Ambassador. We had been seated side by side during heated debates in the Security Council, but he never spoke to me or looked at me. There was no amiable Conor Cruise O'Brien to bridge the gap.

When we assembled for the first meeting of the review conference a participant approached me, wearing a friendly smile on his face and holding out his hand. He looked faintly familiar. Noticing my bewilderment, he introduced himself: "George Tomeh, your neighbour on the Security Council twenty-five years ago." I shook his hand and apologised profusely for not having recognised him; after all, I had never met him face-to-face, only in profile.

I told Tomeh, however, that at one point in the debate a member of his delegation had inadvertently established contact with my delegation. When our verbal clashes had reached the heights of intensity over the question whether the Israeli forces had taken the key town of Kuneitra on the road to Damascus, a member of the Syrian delegation tried unsuccessfully to locate the place on his map. He turned to his neighbour on the right and asked him in Arabic: "Where is this god-forsaken place, Kuneitra?" My Arabic-speaking colleague on the Israeli delegation politely pointed it out. His act of technical assistance was welcomed with an absent-minded "thank you very much" and, later, a side-glance of utter stupefaction.

Ambassador Tomeh greeted the story with hearty laughter and added: "Tell me, Ambassador Rafael, didn't we have a hell of a job defending the positions of our countries?"

"Indeed, we had," I agreed.

"All right then," suggested Ambassador Tomeh, "let's record this as the first Syrian-Israeli post-war agreement and announce it at the conference." We jointly proceeded to the conference table, where I divulged the good news.

The unusual encounter reminded me of Senator Warren Austin, who was America's Permanent Representative to the United Nations in 1948. Exasperated by the fierce exchanges in the Security Council between the Arab and Israeli delegates, he thundered: "Can't you Jews and Arabs settle this bloody conflict in the true Christian spirit?" Could it be that Ambassador Tomeh's friendly gesture was a delayed response to Senator Austin's touching appeal half a century and five major wars later?

CHAPTER 22

YOU NEED BEETHOVEN TO MODERNISE

DANIEL PIPES

IT IS POSSIBLE TO MODERNISE WITHOUT WESTERNISING? THIS IS THE DREAM of despots around the world. Leaders as diverse as Mao on the left and Khomeini on the right seek a high-growth economy and a powerful military – without the pesky distractions of democracy, the rule of law and the whole notion of the pursuit of happiness. They welcome American medical and military technology, but reject its political philosophy or popular culture. Technology shorn of cultural baggage is their ideal.

Sad for them, fully reaping the benefits of western creativity requires an immersion into the western culture that produced it. Modernity does not exist by itself, but is inextricably attached to its makers. High rates of economic growth depend not just on the right tax laws, but on a population versed in the basics of punctuality, the work ethic and delayed gratification. The flight team for an advanced jet bomber cannot be plucked out of a village, but needs to be steeped in an entire approach to life. Political stability requires a sense of responsibility that only civil society can inculcate. And so forth.

Western music proves this point with special clarity, precisely because it is so irrelevant to modernisation. Playing the Kreuzer Sonata adds nothing to one's GDP; enjoying an operetta does not enhance one's force projection. And yet, to be fully modern means mastering western music; competence at western music, in fact, closely parallels a country's wealth and power, as the experiences of two civilisations, Muslim and Japanese, show. Muslim reluctance to accept western music foreshadows a general difficulty with modernity; Japanese mastery of every style from classical to jazz helps explain everything from the historically powerful yen to institutional stability.

MUSLIMS

Among Muslims, choice of music represents deep issues of identity. Secularist Muslims tend to welcome European and American music, seeing it as a badge of liberation and culture. Ziya Gökalp, the leading theorist of Turkish secular nationalism, wrote in the early 1920s that Turks:

> face three kinds of music today: eastern music, western music and folk music. Which one of them belongs to our nation? We saw that eastern music is both deathly and non-national. Folk music is our national culture, western music is the music of our new civilisation. Neither of the latter can be foreign to us.[1]

More recently, as Turkish secularists find themselves under siege, sold-out crowds turn out for concerts featuring western classical music. In the words of a reporter, these have "become a symbolic rallying point for defenders of Turkish secularism".[2] In an event rich with symbolism, the Turkish embassy in Tehran gave a two-hour concert of western classical music in late December 1997, in tribute to the forthcoming (Christian) New Year.[3] Few cultural occasions could quite so sharply delineate the contrasting visions of Atatürk and Khomeini.

In contrast, fundamentalist Muslims, who nurse an abiding suspicion of the West, worry that its music has an insidious effect on Muslims. When Necmettin Erbakan was prime minister of Turkey in 1996-97, he cut back on dance ensembles, symphony orchestras and other western-style organisations. Instead, he fought to increase funding for groups upholding traditional musical forms.

For fundamentalists, listening to western music denotes disloyalty to Islam. A speaker at a fundamentalist rally in Istanbul flattered his audience by telling them: "This is the real Turkey. This is not the aimless crowd that goes out to see [sic] the Ninth Symphony."[4] An Iranian poem characterises the opposite of the downtrodden, faithful Iranians killed by Iraqi troops as an audience of classical music buffs – women with "pushed-back scarves" (i.e., who resist Islamic modesty) and men with protruding bellies (i.e., who profit from the black market). The same poem, titled "For Whom do the Violin Bows Move?" argues that concerts of Mozart and Beethoven promote the "worm of monarchic culture". Anyone who listens to *Eine Kleine Nachtmusik,* in other words, must be a traitor to the Islamic republic. Or to Islam itself: naming the very same composers, a Tunisian claims that "the treason of an Arab . . . begins when he enjoys listening to Mozart or Beethoven".[6]

Of course, if eighteenth-century composers so rile fundamentalist Muslims, what might they think of rock and rap music? American popular music epitomises the values that Muslims find most reprehensible about western culture – the celebration of individualism, youth, hedonism and unregulated sexuality. The Pakistani fundamentalist group Hizbullah has singled out Michael Jackson and Madonna as cultural "terrorists" who aspire to destroy Islamic civilisation. The group's spokesman explains this fear: "Michael Jackson and Madonna are the torchbearers of American society, their cultural and social values . . . that are destroying humanity. They are ruining the lives of thousands of Muslims and leading them to destruction, away from their religion, ethics and morality."[7] Hizbullah finished with a call for the two Americans to be brought to trial in Pakistan.

The Hizbullah statement points to the reasons why fundamentalists mistrust western music: it demoralises Muslims and distracts them from the serious requirements of their faith. Ahmad al-Qattan, a Palestinian preacher living in Kuwait, finds that western music "involves pleasure and ecstasy, similar to drugs", and elaborates:

> I ask a lot of people, 'When you listen to Michael Jackson, or Beethoven, or Mozart, what do you feel?'
> They tell me: 'Oh, I feel my heart torn from the inside.'
> I say, 'To that extent?'
> They tell me: 'Yes, by God, to that extent. I feel that all of a sudden I am flying. One moment I am crying, the next moment I am laughing, then dancing, then I am committing suicide.'
> Our God, we seek refuge with You from singing and its evils.[8]

Ayatollah Khomeini had similar views, as he explained to an Italian journalist:

> Khomeini: Music dulls the mind, because it involves pleasure and ecstasy, similar to drugs. Your music I mean. Usually your music has not exalted the spirit, it puts it to sleep. And it destructs [sic] our youth, who become poisoned by it, and then they no longer care about their country.
>
> Oriani Fallaci: Even the music of Bach, Beethoven, Verdi?
>
> Khomeini: I do not know these names.[9]

But then, unexpectedly perhaps, Khomeini softened his condemnation: "If their music does not dull the mind, they will not be prohibited. Some of your music is permitted. For example, marches and hymns for marching . . . Yes, but your marches are permitted." Others join Khomeini in making this exception. Qattan, for example, also distinguishes between degenerate and useful music: "No Mozart and no Michael Jackson, no singing and no instruments, only war drums."[10] The ecstasy that western music can create is allowable only of it helps march youths to their death.

(Interestingly, marches are the only western music significantly influenced by the Middle East: Gypsies introduced Turkish – or "Janissary" – music to Europe in the eighteenth century. The Austrian army appears to have been the first to have adopted this genre, which involved not just new percussion instruments (tambourines, triangles, cymbals, bass drums and – suggestively – crescents), but also exotic new uniforms. Accented grace notes added to the exoticism. Soon after, these elements entered the orchestra too; Mozart first used Turkish-style music in a sketch dating from 1772, and "Turkish" effects are especially prominent in his *Abduction from the Seraglio* as well as the finale to Beethoven's Ninth Symphony. In a sense, then, the Middle East is letting back in its own innovation.)

Other fundamentalists have divergent ideas on what music is permissible, a debate symbolised by the King Fahd Cultural Centre, a magnificent concert hall seating 3,000 on the perimeter of Riyadh, Saudi Arabia. Shortly before his death in 1975, King Faysal approved the building of this centre as part of the recreational facilities to turn Riyadh, his capital city, into a handsome modern city. Completed in 1989 at a cost of $140 million, it boasts such lavish touches as the finest marble and precious woods, not to speak of a state-of-the-art laser lighting system, a hydraulic stage and other advanced features. But the hall has never staged an event. A foreign diplomat who managed to visit the mothballed facility found that a full-time staff of 180 has, for almost a decade, maintained the building and its gardens in mint condition. This has meant not just tending the flower beds, but air-conditioning the facility all year around so that the delicate woods on the interior do not deteriorate. Why is the cultural centre not used? Because it offends the strict Islamic sensibilities prevalent in Saudi Arabia. According to one report, on hearing about western-style music played by mixed casts (meaning men and women) to mixed audiences, the country's religious leaders "went berserk".[11]

The saga of Riyadh's concert hall neatly illustrates the ongoing debate on western music among fundamentalist Muslims. King Faysal, no slouch in his Islamic faith, thought it a permissible pleasure, but the Saudi religious authorities deemed otherwise. Other fundamentalists too disagree on specifics. The author of an advice column in a Los Angeles Muslim weekly concedes that "Music with soft and good tunes, and melodious songs with pure words and concepts, are acceptable in Islam", provided that this does not lead to "the mixing of men and women".[12] In contrast, `Ali Hoseyni Khamene'i, Khomeini's successor as Iran's spiritual guide, deems "the promotion of music . . . not compatible with the goals of the Islamic system".[13] Accordingly, he prohibits "any swing music that is for debauchery", even when played at separate-sex parties. Egypt's leading television preacher, Sheikh Muhammad ash-Sha`rawi, went further and condemned Muslims who fall asleep to western classical music rather than a recording of Qur'anic recital. Inspired by his words, fundamentalist hotheads in Upper Egypt a few days later stormed a concert and broke musical instruments, leading to their arrest.

With such attitudes prevalent, it is hardly surprising that Muslim practitioners of western music have achieved little. As the historian Bernard Lewis notes: "Though some talented composers and performers from Muslim countries, especially from Turkey, have been very successful in the western world, the response to their kind of music at home is relatively slight."[14] They enjoy neither renown nor influence outside of their native countries and even there are minor cultural figures.

JAPAN

How different is Japan! True, the early reactions to western music were adverse: on hearing a child in song in Hawaii, Norimasa Muragaki, a member of the very first Japanese embassy to the United States in 1860, compared the sound to a "dog howling late at night".[15] Within a few years, however, Japanese heard western music much more favourably, to the point that the music drew some individuals into western religion. In 1884, Shoichi Toyama argued that "Christianity ought to be adopted for, first, the benefit of progress in music, second, the development of compassion for fellow men and harmonious cooperation, and third, social relations between men and women".[16] Note that he lists music first.

Before long, some Japanese discovered that western music expressed their feelings far better than anything in their own tradition. As he left French soil, the leading writer Nagai Kafu (1879-1959) mused wistfully on the beauty of French culture:

No matter how much I wanted to sing western songs, they were all very difficult. Had I, born in Japan, no choice but to sing Japanese songs? Was there a Japanese song that expressed my present sentiment – a traveller who had immersed himself in love and the arts in France, but was now going back to the extreme end of the Orient, where only death would follow monotonous life? . . . I felt totally forsaken. I belonged to a nation that had no music to express swelling emotions and agonised feelings.[17]

Kafu describes emotions almost entirely unknown to Muslims.

The local musical tradition engages an intense give and take with western music. Woodblocks, a traditional Japanese instrument, are a standard of jazz percussion. Traditional Japanese music has influenced many western composers, and John Cage probably the most directly so. The Suzuki Method, which applies the traditional Japanese techniques of rote learning (hiden) to children learning the violin, has won a substantial following in the West. Yamaha sells over 200,000 pianos a year and is the world's largest maker of musical instruments.

Conversely, European classical music and American popular music have become part of the Japanese scene. Tokyo has nine professional orchestras and three operas, giving it the highest density of European classical music talent in the world. Seiji Ozawa, music director of the Boston Symphony Orchestra, rates as the most renowned of Japanese conductors. Classical performers with wide reputations include pianists Aki and Yugi Takahasi and percussionist Stomu Yamashita.

Though Japanese composers are yet little known outside Japan, their pace of activity is considerable. Toru Takemitsu, who makes a speciality of exploring timbre, texture and everyday sounds in both European and Japanese media, is perhaps the most renowned internationally. Akira Miyoshi composes classic western music. Toshi Ichiyanagi, Jo Kondo, Teruyaki Noda and Yuji Takahashi write in an avant-garde manner. Shinichiro Ikebe, Minoru Miki, Makato Moroi and Katsutoshi Nagasawa write for traditional Japanese instruments. The marimbist Keiko Abe is the best known of classical Japanese musicians and Toshiko Akiyoshi is the best known of the jazz players.

European classical music has shed its foreign quality in Japan, becoming fully indigenous. In this, Japan resembles the United States, another country which has imported nearly all of its classical music. Just as Americans have adapted the music to their own tastes and customs – playing the 1812 Overture on the Fourth of July – so have the Japanese.

Beethoven's Ninth Symphony, for example, serves as the anthem of the Christmas and New Year's season. Not only do the country's leading orchestras play the symphony over and over again during December, but gigantic choruses (numbering up to 10,000 participants) rehearse for months before bellowing out the Ode to Joy in public performances.

As for pop music, the Japanese – like nearly all the world – idolise American pop stars and grow their own local talent. But more interesting is their intense engagement with jazz. So large is the Japanese jazz market that it affects music produced in the United States. Jazz coffee shops (which play wide selections of music on state-of-the-art equipment) have proliferated, and Japan hosts three international jazz festivals a year. *Japanese Swing Journal* sells 400,000 copies a month (compared to only 110,000 copies of the best-known American publication, *Downbeat*), and roughly half of some American jazz albums are bought by Japanese. Indeed, according to one American producer, Michael Cuscana of Blue Note records: "Japan almost single-handedly kept the jazz record business going during the late 1970s. Without the Japanese market, a lot of independent jazz labels probably would have folded, or at least stopped releasing new material."[18] This is too big a market to lose, so American and other artists must increasingly pay attention to Japanese taste.

As for Japanese creativity, here too the results have been modest until now – composers and musicians do little more that imitate the styles of foreigners – but the existence of a large and increasingly sophisticated home market offers fertile ground for Japanese musicians to experiment and then to lead. Attempts to combine jazz with traditional Japanese music have begun; these blendings are likely to influence jazz as much as they already have architecture and clothing. It seems safe to predict that the Japanese before long will become a major force in jazz.

The Japanese give in other ways too. The *karaoke* machine plays instrumental versions of popular songs and permits a bar patron to accompany the music as though he were an accomplished singer, providing a good time for all. Not only has *karaoke* become an amusement staple worldwide, but the characteristic Japanese-style bar (with its hostesses, a mama-san and *karaoke* microphone) has begun to appear here and there in the West. *Karaoke* machines are sold in Sears Roebuck stores and have won a large and cheerful, if slightly tipsy, following.

CONCLUSION

Muslim and Japanese responses with western music symbolise their larger encounters with western civilisation. Muslims have historically approached the West warily, fearful of losing their identity. This prevents them from immersing themselves in western learning or gaining the needed skills in technology and business. They remain permanently in arrears, coping with one wave of western influence after another, barely keeping up and exerting virtually no influence over the West.

The Japanese do things differently. First, they throw themselves whole-heartedly into the new subject, not fearing the loss of their own identity. Second, they acquire skills, matching and even beating the West at its own game; what Seiji Ozawa is to music, Toyota is to cars. Third, Japanese evolve original customs of their own, either based on their traditions (*karaoke*) or an amalgam of cultures (Beethoven's Ninth for New Year's). Finally, they develop techniques that westerners adopt; the Suzuki Method in music parallels the just-in-time system in car manufacturing. They have absorbed western civilisation in its entirety, taken what interests them, discarded what does not and mastered it.

Thus does the response to western music exemplify the whole of a civilisation's experience with modernity. Its lack of utility makes it all the more useful as an indicator of achievement. Why this connection? Because, as Lewis observes: "Music, like science, is part of the inner citadel of western culture, one of the final secrets to which the newcomer must penetrate."[19] Music represents the challenge of modernity: competence in this arena implies an ability to deal with whatever else the West might serve up. Muslim resistance to accepting music from the West represents its larger unwillingness, whereas the Japanese have truly entered the inner citadel. In short, whoever would flourish must play Beethoven as well as westerners do.

310

IX

DEMOCRACY, HISTORY
AND CULTURE IN MEXICO,
CHINA AND EUROPE

CHAPTER 23

MEXICO: BETWEEN PAST AND FUTURE

ENRIQUE KRAUZE

AS ONE OF THE EPIGRAPHS FOR MY BOOK, *MEXICO: BIOGRAPHY OF POWER*, I chose a paragraph by the Spanish writer, José Moreno Villa, in which he captures something of the fascinating and terrifying Mexican obsession with history:

> History endures in Mexico. No one has died here, despite the killings and the executions. They are alive – Cuauhtémoc, Cortés, Maximilian, Don Porfirio, and all the conquerors and the conquered. That is Mexico's special quality. The whole past is a pulsing present. It has not gone by, it has stopped in its tracks.

I remember that when I selected these words, I felt that Mexicans were beginning to emerge from this sometimes overwhelming concentration on the past. And I even thought that my work might contribute somewhat to this process of liberation, that it could be a kind of psychoanalysis, in a loose sense, of the nation. Now I am less sure, though not at all despairing. Jorge Luis Borges said that Mexico insisted upon a "contemplation of the discord in its past". And I think he was right. It is not completely impossible that Mexico could even experience the same misfortune as Borges' character, Funes the Memorious, a man who died, literally, from an overdose of memory. The drawing of distinctions between history as mythology and history as reality may be, for some countries, a matter of secondary interest. But not for Mexico.

If someone were to ask me to define my country in a word, I would say "ancient". At first sight, this may seem obvious enough. Everyone knows that Mexico is the country of the Mayas and the Aztecs, the immense stage for the Conquest led by Hernán Cortés, an open-air museum of baroque architecture. But the antiquity of Mexico is very different from that of Egypt or Greece. The Mexican past, in many respects, has not passed. It is still alive, not only because there are still many open wounds, many looming or latent problems derived from our history, but also because significant groups of Mexicans, over and over again, seek the return of earlier historical events, as if evoking them through magic or a kind of religious devotion. In Mexico one cannot speak of the present or speculate about the future without taking the past into account.

This weight of the past has some positive features. In Mexico the past resolved, to a considerable degree, certain problems that are still grave wounds in many countries of Europe and the Middle East. For example (leaving aside for the moment the conflict in Chiapas, to which I will return), history has, at least significantly, freed us from ethnic hatred. In contrast to the United States or Chile, where Indians were decimated or forced onto reservations, in contrast to Peru, where the Indians and the whites have formed two mutually distrustful societies, Mexico has witnessed the continuous process of racial and cultural mixture known as *mestizaje*. It is a phenomenon which has translated, for the most part, into a natural coexistence between people and peoples, apart from their colour or ethnic origin. The same can be said of the religious piety of the Mexicans, a clear and deep fervour, immune to historical and natural calamities and largely free of intolerance. Thanks to the heritage of the past, Mexico does not have irredentist areas or separatist groups (despite much of what is now claimed by the current of neo-indigenism, which I will also talk about later). Born as an independent nation at the beginning of the nineteenth century – before Italy and Germany – and having suffered two major wars against foreign expansionism (with the United States in 1847, which cost the country half its territory, and with France between 1862 and 1867), wars that hardened its inward-looking, suspicious and defensive sense of identity, national cohesion has been, for Mexico, a true act of faith.

Unfortunately, the past has also brought us burdens, dead weights that have hindered our access to the modern world. One of them has been the two-fold tradition of political authoritarianism from which we Mexicans arose as a nation. For the Aztecs, the emperor was virtually a god. By the same token, the Spaniards envisioned political life as a great corporate edifice, which the monarch could manage as his own personal property. A long-lasting political order arose from the confluence of these two

314

currents. It lasted three centuries and its destruction led to decades of anarchy. Spain might have avoided this violent end – if the mother country had relaxed its ties with the colonies beyond the ocean, if it had been willing to concede a steadily increasing autonomy to the elites of New Spain. But the Spanish crown was unwilling to consider these options, and this political blindness precipitated a violent reaction which led, in turn, to the rise of small local kings or contenders for national and personal power: the *caciques* and the *caudillos*.

During the nineteenth century, Mexico lived immersed in a grinding dispute between two conflicting projects. The conservatives wanted to preserve, at all cost, the Spanish and Catholic political inheritance. Their adversaries, the liberals, wanted a country open to the future, inspired by the ideals of the American and French Revolutions. In the violent confrontation between the two tendencies, the country, already backward, lost long and irrecoverable decades.

The solution, as has been customary in Latin America, was the rise of a *caudillo*. General Porfirio Díaz ruled the country for more than thirty years (1876-1910), presiding over a period of accelerated economic development and iron political control exercised through the methods of the past. The Porfirian political order was, in effect, very similar to the colonial way of power: absolute, paternal, corporative. Mexico passed through a temporary compromise between these two tendencies: the country opened up to the world in economic terms, but it maintained a regime of political absolutism, converting the divisions of powers, freedom of the press and the electoral process into mere formalities.

The inability to find a fundamental solution to this fragile compromise resulted in a bloody revolution that lasted ten years (1910-1920) and cost 1,000,000 lives. It was rapidly followed by a series of large-scale brawls (between generals, local powers, unions, various peasant groupings), by the consolidation of regional *caciques* and by a strange and anachronistic religious war between peasants in the west of Mexico and the fiercely anti-clerical government of Plutarco Elías Calles (1924-1928), who proposed to extirpate the deeply-rooted Catholic religion of Mexico. And after two decades of violence a new compromise arose. The country followed the direction of economic growth, but corrected this time by vigorous social policies slanted toward agrarian problems and the urban working class, together with strongly nationalist educational and cultural policies, all overseen by a powerful state apparatus. So was born the "Mexican political system" that for more than half a century freed Mexico from the cycle of dictatorship and anarchy so customary in Latin America. But the system's unreformed insistence on permanence in power has been the principal cause of the severe problems now facing the country.

The system has functioned like a huge business or corporation, whose "stock-holders" come from the so-called "revolutionary family". These "stock-holders" delegated power to an imperial president invested for six years with an absolute and untouchable authority. He had the right to name his successor and his only limitation was that of time: he could not be re-elected. To legitimise his authority, the president counted on the machinery of the state party, the Partido Revoluciónario Institucional (PRI), which practised a refined technology of electoral fraud.

Around this binary star of the president and the PRI, there wheeled, like planets in a solar system, elements of society at various degrees of dependency on the centre. Completely *dependent and subordinate* were the army, the unions, the peasant organisations, the official politicians – deputies, senators, judges, governors – and the immense public bureaucracy. Those groups *not so dependent and subordinate* included the press, the Church, businessmen, university people and the intellectuals. Those few who were not dependants of the system, though they rarely arrived at true insubordination, included the Partido Accion Nacional (PAN) – composed of middle class professionals, the marginal and persecuted parties and partisans of the left – and a few independent writers, who were prophets preaching in the wilderness.

The corporation of government – for all practical purposes each successive presidency – was immensely rich: master of the soil, the subsoil and the lines of communication. The government monopolised all essential activities: electricity, railroads, oil, steel. The politicians of the PRI would use their power like a personal patrimony: to enrich themselves; to buy loyalty through a cascade of money, jobs and perquisites. Mexican life itself took on the form of a pyramid: citizens of all social strata dreamed of rising to a public job within the system and sometimes they achieved it. The system could count on capable administrators and developed impressive mechanisms for self-regulation. Indeed, between 1940 and 1970 the economy expanded at an annual rate of six percent, without any significant inflation or external debt.

It has to be acknowledged that in some ways it was a brilliantly conceived system. Still, it became a victim of its own success. Like an incubator, it was effective for a time, but not for all time. It was – among other limitations – designed for a much smaller number of people.

(Mexico had a population of 25,000,000 in 1950, while today it has 90,000,000). It was an experiment in a protected economy, a guided society and a closed political life. It could not maintain itself in a world open to competition and global communication. The official propaganda asserted that the system offered the best of two worlds: a market economy like the First World (with restrictions, but still active and functional); and a welfare society like the socialist world (without work camps, a secret police or an ideology of the state.) But reality, in the long run, proved the opposite: the system had the economic disadvantages of the socialist system (a burdensome and inefficient bureaucracy, corruption, lack of innovation), without the political advantages of the democratic West.

The massacre of hundreds of students in 1968 was the first grave warning sign. The system would not tolerate dissidence. It became clearer that power, resources and decision-making had to be distributed according to democratic and federalist rules, in forms worthy of a true republic. The moment had arrived to gradually dismantle the corporate edifice, loosen the protections on the economy and transform generalised dependence into free competition.

Unfortunately, between 1970 and 1982 two populist presidents preferred to reinforce the system rather than reform it. The public sector swelled from 600,000 to 4,000,000 employees. The state nationalised or created more than 1,000 enterprises and financed all this massive expansion with foreign loans. A wealth of oil was wasted on pharaonic projects or poured down the sewers of corruption. The system went into economic bankruptcy. Mexico paid the price for periodically entrusting its life's blood to the control of one man. No single party system, without the checks and balances of accountability, is immune to the flaws of its leaders.

A young reformist president, Carlos Salinas de Gortari, tried to change direction. He balanced the budget, privatised state enterprises, deregulated foreign trade and signed the NAFTA agreements. The entire world, and a significant number of Mexicans, applauded him as a great reformer. But the favourable numbers masked a political drama: Salinas was trying to construct a modern economy, but he was reinforcing the most archaic political methods. He fancied himself as a new Porfirio Díaz and cherished an ambition for absolute power, involving his own return to the presidency in the year 2000. With these intentions in mind, he chose his political son, Luis Donaldo Colosio, to succeed him as president; and as part of the same attitude he permitted the corrupt enrichment of his brother, Raul. He wanted to do what no one had done in a very long time: *take total personal control of the system.* But the "stockholders" of the "revolutionary family" blocked his way.

In January of 1994 the political system cracked along both inner and outer fault lines. The "Zapatista" guerrilla actions in Chiapas – with all the theatricality that movement showed from the very beginning – underlined the government's lack of democratic legitimacy. The assassination of Colosio – although the men behind it have never been identified – was a crime, in all likelihood, planned within the depths of the system. From that time on, Mexico entered a profound crisis, perhaps the gravest of this century after the Revolution itself. But observers should pay very close attention to the facts and results, so as not to leap to any mistaken conclusions. Mexico is not living through an Apocalypse, but rather a complete transition that, in all probability, will come out well.

But as was true at the turbulent beginnings of the nineteenth and the twentieth centuries, Mexico is now moving through a time of crisis and potential chaos. We are advancing, with care and with hope, across a minefield. The so-called "Mexican political system" is now bankrupt, but the democratic process has not yet been fully consolidated in my country. Although there are leaders and interests that favour the return to a corporate state, that kind of backward process does seem impossible. The surge toward democracy within Mexican society is too strong, and the world situation is against such corporate states, which have, for the most part, either disappeared (like the communist regimes of Eastern Europe) or are now (as with some of the tigers of Asia) considerably weakened.

A very hopeful sign has been the attitude of President Zedillo. Despite the recent and serious setbacks for the government in Chiapas, the president has shown a real desire to democratise the ruling party and seems ready to confront the old guard of the PRI, who are entrenched in their feudal territories or corporate trade unions. And there are other hopeful signs. The planetary forces that before circled obediently around the presidential sun have been showing increased independence; and this is true, though far from universal, in federal and state legislatures and among governors and city mayors. And it is beginning to be true within labour and peasant organisations, areas that have been corporately controlled by the PRI for more than half a century.

The media – the newspapers, the radio, and to an ever-increasing degree, television – can now report the news and discuss issues of public interest with a degree of political liberty and professional integrity that would have been unimaginable in the old culture of dependence and subordination. Big businessmen seem to be more conscious of their need not only for financial and economic, but also political, autonomy. The intellectuals, who in Catholic societies constitute, for better or for worse, a kind of secular priesthood, no longer have to live on the largesse of the state, because a massive public readership now exists who buy their books and follow the course of their opinions in the daily newspapers, political reviews and radio and television programmes.

The national state and municipal elections of 6 July 1997 were truly an historical moment, not only for their results, which ended the seemingly endless monopoly of the PRI in the lower house and in the government of Mexico City, but also for the quantitative leap in political consciousness displayed by the people of Mexico. Mid-term legislative elections have always been meaningless, an idle holiday for the PRI or a field day for abstentionism and passivity. The sixth of July was entirely different. The centre-right Partido Acción Nacional (PAN), which had been a true leader for decades in the struggle for electoral democracy in Mexico, did less well than expected in the national vote, but still has come a very long way from the days when the system accorded it the crumbs of a few legislative seats and dubbed its partisans "mystics of the vote". It now has a real national presence and, through its city and state office-holders, governs thirty percent of the country.

But the great surprise and political surge of the elections on 6 July 1997 was the performance of the centre-left Partido de la Revolución Democratica, the PRD. It doubled its representation in the Lower House to become the second national power in the legislature, holding a few more seats than the Partido Acción Nacional. Many of its present militants come from two political currents exterior to, and even opposed to, democracy – the Communist Party and the governmental monopoly of the PRI – but the PRD has been successfully realising a lively adventure in democracy. Within the party old habits of dogmatism and intolerance still exist, but such features are equally evident among their conservative opponents in the Partido Acción Nacional. And within both parties extremist ideas and personalities are likely to lose ground, because the Mexican people have shown an aversion toward extremes. The presidency in the year 2000 will belong to the party and candidate that can conquer the ideological centre.

* * *

If there were complete agreement on the need to definitively establish a democratic order – and its necessary concomitant of a free market, though not totally uncontrolled and without regard to the needs of society – then Mexico could easily resolve, or at least soften, the dialectical tension

319

between the gravitational weight of its traditional past and the summons from a future that cannot be postponed. But so high a degree of consensus does not exist, and though the dominant tendency within the country points toward modernisation, the past has reappeared in recent days in a multiple and complex form: as memory and nightmare, as a debt to be paid and as the threat of repression.

One of the forms in which the past has surfaced is that of violence itself, the subterranean river of blood that runs throughout our history. Violence in Mexico assumes many different forms: organised or sporadic, criminal or social, paramilitary or guerrilla. Will Mexico today be able to control the spread of violence? It all depends on how rapidly (and how decisively) citizens and authorities can reconstruct – or, more accurately, construct – a fair and efficient system of criminal justice. It will depend on a truly effective and generalised revival of the economy. And probably most of all, it will depend upon the clarity with which the whole problem of crime is discussed and the dedicated confrontation of all its manifestations, from street muggings to the international scope of the drug trade.

Another form of historical reappearance can be seen in the growing influence of the Church. Many of us certainly applauded the constitutional reforms enacted during the presidential term of Carlos Salinas, which officially granted the Church, its priests and its nuns freedom of action within civil society. But the steady collapse of the political system and the crisis experienced by the Mexican state has awakened sentiments of revenge within some quarters of the Church. It is, at least in part, as if bills are being called in against the state for the century and a half of humiliations that the Church has undergone since the conservative defeat in the Wars of the Reform and French Intervention. And this is true of both the right and left political wings of the Church (with aspects of both sometimes combined in one person, such as Bishop Samuel Ruiz of Chiapas, a champion of the revolutionary ethic of the Theology of Liberation, yet extremely conservative in his strong opposition to all methods of birth control). The right wing of the church, or its parallel current of thought, has been involved in moralistic campaigns, sometimes criminally so, as in its opposition to the use of condoms as a protection against AIDS. The left wing of the church, which includes some of the proponents of the Theology of Liberation, has shown ideological rigidity and a lack of respect for democracy. It is difficult to know just what the growing influence of the Church may mean in our country. But the influence is surely there.

And another central protagonist of nineteenth century Mexico has made a renewed and possibly significant appearance. For half of a century the Mexican army has remained loyally subordinate to the presidential authority of the corporate state. It does not have a tradition of military coups, nor do the generals, at the present moment, seem to have such ambitions. Nor does the current political condition of Latin America encourage or legitimate any such actions. And yet it is certainly true that within the present political and social situation the army is becoming steadily more visible in the national arena. If the collapse of the old system does not lead to the firm establishment of democracy in the presidential elections in the year 2000, or if violence in its various forms geometrically increases, sectors of the army could feel the temptation to maximise their political influence. They might achieve this by supporting the most reactionary elements within the PRI – the so-called dinosaurs – or they could conceivably decide to take the risk themselves of moving into power, imposing "peace, order and progress" as did Porfirio Díaz himself. Will the army remain loyal to its historical limits? I tend to think that it will, but, nevertheless, the issue of the army remains another open question.

* * *

But perhaps the most surprising reappearance from the past has been the "issue of the Indians", which has once again become the order of the day. Indigenism, a noble current of thought and action which was born among some of the religious orders during the period of the Conquest, is again palpably present in a militant sector of the press, in a flurry of books and within the academy. And this renewed presence is a positive fact for at least two reasons. It stands opposed to the tendency toward cultural homogenisation, which marks the process of globalisation within which we are all immersed. What's more, it is an urgent alarm, highlighting the long-standing condition of poverty and exclusion endured by ten percent of the population, the poorest of the poor, the Indians of Mexico.

But together with this valid and necessary call for justice, a disturbing political and intellectual process has begun to unfold. A new ideology, in the classical sense of the term, is being preached, a quasi-religion that is also a "false consciousness of reality". It is an intensification of indigenism that one might call "neo-indigenism". Among its proponents are representatives of the Church in Chiapas. Nor is it strange that this should be so, since they are facing a reality, in terms of social misery, not so different from what Fray Bartolomé de las Casas, the great Apostle of the Indians, had to confront

450 years ago. And the world knows of neo-indigenism through the words and image of Subcommandante Marcos, who has shown true genius as a post-modern communicator. With a single ideological *coup d'état*, he freed himself of the weight of Marxism and adopted the creed of neo-indigenism as a firm basis of legitimacy. And certainly – this is surely a hopeful sign – genuine representatives of the Indians themselves are proposing and supporting the new ideology in state and national assemblies and organisations as a legitimate defence of their wounded dignity. In their keeping, neo-indigenism becomes a will toward political participation that may rapidly translate into tangible benefits for their communities.

Nevertheless, there is another more shallow and distorted side to the new ideology. Numerous sociologists, philosophers, historians, political scientists and newspaper columnists have become prophets of neo-indigenism rather than supporting, with genuine reasoning, the interests of the Indians – and of truth. As a result, this native Mexican movement has echoed throughout the world. Indeed, assisted by several forces – the Priista (PRI) government's repression at the state and local levels, various reactionary groups and their storm troopers in Chiapas society – neo-indigenist ideology has converted Mexico into the world capital of conscience laundering. A German, an Italian, a Frenchman or a Spaniard now has the luxury of being able to transfer the historical sins of his own nation to Mexico, the new Mecca of discrimination, oppression and racism.

At the centre of the neo-indigenist creed resides a fundamental article of faith: Mexico, since its days as a Spanish colony, has been a racist state. By the same token, some have posited that Mexico, because of its discriminatory treatment of the Indians, has not succeeded in becoming a *nation*. I would answer that neo-indigenism elevates to the rank of a universal principle attitudes and practices that have been, to be more precise, specific, partial or relative. The brutality of the Spanish Conquest is unquestionable; there were broad areas of resistance to Spanish colonisation; the centuries-old struggle of various communities to defend their rights to the land is a well-known fact, as is the admirable tenacity with which a number of Indian cultures have defended their identity, sometimes violently, against the threat of homogenisation. But the neo-indigenist creed ignores the *other history*: the vast convergence of races and cultures that has produced modern Mexican civilisation; the conquest as a spiritual phenomenon; the relatively paternal elements within the Spanish domination as compared with other colonising conquests; the constant escape of Indians throughout our history from the confines of their communities toward cities, haciendas and work sites, where life may have been no less difficult, but was certainly free; and the constant process of race-mingling that produced the mestizo culture of Mexico. And it should be remembered that nothing ever occurred in Mexico remotely similar to the systematic extermination of the Indians in Chile and Argentina or the killing circle thrown around the Indians, and their confinement to reservations, that was the pattern in the United States. The greatest horror in Mexico, brought by the white man, yes, but not through his will, were the epidemics of European diseases that killed millions of Indians in the sixteenth century.

Mestizaje itself is a complex and essential phenomenon. In contrast to the more Puritan mentality that tended to prevail north of the Rio Grande, the Thomist Iberian tradition (though ideologically exclusive in religion) tended toward mixing and assimilation south of the river. The Crown itself recommended that Spaniards marry Indian women. The process of *mestizaje* took centuries, but Mexico became a mestizo country, a kind of mestizo family. And the virtues of that blend of races, and the climate of mutual tolerance encouraged by it, come into sharper relief when one considers the two parts of the country where the process was weakest or almost non-existent: Yucatán, the stage for the ferocious interracial War of the Castes in the nineteenth century; and Chiapas, which has witnessed racially-based uprisings and unrest since the sixteenth century. But elsewhere, even in heavily indigenous areas like Oaxaca, incidents of confrontation have certainly occurred, but they have been exceptional, ephemeral, limited. The traditional derogatory racial labels of the nineteenth century have almost entirely disappeared in Mexico, except in certain indigenous enclaves, most notably Chiapas. The very word "mestizo" is now rarely used, but rather replaced by "Mexican", since the immense majority of Mexicans are mestizos.

But certainly, once there is a clear recognition of the basic national unity in *mestizaje* of the Mexican people, the widest possible diversity is highly desirable. Mexico must be free to absorb influences from abroad and must be willing to allow a measure of responsible autonomy to its Indian populations.

But what kind of autonomy? I would say a form of autonomy that can be absolutely free in its internal functioning, but also respects the common national historical inheritance: a federal organisation; a republican and, it is to be hoped, a truly democratic system; the common right to the soil and subsoil of Mexico; and, above all, the liberties of the individual. Such rights must be guaranteed within the entities – cities, villages, territories – that already exist or will come into being. Unfortunately, some of the new prophets of Indian autonomy seem more inclined toward a yearning for an ideal reconstitution of what they see as an ancient (though totally imaginary) Republic of the Indians, rather than appear ready to confront the hard task of conceptually organising viable entities, reconciling the political map of modern Mexico with the various traditional divisions, wherever they exist or would wish to exist. All this would have to be planned very concretely – in every state, every delimited area, every city or village – and put into effect with the greatest caution. Otherwise, we run the risk of a thousand massacres like the recent horror in Actea, Chiapas.

And if such care is not taken, we would also face the prospect of legitimising a new form of quasi-religious fundamentalism that would not only feed ethnic tensions within Mexico, but actively stimulate them, actually create them in areas where they do not exist. And worst of all would be the sowing of additional confusion about the real, the lacerating problem of Mexico, which is not primarily ethnic, but rather social and economic: in a word, poverty. This is a condition that neither respects differences of race nor can be exhaustively explained in merely racial terms; and still less can it be fought and defeated by simply brandishing the banners of race.

* * *

It is likely that the Mexican dialectic between the past and the future will never really disappear. And Mexico owes much of its unique nature, its vitality, to that constant presence. But surely Mexico is advancing toward the future due to the growing political maturity of its citizens, the effect of vast and very real economic forces, its massive means of communication and its frontier with the United States, where millions of Mexicans live as emigrants, labourers and businessmen. Although the elections of 6 July 1997 allowed the country to celebrate a democratic fiesta, we must always remember that Mexico has previously experienced democracy for only two brief periods in its 175 years of independence: during the era of Juárez in the nineteenth century; and ephemerally under Madero after the first stage of the Revolution. Yet it does seem likely that in the year 2000 the PRI will have to pay its debt to history, yield the executive power to another party and go about the business of cleaning up its own political house. It is to be hoped that the nation will then move to confront its wider problems. Likewise, in a country with significant divisions, especially between the more modernised North and the poorer, more traditional South, localism must not dominate the landscape. What must reign instead is a unified will and desire to deal with our central problems, to lower the index of poverty, to promote public education, to move a united, democratic country, gifted with so rich a past, forward into the future, without ever forgetting that past.

CHAPTER 24

CONOR CRUISE O'BRIEN AND CHINA

XIAO-HUANG YIN

I FIRST CAME ACROSS DR CONOR CRUISE O'BRIEN'S NAME IN 1980 IN Bucharest, Romania – a place which seems to have little relationship with his long and extraordinary career as an Irish statesman, diplomat and scholar. I had just graduated from college in China and was working for a year as an assistant to the head of the Chinese trade delegation to Romania, which was China's most important ally in Eastern Europe in the 1970s and 1980s. My work for the delegation and in the Chinese Embassy was quite routine, and Bucharest in those years was certainly not an exciting place to live. I thus spent most of my spare time reading books from the Chinese Embassy's library. Fortunately, the library had a large collection, including many volumes on international affairs and the United Nations. It was in a book about the UN's peacekeeping operation in the Congo from 1960 to 1964 that I first came across the name "Conor Cruise O'Brien". I read this particular book with great interest because China maintained strong relations with African countries in the 1960s and was quite involved in the Congo crisis.

Yet what really fascinated, and puzzled, me about the book was why Conor Cruise O'Brien, an Irish diplomat, was chosen to head the UN's mission in Katanga, a mineral-rich province trying to secede (with western assistance) from the Congo. A senior diplomat in the Chinese Embassy who had served in Africa in the 1960s explained to me that O'Brien, a highly respected figure in the international community, had been active in UN affairs since the 1950s. In addition, O'Brien's background as an

Irishman was also considered helpful to the UN. According to my senior colleague, during the 1950s and 1960s Irish diplomats were frequently chosen by international organisations to address issues involving Third World countries. "Because Ireland suffered under British colonial rule throughout history," the senior diplomat taught me, in a manner which reminded me of lectures given by the Communist Party secretary during my college years, "the Irish tend to be more sympathetic than other westerners to the woes of the people in the Third World." I was not sure how authentic his explanation was, but since then the name Conor Cruise O'Brien has stayed in my mind.

* * *

In the spring of 1987 I was a graduate student at Harvard University. Naturally, I was excited when I learned that Conor had been invited to deliver the prestigious William E Massey Sr, Lectures in the History of American Civilisation at the university. His lectures, which explored the interrelationship between religion and nationalism, were well received by the Harvard community and subsequently published as *God Land: Reflections on Religion and Nationalism.*[1] I still remember the crowded lecture hall and the audience's enthusiastic response to his eloquent remarks and forceful arguments.

Conor's presence at Harvard that spring allowed me to meet and talk with him in person for the first time. During a lunch in his honour hosted by a group of graduate students, Conor and I had a pleasant discussion on a wide range of issues. Our conversation naturally turned to Asian topics once I told Conor that I was Chinese. With his characteristic sense of humour, Conor joked that he had "cruised" to almost every part of the world except East Asia. He also mentioned that during his tenure as vice-chancellor of the University of Ghana he used to play ping-pong with Huang Hua, who was then China's Ambassador in Accra.[2] For this reason, I said to Conor that perhaps he should be credited with the invention of "ping-pong diplomacy" since he began that practice almost a decade before President Richard Nixon's historic visit to Beijing in 1972.

Still, much of our conversation during lunch, and on other occasions during Conor's visit to Harvard, centred on cross-cultural studies. In fact, it was our shared interest in this field that laid down the foundation of our friendship. I was fascinated by Conor's global approach to US-China relations and his insightful analysis of problems that had stymied reform in China during the post-Mao era. When Conor learned that I had written several papers on comparative studies of Chinese and western cultures, he expressed interest and asked me to send him my essays on the subject.[3] His comments on my work on American Puritans and the Chinese Cultural Revolution again impressed me: his cross-cultural approach and global mind allowed him quickly to grasp the essence of issues that, at first glance, appeared outside his areas of expertise and enabled him to throw light on some of the most significant, yet controversial, events in human history.

* * *

We have become friends since we met at Harvard in 1987. About one year later I visited Conor when he was teaching at the University of Pennsylvania. He and his wife, Máire, who is a well-known Irish poet, took me to dinner in Philadelphia. It was in a nice German-style restaurant. The food was delicious – which somewhat changed my bias that Chinese cuisine is the best in the world – and the wine was superb, even to my rather unsophisticated taste. After we returned home Conor and I continued our discussion on China and other issues until well past midnight. He then suggested that we drink a little whiskey before retiring and asked if I wanted to put water into my whiskey. I was a little taken aback because I thought that *everyone* added water to his whiskey. "Not really, my young man," Conor told me. "I know there are people who drink whiskey without adding water." Then, with a smile and a twinkle in his eyes, he whispered, "But they are all dead."

Our shared interests in cross-cultural studies led us, in the ensuing months, to focus on a specific issue: does the western media's coverage of China present a clear and objective picture of what really happens there? Conor and I both concluded that although western commentators thought that they had examined China thoroughly, plenty of "entrenched misunderstanding" persisted and needed to be cleared up. For example, the media failed to adequately explain why, despite similarities between their political systems, the collapse of communist rule in Eastern Europe in 1989 did not simultaneously occur in China. Obviously, western newspapers and television had overlooked two crucial points about China germane to this issue. First, in Eastern Europe a strong middle class had emerged that constituted the mainstream of the democratic movement and initiated political change, yet a similar class had not arisen in Chinese society. In addition, China is a highly homogeneous nation: about 94% of her people are of the Han nationality – the Chinese. And despite regional differences, Chinese people throughout the country share a common cultural heritage. As a result, nationalism has always played a powerful unifying role in modern Chinese history. Indeed, while nationalism in Eastern Europe proved to be a weapon capable of mobilising people against communist governments, which were viewed as Soviet puppet regimes, just the opposite was the case in China. Chinese nationalism has consistently served the interests of the government and is used by the communist movement (which has indigenous roots) as an effective means to unite the nation and fend off western ideas, including democracy.

The Tiananmen Square Incident in 1989 is another case which proved that better media coverage of China was necessary. Western journalists were stunned by Beijing's crackdown on the student demonstrators. They had predicted that the Chinese government would not suppress the protestors' demands for democracy, because, as many reporters believed, political reform was "the common desire of the people all over China". Unfortunately, this was a misperception. But Conor Cruise O'Brien did not fall for it. He opened his column on the Tiananmen Square Incident in *The Times* (London) with the thought-provoking question: "How can you bring about democracy in a country where most people don't actually want democracy?" Having grasped the great divide between the student demonstrators and China's traditionalist masses, Conor argued convincingly that the western media had overestimated the trend for democracy and underestimated the strength of traditional elements in Chinese society. "Enthusiasm for [western-style democracy] is confined to city people, and especially to intellectuals," Conor continued. "Villagers, in China as elsewhere, distrust city people, and intellectuals most of all, especially when they are being enthusiastic."[4]

* * *

What happened in Beijing in 1989 led Conor and I to draft a research proposal on China. Our joint project, entitled "A Tale of Two Chinas", was designed to illuminate the gap between interior provinces and coastal regions and called for comparative studies between ideas prevalent among peasants in rural areas and intellectuals in urban centres. (Please see the attached excerpts of the project proposal at the end of this essay.) We thought that such a study could help people in the west better understand the reality of Chinese society and the essence of the China issue.

Several major newspapers and magazines in the United States and Europe expressed interest in our project. Of course, there were questions about the feasibility of our plan. Mr Jack Beatty, senior editor of the *Atlantic Monthly*, asked if we could get peasants in China to talk. I replied that this would not be a problem. Compared with "town folk", villagers in China are actually more willing to speak out, because, as William Hinton discovered long ago, Chinese peasants have nothing to fear since they have nothing to lose – they are already at the bottom of society.[5]

With financial support from the *Atlantic Monthly* and *The Times* (London), Conor and I made arrangements for our trip to China and we scheduled a six-week visit for the fall of 1991. By then it would have been two years after the Tiananmen affair. We expected that life in China would have calmed down and conditions would allow us to carry out our fieldwork. Unfortunately, just when we were about to set out for that vast land in Asia, Conor experienced health difficulties. His doctors strongly suggested that he avoid such a long and strenuous journey, so, regrettably, we had to cancel our visit.

Although we failed to carry out the project, Conor's sharp observations and his cross-cultural analysis of problems in Chinese life, and the shared experience of drafting our research proposal, deepened my understanding of problems with China's reform. With his encouragement and suggestions, I made a six-week journey across China in the summer of 1993. Motivated by the ideas that Conor and I had delineated in our proposal, I travelled extensively both in cities and throughout the countryside and conducted investigations among not only the educated elite, but also working-class peasants. My fieldwork confirmed Conor's views on China. I discovered that there was, indeed, a large gap in opinion between city dwellers and villagers and that the ordinary people, especially working-class Chinese, were not as enthusiastic about democracy as the western media would think.

Upon my return to the United States I published my conclusions about Chinese society in the *Atlantic Monthly* under the title "China's Gilded Age". The upshot of my argument was that ordinary "people have not forgotten the Tiananmen Square crackdown of 1989, but they now believe that the best prospect for democracy in China is 'peaceful evolution' – the Asian model, emphasising social stability and economic prosperity rather than radical political changes, which many Chinese see

329

as dangerously volatile".[6] In the countryside I encountered villagers embittered by persistent poverty, especially when their lot was contrasted with growing prosperity in cities in coastal regions. Indeed:

> [A] subtle manifestation of rural grievance is that many villagers now hang Mao's picture in their houses. When I asked if they really missed the Great Leader, an old woman hesitated and then said: 'No one likes the old days.' She quickly added in a louder voice: 'But under his leadership at least we all lived the same kind of life. Chairman Mao put the interests of us villagers first. Now the leaders have forgotten us. We are no longer treated the same way as the town folks.'[7]

Prior to its appearance in the *Atlantic Monthly*, I had sent Conor a copy of my original report. He read it with great interest and praised it as "the most illuminating thing I have read on contemporary China".[8] In a subsequent article on the bloody confrontation between the Russian Parliament and President Boris Yeltsin, he argued eloquently, with examples from my fieldwork in China, that without a relatively high level of economic prosperity, "Russia cannot afford the fruit and peril of democracy . . . [And] Russia under Boris Yeltsin will be basically an autocracy, not a democracy, except in outward forms".[9] His pregnant comment has been confirmed by events in Russia during the past several years.

I would like to end this essay by quoting Conor's own words. "There is a saying of Alexander Hamilton's that the Americans might bear in mind in their talks with Boris Yeltsin", Conor pointed out in his discussion of the Russian experience. "Nations have to find their own way, not have their way found for them by other nations."[10] These words are Hamilton's, but they also reflect Conor's views on world affairs. A humane and broad-minded scholar and diplomat, thoroughly at ease with both domestic and international issues, Dr Conor Cruise O'Brien is always ready to explore new fields of study in our "global village". A proud son of Ireland, he has, throughout his entire career, won respect and friendship from people across national and cultural borders.

EXCERPTS FROM "A TALE OF TWO CHINAS: A PROPOSAL BY CONOR CRUISE O'BRIEN AND XIAO-HUANG YIN" (JUNE 1990).

Do the western mass media understand the situation in China? Prior to Beijing's crackdown on the student demonstrators in Tiananmen Square in June of 1989, western journalists believed that they had fully elucidated the case of China. They were confident that they had successfully analysed the main forces at work in Chinese society, particularly the spread of democracy. When the student movement broke out they predicted that the Chinese government would not dare to suppress it, because democratic ideas were irresistible, having already diffused throughout the wider society. Many western reporters, therefore, were stunned when the crackdown occurred.

Undoubtedly, there is a strong demand for political change, but it is far from being "the common desire of the people throughout China". Western observers have overestimated the trend of "bourgeois liberalisation" and have underestimated the strength of traditional elements in Chinese society. In general, the democratic movement has been largely confined to urban centres and its ideas are popular mainly among the educated elite. On the other hand, even at the high tide of the student movement many demonstrators were holding portraits of Chairman Mao, a symbol very different from that of the Goddess of Democracy erected by the students in Tiananmen Square.

The misjudgement of the situation on the part of the western media is largely a result of the narrow, one-sided experience many reporters have had in China. Because of a number of factors – hurdles set up by the Chinese government, their own preferences, language barriers – many western journalists in China like to spend their time in cities such as Beijing and Shanghai, which are highly westernised compared to small towns and rural villages. They also tend to interact mostly with liberal-minded and western-educated intellectuals. Such a practice would, of course, encourage them to embrace an overly optimistic view of the development of democracy in China.

Outsiders, however, have overlooked a basic fact: despite the drastic changes that occurred after the communist victory in 1949, China remains predominantly a peasant nation: as much as 80% of its population live in the countryside, where a strong traditional political culture holds sway.[11] Although peasants welcome economic change ("perestroika"), political reform ("glasnost") is entirely another matter. In their eyes, there is not much difference between an emperor and an "imperial Chairman" – their name for the leader of the Chinese Communist Party. They have also shown little interest in ideas advocated by urban intellectuals. In fact, many peasants are suspicious about students' demands for western-style democracy, because they fear it might destroy traditional values as well as their own social benefits. Indeed, throughout modern Chinese history peasants have repeatedly suffered from the over-enthusiasm of intellectuals. It is these factors that make the Chinese government believe it can suppress the demand for political reform without provoking anger from the majority of the people in China. In other words, because China is a peasant country and a homogeneous society strongly influenced by traditional ethics and culture, it is difficult for western-style democracy to make any substantial progress – unless there is a substantial rise in the standard of living and the emergence of a large middle class. These factors also explain why so many setbacks have beset political reform in China during the brief post-Mao era.

For this reason, examining the widening rift between the intellectuals and peasants in China will help us to clarify western misperceptions of China. With this purpose in mind, we shall carry out investigations in urban and rural areas, respectively, and compare ideas prevalent in large cities and in the countryside. Specifically, we shall first go to major cities, such as Beijing and Shanghai, to interview students, professors, writers, journalists and other professionals. After that we shall visit villages – both near cities and in more remote regions – to talk with different types of peasants: the newly-rich and the poor; the young and the old; and the better-educated and the illiterate. We will thus be able to solicit a wide variety of opinions about social, political and cultural life in China.

CHAPTER 25

THE NECESSITY OF SOCIAL DEMOCRACY

EOGHAN HARRIS

For 25 years (1965-1990) I was the principal pamphleteer of the Workers Party, a small, but influential, Marxist party which grew out of Official Sinn Féin and which prevented the Provisional IRA from gaining ground among working class voters in the Republic during the crucial years 1968 to 1988. Conor Cruise O'Brien had a commanding influence on my ideas at two critical points. First, his newspaper columns, essays and other writings in the 1970's helped me to reject republicanism and, likewise, deeply influenced the historical parts of a revisionist document I authored, The Irish Industrial Revolution (1976), *which became the official policy of the party. Second, Conor's work on Edmund Burke, and his adherence to classical liberalism, eventually convinced me that I must break with Marxism as well. The result was* The Necessity of Social Democracy, *a polemic cast in a popular style and meant to change minds, which I began in 1988 and finished in 1989, just as communism went into crisis. The publication of this pamphlet led to a row and my resignation from the Workers Party after 25 years. Still, Mary Robinson read it and recruited me to run her presidential campaign. So you could say that Conor Cruise O'Brien had an indirect hand in her election, too.*

INTRODUCTION
"It is now the time for individuals."
   – Central Committee of the Communist Party of the Soviet Union, "Address to the People", December 1989.

This is a personal view. There can be no other kind. A person cannot speak like a collective without lying. One of the many lessons of 1989.

Before 1989 socialists always said "We", never "I". This suppression of self, more fitting for Poor Clares than followers of the self-confident Karl Marx, led to a self-satisfied and self-imposed silence in socialist parties, with members surrendering themselves to a higher power – with almost sado-masochistic relish in some cases.

Silence and suppression of self killed socialism.

This polemic has one main theme: that the individual person – not the crowd, collective or class – is the subject and object and the whole point of history.

The person is the point of politics.

Socialism put down the person. But if the person is put down so is private conscience. Criticism is then left to collectives like the "party". But the collectives, the communist parties in Eastern Europe, did not criticise in the crunch, were cowards in the crunch, and so socialism became corrupt and complaisant and died.

All for want of plain speaking.

This critique may not be correct. That is for you to debate and decide. But you should insist on the debate being conducted in plain language without dogmatic jargon.

Simplicity is a duty to democracy.

A POLITICAL PROGNOSIS

This paper puts three points. First: that socialism, as we understand it, is dead. Second: that socialism committed suicide by neglecting three principles: the primacy of the person over the collective; the dominance of dialectics over dogma; and the principal place of politics in historical change. Third: that socialist values, but not socialism, can rise from the ashes as a democratic political idea, which can complete the Marxist project to move mankind from the "realm of necessity to the realm of freedom".

That idea is called social democracy.

What is social democracy? Social democracy is socialism shorn of its static statist structures so that it becomes once again a theory and practice of social change, a praxis in which democracy (the working class) and civil society (not the state) are the agents of change and the state is the instrument and not the master of civil society.

Social democracy in each society has a specific project.

In Ireland that project is to find a democratic solution to the National Question. Part of that solution is a policy of peace and plenty for the people of the two states on the island. A policy of public intervention.

Socialism cannot carry out this project.

THE DEATH OF SOCIALISM
"His theory, insofar as I can understand it, seems to discount the testimony of human experience . . . "
– Flann O'Brien, *The Third Policeman*.

Is socialism dead as a dogma?

If we say "no" then everything's fine. Just ignore the fact that almost every communist party in Eastern and Western Europe is changing its name and politics.

If you think it is not dead, just badly injured, and will be up again on the third day, perhaps you should join the St. John's Ambulance Brigade? Why not stick a "democratic socialist" tag on its toe? Or be brave and go for the more aggressive "socialist democracy" label: "Very popular this year with small parties far from power, sir."

But if you are the kind of socialist who hates messing around when change is necessary then please read on.

Is socialism dead? Yes or no?

335

Yes. Sorry for your trouble. Yours and mine. Because no more than you do I like church bells ringing out to celebrate the end of communism. But there it is. Dead as doornails. Five socialists states are no more.

No wonder socialists are in shock.

Some people can't face a death. Elvis lives. Lennon lives. You can see socialists like that, giving the corpse cardiac shocks from the portable "democracy" resuscitator, hoping it will sit up and speak like a democrat.

It might. But who'll believe it? Vaclav Havel of Czechoslovakia outlined the problem in October 1989: "In my country for ages now the word socialism has been no more than an incantation that should be avoided if one does not wish to appear suspect."

Havel is saying that you can't use the word "socialist" any more in his country. Even if you are a socialist. This should be easy for us to understand. Would we use the word "republican" to describe ourselves in public? Not now. But remember the rearguard attempt to hang on to it on the grounds that "real republicans" were not sectarians? Until a river of Protestant blood forced us to dump the dirty word "republican" like nuclear waste. A century from now it will still be toxic.

Socialism is a sick word. And we are not immune from the fall-out in Ireland. Who knows what more there is to come? And we can guess what use our political enemies will make of the socialist smear in the future.

Let me make a suggestion about the word socialism. Walk away from it. Start again. But this time let's not be infallible. Let's just do our best this time.

Social democracy is a chance to do our best.

In 1989 socialism broke down like a car on a level crossing. The train is coming fast. What do we do?

First, we must figure out what is wrong with the car. Second, we must fix it. Third, if we can't fix it we don't start pushing it. We get out and dump it.

Let's open the bonnet.

* * *

I am a Marxist. Marxism to me is, first and foremost, a moral system. When it is not moral I do not believe in it. I believe broadly in Marx's idea of historical materialism, which means, simply, history viewed dialectically from a material standpoint. I believe in class struggle – but that in a democracy it may not be a decisive element if social democracy is successfully pursuing a system of advance based on merit. And we must be adamant that lumpen proletarian underclasses thrown up by capitalism are not made the subject of romantic crusades as if such groups were the historic "proletariat" of Karl Marx's vision. I do not believe the material base determines history, but neither in my view did Marx – I think he wrote in a deterministic style to frighten the bourgeoisie – a deterministic style is good for morale as readers of the *Irish Industrial Revolution* will remember. I believe strongly in Hegelian dialectics as applied to political struggle. This is a dialectic document – that is I expect the consensus will emerge from conflict on these issues. I never believed in state ownership of industry but I do believe in forms of public ownership. I believe that nothing is determined except death and change. I do not think "socialism" is worth the shedding of one drop of Protestant blood. I believe that the person and private conscience are the two great levers of history. So for me personal freedom is political, and politics is the pursuit of personal freedom.

I am as much a Protestant as a Marxist in that regard.

* * *

What went wrong with "the socialist" dream?

Why did socialism in Eastern Europe not lead to a higher form of society? How did a system that set out with such a high ideal of humanity end up so inhuman? Was it the theory? Or man? The answer, as usual, is dialectical. The problem was Marx's theory of man.

Man is a creature of need in a field of scarcity.

That was Marx's basic view of the historical project of humanity. Man would have to overcome Nature and Capitalism to reach the Realm of Freedom. This theory assumed that man would act according to reason.

Which may not be a correct assumption to say the least.

There are basically two views of human history. Call them the Limitless Vision and the Limited View. Where these two theories differ is in their view of the perfectibility of man. The Limitless Vision says man is infinitely perfectible and can create a paradise on earth. The Limited View says man is flawed and can create a hell on earth if not kept under control.

This simplification cuts a few corners but nevertheless the struggle between Limitless Vision and Limited View is a constant and recognisable conflict in modern history and can be broken down into names: Plato versus Aristotle; Whig versus Tory; Robespierre versus Edmund Burke; and indeed Lenin versus Stalin.

The Limitless Vision starts with Plato's *Republic* – which in passing we should point out is a place that badly needed a reform movement – and stretches through visionaries like Robespierre and Lenin to Utopian communists like Castro in our own day. But there are dictators and dictators and Hitler and Stalin can't be put in the same pot. You could survive in the Soviet Union if you conformed. But a Jew died no matter how badly he wanted to join the Nazis. Stalin, as his toughest critic Isaac Deutscher pointed out, cannot be judged a reactionary because his vision was progressive in aim although cruel in execution, whereas Hitler left nothing behind. A revolutionary like Lenin, no matter how harsh, commands respect as well as revulsion. We sense the grim grandeur of his bleak vision of mankind's march to the New Jerusalem, the City of God, to the Realm of Freedom where man is perfect and at peace.

It's a vision to die for. People still die for it.

The Limited View has no such grandeur. It walks, indeed trudges, where others ride on a white horse. But it's a steady walk, starting with Aristotle and ending with Edmund Burke, and moving on to the future at a snail's pace. The Limited View says man is fallible and flawed. Since that is so his political projects will be flawed too.

Best to settle for something less. Like capitalism and democracy, defined as lots for some and a little for all.

It's a theory to live with, not for. Living without a vision is like living without hope for humanity. Dead.

Which of these two views is true? Both of them. That's if you think dialectically and not dogmatically. It is perfectly plain that since the beginning of recorded history man has insisted on acting against his own best interests. It is the right most frequently exercised by the human race. Christians call it original sin. Communists call it anti-socialist behaviour. Call it messing if you like. But whatever we call it we can't pretend man is perfect. Otherwise we Marxists would not be having so much trouble right now, and listening to Edmund Burke saying "I told you so".

Edmund Burke, our greatest political genius, the man who flatly told the electors of Bristol that just because they had elected him did not mean they owned his conscience or voice, put the big question succinctly at the time of the French Revolution: "How can man, who is not himself perfect, make a perfect revolution?"

No answer yet. Asinine answers used to be plentiful. At a Writers' Congress in Moscow in the 1950s, the French Communist writer, André Malraux, listening to another interminable harangue promising universal happiness in a future workers' paradise, suddenly said: "What about a child run over by a tram car?" There was a stunned silence. But dogmatists are as resourceful as theologians and one such jumped up to give the party line to thunderous applause: "In a perfect planned socialist transport system there will be no accidents . . . "

Except, we might add, accidents caused by the train of history running over the stalled socialist car.

The dialectical truth is that we don't know how perfectible man is until we are perfecting so to speak. We learn by doing. Perfectibility is not a final state but a process. What we do know is that humanity throughout history has insisted on a Limitless Vision by night and a Limited View by day so to speak. Which explains the guilty uproar in the Senate recently when Professor John A Murphy pointed out that in this century nothing in the

West could surpass the shining vision of the Bolshevik Revolution of 1917.

THE PRIMACY OF THE PERSON
Politics are about the person. And politics are always personal. And when they are not they are inhuman.

Three more lessons from 1989.

Socialism said that politics was about the collective, about society, about the proletariat, about any number greater than one. And in 1989 the people of Europe, for the second time in two hundred years, told us that was not so, and that politics is always about the person.

The individual person is the whole point of history. This is the message from the French and Russian revolutions. In 1789 the people of France told princes that from now on history would be about the freedom of the individual person and not just a history of nobles. Two hundred years later, in 1989, the people of Eastern Europe told the party the very same thing.

People won't tell us a third time.

The passion for personal freedom is the greatest of all political passions. It drove the French Revolution of 1789 to cut the head from kings, and it drove the Gorbachev revolution of 1989 to cut the ground from under the feet of dogmatists. The passion for democracy is the passion for the sense of personal liberty at the heart of democracy. And that personal liberty is about the sense of self.

We may not be immortal. But we feel immortal. We feel, each of us, that there will never be another like us. That is the feeling of every man and woman born on this earth and it is a feeling so universal, so timeless and so full of truth that we must respect it.

1989. The year we were told to respect the self.

Revolutionaries who suppress self in the name of the revolution are certain to repress and resent the sign of self in others; socialists who think little of themselves are likely to think a lot less of others; socialists who give up their own right to speak in the name of history are likely to lock up others who exercise that right and who make them guilty.

* * *

Persons are the beginning and the end of politics.

This is the view of people on the street and is completely correct. The source of all political authority is the personal conscience of each citizen counted one by one. This view is still a sin on "the left" where the cult of the collective is fine but not the cult of personality, which is only a person speaking the truth as that person sees it. The cult of the personality in practice is aimed at "political" leaders because politics is suspect on the left. This is another dreary dogma that cuts off from real life.

* * *

A spectre is haunting Europe. The spectre of social democracy, child of socialism and democracy.

Social democracy is socialism purged and purified. We cannot shirk this cleansing procedure, which must be conducted in three dialectical stages: by criticising, by annulling, by transcending. We must criticise all aspects of our heritage without any cover-ups; we must annul what is wrong and we must transcend what is left and step up on dead dogmas to catch sight of the future.

The future is social democracy.

What is Social Democracy?
Social Democracy can be defined as the struggle for socialist values in a democratic society with a market economy; a process of progressive advances rather than static state of arrival; a permanent puncturing of private greed by principles of public good – the Marxist theory of social change married to social democratic politics, the historic struggle to move mankind to the realm of freedom.

But with the person at the centre of history.

341

What is the goal of social democracy?
Liberty, Equality, Fraternity.

What is its project in Ireland?
It must be a project that makes sense to our people and makes sense of our peoples' history. It must be democratic, which is not merely a matter of addition but a dialogue between party and people that respects human and minority rights. It must be hegemonic, that is it must subsume and subordinate other projects to it.

The National Question is that project.

What is the National Question?
The National Question, in today's terms, can only be defined as the Democratic National Question. This has three aspects: it means supporting the democratic right of Northern Unionists to decide their own political destiny; defeating the Catholic sectarian campaign of the Provo IRA to set up a one-party state; and uniting all the progressive forces on the island in pursuit of peace and plenty in the context of a social-democratic Europe from the Atlantic to the Urals.

X

THE EUROPEAN
LITERARY IMAGINATION

CHAPTER 26

ALBERT CAMUS AND THE
DUBIOUS POLITICS OF MERCY

SUSAN DUNN

A FEW YEARS AFTER THE LIBERATION OF FRANCE, A WAR-WEARY ALBERT Camus, facing new Cold War realities, looked back at the execution of Louis XVI and surprised his readers by declaring that the king's death was the most significant and tragic event in French history. The execution of Louis XVI, he felt, marked a turning point. It underscored the irrevocable destruction of a world that, for a thousand years, had embraced a sacred order. Celebrated by some as man's seizing control of his political and historical fate, the regicide was mourned by others like Camus as the permanent loss of a moral code of mercy and compassion sanctified by a transcendent God.

"The condemnation of the King is at the crux of our contemporary history", Camus wrote. "It symbolises the secularisation of our history . . . Up to now God was a part of history through the medium of the kings. But His representative in history has been killed, for there is no longer a king."[1] For Camus, the regicide constituted a direct and fatal attack upon the divine mystery that had been the safeguard of certain universal moral, spiritual and political values – compassion, mercy and pardon.

Henceforth, reason and history reigned; morality was displaced by expediency. There was no longer any authority higher than man himself;

everything that had been God's now belonged to man. Camus traced a straight path from Rousseau's *Social Contract* to the regicide and Terror, then to nineteenth-century ideologies of historical necessity and, finally, to twentieth-century totalitarianism. The absence of totalitarianism in France and the commitment of modern France to democratic institutions notwithstanding, Camus located in the regicide the origin of the nihilistic reign of godless "history".

"It is certainly a deplorable scandal," Camus objected, "that the assassination of a weak but good-hearted man has been presented as a great moment in French history."[2] Aggressively distancing himself from the French Revolution and the violent foundation of the First Republic, Camus goes so far as to call the king's death an "assassination". Although the legal basis for the prosecution of the king may have been questionable, and although the trial was flawed for a variety of reasons, the king, nevertheless, had been represented by legal counsel and his fate voted upon. This elaborately staged and politically motivated public execution can be termed an assassination only by a writer who wishes to depict Louis' death as a cowardly act, supremely traumatic for France. France had sacrificed God's "lieutenant" on earth, the compassionate, merciful father of the desperate and dispossessed. "Like God Himself", noted Camus, the king traditionally was "the last recourse for victims of misery and injustice". In principle, the people could appeal to the king for help against their oppressors, he explained. "If the king only knew . . . " was the hopeful refrain. Did the king, in fact, rescue his people? Yes, replied Camus. "When the monarchy did know," he claimed, "it often tried to defend the lower classes against the oppression of the aristocracy and the bourgeoisie."[3]

Camus, of course, understood that the king's mercy and generosity depended on his will alone. The king's arbitrary "grace" could hardly be equated with justice, for "even though it is possible to appeal to the king, it is impossible to appeal against him".[4] And yet, a king who could bestow pardon and who incarnated God's mercy appeared to Camus to wreak considerably less havoc on humanity than Jacobin or Soviet versions of justice. Given the choice between revolutionary-style justice and monarchical grace, arbitrary grace seemed infinitely less threatening and less potentially violent than the French or Russian Revolution's desacralised principles of rational and merciless justice.

346

Camus' positive remarks about monarchy, in general, and about the hapless Louis XVI, in particular, may startle modern readers. But his sympathy for Louis XVI and his criticism of regicide do not signal an improbable reactionary embracing of right-wing politics. Camus was never a monarchist and always felt a greater affinity for the political left than for the right. He dwelt on the king's death to dramatise his hard-line opposition to historicism and totalitarianism as well as to express his own longing for a politics of clemency and compassion. He provocatively expressed nostalgia for a past that never existed, a theocratic regime in which political power was finite and the moral authority of God and king infinite. It was always the myth, never the reality of monarchy, that attracted Camus.

As one of France's leading intellectuals and political commentators in the 1940s and 1950s, Camus wanted most of all to present himself as a moral authority and as a voice of humane, non-ideological reason. And it was precisely the benevolent values – mercy, compassion, pardon – that he associated with monarchy that he attempted to inject into discussions of the political crises of his times, the post-war "purge" of collaborators and the Algerian War. But would his esteem for the essentially non-political values of pity, clemency and reconciliation help him to take meaningful political positions or ultimately force him to withdraw from the political arena?

* * *

Clemency, mercy and grace had not always been part of Camus' vocabulary, for there was a time when he demanded strict justice, dismissing pleas for mercy. In the months following the liberation of France in 1944 he was adamant in his support for the punishment of collaborators, known as the "purge" or *l'épuration*. At that time radical revolutionary measures seemed entirely appropriate to him, and he summoned to the rescue the most intransigent of the Jacobins. "This country does not need a Talleyrand", he asserted. "It needs a Saint-Just."[5] Insisting on the necessity of remembering past crimes, he refused to consider amnesty or pardon. "Who would dare speak here about pardon? Who would ask us to forget?" he demanded. "It is not hatred which will speak tomorrow, but justice itself, founded on memory."[6]

Camus insisted that France needed to deal in a stern and judicious manner with French men and women guilty of collaboration. "France carries within her, like a foreign body . . . men of treason and injustice", he judged. Still, "we have never called for mindless or convulsive vengeance . . . We want France to keep her hands pure. But precisely because of that, we wish for prompt justice . . . and then . . . the rational forgetting of the errors that so many French people nevertheless committed".[7] This eminently reasonable and justifiable desire to confront the past and legally assign guilt and responsibility is oddly tempered with references to purity and to remembering as the condition for the evidently more important stage of forgetting.

In January 1945 Camus passionately took issue with François Mauriac, who was repelled by the policy of the purge and urged forgiveness. Deriding Mauriac's plea for Christian charity, Camus declared that 1944 was a year to settle scores. "Charity has nothing to do with this", he declared. "As a *man*, I might admire Mr. Mauriac for knowing how to love traitors, but as a *citizen*, I deplore it, because this love will result in a nation of traitors and mediocrities and a society of which we want no part."[8] But, again, in Camus' vehement defence of the purge one detects a latent ambivalence.

Camus' dismissal of charity and pardon is less resolute than it appears. The distinction he creates between the moral man, who might forgive his enemies, and the politically-minded citizen, who demands their punishment, suggests that he had not fully resolved for himself these political and ethical issues. Although in early 1945 he identified with the citizen, he nevertheless intimates that the moral man may occupy the higher ground. And, in fact, just half a year later he would decide that the purge was a misguided failure.

What was the purge? Not to be confused with the summary executions of collaborators, which did also take place, the purge consisted in the legal trials of tens of thousands of people accused of collaboration. As Peter Novick points out in *The Resistance Versus Vichy*, the Resistance wanted a sweeping purge of collaborators that would cleanse and regenerate France. De Gaulle, on the other hand, stressed the need to forgive and forget, reminding people that "France needs all her sons".[9] As far as de Gaulle was concerned, the collaborators who should be tried constituted only "a tiny number of scoundrels" and "a handful of *misérables*". Thus, from the beginning, the lines were clearly drawn between those demanding punishment and those wishing immediate reconciliation.

The trials presented many significant legal, procedural and moral questions, such as whether or not Vichy had been the legal government of France; whether the pre-war penal code would be used or whether retroactive laws needed to be enacted; whether a jury consisting of *résistants* could be impartial; whether an individual's *acts* or *character* would be on trial; whether the basis of guilt would be legal or moral. The purge was made all the more difficult because the police and the judiciary themselves would have needed to be purged for the trials to be completely fair. In addition, it was a monumental task to establish 200 new courts, each with its own investigative and prosecuting staff.[10]

The trials dragged on until 1949. Approximately 124,751 cases were tried: 2,853 death sentences were handed down, of which 767 were carried out; an additional 3,910 death sentences were made *in absentia;* also handed down were 38,266 prison and hard labour sentences; and 49,723 people were condemned to "national degradation", that is, the deprivation of their civil rights and property. But because of various amnesty laws, by 1951 only 4,000 people (out of almost 40,000) remained in prison; the rest had been released or pardoned.

The purge ended with widespread frustration and disappointment. In general, the trials were criticised for "incoherence": many important verdicts were capricious, disproportionately lenient or harsh.[11] But for all the imperfections, inconsistencies and miscarriages of the purge, surely more egregious would have been a refusal to hold any trials at all.

At the time of the Liberation Camus had vigorously supported the purge, associating it with his expectations for the wondrous rebirth of France. In his *Combat* articles of 1944, over and over again he expressed the belief that the heroic Resistance movement would somehow be transformed into a political and moral revolution, and inseparable from that vision for the future of France was the necessity of the purge. In 1944 he wrote that the purge was "the only chance we have left to prevent France and the rest of Europe from becoming that desert of mediocrity and silence in which we are no longer willing to live".[12]

But, ultimately, Camus was more drawn to the idea of a purifying and rejuvenating revolution than interested in trials that would inevitably be divisive and prey to the fallible procedures inherent in any system of legal justice. Disgusted especially with one sentence he considered too harsh,[13] he quickly decided that the purge was harmful to France. In March 1945 he diagnosed the purge as a symptom of the contagion of the Nazis' violence and hatred. "To the hatred of their persecutors," he deplored, "the victims responded with their own hatred. And the persecutors having departed, the French remain on their soil with their hatred in need of an object. They still look at one another with the remains of their anger."[14] In August 1945 he condemned the purge, calling it a disaster. "There is no doubt that the purge in France is not only a failure but entirely discredited", he concluded. "The word purge was already sufficiently painful in itself. The thing has become odious."[15]

Camus determined that charity, not punishment, should be the order of the day. In 1948, referring to his earlier disagreement with François Mauriac, he acknowledged that "Monsieur Mauriac was right, not I".[16] In fact, in that same speech he goes so far as to dismiss apologetically his earlier demand for retributive justice by attributing it to nothing more than "the difficult *memory* of two or three murdered friends".[17] Amnesia was preferable to memory, and amnesty and reconciliation were evidently preferable to punishment and divisiveness.

Amnesty has historically been used after wars and uprisings to restore harmony. Victor Hugo had pleaded for amnesty after the Franco-Prussian War. And in 1834, after a revolutionary uprising in Lyons, Lamartine had also sought national reconciliation, arguing that one half of the nation could not try the other half.[18] Concerning the Nuremberg Trials, Camus made a comment similar to Lamartine's. "Jodl was hanged at Nuremberg", he commented. "But 70 million inhabitants could not be hanged."[19] Yet neither in France nor in Germany was the issue the hanging of half or most of the population; it was a question of punishing collaborators and war criminals. The crimes they committed against innocent people cannot be compared to the politically-motivated accusations against the insurgents of Lyons or the Communards.

In America presidents traditionally granted amnesty at the end of the country's wars. The purpose of amnesty was to signal a war's end, never to cancel or undermine retributive justice. President Thomas Jefferson pardoned deserters from the Continental Army. Abraham Lincoln pardoned Civil War deserters (on the condition that they return to their units and continue to fight) as well as supporters of the Confederacy.[20] As Alexander Hamilton had recommended, it was useful to "restore the tranquillity of the commonwealth" by a "well-timed offer of pardon to the insurgents or rebels".[21] However, to serve truly the public interest pardon must promote justice as well as harmony. In the case of the Civil War, pardon was a way to acknowledge that the punishment of soldiers who were guilty only of desertion would have been ill-desert; and it was equally necessary to recognise that Confederate soldiers were not really traitors.[22] But soldiers who were guilty of crimes other than desertion were punished, as the Andersonville Trial illustrated.

As for President Carter's 1977 amnesty for Vietnam draft evaders, he was recognising that many of them had done not only what they sincerely believed, but also what may have arguably been right; thus amnesty was a way of preventing the punishment of innocent people.[23] As in the Civil War, soldiers accused of war crimes in Vietnam were put on trial. Amnesty was not intended to prevent retributive justice or thwart the punishment of those who were morally or legally deserving of punishment.

But it was punishment that Camus could simply not countenance. In an article critical of the purge he wrote that "punishment must be taken into consideration. And this horrible word has always repelled hearts that are in the least bit sensitive".[24] Sensitive hearts, however, might be infinitely more repelled by crime and a judicial system that does not hold people accountable for their actions than by just punishment.

Ultimately, Camus was appalled by the thought of occupying the judge's bench. He dreamed of distributing charity, not sentences. Yet in the name of charity, after the most evil crimes ever committed against millions of innocent human beings, he would have dispensed with legal justice and even with the remorse and expiation of the culprits. This would, indeed, have been the reign of God the Father, not God the Judge. Pardon would have been as gratuitous, arbitrary and non-rational as the gift of a king who touches and heals his subjects.

Memories of the occupation, Vichy and the Holocaust notwithstanding, Camus stated that hearts poisoned by anger could be cured only through "that superior effort which will transform our appetite for hatred into a desire for justice".[25] Disparaging a rightful desire for the legal punishment of collaborators and war criminals by falsely labelling it "an appetite for hatred", Camus indicates that there is a higher form of justice than the rule of law. What is this new justice?

Camus oddly defined justice not in terms of legal procedure, but in terms of "solidarity" and compassion. "If justice has any meaning in this world," he wrote, "it signifies nothing other than the recognition of human solidarity; in its essence, it cannot be separated from compassion."[26] "Justice is simultaneously an idea and a warmth of the soul", he wrote in *Combat* in 1944,[27] reducing justice to vague emotional feelings of well-being.

Thus, just six months after the liberation of France and two months before the surrender of Germany, Camus saw fit to displace legal justice as well as any concept of desert with vague notions of "friendship"[28] and "warmth of the soul". The position he arrived at was legally meaningless and politically and morally troubling.

* * *

Ten years later, during the Algerian war, Camus' antipathy for violence, his ethical principles and his strong emotional ties to Algeria brought forth so many contradictions that the situation in Algeria became a political, moral and personal quagmire for him. In 1958 he announced his voluntary withdrawal from the political debate: "I decided to take no further part in the constant polemics that had no result other than to harden the uncompromising points of view at loggerheads in Algeria and to split even wider a France already poisoned by hatred and factions." He added that he was personally "interested only in the actions that here and now can spare useless bloodshed".[29] In his writings he was as concerned with the ethical conduct of all sides involved in the conflict as with the political future of Algeria.

Having tortuously examined the moral short-comings and political failures of all factions, Camus renounced active participation and offered himself as a voice of reason. As an intellectual he could best contribute to the Algerian situation, he felt, by "clarifying definitions in order to disintoxicate minds and calm fanaticisms".[30] But although Camus abstained from making an unambiguous partisan declaration, his position was clear: he supported a French-imposed solution to the war in Algeria and he supported non-violence.

Camus' commitment to the survival of the French community in Algeria and his refusal to countenance Algerian independence have compromised his stature as a political thinker. Only in 1958 did he finally denounce colonialism as an institution and even when he came to this conclusion he still would not entertain the possibility of complete Algerian separation from France. Algerian independence, he wrote, "is a purely emotional slogan".[31] Even more problematic was his remark that the presence of his mother in Algeria was sufficient to counterbalance for him the entire colonial situation. "I believe in justice," he declared, "but I will defend my mother before justice."[32]

Mother or Justice? Loyalty or principles? Camus was "as much a man of honour as a man of principles", Michael Walzer aptly noted, "and honour begins with personal loyalty, not with ideological commitment".[33] Yet what makes Camus' writings about Algeria questionable may not be his emotional connectedness to the situation in Algeria, which he himself alluded to as a personal tragedy,[34] but the contradictions in his politics and the inherent weakness of some of his positions – his ambivalent attitude toward the Arab community in Algeria, his strange inflation of France's role in Algerian history, his anachronistic Francocentric references to the unique, pivotal role of France in world history and politics. France, he declared, "can offer the Arab people their best hope for the future".[35]

Camus never had the political insight or the political courage of Conor Cruise O'Brien and Máire MacEntee when they represented Ireland at the United Nations in the late 1950s. They did not shrink from proposing a just solution to the Algerian problem under international auspices or from supporting independence for Algeria; likewise, they endorsed the principle of self determination for all nations.[36] Indeed, Conor Cruise O'Brien later noted Camus' denunciation of violent revolt in Algeria and his approval of it in Hungary, his silence when violence was used to defend the status quo, except where the status quo still asserted a legitimacy based on revolution.[37]

Attempting to understand Camus' political thought, one inevitably becomes mired in his conflicts and discouraged by his righteous and moralising tone. But if it is possible to see beyond his irresolvable and disputable positions, from which he fully realised he could not disentangle his own feelings, we might nevertheless discover a modern writer who was searching for moral principles according to which people could conduct their lives, principles that would shield the innocent from suffering and violence and protect societies from ideologies that justify murder.

* * *

Jean-Paul Sartre, Camus' great rival, did not disguise his contempt for Camus' eagerness to be the "Attorney General for the Republic of Pure Souls".[38] In his preface to Frantz Fanon's *Les Damnés de la Terre*, Sartre defended political violence as a legitimate means for national liberation. He celebrated the creative potential of violence, arguing that violence was the only force that can purge society, terminate centuries of colonial tyranny and simultaneously produce a new social order. "No gentleness can efface the marks of violence", Sartre wrote. "Only violence itself can destroy them."[39]

Sartre celebrated the act of murdering a European colonialist. Such a murder, he felt, was rich in meaning and consequences. It signified the death of the oppressor as well as the symbolic death of the murderer himself, who, by murdering the colonial oppressor, is reborn a free man. A phoenix, he rises from the corpses of his victims. "To shoot down a European is to kill two birds with one stone", Sartre explained. "There remain a dead man and a free man; the survivor, for the first time, feels a *national* soil under his foot."[40] Fraternity, Sartre went on to argue, is located in the shared experience of murder. "They are brothers inasmuch as each of them has killed and may at any moment have to kill again."[41]

Who was more deluded? Camus dreaming of a harmonious and just French-imposed political reconciliation in Algeria or Sartre rhapsodising about blood, death and resurrection? Politically and morally, Sartre's praise of violent revolution, along with his belief that violence is the *sine qua non* of political change, are mistaken at best.[42] Camus' colonialist assumptions about French Algeria were also untenable. He simply could not imagine, as Conor Cruise O'Brien suggests, that there were Arabs who felt that:

> the French were in Algeria in virtue of the same right by which the Germans were in France: the right of conquest. The fact that the conquest had lasted considerably longer in Algeria than it was to last in France changed nothing in the essential resemblance of the relations between conqueror and conquered.[43]

As for the conquered, colonised peoples, neither Sartre, excited by revolutionary violence, nor Camus, spellbound by innocence, could offer them help of any value. But Camus' abhorrence of violence in Algeria was at least a moral (if otherworldly and apolitical) response to colonial and anti-colonial terror.

What moral values, Camus wondered, could be higher than mercy and compassion? What political principle higher than pardon? The idea of clemency pulled him like a magnet, but he found himself imprisoned in a historical period that recognised only guilt and blame. In his ironic last novel, *La Chute*, there is only too much blame to go around. In *La Chute* Camus depicts a cold, fog-enshrouded place in which there is no innocence and no mercy, only desperate, guilt-ridden individuals who are nostalgic for kindness and pardon.

In the godless and kingless world of *La Chute*, compassion and pardon have survived only as empty, cynical words, their emotional substance and depth having long disappeared. True pardon, remarks Jean-Baptiste Clamence, the narrator, is not an empty ritual, but lies in the genuine synthesis of forgiving and forgetting, in political and moral amnesty. But even Clamence can offer no clemency. Of short memory, he simply forgets in spite of himself; pardon is neither his intention nor his gift. "My forgetfulness was praiseworthy", he says. "I wasn't good enough to forgive offences, but eventually I always forgot them."[44] An irremediable fall from grace, a relentless consciousness of guilt in a world that knows neither compassion nor pardon constitute the sad human condition.

The modern world, having exiled the king, exiled itself from his kingdom of misericord. In the sunless universe of *La Chute*, the sun-king is absent and a tortured and pitiless "sun-citizen"[45] reigns in his place. It is not surprising that Camus had originally intended this novel about exile to be one of the short stories in his last collection, *L'Exil et le royaume*, for Clamence's "fall" mirrors an entire civilisation's exile from the kingdom of grace, of which the execution of Louis XVI was emblematic.

The decapitation of Louis XVI was the single most crucial event in Camus' vision of the history of the Occident. No institution and no ideology could henceforth replace the king, who, like God, rescued the poor and comforted the suffering. Perhaps only a prophet or a priest might try to rekindle the king's message of charity. Not unlike his great predecessor Victor Hugo, Camus envisioned his role as a moral guide in the swamp of history and politics. However conflicted and disturbing some of his political positions were, it was nevertheless his laudable hope to provide the world a glimpse of what the "kingdom" might have been. As our century draws to a close, as the Cold War's passionate debates between opposing ideologies have given way to the common passion for prosperity, as the dispossessed are ignored and forgotten, a reminder of Camus' attempt to inject compassion and mercy into politics might not be unseasonable.

CHAPTER 27

MARIA CROSS ROADS:
A STUDY OF "DONAT O'DONNELL"

OWEN DUDLEY EDWARDS

I do not claim . . . that anything is proved, in the scientific sense, at all.

The only requirement of the scientific spirit to which I have tried to conform is that of respect for the facts . . . It is quite possible that the living writers discussed will not, if they read the essays on themselves, agree. This need not unduly perturb the critic. GK Chesterson, in his introduction to *The Old Curiosity Shop*, gave a valuable definition which has been too little heeded by subsequent Catholic critics. 'The function of criticism,' he wrote, 'if it has a legitimate function at all, can only be one function – that of dealing with the subconscious part of the author's mind, which only the critic can express, and not with the conscious part of the author's mind, which the author himself can express. Either criticism is no good at all (a very defensible position) or else criticism means saying about an author the very things that would have made him jump out of his boots.'

– "Donat O'Donnell" [Conor Cruise O'Brien],
*Maria Cross: Imaginative Patterns in a Group
of Modern Catholic Writers*

The highest, as the lowest, form of criticism is a mode of autobiography.
– Oscar Wilde, *The Picture of Dorian Gray*

URBS ET ORBIS

"The Irish state in the aftermath of the [Second World War] felt its isolation, psychologically and intellectually", wrote Máire and Conor Cruise O'Brien in *A Concise History of Ireland*. What's more:

It had had for years a censorship of literature, aimed against obscenity but so interpreted as to attempt to exclude all modern imaginative prose writings of importance. This censorship law, together with laws against divorce and contraception, had been passed, under clerical pressure, in the period after the Civil War . . . To the censorship of literature had been added, during [World War II], a strict censorship of the press. With the ending of press censorship, Irish people found themselves strangers, and not very popular ones, in a strange post-war world.

Ireland crawled suspiciously out of its burrow in 1945, showing little confidence in a new world order baptised by atom bombs dropped on Hiroshima and Nagasaki. Luck, and a ferociously unspoken policy of covert aid to the British and Americans, preserved 26-county neutrality, but after the war those who had ears knew quickly enough of the successive invasion threats from the IRA, its Nazi allies, its British opponents and its American critics, more or less in that order. Popular – though far from unanimous – sympathy for Britain was warped by an intemperate anti-Irish radio rant from Winston Churchill at the war's end, while the always more popular Americans weakened their standing through the antics of an ambassador (David Gray) who had advocated replacing the de Valera government with a puppet dictatorship. Paradoxically, Irish popular loyalties towards specific Allies weakened any general identification with the victors. General Charles de Gaulle of the Free French – Catholic, aristocratic and vaguely credited with descent from the Wild Geese – was the most obvious point of Irish identification among Allied leaders, but his nationalistic French ruptures from the supposedly more cosmopolitan nationalists Churchill and Roosevelt, and his rapid polarisation in French politics from an indistinguishable vociferous rabble of Fourth Republic leaders, appealed simultaneously to Irish nationalists, liberationists, Catholics and ironists. Irish links with Britain had been powerfully strengthened by Irish volunteers in the British armed services, but the returning soldiers carried a flavour of anti-American sentiment on the rise in the Britain of 1945, and this invited the disapproval of the Irish to whom the United States combined the attractions of a mildly improper dream, an ambiguous Fairy Godmother and a long-lost child of possibly lucrative loyalties. The causes of India and Israel made appeals to the more and less peaceable critics of Pax Britannica, and Holy Mother Church was ready to turn her incessant denunciation of the USSR into thinly-veiled acidities against its recent allies: the socialist British and the liberal Americans. As for Ireland herself, according to *A Concise History of Ireland,* "de Valera, whose leadership had been accepted by almost all in the war period, now began to lose support. The young men whom he had interned (with general approbation at the time) now began to attract, by a familiar process, some retrospective and retroactive sympathy".

Seán and Mary Citizen still went to "the pictures", though their increasingly distant cousins Shane and Miriam Fitzperson went to "the cinema" or "the films", and in both instances absorbed, with individual reservations, the romantic legitimisation of popular sentiment as filtered through the moving image. *I See a Dark Stranger* (1945) gave splendid play to the English sense of humour, as Frank Launder and Sidney Gilliat contrasted innocent Irish republicanism (Deborah Kerr) with evil Nazism temporarily mesmerising it, but in acquitting the Irish Catholics of pro-Hitler sympathies, the film involuntarily sanitised the IRA. *Odd Man Out* (1946), directed by Carol Reed, made the hopeless flight of the IRA gunman (James Mason) dry up any audience scruples for his victims. The Boulting Brothers produced Graham Greene's *Brighton Rock* (1947) to a screenplay from the author and Terence Rattigan which saved Rose, its heroine (Carol Marsh), from hearing on a record her dead, Satanically-beautiful husband, Pinkie Brown (Richard Attenborough), expectorating his contempt for her love, which he had conjured up to prevent her from testifying to one of his murders. The Irish audience knew the value of illusions to preserve widows' love for dead killers, however patriotic, and also knew Greene's book text as a "shilling Penguin". John Ford, famed for *The Informer* (1935), gave an Irish directorial sanctification to *The Fugitive* (1948), whose even more sanitised version of Greene's *The Power and the Glory* cleaned up his whiskey-priest (Henry Fonda) before sending him on the run in twentieth-century Mexico (easily conflated with later twentieth-century communist Eastern Europe or early-eighteenth-century Protestant Ireland). Reed's *The Fallen Idol* (also 1948) turned an innocent, bourgeois child (Bobby Henrey) into a liar defending what he takes to be a murderer (Ralph Richardson), albeit only in Greene's original story ("The Basement Room") is the boy's friend a real killer. Reed's *The Third Man* (1949) for once found itself darkening a Greene happier ending, with its heroine (Alida Valli) rejecting the man (Joseph Cotton) who has betrayed his friend (Orson Welles) to the British authorities for adulterating penicillin and thereby destroying the lives of hospital patients.

* * *

Dublin revelled in all of these films, especially the last, reinforcing as it did the nationalist creed of implacable enmity to the informer. Its leading liberal intellectual journal, the *Bell*, had greater reservations about the facilely fashionable, as its youthful critic "Donat O'Donnell" – Conor Cruise O'Brien – made clear in a May 1947 review of *Odd Man Out:*

> there are two themes in *Odd Man Out* which never fuse . . . the real streets of a city, rain on dark uniforms, running mobs of children, the external world [and] . . . the inner drama of Johnny's destiny . . . Johnny is leader of an organisation at war with the rulers of the city. His natural immediate environment is the people that make up, support or tolerate that organisation. If he is to live convincingly these people must live too. Therefore, as the city chosen is Belfast, an attempt must be made to portray Republicans and Catholics in that city, and the city's deeply divided, suspicious, almost racialistic life. If that line had been taken, the talents that produced *Odd Man Out* would have made a magnificent film and also, in the literal sense, a riot.
>
> The makers of the film, including the writer of the scenario-novel, Mr FL Green, fought shy of this. They gave Johnny instead a vague fantastic environment: a few non-political, non-sectarian lay-figures as 'the organisation', and three neurotic isolated 'characters' from nowhere as the main landmarks in the story. Then, having deprived him of a credible environment, they are forced to make an attempt, in the German manner, at soul-photography – an attempt which is doomed from the start – so the gap between man and city is never filled, Johnny never comes to life, and *Odd Man Out* is a failure . . . It contains many scenes of beauty, but not unfortunately the one thing that was needed to relate these specific scenes: a serious and intelligent regard for truth.

The last words of a film review are not a bad location for a manifesto.

James Joyce's "The Dead", the last story of *Dubliners*, shows the Dublin would-be intellectuals of 1904 fumbling for a culture between the counterpulls of the Galway Gaedhealtacht's vaunted integrity, the social and financial attractions of London fashions, the comparative charms of France and Germany, the traditions and sacrosanct strength of Catholic Rome, the Anglo-Irish colonial heritage now usurpable by the Catholic bourgeoisie and the unanswerable tyranny of dead, martyred youth consecrated to altruistic love. Conor Cruise O'Brien for most of his life believed the Gaedhealtacht advocate in "The Dead", Molly Ivors, to be based on his mother, Kathleen Sheehy, but recently has allowed the anti-social vehemence to suggest a blend with his more recriminatory, if less Gaelicist, aunt Hanna Sheehy-Skeffington. Dublin's would-be intellectuals of 1945 were caught in a similar polylateral of forces. There were not wanting some Germanophiles among the Gaelicisers; Catholicism bred its share of Hispanophiles and Italophiles as well as Francophiles; Castle Catholics had long outlived the viceregal court; the College of the Holy and Undivided Trinity of Queen Elizabeth kept its ancient loyalities where they had been in 1904 (coincidentally, the last date of firm Tory rule over Ireland); fierce chauvinists denounced the government's compulsory Irish policy as wretchedly insufficient; American dollars, publishers and celluloid blandished; Rome rang its ancient bells, not every peal being permitted by the Irish hierarchy to sound in the ears of the Irish faithful; Belloc was old and Chesterton was dead; and what was Paddy to read?

The answer to that question was probably banned by the Censorship Board.

* * *

"Donat O'Donnell" welcomed the *Bell*'s contrast to its highbrow London counterpart *Horizon* (which was edited by Cyril Connolly). As he observed in the eponymous journal in March 1946:

> although it represents whatever is most consciously intellectual in modern Ireland . . . in its caution, its realism, its profound but ambivalent nationalism, its seizures of stodginess and its bad paper . . . [it] reflects the class who write it and read it – teachers, librarians, junior civil servants, the lettered section of the Irish petty bourgeoisie . . . They are earth-bound, for good or ill, and the *Bell*, making the best of it, deliberately sets out to reflect Irish life, rather than attempt the very different task of pursuing the true, the good and the beautiful.

"L'art pour l'art est un vain mot. L'art pour le vrai, l'art pour le beau et le bon, voilà la religion que je cherche", wrote Georges Sand to Alexandre Saint-Jean in 1872, and if "O'Donnell's" invocation of an uncredited French liberalism half unfurled his manifesto, its symbols were elegantly clashed. The *Bell*, established by Seán O'Faoláin in October 1940, was courageous: "Donat O'Donnell" wished to make it more so and was now saying that his contributions would make it more so. His own writings for it would say relatively little reflecting "Irish life", of which his own knowledge was limited in the present and profound for the past. Writer and journal had reasons for caution: O'Brien, as a twenty-seven-year-old junior civil servant (lately in the Department of Finance, for the past few years in External Affairs), was vulnerable, although given licence by his

pseudonym as was, for instance, "Myles na gCopaleen", aka "Flann O'Brien" (Brian Nolan); and the *Bell*'s most obvious precursor, *Ireland Today*, had been terminated by lay Catholic pressure against its advertisers and distributors over articles hostile to the Franco rebels in the Spanish Civil War written by O'Brien's first cousin and mentor, Owen Sheehy-Skeffington. Sheehy-Skeffington was strongly anti-communist, but for all of his emphasis on the Francoite oppression of the Basque Catholics and their priests, rabid Irish Catholic opinion in 1936-39 largely swallowed Franco's self-identification with the cause of Catholicism and condemned Sheehy-Skeffington not simply as anti-Catholic (which he was), but as pro-communist (which he wasn't). Seán O'Faoláin, an ex-Catholic who reconverted in the late 1940s to "European", not "Irish", Catholicism, had been hostile to both Franco and to the Spanish Republic (chiefly to its more pro-communist Popular Front supporters); Peader O'Donnell, the *Bell*'s managing editor and O'Faoláin's successor as editor in April 1946 (O'Faoláin remaining literary editor), had been a pro-communist supporter of the Spanish Republic. Sheehy-Skeffington preceded his cousin's advent to the *Bell*, becoming a regular – and, even from the perspective of fifty years later, brilliant – analyst of foreign affairs, occasionally inviting Peader O'Donnell's reprobation due to his support for insurgent Israel (O'Brien's *The Siege* vindicated a legacy inherited from his closest and dearest kinsman, original though its inception was).

On leaving office O'Faoláin nominated an editorial board which conveyed the phalanx of mutual support against the world and mutual disputants at their own pleasure: himself, Peader O'Donnell, "Donat O'Donnell", Thomas Woods (or "Hogan"), Valentin Iremonger, Owen Sheehy-Skeffington and the economist Patrick Lynch. Still under thirty, "Donat O'Donnell" was the youngest of them. All or any might have advised on any *Bell* contribution, either by editorial or by authorial referral. All were brilliant; all were visionaries; all were extremely funny; all despised pomposity; all believed in simultaneously challenging orthodoxies as writers and undermining them as public servants; all were worshipped by the present writer, 20 years junior to their youngest.

If it was to retain the respect of its readers, what the *Bell* needed urgently was to be sent up rotten in its own pages. It might mingle its courage with caution, and its caution with courage, and survive, but if nihilistic Dublin labelled it as taking itself too seriously it was doomed. In the *Bell*'s pages O'Brien's Trinity College roommate, Vivian Mercier, might analyse the "six jokes" of the humourous journal *Dublin Opinion*;

his colleague at External Affairs and (with Sheehy-Skeffington) future consultant on *Maria Cross*, Thomas Woods, might even analyse Myles na gCopaleen (himself an early contributor, but now dubbing O'Faoláin "*Bell*-bottomed" in his *Irish Times* column). But it was left for "Donat O'Donnell" to delight the *Bell*'s audience in May 1945 with a parody of the journal drastic enough to pre-empt further strikes from beyond its columns. Myles himself could hardly better the prediction of Trinity's frosty Classicist WB Stanford, regaling *Bell* readers on Gaelic football and hurling, as "An Olympian at Croke Park" (Benjamin Jowett reviewing Glasgow Celtic would be more probable), while "Crubeens v Boxty: A Symposium" collapsed the *Bell*'s North-South confrontations into culinary affrays about the respective merits of pigs' feet and bread made of the raw pulp of potatoes (both much extolled by the synthetic folk guru). The *Bell* had found its *enfant terrible* and its Minister for External Cultural Affairs. The *Bell*'s understandably savage indignation against Irish obscurantist complacency risked over-valuation of the overseas cultures contrasting so favourably with Ireland's own: Seán O'Faoláin's rediscovery of his religion in Europe, and Peader O'Donnell's fitful yearnings to resume Sovietisation of Irish republicanism, needed a younger and less romanticised eye with which to pursue the true, the good and the beautiful. Or, as the neo-Platonists of Crubeens and Boxty might prefer to put it, "Donat O'Donnell" was the man to judge the horn-length of cows across the sea.

* * *

"O'Donnell's" March 1946 *Horizon* essay struck a note on the English to which he would return, class:

> The English, unlike most other European nations, have retained their old upper classes, a little battered, but still in working order. Symbolically, their Prime Minister [Clement Attlee], though a Socialist, is still a Public School man. Inherited wealth, in its forms of freedom, leisure and detachment, has formed the minds of intellectual life to a greater degree than is the case in any other country, save, possibly, Franco Spain.

This judgement, like others "Donat O'Donnell" would make in these years, reminds us of subsequently forgotten truths. The triumphs of the welfare state, admirable to the British and exemplary to the Irish, cloud our recollection of the strength of the English class system at its origin and the durability – not simply the reenactment – of class influence on subsequent decades. (In recent years Scots and Welsh often seem much more alive to the survival of English class-consciousness than do many Irish.) It also shows a writer using Ireland's relative detachment from Europe to achieve a comparative perspective markedly lacking in much English – and indeed Irish – self-analysis. Most valuable, perhaps, was "O'Donnell's" comforting reassurance, derived from *Horizon*-scans, that what he termed "the spoiled child's universe" was visible in Britain as well as in Ireland:

> Bill was a neurotic case described by Miss Anna Kavan (February 1944) as 'one of the heroes of our time'. His heroism consisted in protesting against the war and the modern world in general by means of a nervous breakdown. Miss Kavan suggested that his example deserved to be widely emulated, and subsequent correspondence showed that several *Horizon* readers warmly agreed with this rather surprising view. No letter of different tendency was published.

Post-colonialism invited the Irish to assume either perpetual superiority to their former rulers or perpetual inferiority. "O'Donnell" gave no comfort to either delusion. His early *Bell* work had included press analyses: in the future he would make some of them the most incisive and extensive investigations of foreign cultures by studying runs of symptomatic journals – the *New Yorker, New Statesman, Encounter*. Some of this skill in critical summation may have derived from his duties for the press division of External Affairs – "Mr O'Brien, the *Irish Catholic* is waitin' at the desk." "Offer him £5 for his horse." – but aptitude seems to have preceded the activity. "O'Donnell" had a fast hand with *Who's Who*, whence he seemed to acquire more sociological depth than did any of his contemporaries:

> literary criticism is the characteristic cultural activity of the rentier world.
> The creative work appearing in *Horizon* gives less evidence of vitality. It is . . . small in bulk . . . The quality of the work is, as one would expect, distinguished – except for one or two cases where a well-known name has apparently been held to cover a multitude of words – but it is notable that almost all the work that has been better than just correct has been of foreign extraction . . .
> Of thirteen recently-published *Horizon* writers whom I can find in *Who's Who*, seven were educated at Eton and/or Oxford and at least four of the others obviously belonged to the same social class. I have no reason to suppose that the proportion is greatly different for the British-born *Horizon* writers who have not yet made *Who's Who*. This Brahmin class on which *Horizon* is founded is a narrow one; it has done, and is still doing, a great deal to justify the heavy capital investment which English society

as a whole has put into its education and upkeep. But it seems to be getting a little tired, and England is certainly tired of investing in it. The world of *Horizon*, the world for which art is a religion that one seldom gets round to practising, has, like art, been long-lived, but it is dying . . . having collected for the admiration of posterity the folklore of a society soon to be, like our ancient Gaelic aristocracy, ploughed under.

ON ORWELL ROAD

"Donat O'Donnell" subsequently directed part of his research towards several illustrious European writers: as it happened, one was an Etonian – Eric Blair, aka George Orwell; and another was an Oxonian – Evelyn Waugh. His Orwell essay, entitled "Raffles, Stalin and George Orwell" and published in May 1946, was a formal review of *Critical Essays* and *Animal Farm*. It captures Orwell at the pre-*1984* phase, while his *Tribune* socialism was in reformation. Amid so much subsequent canonisation or demonisation of Orwell, "O'Donnell's" cool head and infectious grin bring an almost mathematical precision to the evaluation:

An old Etonian post-Marxist ex-policeman is clearly an unstable and contradictory character. Such a man – one could argue from the case history alone – must be torn by doubts and dissaffections, and in particular by the conflict between his intellectual convictions and his social background and training. He is likely to be unhappy, perhaps near to despair, and, carrying his internal war outwards, to belabour alternately the blimps and the leftists, the thieves and the police. His bilious temperament will make him a critic or a satirist, and the contradictions of his own nature help him to interpret the bewildering symptoms of a society which is itself suffering from the neuroses of sharp transition.

Mr George Orwell, the man burdened with these qualifications, is probably the most interesting critic now writing. He is indeed more than a critic – he is a pioneer – thoroughly unscientific like most pioneers – in a field of anthropology. He takes a subject . . . and analyses not its artistic value but its relation to society.

The last of the subjects from *Critical Essays* "O'Donnell" listed was "the poetry of Yeats". Almost twenty years later O'Brien himself would open up that question and thereby transform scholarly investigation of Yeats, however ungrateful some of his emulators: Orwell's Yeats essay had, indeed, originally seen print in *Horizon* (January 1943). "O'Donnell's" dissection of *Horizon* thus proves a slight case of gerontophagy: if he saluted Orwell as a pioneer in literary anthropologising, he showed himself a good second. Understandably, "Donat O'Donnell" did not place Orwell's Yeats analysis among his finest, although "O'Donnell" firmly put Orwell alongside Peter Quennell's "Four Portraits", Arturo Barea's "Notes on Lorca" and AJ Ayer's exegesis of Sartre as *Horizon*'s "high spots" in its literary criticism. Orwell on Yeats evidently elicited an "O'Donnell" giggle: Mr Orwell sees in him "something that links up . . . with Rackham's drawings, Liberty art fabrics and the *Peter Pan* Never-Never Land". "O'Donnell's" *Bell* essays on *Horizon* and Orwell did not show the long root germinating in the mind of O'Brien, yet it must have been fed by Orwell's final words on Yeats:

> By and large the best writers of our time have been reactionary in tendency, and though Fascism does not offer any real return to the past, those who yearn for the past will accept Fascism sooner than its possible alternatives. But there are other lines of approach, as we have seen during the past two or three years [1939-42]. The relationship between Fascism and the literary intelligentsia badly needs investigating, and Yeats might well be the starting-point. He is best studied by someone . . . who . . . knows that a writer's political and religious beliefs are not excrescences to be laughed away, but something that will leave their mark on the smallest detail of his work.

Orwell's main charges against Yeats won some subsequent mockery from O'Brien in his seminal "Passion and Cunning": Orwell had found Yeats' "quaintness" linked to "his rather sinister vision of life", which, said the O'Brien of 1965, "does not fit very well, for the 'quaintness' was at its height in the 1890s . . . Unfortunately for Orwell's thesis . . . Yeats' greatest poetry was written near the end of his life, when his ideas were at their most sinister". That Orwell was "critical", and up to a point percipient, about Yeats' tendencies O'Brien readily granted. He also drew on two other sources from the 1940s while writing "Passion and Cunning". One (certainly known to Orwell) was Seán O'Faoláin's "Yeats and the Younger Generation" (*Horizon*, January 1942), which spoke of Yeats' fascist "tendencies": Orwell, without acknowledgement, had made free with virtually the same words while addressing virtually the same audience a year later. In 1965 O'Brien also cited Frank O'Connor, who had written in the *Bell* a year earlier than his friend O'Faoláin that Yeats "was a Fascist and authoritarian". The *Bell's enfant terrible* was, nevertheless, its *enfant*, and Orwell was simply misdating eggs to be hatched in Ireland, but it was the Orwell challenge that sparked off O'Brien's later and sounder anthropological discipleship. It could hardly have got started by a zeal for regurgitating O'Connor/O'Faoláin. In 1965 and after, as in 1946 and before, O'Brien – "O'Donnell" – was nobody's clone.

In any case, in 1946 "O'Donnell" found in Orwell's obsessions – the reactionary traditionalism of *The Gem*, *The Magnet*, the Donald McGill postcards, Kipling and Wodehouse – a "post-Marxist" hankering "for the age of cricket". Further, Orwell on the superiority of public school criminality (Raffles) to modern sadism (*No Orchids for Miss Blandish*) was "an Etonian panacea" based on the Englishman's growing conviction that "snobbishness, like hypocrisy, is a check upon behaviour whose value from a social point of view has been under-rated". "O'Donnell" added, from the high ground of burlesque: "And yet this is a monstrous proposition, and arrived at by sleight-of-hand. For after all, the world of Rackham and Raffles was also the world of that highly parasitic nobleman, Count Dracula, and under the shadow of the last Eminent Victorian, Jack the Ripper."

"Donat O'Donnell" concluded his review article on Orwell with an appreciation of *Animal Farm*: "a very amusing book . . . the aptness of much of [whose] satire is undeniable. But its general lesson is the perniciously untrue one contained in the French platitude: *Plus ça change plus c'est la même chose*". Orwell's disillusion over a Russian Revolution that was "confidently expected [to] lead to Utopia" meant, said "O'Donnell", his repeatedly "flogging the dead horse that was to have brought [him] there". Moreover:

> A generation that came to maturity at a time when it was quite clear that no millennium was at hand is inclined to feel surprise at the odd and even reactionary activities of these 'disillusioned' leftists, whose disappointment leads them to advocate . . . a revival of pre-1914 morality . . . The saturnian reign of Edward VII, not the future Socialist Commonwealth, became his mental refuge from the world of Stalin, Miss Blandish and Salvador Dali. The trouble with this type of private myth is that it leads to peevish and sterile negativism, with which Mr Orwell is increasingly threatened.
>
> And yet he knows better and . . . has lucidly condemned what is now his own position: 'Perhaps some degree of suffering is ineradicable from human life, perhaps the choice before man is always a choice of evils, perhaps even the aim of Socialism is not to make the world perfect but to make it better.'
>
> Perhaps we could do without the perhaps.

* * *

Did Orwell read the *Bell*? He seems vaguely to resent Ireland (which "Donat O'Donnell" might have been tempted to credit to the "ex-policeman" rather than the "post-Marxist" facet). But so detailed an essay from a critic so close to his own ground would have invited attention, and his relations with FJ Warburg of Secker and Warburg, publishers of *Animal Farm* and *Critical Essays*, were close enough to ensure his ready access to the file of reviews. The result may have had one effect on *1984*. The pursuit of nostalgic celebration of an over-valued past becomes one of Winston Smith's strongest expressions of rebellion against Oceana and the one which traps him – the junk-shop proprietor "Mr Charrington" proving the member of the Thought Police who sets him up for transgression and arrest. It was logical in Orwell to give Smith his own deepening quest, but to make it the hinge of his destruction – "O'Donnell" having predicted it would destroy Orwell himself – could have followed brooding on the *Bell* review essay.

We have to consider one further point. Literary London was as full of gossip-mongers as literary Dublin. Quite apart from Orwell, Cyril Connolly should have been interested in identifying his irreverent Dublin critic, and his own contributor Seán O'Faoláin was an obvious source of the information. It was no secret, after all. Did Orwell feel indignant about a review essay whose recognition of "the most interesting critic now writing . . . more than a critic he is a pioneer . . . in a field of anthropology" was undercut by the observation that "this seems to hold good for Orwell himself . . . this Etonian panacea . . . peevish and sterile negativism". In *1984* Winston Smith is lured by one he trusts to admit readiness to perpetrate crimes as evil as those against which he rebels.

And the name of that inspirer of confidence who masterminds Smith's destruction is O'Brien. The most plausible explanation is that of coincidence. No doubt it is also coincidence that Orwell began to work on Catholic novelists in 1948, by which time "O'Donnell" was known to have a book in progress on imaginative Catholic writers. Orwell took up Mauriac, followed him with Léon Bloy, wrote an article on Graham Greene, commenced an essay on Evelyn Waugh, "tried" Péguy, who made him "feel rather unwell". "I think it's about time," he told Julian Symons on 10 July 1948, "to do a counter-attack against these Catholic writers." He would certainly have assumed "O'Donnell" was a "Catholic writer" and that any book from him would be in what Orwell now saw as their camp. Orwell had written as early as 1946 on George Bernanos. So the long arm of coincidence extends to his pursuit of six of the eight subjects of *Maria Cross*, several of whose chapters had already won publication. And the summer and early autumn of 1948, when Orwell was turning over his attack on the Catholic writers, was the time in which he concluded writing *1984*, which immortalised his own O'Brien. If Orwell had investigated "O'Donnell" and discovered he was really called O'Brien, no doubt he had likewise discovered that underneath his cool prose this O'Brien was also a worker for the Catholic government geographically closest to Britain.

In a small, populist state like Ireland the extra-curricular literary career of civil servant was popularly regarded as absurdly irrelevant to his activities for the government. A critical essay from "Donat O'Donnell" would be no more felt to foreshadow government thought (if such a thing existed) than would a book review by "Thomas Hogan" or a satirical column by "Myles na gCopaleen". But in a London whose BBC news management would inspire aspects of "The Ministry of Truth" in *1984*, a book review from "a chap in the FO" would be darkly portentous: the anonymous *Times* piece would be more probable than a pseudonym, once again with wide currency as to its true authorship. War propaganda had commissioned significant fiction, criticism and films – e.g., the paternity of Graham Greene's "The Lieutenant Died Last" to the film warning against German invasion, *Went the Day Well* (1942), had been widely acknowledged. The British Left remembered its lost Protestantism in mildly paranoid anti-Catholicism, often illustrated by dark suspicions of Roman Catholics in the Foreign Office or (as in Greene's case) the Secret Service.

And Orwell had laid out the battle lines as recently as 1946 in his essay "The Prevention of Literature":

> Although the point of emphasis may vary, the writer who refuses to sell his opinions is always branded as a mere egoist. He is accused, that is, either of wanting to shut himself up in an ivory tower, or of making an exhibitionist display of his own personality, or of resisting the inevitable current of history in an attempt to cling to unjustified privileges. The Catholic and the Communist are alike in assuming that an opponent cannot be both honest and intelligent.

Certainly "O'Brien" in *1984* is related in some way to Orwell's lifelong suspicions of Catholic conspiracy. Can we point to any other source for his name than that of the other O'Brien who also appeared to have a nominal job as a propagandist covering a much more powerful post as formulator of state policy?

On the other hand, as *1984* reminds us, two and two make five.

"Donat O'Donnell's" critique of Orwell for excessive nostalgia was exactly that, with subliminal implications – as Irish eyes, smiling or otherwise, would promptly recognise – to warn Irish readers of the dangers of enthroning nostalgia in Ireland no less than in Britain. His was the generation which three years earlier had heard Eamon de Valera on Radio Éireann hymn the ideal of a rural paradise probably not more than two hundred years behind the times. Far from being de Valera's actual agenda, it was a means of fixing the eyes of the electorate on a sufficiently spiritual Utopia, while the boys got on fixing the jobs. "O'Donnell" had little desire to encourage this cult, however much it might constrain his official person as O'Brien: Big Brother – in this case *Pater Patriae* or, alternatively, *Múinteoir na Tíre* – might not be watching him, but instead had those who would do all the watching necessary. If *Bell* readers saw a parable for de Valera in a reproof for Orwell, that was their business.

The danger of an Evelyn Waugh cult for Irish Catholics was also quite serious. The de Valera nostalgia was, if anything, likely to enhance the attractions of its converse, and even in religion *Brideshead Revisited* (1945) was its converse, the simplicity of the de Valera private peasant worship contrasting with the ostentation of English aristocratic luxuriation in the highest of all social codes. The affirmation of one's own religion as the highest peak of English culture offered the most satisfactory terms any cultural diplomat could surely ask. Roman Catholicism, the heart of Irish Catholic identity, was hereby enthroned as the stone of the English Catholic aristocratic corner; displacement by a materialistic English bourgeoisie could resemble the post-Reformation displacement of Gaelic aristocracy by equally materialistic and no doubt bourgeois English Protestant conquistadors (however subsequently ennobled); Irish post-colonialism could happily dissolve its tensions by emulating the lifestyle of its former rulers as its own vindication. It was as though Amerindians might find their cultural future, and its pre-eminence, assured by the sight of President Calvin Coolidge donning a feathered head-dress as an honorary chieftain. The rumour that Waugh, this evangelist of Recusant Debrett, might bring his cultural vindication to dwell in Ireland itself surpassed Coolidge's choice of South Dakota whence to issue his refusal to run for reelection. Land, so to say, deepened the affirmation in literature. University College Dublin could acquire airs surpassing those of Trinity. Brideshead could be relocated.

O'Brien may not have known of the proposed Waugh pursuit of an

Irish Sabine Farm, but he saw enough to diagnose the virulence of the Brideshead infection. His antidote assumed the form of a book review published in the *Bell* in December 1946 under the title "The Pieties of Evelyn Waugh". He showed, indeed, the same positive criticism of criticism he had revealed with Orwell: take what was good about it, learn from what was bad about it. In this case, the taking and learning was from Edmund Wilson of the *New Yorker*, but the effect was comparable. Wilson, as he frequently did, got to the heart of the question, but, having made the crucial incision, withdrew his knife prematurely with only a superficial extraction. It would not be enough to denounce Waugh as a snob: in a reply to "Donat O'Donnell" printed in the *Bell*, Waugh himself would handsomely admit it: "I think perhaps your reviewer is right in calling me a snob; that is to say I am happiest in the company of the European upper-classes; but I do not think this preference is necessarily an offence against Charity, still less against Faith." And Wilson's charge had no consistency on its side, as "O'Donnell" showed: "Mr Edmund Wilson . . . condemned the snobbery of *Brideshead Revisited*, but he had swallowed with delight the snobbery of the earlier novels, from *Decline and Fall* to *Scoop*. Snobbery was quite acceptable as an attitude: the critic objected only when it was formulated as doctrine." What "O'Donnell" did was to show not only the literary extent, but also the racial depth, of Waugh's snobbery, such as to make it incompatible with any sense of post-colonial identity. To do so he had to operate with a boldness and skill which could graze the very nerve. The charms of *Brideshead Revisited* were not to be denied – the Irish critic paid generous tribute to Waugh's literary craftsmanship, where his disillusioned American counterpart weakened his case by pedantic carps. "O'Donnell" had to guard against handing a victory, even on colonialism, to Evelyn Waugh by insensitive over-vehemence.

If the Irish Catholic bourgeoisie chose to flower (even deflower) itself into Anglo-Saxon aristocratic attitudes, Waugh himself might be vouchsafed some pardon. Whatever fantasies his prose might draw around Irish readers, Hibernophiles would have their work cut out to prove him a kindred spirit. Perhaps the use of the name "Connolly" in contemptible contexts might be attributable to the author's perpetually changing affections for Cyril Connolly, whose Irish antecedents were obliterated far beneath impeccable Etonian origins. But in *Black Mischief* (1932), the General is introduced by a judicious addition of English insult to Irish injury: "He was a stock Irishman in early middle age who had seen varied

371

service in the Black and Tans, the South African police and the Kenyan Game Reserves before enlisting under the Emperor's colours." The Black and Tans were an instrument of British oppression, not of Irish *esprit de corps*, as Waugh clearly knew all too well: their Irish recruits remained unknown for reasons of prudence both Irish and British, although on 3 January 1946, the year "O'Donnell" was writing, the most famous Irish Black and Tan was hanged by the British authorities for his services to the Third Reich, namely, William Joyce (Lord Haw Haw). General Connolly at least exhibited no racial exclusiveness akin to Joyce. When His Britannic Majesty's Minister's wife calls on the General:

> Sentries presented arms in the courtyard, a finely uniformed servant opened the door, but this dignified passage was interrupted by a resolute little Negress in a magenta tea-gown who darted suddenly across the hall and barred her way to the drawing room.
> 'I am Black Bitch,' she had explained simply. 'What do you want in my house?'
> 'I am Lady Courtney. I came to see General Connolly.'
> 'The General is drunk today and he doesn't want any more ladies.'

By the same token, in *Put Out More Flags* (1942) there is little reason to doubt Irish origin for the Connolly children – "one leering, one lowering, and one drooling" – by whose strategic relocation Basil Seal blackmails designated hosts. As "O'Donnell" observed, "the purest comedy lies in lurid descriptions of the appearance and behaviour of three proletarian evacuee children". Waugh had written, for example: "The Connolly's were found at last and assembled. Doris had been in Barbara's bedroom trying out her make-up, Micky in the library tearing up a folio, Marlene grovelling under the pantry sink eating the remains of the dogs' dinners." Doris is sex-mad, Micky a destroyer, preferably of life, Marlene retarded. It put the Irish firmly on the receiving end of Waugh's snobbery.

Yet TJ Barrington, afterwards the Director of the Irish Institute of Public Administration, protested to the *Bell*. He objected to "O'Donnell's" interpretation of *Black Mischief* as "largely based on a sly appeal to the white man's sense of racial superiority". Barrington wrote: "A Coloured man, or an unprejudiced one, might be pardoned for believing . . . that Waugh is being sly about the whites." Similarly, the joke was not, Barrington felt, against the evacuees. "O'Donnell" replied:

> Mr Waugh laughs at Basil Seal and various Bright Young Things, but there is affection, nostalgia, even admiration, in his laughter. Basil Seal may eat his fiancée by accident, but his creator does not think any the less of him

for that. When Mr Waugh turns, however, to Seth, the black king with 'western' ideas, there is something different, something brutal, about his laughter. Clearly to him Seth is in himself a . . . more sophisticated version of the chimpanzee – with – a – clay – pipe joke. Similarly with the evacuees and their hosts . . . Mr Waugh's evacuees are grotesque half-animal human beings whose parody of human behaviour and persecution of real though silly human beings provide the fun.

Neither Barrington nor "O'Donnell" discussed the Irishness of these various Connollys, but Barrington's own reaction showed how wise had been "O'Donnell's" initial anxieties about Waugh. The wartime isolation of the Irish, those "happy drab escapists" (*Put Out More Flags*), made for an ugly future if its Ireland imagined that anti-black jokes would be regarded as anti-white by "A coloured . . . or an unprejudiced man". Waugh would demolish Barrington's defence against the charge of snobbery by admitting it, but until his entry into the controversy his fashionable Catholicism granted him some immunity against Irish racial or class sensitivity.

Today any rational discussion of such questions would put them at the heart of an author's Catholicity. Racial or class contempt is as anathema to the conservative Pope John Paul II as it was to the radical Pope John XXIII. But "O'Donnell", like John XXIII after him, was a pioneer. He made no pretence of Catholicism (indeed, he clearly wrote on the scholarly principle that private observance and belief were irrelevant, provided the scholar understood the doctrine under analysis): but O'Brien's Protestant education and secular beliefs were well-known, and Barrington pleasantly implied similar views for "O'Donnell". And Barrington also argued that "O'Donnell" questioned whether Waugh was sufficiently Catholic:

> Donat O'Donnell's central argument is entertaining. It is calculated to shake the boys on the pious papers, *The Tablet, America,* and the rest, who, because of *Brideshead Revisited,* hailed Waugh as a great apologist for the Catholic Church. What a jolt for them to learn from Donat O'Donnell that . . . Waugh's Catholicism . . . is 'mingled' with 'a highly personal system of belief and devotion' and is 'superimposed' on a 'fixed and intolerant mythology' which is Waugh's 'private religion'. In short, Waugh's Catholic apologetics do not click because Waugh is a heretic.

In point of strict theological pedantry, Barrington was wrong: "O'Donnell" did not accuse Waugh of breaking from Catholicism on a doctrinal issue, simply of never having joined it. Waugh's own letter, almost unbelievably polite, took up that point:

I am most grateful for the attention given my work in your pages and would not intrude in the discussion but for the fear that a hasty retreat might conceive the doubt, which your reviewer scrupulously refrains from expressing, of the good faith of my conversion to Catholicism . . . I can assure you that [my snobbery] had no influence on my conversion.

But what concerned "O'Donnell" was the dangers of Catholics – especially Irish Catholics – taking the social *and theological* arguments of *Brideshead Revisited* as new gospel.

Ireland in 1945 was an ex-aristocratic society, precisely the point at which aristocratic yardsticks and manners might seem most appealing. The Jacobitism which "O'Donnell" saw in Waugh, and which clung iconographically to stately Catholic homes and schools in England, had received new blood when the Jacobite claimants effectively died out and fifty years later their distant cousin Queen Victoria festooned herself with Jacobitism. "O'Donnell" and his *Bell*fellows might hope for an alienation of the intellectuals, but not in a Never-Never Land of this kind. For a historian, O'Brien has always shown singular powers of prophesy, and while seeing the roots of Waugh's romanticism in his early Pre-Raphaelite studies and his fictive aristocrats only capable of living by destruction, "O'Donnell" noted qualitative change in *Brideshead Revisited* and marked its direction:

just as snobbery and adolescent cruelty gave edge and tension to his early work, so now the intense romantic and exclusive piety of his mature years gives him strength and eloquence. The clear focusing of remembered detail, the loving reconstructions of youth, and the great extension of metaphor in *Brideshead Revisited* all recall Proust more than any living writer, and the texture of Mr Waugh's writing is both finer and stronger than is usual in Proust . . .

The resemblance is neither accidental nor merely superficial and has nothing to do with plagiarism. The outward lives of the two men are very different – one can hardly imagine Proust in the Commandos – but their mental worlds are, up to a point, surprisingly similar . . .

The difference between the two men may in part be explained by the historical setting. Proust lived and wrote at a time when the upper classes were menaced, but not severely damaged . . . In our time, however, the upper classes, even in England, are not merely menaced; they have been gravely damaged. They feel not merely frustrated or irritated but actually oppressed by the high level of modern taxation and they see their equals levelled all over Europe. Proustian detachment and sense of nuance tend to perish in this atmosphere, and the wistful romantic easily develops, as Mr Waugh has done, into an embattled Jacobite . . . Mr Waugh . . .

emerged an English gentleman, with slight symptoms of hysteria. [This was written ten years before *The Ordeal of Gilbert Pinfold.*] Cream and dappled unicorns clearly have no place at a public school, and an inner life that includes such creatures will feel itself menaced. If it does not die, it will take on a new intensity, becoming a fixed intolerant mythology.

"O'Donnell" picked up the contrast between the Flytes of Brideshead and the vulgar Hooper who so edges the narrator's teeth in his wartime return to their Catholic aristocratic shrine, the frame of the book: "Is Lord Marchmain's soul more valuable than Hooper's? To say so in so many words that it was would be heresy, but *Brideshead Revisited* almost seems to imply that the wretched Hooper had no soul at all, certainly nothing to compare with the genuine old landed article." (This was wicked in "O'Donnell", suddenly making Waugh sound like the devoted guide showing round a busload of tourists in need of reverential stimulus: I remember Anthony Burgess' remark that Waugh "liked to be thought aristocratic although his people were firmly middle class – *publishers*, for God's sake!") Barrington complained that "Donat O'Donnell overplays the Hooper card", a natural reaction given the brevity and innocence of Hooper's lines. But "O'Donnell" knew his man: once again, Waugh vindicates his dissector's prescience, this time in his preface to the revised edition of *Brideshead Revisited*, dated 1959, in which he reflects with faint optimism:

> Brideshead today would be open to trippers, its treasures rearranged by expert hands and the fabric better maintained than it was by Lord Marchmain. And the English aristocracy has maintained its identity to a degree that then seemed impossible. The advance of Hooper has been held up at several points.

Hooper had become the symbol of the new democratisation that Orwell had hoped – in *the Lion and the Unicorn* (1941) – the war would bring. Barrington complained of "O'Donnell's" insistence that "Mr Waugh's . . . almost idolatrous reverence for birth and wealth has not been destroyed by the Catholic faith; on the contrary, *Brideshead Revisited* breathes from beginning to end a loving patience with mortal sin among the aristocracy and an un-Christian petulance towards the minor foibles of the middle class". "That is brilliantly said," Barrington nodded, "but it is brilliantly wrong." "Surely it is a commonplace," replied "O'Donnell", "that Christianity should destroy idolatrous reverence for anything, birth included."

"Such," concluded "O'Donnell's" original article, "is Mr Waugh's private religion, on which he has superimposed Catholicism, much as newly-converted pagans are said to superimpose a Christian nomenclature on their ancient cults of trees and thunder." "O'Donnell" himself may have startled those conversant with his true identity by the severely religious nature of his argument. The critique of Waugh's indulgence for the aristocratic penitent suggests nothing so much as Pascal's denunciations of Jesuit indulgence towards wayward souls in high places. "O'Donnell" clearly saw where Waugh was going: towards imprisonment in the part he had chosen to play. It had its own tragedy – the satirist self-trapped, becoming the original butt of his own satire – and Waugh was to become its chronicler in *The Ordeal of Gilbert Pinfold*. Reviewing this novel in the *Spectator* (July 1957), "O'Donnell" justly found it "almost entirely unfunny, and a little embarrassing". But however unconsciously crafted, it is also an astoundingly confessional work. Waugh's self-portrait in the first chapter is, as "O'Donnell" would remark, "painted by no satiric or malevolent hand". But the delusions of persecution, and the self-hatreds and lost hopes they reveal, confront the author with himself in a far more brutal light. It is not edifying: it becomes miserably close to self-pity in its attempts to avoid self-realisation. The dedication hopes that the "abounding sympathy" of the dedicatee "will extend even to poor Pinfold". In *Brideshead* we are to extend that pity to Lord Sebastian Flyte, whom "O'Donnell" found "beautiful and charming" and who is surely the most likeable character Waugh ever made; Lord Marchmain may also require it of us, less easily. But as "O'Donnell" said grimly, "The Waugh of before *Brideshead Revisited* seldom wrote about himself; the Waugh of after *Brideshead* seldom writes about anything else". Or, as O'Brien under his own name declined further discussion of Waugh in the reprint of *Maria Cross*: "his principal work in recent years has been the trilogy *Men at Arms*, which I gave up reading about half-way, feeling Hooperish and as if eavesdropping. There is no reason why Mr Waugh should not talk, in print, to himself and a few friends, but it would be pointless for a critic to comment on the monologue".

"O'Donnell" may have had a hidden agenda. Waugh's Catholicism was questionable, but from any standard of public moral health it was at its most pernicious in its fanatical insistence on its truth. Waugh proclaimed he had found the right formula in Catholicism: all others were damnable. It might be felt that Irish Catholicism had known this for centuries and that it had relieved some of the worst privations of the penal laws. But that made its reinforcement from so socially exotic a quarter an extremely deplorable business. In the world after 1945 Ireland at last had the chance of developing multi-culturally – as the *Irish Times* drifted into acceptance of the new state; as some Trinity dons accepted Irish government commissions; and more Trinity graduates sought jobs in the Irish civil service; and a new generation less implicated in the religio-political confessionalism of the state emerged from the University Colleges; as the end of American isolation opened up cultural exchanges; and thinking Catholics began to feel the first stirrings of ecumenism as it would fructify in the Second Vatican Council. The thought of Ireland's new St Patrick, her influx of Catholic artistic leadership from abroad, her Pied Piper of the post-war world proclaimed in this high-living anchorite hell-driven to assert and maintain an exclusivist triumphal Church – all of this was anathema to the great-nephew of the Land League Priest, Father Eugene Sheehy. It seems probable that his great-uncle was forcefully present in the mind of the critic. "There was once an Irish priest who refused to pray for the conversion of England, and Mr Waugh, I fear, might refuse to pray for the conversion of Hooper": thus "O'Donnell". There were probably many such priests, but there was only one well-known in the immediate history of O'Brien's family.

In retrospect, it may not have been the least of Evelyn Waugh's achievements to have unleashed the hidden priest in "Donat O'Donnell". This heretical theologian was fiercely critical of the nostalgic anti-Catholicism of Orwell, the pseudo-Catholicism of Waugh and the suffocating Catholicism of Ireland. Thus neither author nor nation were spared "O'Donnell's" baptism by fire, including the other writers – Greene, Mauriac, Péguy, O'Faoláin and more[1] – whose Catholic imaginations are exposed by the light of the sun in *Maria Cross*.

377

NOTES

CHAPTER I: RICHARD ENGLISH AND JOSEPH MORRISON SKELLY, IDEAS MATTER

1. For a comprehensive review of Conor Cruise O'Brien's career, see Donald Harman Akenson, *Conor: A Biography of Conor Cruise O'Brien: Volume I: Narrative* (Montreal: McGill-Queen's University Press, 1994).

2. See, for example, "Select Bibliography of Works by Conor Cruise O'Brien" at the end of this volume and the comprehensive bibliography in Donald Harman Akenson, *Conor: A Biography of Conor Cruise O'Brien: Volume II: Anthology* (Montreal: McGill-Queen's University Press, 1994), pp. 311-51.

3. Isaiah Berlin, "The Pursuit of the Ideal", in Isaiah Berlin, *The Crooked Timber of Humanity: Chapters in the History of Ideas* (New York: Alfred A Knopf, 1991), p. 1.

4. Walter Bagehot, *Physics and Politics* (New York: Alfred A Knopf, 1948), p. 169.

5. William Butler Yeats, *Explorations* (London: Macmillan, 1962), p. 263.

6. See, for example, Conor's correspondence with Isaiah Berlin, which is reprinted in Conor Cruise O'Brien, *The Great Melody: A Thematic Biography and Commented Anthology of Edmund Burke* (London: Sinclair-Stevenson, 1992), pp. 603-18.

7. Mark Lilla, "A Tale of Two Reactions", *New York Review*, 14 May 1998, p. 4.

8. Quoted in Conor Cruise O'Brien, "Introduction", in Matthew Arnold(ed.), *Irish Affairs: Edmund Burke* (London: Cresset Library Edition, 1988), p. xiii.

9. Isaiah Berlin, "My Intellectual Path", *New York Review*, 14 May 1998, p. 58.

10. *Ibid.*, p. 57.

11. Isaiah Berlin, *The Hedgehog and the Fox* (New York: Simon and Schuster, 1966), pp. 1-2.

12. Seneca, *Epistles*, 12, 11.

13. For Conor Cruise O'Brien's treatment of Rousseau, see his essay "Virtue and Terror: Rousseau and Robespierre", in Conor Cruise O'Brien,

Passion and Cunning: Essays on Nationalism, Terrorism and Revolution (London: Weidenfeld and Nicolson, 1988), pp. 62-72; for his analysis of Nietzsche, see his *The Suspecting Glance* (London: Faber and Faber, 1972), pp. 51-91.

14. Paul Johnson, *Intellectuals* (New York: HarperPerennial, 1990), p. 342.

15. Berlin, "Intellectual Path", p. 60.

16. Quoted in O'Brien, *The Great Melody*, p. 435.

17. Conor Cruise O'Brien, "Paradise Lost", *New York Review*, 25 April 1991, pp. 52-60: reprinted in O'Brien, *The Great Melody*, pp. 605-618.

18. Conor Cruise O'Brien, "Nationalism and the French Revolution", in Geoffrey Best(ed.), *The Permanent Revolution: The French Revolution and its Legacy* (London: Fontana Press, 1988), p. 28.

19. Quoted in O'Brien, "Virtue and Terror", p. 71.

20. Quoted in Susan Dunn, *The Deaths of Louis XVI: Regicide and the French Political Imagination* (Princeton: Princeton University Press, 1994), p. 165, n. 1.

21. Conor Cruise O'Brien, "Foreword", in Dunn, *The Deaths of Louis XVI*, p. ix.

22. Conor Cruise O'Brien, "Ireland's Fissures, and My Family's", *Atlantic Monthly*, 273, 1 (January, 1994), p. 70.

23. Conor Cruise O'Brien, "Religion and Politics", *The New University of Ulster Tenth Annual Convocation Lecture* (Coleraine: New University of Ulster, February, 1984), p. 5.

24. O'Brien, "Foreword", in Dunn, *The Deaths of Louis XVI*, p. xi.

25. O'Brien, "Religion and Politics", p. 1.

26. Michael Novak, "The Most Religious Century", *New York Times*, 24 May 1998.

27. Conor Cruise O'Brien, *Ancestral Voices: Religion and Nationalism in Ireland* (Dublin: Poolbeg Press, 1994), p. 5.

28. See, for example, Joseph Morrison Skelly, *Irish Diplomacy at the United Nations, 1945-65: National Interests and the International Order* (Dublin: Irish Academic Press, 1997), pp. 68-77.

29. *Daily Mail*, 15 September 1961: quoted in Conor Cruise O'Brien, *To Katanga and Back: A UN Case History* (London: Hutchinson, 1962), p. 12.

30. See Conor Cruise O'Brien, *Ireland, the United Nations and Southern Africa* (Dublin: Irish Anti-Apartheid Movement, 1967).

31. See Conor Cruise O'Brien, "What Can Become of South Africa?" *Atlantic Monthly*, 257, 3 (March, 1986), pp. 41-68. David Welsh recounts

Conor's visit to South Africa in his contribution to this volume; Alex Kwapong recalls Conor's tenure as vice-chancellor of the University of Ghana.

32. Conor Cruise O'Brien, *Herod: Reflections on Political Violence* (London: Hutchinson, 1978), p. 13.

33. Conor Cruise O'Brien, "The Liberal Pole", in O'Brien, *Passion and Cunning*, p. 74.

34. Conor Cruise O'Brien, *On the Eve of the Millennium: The Future of Democracy through an Age of Unreason* (New York: The Free Press, 1994), p. 16. For a similar, yet more recent, argument, see Dr O'Brien's remarks in the *Sunday Independent*, 3 May 1998.

35. O'Brien, *On the Eve of the Millennium*, pp. 163-4.

36. O'Brien, *Suspecting Glance*, p. 56. See also O'Brien, "Foreword", in Dunn, *The Deaths of Louis XVI*, p. xi; O'Brien, "Nationalism and the French Revolution", pp. 46-8.

37. O'Brien, *On the Eve of the Millennium*, p. 30.

38. O'Brien, *Suspecting Glance*, p. 87.

39. *Ibid.*, p. 11.

40. Conor Cruise O'Brien, "Passion and Cunning: An Essay on the Politics of WB Yeats", in A Norman Jeffares and KGW Cross(eds.), *In Excited Reverie: A Centenary Tribute to William Butler Yeats, 1865-1965* (London: Macmillan, 1965): reprinted in O'Brien, *Passion and Cunning*, p. 54.

41. Conor Cruise O'Brien, *Camus* (Glasgow: Fontana, 1970), p. 104-5.

42. O'Brien, *Suspecting Glance*, p. 63

43. *Ibid.*, p. 51.

44. Shelby Steele, *The Content of Our Character: A New Vision of Race in America* (New York: St. Martin's Press, 1990), p. xii.

45. Conor Cruise O'Brien, "The Ferocious Wisdom of Machiavelli", in O'Brien, *Suspecting Glance*, p. 15.

46. *Ibid.*, p. 16.

47. Conor Cruise O'Brien, "Foreword", in Frank Callanan, *The Parnell Split* (Cork: Cork University Press, 1992), p. xi. For a discussion of Vico's concept of *fantasia*, see Isaiah Berlin, "Giambattista Vico and Cultural History", in Berlin, *The Crooked Timber of Humanity*, pp. 62-5.

48. Akenson, *Conor: Volume II*, p. x.

49. Conor Cruise O'Brien, "The Artist as Pompous Prig", *Sunday Tribune*, 31 January 1982: reprinted in Akenson, *Conor: Volume II*, pp. 267-9.

50. Conor Cruise O'Brien, *The Times*, "An Exalted Nationalism", 28

January 1989: reprinted in Akenson, *Conor: Volume II*, pp. 285-8.

51. See, for example, Jan Lewis and Peter S Onuf, "American Synechdoche: Thomas Jefferson as Image, Icon, Character, and Self", *American Historical Review*, 103, 1 (February, 1998), pp. 125-136.

52. Quoted in O'Brien, "Introduction", in Arnold, *Irish Affairs*, p. xi.

53. See *Sunday Independent*, 3 May, 10 May 1998; *Irish Times*, 8 May 1998; *Observer*, 10 May 1998.

54. Conor Cruise O'Brien, *The Siege: The Saga of Israel and Zionism* (London: Weidenfeld and Nicolson, 1986), p. 19

55. Quoted in Akenson, *Conor: Volume I*, pp. 111-12.

56. Conor Cruise O'Brien, *The Long Affair: Thomas Jefferson and the French Revolution, 1785-1800* (Chicago: University of Chicago Press, 1996), p. 315.

57. Conor Cruise O'Brien, *Booknotes*, 17 November 1996: transcript available at www.booknotes.org.

58. Paul Johnson, *Intellectuals*, p. 336.

59. See, for example, *States of Ireland* (London: Hutchinson, 1972); *Neighbors: The Ewart-Biggs Memorial Lectures, 1978-79* (London: Faber and Faber, 1980); *Ancestral Voices*.

60. See, for example, O'Brien, "Ireland's Fissures, and My Family's", pp. 50-72.

61. O'Brien, *Herod*, p. 11.

62. *Ibid.*, p. 13.

63. Conor Cruise O'Brien, "Introduction", in Conor Cruise O'Brien and William Dean Vanech, *Power and Consciousness* (New York: New York University Press, 1969), pp. 4-5.

64. Conor Cruise O'Brien, *The Second Ian Gow Memorial Lecture* (London: Friends of the Union, 1992), p. 3.

65. See, for example, Conor Cruise O'Brien, "Foreword", in Robert McCartney, *The McCartney Report on Consent* (Belfast: The United Kingdom Unionist Party, 1997).

66. See, for example, Conor Cruise O'Brien, "Challenging Times", *Irish Independent*, 15 August 1998.

67. Conor Cruise O'Brien, "I'm Happy Defending the Union with Ian". *Sunday Independent*, 3 May 1998.

68. Conor Cruise O'Brien, "Intern them Now", *Irish Independent*, 17 August 1998.

CHAPTER IV: JOHN A MURPHY, MYSELF AND "THE CRUISER"

1. John A Murphy, "Further Reflections on Nationalism", *The Crane Bag*, 2, 1 & 2 (1978), p.158.

2. His views were a "culture shock" for the lady who is now President of Ireland: see interview with Mary McAleese, *Magill*, February 1998.

3. For a general comment on all this, see my introduction to James Stephens, *The Insurrection in Dublin* (Gerrards Cross: Colin Smythe Ltd, 1978).

4. I took issue with Conor on these points in my address to the annual convention of the Association of Secondary Teachers Ireland, reported in the *Irish Press*, 5 April 1972, and in *The Secondary Teacher*, (Summer, 1972). A more professional approach to history teaching had been introduced over the previous decade and, as one of the advisors to the Department of Education on this development, I suggested in my criticism that "even politicians with an academic background are out of touch with such developments".

5. *Irish Press*, 19 April 1977. The television debate was on 15 April. See also television reviews by Tom O'Dea, *Irish Press*, 23 April 1977, and Ken Gray, *Irish Times*, 16 April 1977.

6. Conor Cruise O'Brien, "Nationalism and the Reconquest of Ireland", *The Crane Bag*, 1, 2 (1977), pp. 8-13; John A Murphy, "Further Reflections", pp. 156-163. See also Paul Durcan's comments on above, "Murphy v O'Brien", *Cork Examiner*, 2 October 1978.

7. John A Murphy, "Further Reflections", p. 157.

8. *Ibid.*

9. *Ibid.*, p. 158.

10. *Ibid.*, p. 159.

11. *Sunday Press*, 23 May 1982.

12. *Irish Times*, 1 June 1982.

13. *Ibid.*, 7 June 1982.

14. A reference to his public nickname (see below) and to the sinking of the *Belgrano*.

15. *Irish Times*, 15 June 1982.

16. "Cult of Blood Sacrifice", *Irish Times*, 24 April 1984.

17. "Easter 1916 – the View from 1984", *Sunday Independent*, 22 April 1984.

18. John Boland, *Evening Press*, 18 August 1982.

19. "A Quest for Identity", *Irish Times*, 31 August 1982.

20. This article is being written in March-April 1998.

21. *Sunday Independent,* 18 January 1998.

22. *Ibid.,* "I'd Love to be Proved Wrong", 25 January 1998.

23. *Today FM,* "The Last Word", 29 January 1998.

24. 6 February 1998.

25. Posts and Telegraphs, the government department then responsible for broadcasting.

26. Ó Ríordáin returned again and again to the "Crús" topic in his *Irish Times* column in the early 1970s: see, for example, "Dev & Jack & Crús", 2 October 1971; "Ionsaí an Aire", 26 August 1972; "An Cliche Crús", 13 July 1974; "Crús", 2 November 1974; and, especially, "Mairbhghin Uí Chuanaigh", 28 September 1974.

27. The author prefers not to be mentioned.

28. Breandán Ó hEithir, *The Begrudger's Guide to Irish Politics* (Dublin, 1986). I have taken some slight liberties with the stanza as quoted.

29. See my assessment, "The Slow Narrowing of a Liberal", *Sunday Independent,* 3 May 1987.

30. *Irish Times,* 7 June 1982.

31. *Ibid.,* 24 June 1978 (on Herod); *Sunday Independent,* 3 April 1988 (*Passion and Cunning*); *ibid.,* 1 November 1992 (*The Great Melody*).

32. *Irish Independent,* 29 November 1997.

CHAPTER IX: FRANK CALLANAN, "IN THE NAME OF GOD AND OF THE DEAD GENERATIONS": NATIONALISM AND REPUBLICANISM IN IRELAND

1. *New York Review,* 29 April 1982: reprinted in Conor Cruise O'Brien, *Passion and Cunning: Essays on Nationalism, Terrorism and Revolution* (London: Weidenfeld and Nicolson, 1988), pp. 213-25. A foreshortened text of the essay is included in Seamus Deane(ed.), *The Field Day Anthology of Irish Writing* (Derry: Field Day, 1991), iii, pp. 595-602.

2. Sir Charles Russell, *Speech Before the Parnell Commission* (London, 1889) pp. 223, 442. Russell wisely refrained from any sustained endeavour to bring the judges of the Special Commission to a more sophisticated view of Fenianism, limiting himself to the proposition that the Fenian organisation at the time of its inception was "not a party of assassination", but "a revolutionary party that looked to physical force for the redress of Irish grievances": *ibid.,* p. 37.

3. *Times, Special Commission,* xxv, p. 141. In the quotations from the evidence, I have used the Times volumes of the proceedings published in

small format softback booklets, as if they were an elaborate appendix to the original *Times* articles which had been republished in the same format, and the Special Commission's report of its own proceedings.

4. *Times, Special Commission*, xxv, pp. 141, 169. The last quotation, which appears in para. 80, 447 of the official report of the Commission's proceedings (volume 8) is not quoted in the *Times* reports.

5. *Special Commission Proceedings*, 9, para. 87, 652.

6. *Special Commission Proceedings*, 1, paras. 761-2. Parnell's perverse conviction that O'Shea was responsible for the forged letters which endured even after Pigott admitted his guilt [Frank Callanan, *TM Healy* (Cork: Cork University Press, 1996), pp. 190, 204, 208-9, 220] may have owed something to the almost identical configuration of the shapes thrown by the two gallants in homage to the patriotic ardour of the Fenians. Pigott went so far as to assert that the Land League agitation was "originated chiefly with the set purpose of diverting Fenians from the errors of their revolutionary ways into the peaceful paths of constitutional agitation". The new departure was a device whereby honourable patriots enlisted in the corrupt cause of the Land League ("managed by business men for business men"): Richard Pigott, "The Irish Question", *Macmillan's Magazine*, xiv (December, 1887), pp. 168, 173.

7. *Special Commission Proceedings*, 7, para. 59, 842.

8. *Special Commission Proceedings*, 7, paras. 59, 219-59, 223. It will be appreciated that in forensic advocacy, twice is rendered "more than once".

9. *Special Commission Proceedings*, 7, para. 59, 632. For Parnell's contemporary use of the term "nationalist", see ibid., paras. 60, 025-29. Parnell's interview with the American newspaperman James Redpath, in the Nation of 2 October 1880, in which he asserted that there was "no conflict" between his movement and the Fenians, referred to the Fenians throughout as "Nationalists", was noted in the report of the Commissioners (*Times, Special Commission*, part xxxv, pp. 49-1). Parnell's cross-examination on the subject can be found in the *Special Commission Proceedings*, 8, paras. 60, 741-770.

10. Henry James, *The Work of the Irish Leagues* (London, n.d.) p. 39. This was, of course, inaccurate; Parnell had dated the terminological shift from the foundation of the National League (1882), not that of the Land League (1879). A major re-assessment of the gains derived by the Conservative government from the Special Commission is to be found in the chapter entitled "Parnellism and Crime: Constructing a Conservative Strategy of Containment, 1887-90", in Professor Margaret O'Callaghan's *British High*

Politics and a Nationalist Ireland (Cork: Cork University Press, 1994).

11. *Times Special Commission*, part xxv, pp. 16, 37, 40-1.

12. Conor Cruise O'Brien has stood aloof from this dispute. He wrote in 1982 "there is a real continuity in Irish nationalism: not an ideological continuity, but a continuity of the traditions and feelings of a people": "Ireland: Shirt of Nessus", p. 214. This aloofness led to criticism from Ernest Gellner, the chief "modernist", in his review of Cruise O'Brien's *God Land: Reflections on Religion and Nationalism*, republished as "The Sacred and the National", in Gellner's *Encounters with Nationalism* (London: Blackwell, 1994), pp. 59-73. Of Gellner, Cruise O'Brien had written privately in 1965 that he "strikes some faintly suspicious chord, but I can't say what": quoted in Donald Harman Akenson, *Conor: A Biography of Conor Cruise O'Brien: Volume I: Narrative* (Montreal: McGill-Queen's University Press, 1994), p. 321.

13. For his most recent consideration of this issue, see his article in the *Irish Independent: Supplememt*, 23 May 1998.

14. Patrick Pearse, *Collected Works of Padraic H Pearse: Political Writings and Speeches* (Dublin and London: Phoenix, 1922), p. 127.

15. Pearse, *Political Writings*, p. 137.

16. Pearse, *Political Writings*, p. 205. Only the most depraved revisionist will be reminded by this sacral reminiscence of Pearse's boyhood of Allingham's lines:

> Up the airy mountain,
> Down the rushy glen,
> We daren't go a hunting,
> For fear of little men.

17. Pearse, *Political Writings*, p. 155.

18. *Ibid.*, p. 176.

19. *Ibid.*, p. 238.

20. *Ibid.*, p. 237, 370.

21. For students of Irish nationalism and republicanism in this era, Zeev Sternhell's *La droite revolutionnaire, les origines françaises du fascisme 1885-1914* (Paris: Editions du Seuil, 1978) is rich in points of comparison.

22. For a very recent manifestation of the cult of Pearse, see Declan Kiberd, "Romantic Ireland's Dead and Gone", *Times Literary Supplement*, 12 June 1998. This review includes a remarkably crass equation of Pearse as a supposed artificer of Irish modernity with James Joyce. Cultural nationalism has migrated to literary criticism, now the last fastness of the non-refutable.

23. See TW Moody (ed.), *The Fenian Movement* (Cork: Mercer Press, 1968), p. 102.

24. In 1886, even then treating the Fenians as a historical phenomenon, John O'Leary stated: "Everywhere, too, in Ireland, I hear much talk of the Fenians, but I find that even less is known about them than about the Young Irelanders, with more excuses however in that there is as yet little authentic account of them": John O'Leary, *What Irishmen Should Know*, lecture delivered at Cork, February 1886 (pamphlet, Dublin n.d.), p. 5. O'Leary was using the term Fenian to refer to those who had been involved in the famously abortive rising of 1867. Its failure did not, however, mark the end of Fenianism. The rallying of Fenians to Parnell in the split of 1890-1 represents perhaps the last discernibly Fenian incursion in the course of Irish history.

25. Flaubert memorably defined conspirators in the *Dictionnaire des Idées Recues* as persons who "feel a compulsion to write their names on a list". In this respect at least Fenianism partook of the character of revolutionary movements in nineteenth century continental Europe.

26. TW Moody, *The Fenian Movement*, p. 9. The fact that in the intervening period the latter half of the nineteenth century has become something of a deserted village in the history-writing of modern Ireland has compounded the effect. Moody's own general assessments of Fenianism, while concise and exact, are disappointingly brief and cautious: *ibid.*, pp. 99-111; TW Moody, *Davitt and the Irish Revolution* (Oxford: Clarendon Press, 1981), pp. 41, 43.

27. In his essay, "Passion and Cunning: An Essay on the Politics of WB Yeats", Conor Cruise O'Brien mordantly observes of the high – almost impossibly high – Fenian, John O'Leary, that his adherents, "shunning alike agrarian agitation, terrorism and moderation, were left alone by the police": O'Brien, *Passion and Cunning*, p. 12.

28. Martin McGuinness was quoted in the prelude to the Good Friday agreement as declaring that Unionist attempts to divide "nationalist Ireland", and "to split Bertie Ahern, Gerry Adams and John Hume" had failed miserably: *Irish Times*, 4 April 1998.

CHAPTER X: PATRICK LYNCH, MORE PAGES FROM AN IRISH MEMOIR
1. "Pages from an Irish Memoir", in Patrick Lynch and James Meenan(eds.), *Essays in Memory of Alexis Fitzgerald* (Dublin: Incorporated Law Society of Ireland, 1987).

2. I would like to thank Dr Deirdre McMahon for kindly directing me to Reference 130/90, Dominions Office Files, Public Records Office, Kew.

CHAPTER XII: ROBERT MCCARTNEY, THE UNION AND THE ECONOMIC FUTURE OF NORTHERN IRELAND

1. *Belfast Newsletter*, 24 February 1998.
2. The case for joint, or shared, authority is made in Brendan O'Leary, et al, *Northern Ireland: Sharing Authority* (London: Institute of Public Policy Research, 1993). Arguments against joint authority are lucidly stated in the Cadogan Group's *Blurred Vision: Joint Authority and the Northern Ireland Problem* (Belfast: Cadogan Group, 1994).
3. See Patrick J Roche and J Esmond Birnie, *An Economic Lesson for Irish Nationalists* (Belfast, 1995), pp. 35-6.
4. *Northern Ireland Sales and Exports, 1994/95-1995/96* (Belfast: Industrial Development Board, May, 1997), p. 17.
5. *Ibid.*, p. 17.
6. *Ibid.*, p. 17.
7. *Belfast Telegraph*, 7 March 1998.
8. *Northern Ireland Sales and Exports, 1994/95-1995/96* (Belfast: Industrial Development Board, May, 1997), p. 17.

CHAPTER XIV: DEIRDRE LEVINSON, POLITICS AS PSYCHOLOGY AS POLITICS: A READING OF *MACBETH*

1. My text is the Arden edition of *Macbeth*, edited by Kenneth Muir. Assuming the reader's familiarity with the play, I have not footnoted quotations from it.
2. I am indebted for this precise term to Stanley Cavell's book, *Disowning Knowledge in Six Plays of Shakespeare* (Cambridge: Cambridge University Press, 1987).

CHAPTER XV: JOHN LUKACS, POLITE LETTERS AND CLIO'S FASHIONS

1. T O'Raifeartaigh(ed.), *The Royal Irish Academy: A Bicentennial History, 1785-1985* (Dublin: The Royal Irish Academy, 1985). This essay was first delivered as a Royal Irish Academy Discourse on 8 June 1989.
2. *Ibid.*, p. 9.
3. *Ibid.*, p. 188.

4. *Ibid.*, p. 195.

5. Jakob Burckhardt, *Briefe*: edited by Max Burckhardt (Basel: B Schwabe, 1949-86), iv, pp. 125, 169, 260. For further discussion, see John Lukacs, *Historical Consciousness* (second edition, New York: Schocken Books, 1985), pp. 37, 98, 227-36.

6. For elaboration of this point, see Lukacs, *Historical Consciousness*, pp. 108-14.

7. FSL Lyons, *Culture and Anarchy in Ireland, 1890-1839* (Oxford: Oxford University Press, 1980), p. 1.

8. TS Eliot, *Notes Towards the Definition of Culture* (London: Faber and Faber, 1948), p. 22.

9. Lyons, *Culture and Anarchy*, p. 22.

10. Angus McIntyre, *The Liberator* (London: Macmillan, 1965), pp. 127-8.

11. Lyons, *Culture and Anarchy*, p. 22.

12. *Ibid.*, p. 72.

13. CP Snow, *The Two Cultures and the Scientific Revolution*, Rede Lecture, Cambridge University (Cambridge: Cambridge University Press, 1959).

14. Jose Ortega y Gasset, *Meditations on Quixote* (New York: Norton, 1961), p. 118.

15. Thomas Hardy, "Candour in English Fiction", in Thomas Hardy, *Personal Writings*: edited by Harold Orel (London: Macmillan, 1967), p. 127.

CHAPTER XVI: DÁIRE KEOGH, "BURKE'S POLITICAL TESTAMENT": THOMAS HUSSEY AND THE IRISH DIRECTORY

1. Conor Cruise O'Brien, *The Great Melody: A Thematic Biography and Commented Anthology of Edmund Burke* (London: Sinclair-Stevenson, 1992), p. 572. For Thomas Hussey, see Dáire Keogh, "Thomas Hussey, Bishop of Waterford and Lismore 1797-1803 and the Rebellion of 1798", in W Nolan(ed.), *Waterford: History and Society* (Dublin: Geography Publications, 1992), pp. 403-24; William Murphy, "The Life of Dr Thomas Hussey (1746-1803), Bishop of Waterford and Lismore" (unpublished MA thesis, University College Cork, 1968).

2. William Wardlaw to Lord Germain, 8 June 1779, Historical Manuscripts Commission, Report on Stopford Sackville MSS, i (1904), p. 323.

3. C Butler, *Historical Memoirs of the English, Irish and Scottish Catholics since the Reformation* (London, 1822), iv, p. 39.

4. R Cumberland, *Memoirs* (London, 1806), p. 139; S Flagg Bemis, *The Hussey-Cumberland mission and American independence* (Princeton: Princeton University Press, 1931).

5. DA Chart(ed.), *The Drennan Letters* (Belfast: HMSO, 1931), p. 228.

6. Butler, *Memoirs*, iv, p. 43; Eamon O'Flaherty, "The Catholic Convention and Anglo-Irish Politics, 1791-3", in *Archivium Hibernicum*, xi (1985), p. 16; P O'Donoghue, "The Holy See and Ireland, 1780-1803", in *Archivium Hibernicum*, xxxiv (1977), pp. 99-108.

7. Burke to Hussey, 4 Feb. 1795, in Thomas Copeland(ed.), *The Correspondence of Edmund Burke* (Cambridge: Cambridge University Press, 1958-78) [hereafter *Corr.*], viii, p. 136.

8. Hussey to R Burke, 28 August 1790, *Corr.*, vi, p. 134.

9. Edmund Burke, "Letter to Sir Hercules Langrishe on . . . the Roman Catholics of Ireland", [1792], cited in RB McDowell, *The Writings and Speeches of Edmund Burke* (Oxford: Oxford University Press, 1991), ix, p. 597.

10. See LM Cullen, "Burke's Irish Views and Writings", in Ian Crowe(ed.), *Edmund Burke: His Life and Legacy* (Dublin: Four Courts Press, 1997), pp. 62-75; Eamon O'Flaherty, "Burke and the Catholic Question", *Eighteenth Century Ireland*, xii (1997), pp. 7-27.

11. Burke to John Corry, 14 August 1779, *Corr.*, iv, p. 119.

12. Hussey to Burke, 19 February 1795, *Corr.*, viii, p. 152.

13. Hussey to Burke, 3 March 1795, *Corr.*, viii, p. 169.

14. Deirdre Lindsay, "The Fitzwilliam Episode Revisited", in D Dickson, D Keogh and K Whelan(eds.), *The United Irishmen: Republicanism, Radicalism and Rebellion* (Dublin: Lilliput Press, 1993), pp. 197-209.

15. Portland to Camden, 26 March 1795, London, Public Records Office, Home Office, 100/56/455-6.

16. Hussey to Burke, 30 November 1796, *Corr.*, ix, p. 141; P Corish, *Maynooth College, 1795-1995* (Dublin: Gill and Macmillan, 1995).

17. Portland to Pelham, 1 November 1796, WJ Fitzpatrick, *Secret Service under Pitt* (London, 1892), p. 285.

18. Burke to Fitzwillam, 10 February 1795, *Corr.*, viii, p. 145.

19. Hussey to Burke, 30 November 1796, *Corr.*, ix, p. 141.

20. O'Brien, *The Great Melody*, p. 572.

21. Conor Cruise O'Brien, "Introduction", in Matthew Arnold(ed.), *Irish Affairs: Edmund Burke* (London: Crescent Library Edition, 1988), p. xxvi.

22. Hussey to Burke, 30 November 1796, *Corr.*, ix, p. 142.

23. I am grateful to Professor Thomas Bartlett for this suggestion.

24. Burke to Charles O'Hara, 27 November 1767, *Corr.*, i, p. 337.

25. *Report on the debates . . . of 1793*, pp. 310-11.

26. TW Tone, "Statement of the light in which the late act for the partial repeal of the penal laws is considered by the Catholics of Ireland", in Thomas Bartlett(ed.), *Life of Theobald Wolfe Tone* (Dublin: Lilliput Press, 1998), pp. 408-12.

27. Burke to Unknown Bishop [Hussey?], 6 June [1797], *Corr.*, ix, p. 369; K Whelan, *The Tree of Liberty: Radicalism, Catholicism and the Construction of Irish Identity 1760-1830* (Cork: Cork University Press, 1996), p. 115.

28. See Thomas Bartlett, "Counter-insurgency and Rebellion: Ireland, 1793-1803", in T Bartlett and K Jeffery(eds.), *A Military History of Ireland* (Cambridge: Cambridge University Press, 1996), pp. 247-93.

29. Camden to Portland, 17 June 1796, London, Public Records Office, Home Office, 100/69/398.

30. See Dáire Keogh, *A Patriot Priest: The Life of James Coigly 1763-98* (Cork: Cork University Press, 1998).

31. Burke to Hussey, 18 January 1796, *Corr.*, viii, p. 378; John Lennon, *The Irish Repealer's Mountain Harp of the Triumphant Year 1843* (Dublin, 1843), v: cited in Whelan, *Tree of Liberty*, p. 123.

32. Burke to Hussey, 9 December 1796, *Corr.*, ix, p. 162.

33. O'Brien, *The Great Melody*, p. 573.

34. See MJ Powell, "The Reform of the Undertaker System: Anglo-Irish Politics, 1750-67", *Irish Historical Studies*, xxxi, 121 (May, 1998), pp. 19-37.

35. Burke to Hussey, 9 December 1796, *Corr.*, ix, p. 165.

36. Burke to Hussey, 9 December 1796, *Corr.*, ix, p. 166; see James Conniff, "Edmund Burke on the Coming Revolution in Ireland", *Journal of the History of Ideas,* 47 (1986), pp. 37-59.

37. LM Cullen, "Burke's Irish Views and Writings", pp. 73-4.

38. Hussey to JB Clinch, 10 January [1799], Madden MSS, Trinity College Dublin, 873/197.

39. Burke to Unknown [February, 1797], *Corr.*, ix, pp. 253-63.

40. *Irish Magazine* (February, 1808). John Healy was more emphatic, claiming that Hussey had received Burke into the Catholic Church: *Maynooth College, Its Centenary History* (Dublin, 1895), p. 100.

41. O'Brien, *The Great Melody*, p. 577.

42. Conniff, "Burke on the Coming Revolution", pp. 44-5.

43. Source: Draft (corrected by Burke) in Fitzwilliam MSS (Sheffield

Archives); reprinted in *Corr.*, ix, pp. 161-72.

44. Burke is referring to the harsh, illegal measures used in the suppression of Defenderism in South Ulster and North Leinster.

45. During the Armagh expulsions of 1795 and 1796, the Orange Order banished hundreds of Catholic families into Leinster and Connacht.

46. When United Irishmen were taken into custody, neighbours would dig their potatoes or reap their corn in solidarity – such assemblies could consist of between 500 and 2,000 people. After the diggers starting marching in quasi-military formations, the government banned such gatherings by an order of 6 November 1796, but this was largely ignored in the north: see ATQ Stewart, *Summer Soldiers: The 1798 Rebellion in Antrim and Down* (Belfast: Blackstaff, 1995), pp. 26-30.

47. In December 1796 the Senate of Bologna issued a proclamation announcing that the constitution of that new republic was complete and that it had been sent to Napoleon Buonoparte for his approval.

48. James Harris, first Earl of Malmsbury (1746-1820), went to Paris in October 1796 in an attempt to negotiate peace between Great Britain and France. His efforts proved unsuccessful due to his insistence that the Low Countries be restored to Emperor of Austria.

49. The British had taken Corsica in February 1794, but retreated in haste in August 1796 just as a French force arrived from Italy.

50. Lazare Hoche (1768-97). As commander of the Army of the Ocean, he had brought the civil war in Brittany and the Vendée to an end, defeating an *emigré* royalist army at Quiberon Bay in July 1795. Commander of the ill-fated Bantry expedition of December 1796, he was the main hope of the United Irishmen in France until his early death in 1797.

51. Urbain-René de Hercé (1726-95), Bishop of Dol, was executed in the wake of Hoche's victory at Quiberon.

52. Burke here refers to the so-called "Constitution of 1782".

53. William Henry Cavendish Bentick, third Duke of Portland: Home Secretary; Lord Lieutenant of Ireland, 1782; twice Prime Minister, 1783 and 1807.

54. John Jeffreys Pratt, second Earl of Camden (1759-1840), Lord Lieutenant of Ireland, March 1795 to June 1798.

55. James Hyland.

56. William Wentworth Fitzwilliam (1748-1833), Lord Lieutenant of Ireland, December 1794 to March 1795.

57. "Brief and unblest the loves of the Irish people": see Tacitus, *Annals,* II, 41.

58. It is not actually known what happened to James Hyland.

59. Apparently, in the summer of 1795 Reverend Hussey was able to secure the appointment of Catholic chaplains to a few Irish militia regiments then encamped at Loughlinstown, just outside of Dublin: *Hibernian Journal,* 6 July 1795.

60. In 1796 Catholic chaplains were appointed to regiments of the British Army, as opposed to regiments of the Irish militia: *Dublin Gazette,* 6-9 August 1796.

61. As part of Camden's assault on sedition, the Irish parliament passed an Indemnity Act in the spring of 1796 to prevent the prosecutions relating to the illegal methods used by the Crown forces in their suppression of Defenderism in Connacht and Ulster.

62. An act for the more easy and speedy trial of such persons as have levied, or shall levy War against His Majesty: 19 Geo. II, c. 9.

CHAPTER XVII: JOHN PATRICK DIGGINS, A "VANQUISHED ARISTOCRAT" IN DEMOCRATIC AMERICA: ALEXIS DE TOCQUEVILLE

1. Alexis de Tocqueville, *Memoir, Letters, and Remains* (Boston: Ticknor and Fields, 1862), ii, p. 91.

2. F Scott Fitzgerald, *The Crack Up*: edited by Edmund Wilson (New York: New Directions, 1945), p. 69.

3. Edmund Burke, "Speech on Conciliation with the Colonies", in Walter J Bate(ed.), *Selected Writings of Edmund Burke* (New York: Modern Library, 1960), pp. 170-6.

4. Quoted in Andre Jardine, *Tocqueville: A Biography*: translated by Lydia Davis and Robert Hemenway (New York; Farrar Strauss, 1988), pp. 86-87

5. Quoted in Jardine, *Tocqueville*, p. 93.

6. Jardine, *Tocqueville*, p. 176.

7. Alexis de Tocqueville, *Democracy in America*: edited by JP Mayer and translated by George Lawrence (Garden City, NY: Anchor, 1969), p. 12.

8. Quoted in Jean-Claude Lamberti, *Tocqueville and the Two Democracies* (Cambridge, MA: Harvard University Press, 1989), p. 234.

9. Ernest Gellner, *Plough, Sword and Book: The Structure of Human History* (Chicago: University of Chicago Press, 1988), pp. 189-197.

10. Henry Adams, *The Education of Henry Adams* (New York: Houghton Mifflin, 1946), p. 7.

11. Quoted in George Wilson Pierson, *Tocqueville in America* (New Haven: Yale University Press, 1986), p. 117-18.

12. Tocqueville, *Democracy*, p. 51.

13. *Ibid.*, p. 50-7.

14. Karl Marx, "Economic and Philosophical Manuscripts", in Lloyd D Easton and Kurt H Guddat(eds.), *Writings of the Young Karl Marx on Philosophy and Society* (Garden City, NY: Anchor, 1967), p. 301.

15. On Adams and Verblen, see John Patrick Diggins, *The Lost Soul of American Politics: Virtue, Self-Interest, and the Foundations of Liberalism* (New York: Basic, 1984); *The Bard of Savagery: Thorstein Veblen and Modern Social Theory* (New York: Seabury, 1978).

16. Quoted in Lamberti, *Tocqueville and the Two Democracies*, pp. 81-2.

17. Tocqueville, *Democracy*, pp. 48-9.

18. James T Schleifer, *The Making of Tocqueville's Democracy in America* (Chapel Hill: University of North Carolina Press, 1980).

19. John Stuart Mill, "M de Tocqueville on Democracy in America", in Geraint L Williams(ed.), *John Stuart Mill: On Politics and Society* (Glasgow: Fontana, 1976), pp. 227-8.

20. Rene Girard, *Deceit, Desire and the Novel* (Baltimore: Johns Hopkins University Press, 1961), pp. 120-121; for an analysis of the Augustinian angst in Tocqueville, see Joshua Mitchell, *The Fragility of Freedom: Tocqueville on Religion, Democracy, and the American Future* (Chicago: University of Chicago Press, 1995). Tocqueville believed that America's religious origins, specially Puritanism, held the key to explaining America; curiously, the great American intellectual historian, Perry Miller, started his account of the country by explicating the "Augustinian Strain of Piety". See Perry Miller, *The New England Mind: The Seventeenth Century* (Boston: Beacon, 1971). pp. 3-34.

21. Louis Hartz, *The Liberal Tradition in America* (New York: Harcourt, 1955), p. 86.

22. The point comes up in several essays in Abraham S. Eisenstadt(ed.), *Reconsidering Tocqueville's Democracy in America* (New Brunswick: Rutgers University Press, 1988).

23. Tocqueville, *Democracy*, p. 251.

24. John Adams to Thomas Jefferson, 15 November 1813, in Lester J Cappon(ed.), *The Adams-Jefferson Letters* (New York: Simon and Schuster, 1971), pp. 397-402.

25. Quoted in Pierson, *Tocqueville*, p. 750.

26. Tocqueville, *Democracy*, pp. 493-496.

27. In fairness, I am referring to the early Foucault, whose works conveyed the illusion of inevitability. In his later years Foucault saw history as

contingent, though there still remained a sense of necessity, whose law eluded explanation. See Keith Michael Baker, "A Foucauldian French Revolution?" in Jan Goldstein(ed.), *Foucault and the Writing of History* (Cambridge, MA: Blackwell, 1994), pp. 187-205.

28. Tocqueville, *Democracy*, pp. 494-6.

29. Freidrich Nietzsche, *On the Advantages and Disadvantages of History for Life*: translated by Peter Preuss (Indianapolis: Hackett, 1980), pp. 51-3.

CHAPTER XVIII: K ANTHONY APPIAH, THE ARTS OF AFRICA

1. Tom Phillips(ed.), *Africa: The Art of a Continent* (London: Prestel, 1995); *Africa: The Art of a Continent: One Hundred Works of Power and Beauty* (New York: Guggenheim Museum; Abrams, 1996).

2. Sylvia Boone, *Radiance from the Waters* (New Haven: Yale University Press, 1986), p. 157.

3. Boone, *Radiance from the Waters*, p. 159.

4. Boone, *Radiance from the Waters*, pp. 28.

5. Nancy Cunard(ed.), *Negro*: abridged with an introduction by Hugh Ford (New York: Frederick Ungar, 1970), p. 431. A new edition has just been published by Continuum.

6. In the interest of full disclosure, I should say that I wrote for the catalogue of the Royal Academy show (on the basis of a sample of images) and that I was involved in some of the programming associated with the show at the Guggenheim.

CHAPTER XIX: ALEXANDER KWAPONG, CONOR CRUISE O'BRIEN: A LEGON PERSPECTIVE

1 Donald Harman Akenson, *Conor: A Biography of Conor Cruise O'Brien: Volume I: Narrative* (Montreal: McGill-Queen's University Press, 1994), p. 214.

2. *Ibid.*, p. 214.

3. Conor Cruise O'Brien, *To Katanga and Back: A UN Case History* (London: Hutchinson, 1962), p. 44.

4. Cited in Akenson, *Conor: Volume I*, p. 208-9.

5. Nuala O'Faolain, "Black and White Views Leave Us Blinkered", *Irish Times*, 15 December 1997.

6. Mr Geoffrey Bing, a former British Labour Party Member of Parliament who was at the time the Attorney General in the Ghanaian government, later admitted that he had actually proposed the termination of the faculty

contracts; it is also generally assumed that he recommended Conor Cruise O'Brien to Nkrumah: Geoffrey Bing, *Reap the Whirlwind* (London, 1965), p. 361.

7. Conor Cruise O'Brien, "Two Addresses", in Conor Cruise O'Brien, *Writers and Politics* (London: Chattos and Windus, 1965), p. 240.

8. O'Brien, "Two Addresses", p. 242.

9. *Ibid.*, p. 243.

10. *Ibid.*, pp. 256-7.

11. See Akenson, *Conor: Volume I*, pp. 233-71; O'Brien, "Two Addresses", pp. 245-51.

CHAPTER XX: DAVID WELSH, CONOR CRUISE O'BRIEN AT THE UNIVERSITY OF CAPE TOWN: THE GREAT CACOPHONY

1. Conor Cruise O'Brien, "What Can Become of South Africa?", *Atlantic Monthly*, 257, 3 (March, 1986), pp. 41-68.

2. Figures kindly supplied by the Registrar.

3. Dr Saunders served from 1981 to 1996. Despite some criticism of him in this contribution I remain full of admiration for his skilful steering of the University of Cape Town through difficult times. He is the first to admit that the O'Brien saga was "an imperial failure". We remain friends.

4. Conor Cruise O'Brien, "Tutu's Enthornment", *New Republic*, 27 October 1986, pp. 9-12.

5. *Die Burger* (Cape Town), 18 October 1986: translated from Afrikaans by the author.

6. *Report of the Commission of Enquiry into the Events which occurred on the campus of the University of Cape Town on 7 and 8 October 1986* (University of Cape Town, 18 December 1986), p.17.

7. Undated pamphlet.

8. Undated pamphlet.

9. *Cape Times* (Cape Town), 10 October 1986.

10. Statement by the Vice-Chancellor, 22 October 1986.

11. There is no intention of reflecting on their judicial integrity in their subsequent capacities.

12. Council Minutes, 12 January 1987.

13. *Cape Times*, 22 January 1987.

14. *Report of the Commission of Enquiry*, p. 38.

15. *Ibid.*, p. 40.

16. *Ibid.*, p. 17.

17. *Ibid.*, p. 40.

18. Memorandum on the report, submitted to the University Council, 12 January 1987, p.7.

19. Reconstructed from speech notes.

20. David Welsh, "The O'Brien Affair: A Speech to the Cape Town Press Club", *Reality*, May, 1987.

21. *The Argus* (Cape Town), 13 October 1986.

CHAPTER XXI: GIDEON RAFAEL, ENCOUNTERS

1. Conor Cruise O'Brien, *The Siege: The Saga of Israel and Zionism* (New York: Simon and Schuster, 1986), p. 13.

2. *New York Times*, 13 August 1953.

3. O'Brien, *The Siege*, p. 15.

CHAPTER XXII: DANIEL PIPES, YOU NEED BEETHOVEN TO MODERNISE

1. Ziya Gökalp, "Milli Musiki", in Ziya Gökalp, *Türkçülügün Esasları*: edited by Mehmet Kaplan(second edition, Istanbul: Milli Egitim Basımevi, 1972), pp. 146-7.

2. *New York Times*, 28 July 1997.

3. *Turkish Daily News*, 29 December 1997.

4. *Ibid.*

5. Quoted in Robin Wright, *In the Name of God: The Khomeini Decade* (New York: Simon and Schuster, 1989), p. 192.

6. Al-Wasti, cited by Norman Daniel in Derek Hopwood(ed.), *Euro-Arab Dialogue: The Relations between the Two Cultures* (London: Croom Helm, 1985), p. 88.

7. Ne`matullah Khan, *Philadelphia Inquirer*, 13 February 1995. This attitude toward American popular music highlights the ironical fact that many American jazz musicians converted to Islam in the 1950s and 1960s. Their numbers included such luminaries as Mur Alahi, Art Blakey, Fard Daleel, Mustafa Daleel, Talib Daoud, Ahmad Jamal, Yusef Lateef, Muhammad Sadiq, Sahib Shihab, Dakota Stanton and McCoy Tyner. Other superstars said to have converted include John Coltrane, Dizzy Gillespie and Charlie Parker. Islam, incredibly, was known as the religion of bebop.

8. Quoted in "Campaign against the Arts", *TransState Islam*, Summer, 1995, p. 16.

9. Oriana Fallaci, "An Interview with Khomeini", *New York Times*, 7 October 1979.

10. Ahmad al-Qattan, *Hukm as-Islam fi'l-Ghina*: tape-recorded sermon from a mosque in Kuwait.

11. *Washington Post*, 14 January 1997.

12. Muzammil H. Siddiqi, "Shab-e-Barat and Mehndi", *Pakistani Link*, 22 December 1995.

13. *Sobh*, August-September, 1996: text in *Akhbaar Ruz*, 28 August 1996.

14. Bernard Lewis, *The Muslim Discovery of Europe* (New York: WW Horton, 1982), p. 274.

15. Text in Donald Keene, *Modern Japanese Diaries: The Japanese at Home and Abroad as Revealed Through Their Diaries* (New York: Henry Holt, 1995).

16. Quoted in Donald H Shively, "The Japanization of the Middle Meiji", in Donald H Shively(ed.), *Tradition and Modernization in Japanese Culture* (Princeton: Princeton University Press, 1971), p. 92.

17. Nagai Kafu, *Furansu Monogatori* (Tokyo, 1909): translated by Mitsoku Iriye, and excerpted in William McNeill and Mitsuko Iriye(eds.), *Modern Asia and Africa* (New York: Oxford University Press, 1971), p. 169.

18. *Wall Street Journal*, 7 January 1988.

19. Lewis, *Muslim Discovery*, p. 274.

CHAPTER XIV: XIAO-HUANG YIN, CONOR CRUISE O'BRIEN AND CHINA

1. Conor Cruise O'Brien, *God Land: Reflections on Religion and Nationalism* (Cambridge, MA: Harvard University Press, 1988).

2. Huang Hua served as Beijing's first Ambassador to the United Nations when the People's Republic of China first entered the UN in 1971 and he eventually became China's Foreign Minister before his retirement in the mid 1980s.

3. See Xiao-huang Yin, "*The Scarlet Letter* in China", *American Quarterly*, 39, 4 (Winter, 1987), pp. 551-562; "'Pure' Poetry and 'Red' Verse: A Comparative Study of Poetic Works by Puritans and Red Guards", *The World & I*, 6, 12 (December, 1991), pp. 582-597; "Progress and Problems: American Studies in China During the Post-Mao Era", in Huck Gutman(ed.), *As Others Read Us: International Perspectives on American Literature* (Amherst: University of Massachusetts Press, 1991), pp. 49-64.

4. Conor Cruise O'Brien, "Where Deng Scores over Democracy", *The Times*, 27 June 1989.

5. William Hinton, an American agricultural expert, lived in China for more than a decade after the Communist victory. He has written extensively on peasants in China and is best known for his work *Fanshen: A Documentary of Revolution in a Chinese Village* (New York: Monthly Review Press, 1966), which examines changes and continuity in rural life in China after the liberation in 1949.

6. *Atlantic Monthly*, 273, 4 (April 1994), p. 44. My report also has been anthologised in several major textbooks on modern China.

7. *Ibid.*, pp. 48-52.

8. Conor Cruise O'Brien, "The Fruit and Peril of Democracy", *Independent*, 8 October 1993, p. 26.

9. *Ibid.*

10. *Ibid.*

11. Despite the growth of the urban population in recent years, the 1996 census shows that peasants alone still account more than 70% of the Chinese population.

CHAPTER XXVI: SUSAN DUNN, ALBERT CAMUS AND THE DUBIOUS POLITICS OF MERCY

1. Albert Camus, *The Rebel* (1951): translated by Anthony Bower (New York: Vintage, 1956), p. 120.

2. Camus, *The Rebel*, p. 120.

3. Camus, *The Rebel*, p. 141.

4. Camus, *The Rebel*, p. 113.

5. Camus, *Combat*, September 11, 1944: quoted in Emmett Parker, *Albert Camus: The Artist in the Arena* (Madison: University of Wisconsin Press, 1966), p. 67.

6. Camus, *Combat*, 30 August 1944: *Essais* (Paris: Gallimard, 1965), p. 259.

7. Camus, *Combat*, 25 October 1944: *Essais*, pp. 1536-1537.

8. Camus, *Combat*, 11 January 1945: *Essais*, pp. 285-287 (italics mine).

9. Peter Novick, *The Resistance Versus Vichy: The Purge of Collaborators in Liberated France* (New York: Columbia University Press, 1968), p. 157.

10. *Ibid.*, pp. 140-158.

11. *Ibid.*, pp. 164-166.

12. Camus, *Combat*, 25 October 1944: *Essais*, p. 1537.

13. Camus, *Combat*, 30 August 1945: *Essais*, p. 290.

14. Camus, *Combat*, 15 March 1945: *Essais*, p. 314.

15. Camus, *Combat*, 30 August 1945: *Essais*, p. 289.

16. Camus, "Fragments d'un exposé fait au couvent des dominicains de Latour-Maubourg en 1948", in his Essais, p. 372.

17. *Ibid.*, p. 371 (italics mine).

18. Lamartine, "De l'Amnistie, Discours à la Chambre des Députés", 30 December 1834 (Paris: Gosselin), pp. 6, 8, and 14.

19. Camus, *Combat*, 7 May 1949: *Essais*, p. 323.

20. See Kathleen Dean Moore, Pardons: *Justice, Mercy, and the Public Interest* (Oxford: Oxford University Press, 1989), p. 51.

21. Alexander Hamilton, *The Federalist* (New York: Random House, n.d.), Number 74, p. 484.

22. Moore, *Pardons*, pp. 201-202.

23. *Ibid.*, pp. 81-82.

24. Camus, *Combat*, 5 January 1945: *Essais*, p. 1550.

25. Camus, "Défense de l'intelligence", *Actuelles I*, in his *Essais*, p. 315.

26. Camus, *Réflexions sur la guillotine*, in his *Essais*, p. 1052.

27. Camus, *Combat*, 22 November 1944: *Essais*, p. 268.

28. Camus, "Défense de l'intelligence", 15 March 1945, *Essais*, pp. 314, 315, 316.

29. Camus, *Chroniques algériennes, Actuelles III*, in his *Essais*, pp. 891-892.

30. *Ibid.*, p. 899.

31. Camus, "Algérie 1958", *Actuelles III*, in his *Essais*, p. 1012.

32. Camus, "Interview in Stockholm", 14 December 1957, in his *Essais*, p. 1883. Conor Cruise O'Brien, in his book on Camus, drew my attention to this quotation.

33. Michael Walzer, *The Company of Critics* (New York: Basic Books, 1988), p. 150.

34. Camus, *Chroniques algériennes, Essais*, pp. 963-64.

35. Camus, "L'Algérie déchirée", in his *Essais*, p. 980.

36. See Joseph Morrison Skelly, *Irish Diplomacy at the United Nations, 1945-65: National Interests and the International Order* (Dublin: Irish Academic Press, 1997), pp. 125-133.

37. Conor Cruise O'Brien, *Camus* (Glasgow: Fontana, 1970), p. 59.

38. Jean-Paul Sartre, "Letter to Camus", *Les Temps Modernes*, viii, 82 (August, 1952), p. 338.

39. Jean-Paul Sartre, "Preface", in Frantz Fanon, *The Wretched of the Earth* (1961): translated by Constance Farrington (New York: Grove Press,

1966), p. 21.

40. *Ibid.*, p. 22

41. Sartre, "Preface", in Fanon, *The Wretched of the Earth*, p. 22.

42. Sartre, *Situations II* (Paris: Gallimard, 1948), p. 309.

43. Conor Cruise O'Brien, *Camus*, p. 48.

44. Camus, *The Fall* (1956): translated by Justin O'Brien (New York: Vintage Books, 1956), p. 49.

45. Camus, *La Chute* (Paris: Gallimard Folio, 1956), p. 100. The expression "citoyen-soleil" was not retained in the Justin O'Brien translation.

CHAPTER XXVII: OWEN DUDLEY EDWARDS, MARIA CROSS ROADS: A STUDY OF "DONAT O'DONNELL"

1. O'Donnell's [Conor Cruise O'Brien's] treatment of these writers, and the wider context of *Maria Cross*, will be explored in a forthcoming book-length study.

SELECT BIBLIOGRAPHY OF WORKS
BY CONOR CRUISE O'BRIEN

Maria Cross: Imaginative Patterns in a Group of Modern Catholic Writers (New York: Oxford University Press, 1952; London: Chatto and Windus, 1953).

Parnell and his Party, 1880-90 (Oxford: Clarendon Press, 1957).

The Shaping of Modern Ireland (London: Routledge and Kegan Paul, 1960).

To Katanga and Back: A UN Case History (London: Hutchinson, 1962).

Writers and Politics (London: Chattos and Windus, 1965).

Murderous Angels: A Political Tragedy and Comedy in Black and White (Boston: Little Brown, 1968; London: Hutchinson, 1969).

The United Nations: Sacred Drama: drawings by Feliks Topolski (London: Hutchinson, 1968).

Power and Consciousness: with William Dean Vanech (New York: New York University Press, 1969).

Camus (London: William Collins, 1970); American edition entitled *Albert Camus of Europe over Africa* (New York: Viking, 1970).

A Concise History of Ireland: with Máire MacEntee O'Brien (London: Thames and Hudson, 1972).

States of Ireland (London: Hutchinson, 1972).

The Suspecting Glance (London: Faber and Faber, 1972).

Herod: Reflections on Political Violence (London: Hutchinson, 1978).

Neighbours: The Ewart-Biggs Memorial Lectures, 1978-79 (London: Faber and Faber, 1980).

The Siege: The Saga of Israel and Zionism (London: Weidenfield and Nicolson, 1986).

God Land: Reflections on Religion and Nationalism (Cambridge, MA: Harvard University Press, 1988).

Passion and Cunning: Essays on Nationalism, Terrorism and Revolution (London: Weidenfield and Nicolson, 1988).

The Great Melody: A Thematic Biography and Commented Anthology of

Edmund Burke (London: Sinclair-Stevenson, 1992; Chicago: University of Chicago Press, 1992).

Ancestral Voices: Religion and Nationalism in Ireland (Dublin: Poolbeg Press, 1994).

On the Eve of the Millennium: The Future of Democracy through an Age of Unreason (New York: The Free Press, 1994).

The Long Affair: Thomas Jefferson and the French Revolution (Chicago: University of Chicago Press, 1996).

Memoir: My Life and Themes (Dublin: Poolbeg Press, 1998).

ACKNOWLEDGEMENTS

The editors wish to express their appreciation to several people for their generous advice and timely assistance: Joe and Alexander Kearney, Patrick Lynch, Mary Maloney, James McGuire, Anne Moore and Patrick Roche. The entire team at Poolbeg Press has guided this project to completion with enthusiasm, dedication and professionalism of the highest order. We are deeply grateful to the late Kate Cruise O'Brien for her early interest in this project. A special debt of gratitude is owed to Professor Tom Mitchell, Provost of Trinity College Dublin. Members of the staff of Ryan Library, Iona College, have been most helpful, especially Barbara Carlucci, Joy Collins, Gabriela Cipollone, Greg Maroni, Robert Montelleone and Natalka Sawchuck. Finally, we thank the following:

Faber and Faber for permission to reprint a passage from Seamus Heaney's poem "From the Republic of Conscience", which appears in *The Haw Lantern*.

Robert Greacen for permission to reprint passages from his poems "Ulster" and "Derry".

The Trustees of Olive, Countess Fitzwilliam's Wentworth Settlement and the Head of Leisure Services, Sheffield, for permission to quote from Maunscript WWM Bk P 1/3321 (letter of Edmund Burke to Bishop Hussey) in the Wentworth Woodhouse Muniments in Sheffield Archives.

Lilliput Press for permission to reprint an earlier version of John Lukacs' "Polite Letters and Clio's Fashions", which appeared in Ciaran Brady(ed.), *Ideology and the Historians: Historical Studies XVII* (Dublin, 1991).

The Irish Review for permission to reprint passages from Roy Foster's essay "Writing a Life of WB Yeats".

INDEX